Religious Change in Post-Mao China

Religious Change in Post-Mao China

Toward a New Sociology of Religion

YANFEI SUN

The University of Chicago Press

Chicago and London

The University of Chicago Press, Chicago 60637
The University of Chicago Press, Ltd., London
© 2026 by The University of Chicago
Published 2026
Printed in the United States of America

35 34 33 32 31 30 29 28 27 26   1 2 3 4 5

ISBN-13: 978-0-226-84585-2 (cloth)
ISBN-13: 978-0-226-84587-6 (paper)
ISBN-13: 978-0-226-84586-9 (ebook)
DOI: https://doi.org/10.7208/chicago/9780226845869.001.0001

Library of Congress Cataloging-in-Publication Data

Names: Sun, Yanfei, author.
Title: Religious change in post-Mao China : toward a new sociology of religion /
    Yanfei Sun.
Description: Chicago : The University of Chicago Press, 2026. |
    Includes bibliographical references and index.
Identifiers: LCCN 2025028413 | ISBN 9780226845852 (cloth) |
    ISBN 9780226845876 (paperback) | ISBN 9780226845869 (ebook)
Subjects: LCSH: Christianity—China. | Buddhism—China. | China—Religion.
Classification: LCC BL1803.S87 2026 | DDC 200.951—dc23/eng/20250614
LC record available at https://lccn.loc.gov/2025028413

Authorized Representative for EU General Product Safety Regulation (GPSR)
queries: **Easy Access System Europe**—Mustamäe tee 50, 10621 Tallinn, Estonia,
gpsr.requests@easproject.com
Any other queries: https://press.uchicago.edu/press/contact.html

Contents

Introduction

This book aims to map and analyze the changes and developments of major religions in post-Mao China,[1] within the regions predominantly inhabited by the Han Chinese population.[2] The central inquiry revolves around questions addressed in different chapters: Why was Protestantism able to experience extraordinary growth under the restrictive religious policy regime of post-Mao China?[3] Why did the growth of Catholicism lag so far behind that of Protestantism in post-Mao China, despite the historical advantages it enjoyed in converting the Chinese? How can we make sense of the profound changes experienced by Chinese popular religion in its post-Mao revival? Why did the new religious movements (NRMs) fail to become major players in the religious landscape of post-Mao China? Why did the Chinese Buddhist community in post-Mao mainland China largely refrain from reform efforts to strengthen its competitiveness, despite facing pressures from rivals, notably the rapidly rising Protestantism? What changes have occurred in China's religious policy under President Xi Jinping from 2012 onward, and what are their ramifications?

I formulate and tackle these questions by taking an ecological perspective, guided by a theory that can be encapsulated as the *institutions-in-context* approach, which I will expand upon in this introduction.

I perceive all religions coexisting in a specific time and space as constituting a *religious ecology*. Within this religious ecology, each religion holds a distinct yet changeable niche, interconnected and interacting with other religions and forming unique relationships with the environment.[4] In this book, the application of the ecological perspective manifests primarily in three interrelated aspects. First, I insist that each religion's growth and strength should be understood in relation to other religions. Second, I maintain that each religion's growth dynamics are shaped by its relationship to and interactions with other religions, as well as the environment. Third, to have a good grasp of religious change, I argue that one ought to understand the waxing and waning of all the major religions and the changing positions of the religions in relation with each other: that is, to understand the configuration of the religious ecology. In this book, I seek to understand how the changing growth dynamics of each religion under investigation contribute to the evolving nature of the Chinese religious ecology and how the religious ecology emerging in the post-Mao era diverges from the historical religious ecology that crystallized during late imperial China (1368–1912).[5]

Changes in the religious ecology of a society can have profound and far-reaching consequences, at times even prompting a restructuring of that society. Throughout history, examples such as the spread of Buddhism across Asia; the Islamization of Central Asia, North Africa, and the Indonesian-Malay Archipelago; and the Christianization of Europe, the Americas, Africa, and Oceania demonstrate how changes in religious ecology could fundamentally transform the societies involved. More recently, the rise of Protestantism in South Korea and the rapid ascent of Pentecostalism in Catholic Latin America have also generated transformative consequences for their societies. These examples are illustrative of the pivotal role of religion as "switchman" or "tracklayer" for societies and civilizations.[6] Therefore, examining the substantial changes in religious ecology in post-Mao China is crucial, and given China's global significance, the observed changes might have world-historic implications.

Methodological Considerations

Formulating concrete and meaningful research questions is crucial to any sociological inquiry. In this book, I have employed juxtapositions and comparisons on at least four levels to generate, adjust, and refine my questions. Consequently, the book raises many research questions.[7]

First, I compare the divergent growth trajectories of religions in post-Mao China. Although various religions revived after the cessation of Maoist religious policies, not all experienced the same kind of resurgence. Some saw a quicker revival and more robust growth than others.

Second, I examine the post-Mao religious situation in comparison with earlier periods, particularly late Qing and Republican China, to identify emergent patterns and trends.

Third, because the religious ecology of mainland China before 1949 shared many similarities with that of Taiwan, Taiwan serves as an important reference point in my research.

Fourth, I explore internal variations within specific religions, such as differing growth dynamics across schools or traditions, between officially sanctioned and unsanctioned sectors, and between established institutions and emerging new movements.

One issue that particularly warrants elaboration is the selection of an appropriate reference point as the benchmark for evaluating and contextualizing the post-Mao religious changes. In this book, I have chosen the religious situation of late imperial China, particularly the late nineteenth and early twentieth centuries (i.e., the late Qing period), as the primary benchmark for assessing religious changes in post-Mao China. I avoided using the religious landscape of Republican China as the baseline, because that period already saw emerging religious developments diverging from late imperial patterns, albeit on a smaller scale. The late Qing period, on the other hand, predates the significant reforms and revolutions of the twentieth century, making it a more appropriate reference point for examining long-term changes. Using the religious landscape of the Maoist era, characterized by the severe suppression of all religions under radical policies, as the baseline would be even more misguided. Such a choice might lead to a simplistic celebration of the revival of religions in post-Mao China without adequately considering the varied growth trajectories of different religions and their contributions to the transforming religious ecology.

Hence, by juxtaposing the religious situation in post-Mao China with that of the late Qing, we can gain better insights into how the current religious ecology diverges from the historical patterns. But I also compare the post-Mao situation with that of Republican China and, at times, of Taiwan after 1949, for three purposes: first, to show how the religious developments of post-Mao China have diverged from other alternative paths; second, to demonstrate the profound impact of the shifts in the state's policies and actions on the growth dynamics of various religions and thus the restructuring of the religious ecology; and third, to illuminate how the institutional legacies of the Republican and the Maoist states continue to shape the post-Mao state and its religious policies.

As stated above, the religious ecology perspective adopted in this book has compelled me to examine the growth dynamics of the major religious forms in post-Mao China both together and in relation to each other. Most books on religions in post-Mao China choose to examine one religion or one aspect of a single religion.[8] Noteworthy monographs exist on Protestantism, Catholicism, Chinese popular religion, Chinese Buddhism, and NRMs.[9] Yet focusing solely on one religion would hinder our ability to achieve a comprehensive understanding of the changes in the religious ecology of a given society and risk arriving at a partial or even inaccurate assessment of the development of any single religion.

For instance, an exclusive examination of Chinese popular religion in post-Mao China has led scholars to conclude that it has rebounded from the destructions of the Mao era and is currently thriving.[10] However, juxtaposing its growth patterns with those of Protestantism would reveal the deep-seated problems that Chinese popular religion is facing, allowing for a more realistic assessment. Consider another example: according to the Pew Research Center in 2010, Protestants in mainland China constituted approximately 4.3 percent of the population, whereas in Taiwan it was about 4.1 percent.[11] These numbers might lead us to believe that Protestantism in the two societies was of comparable strength. However, by placing the religion within the context of the respective society's religious ecology, we can see that the growth of Protestantism in Taiwan has been overshadowed by the more vibrant presence of Buddhism, Daoism, popular religion, and NRMs. In contrast, Protestantism in post-Mao mainland China has experienced robust development that eclipses all other religions.

In short, the comparative historical approach, combined with the religious ecology perspective, prompts me to contextualize the growth dynamics of each religion by comparing and relating it with its past and with other religions, and, at times, to juxtapose multiple trends within one religion to understand the sources of variations and the loci of change.

To investigate the growth dynamics of different religions within the Chinese religious ecology, I needed a strategy to navigate the numerous challenges that this research project entailed. This proved to be more challenging than anticipated. For nearly twenty years, I have grappled with three types of challenges, for which there are no straightforward solutions.

First, each religion possesses its own distinct teachings and history, accompanied by unique jargon, idioms, discourses, and practices. To enhance the effectiveness of conducting fieldwork and archival research, I have invested considerable effort in familiarizing myself with the names of relevant individuals, significant events, key scriptural texts, and critical ideational developments, as well as essential government documents concerning each religion. I also tried to acclimate myself to the customs and mannerisms of practitioners of each religion and to grasp the broader and specific contexts underlying the narratives provided by informants, government documents, and archival materials.

Second, this study involves comparing the growth dynamics of nearly all major religions in China. However, a question arises: How should these comparisons be made? Should they be based on membership? Religions such as

Buddhism and Chinese popular religion do not operate on a membership basis. Should they be based on social impact? Assessing social impact is challenging. Though I have not completely resolved these issues, I have worked to find ways to mitigate the tensions.

Third, the religions under investigation have different modes of operation: some are membership-based, others are not; some are coterminous with the local community, others are translocal; some revolve around religious virtuosi, others are lay-centered. Therefore, they require distinct analytic methods. Throughout the study, I have striven to identify appropriate methods and units of analysis to take into account the distinctiveness of each religion under investigation, and I also ensure they can be meaningfully compared with other religions. Although I cannot claim to have discovered the optimal solution, it is important to acknowledge the challenges encountered in this endeavor.

It is crucial to note that I embarked on this project as an enthusiastic novice but now find myself approaching the midpoint of my career. Over the past two decades, my understanding of myself, my aspirations, my grasp of sociology as a discipline, my proficiency in ethnographic skills, and my capacity to analyze fieldnotes and other gathered materials—commonly referred to as data—have all undergone substantial change. Although documenting this aspect of my rich experience and reflection is outside the primary focus of this book, I will include a coda on my fieldwork experiences in appendix I to provide further context.

Theoretical Framework:
Explaining the Growth Dynamics of Religions

The questions concerning the growth trajectories of religions, encompassing the rise, expansion, transformation, resurgence, and decline of each, are crucial for understanding the nature and extent of religious changes in a society. These inquiries are of paramount importance because the subsequent changes in the religious ecology have the potential to shape the course of history. Despite their significance, explaining the differential growth dynamics of religions seems conspicuously absent in both classical theories and the secularization theory that dominated the field of sociology of religion from the 1950s to the late 1980s.

Classical scholars who wrote extensively on religions devoted scant attention to the questions regarding the rise and decline of religions. Durkheim's primary focus was to uncover the function of religion in bringing individuals together to form and sustain a society.[12] Weber wrote even more extensively on the topic of religion. His major works on this topic, including *The Prot-estant Ethic and the Spirit of Capitalism* ([1905] 2001), *The Religion of China* ([1915] 1951), *The Religion of India* ([1916] 1958), and *Ancient Judaism* ([1917–19] 1952), have an overarching theme: exploring how dominant religions shaped various aspects of the respective societies, including, above all, the economic sphere.[13]

Neither Durkheim nor Weber focused their investigations on the rise and decline of specific religions or on changes in religious ecology. This omis-sion may be explained in part by the apparent dominance of major religious traditions in the societies they examined.[14] More fundamentally, however, their limited attention to these questions stemmed from the fact that both thinkers were intellectual heirs of the Enlightenment, subscribing to the be-lief that modernity would inevitably erode the influence of traditional reli-gious worldviews. This pessimism, in turn, played a significant role in shap-ing secularization theory, which once held considerable sway in the sociology of religion.

Secularization theorists, drawing on Durkheim and Weber's prophecies, focused on elucidating how modern conditions would lead to a general de-cline in the importance of religion.[15] Because this theory suggested that all re-ligions were destined to diminish and decay, it effectively discouraged schol-ars from exploring the growth dynamics of different religions.

However, despite the prevailing predictions of secularization, scholars ob-served that people continued to engage with and commit to various religions. To make sense of this discrepancy, deprivation theory emerged.[16] Influenced by Durkheim's concept of *anomie*, and Merton's adaptation and development of the anomie theory, proponents of deprivation theory argue that individu-als or social groups turn to religion as a coping mechanism when they experi-ence deprivation in various aspects of their lives, such as economic, social, or psychological conditions.[17]

Deprivation theory offers valuable insights by linking individual and group religiosity to broader social contexts that may generate various forms of grievance or deprivation. However, it falls short in addressing more criti-cal questions, such as why deprived individuals gravitate toward one religion over another and why certain religions benefit more from the conditions of deprivation. This inadequacy points us toward a dominant perspective in the sociology of religion, which I refer to as the institutional approach.

In the 1950s and 1960s, the United States and Europe witnessed the pro-liferation of NRMs of various kinds. Researchers studying these movements developed theories that highlight the micro-level factors and processes lead-ing to individual conversion. However, their findings also indicate that the success of NRMs largely depends on their ability to establish institutions that foster personal bonds between existing members and potential recruits, and to socialize these recruits into active members through intensive interactions.[18]

Church scholars in the United States have observed significant internal variations in the vitality of Protestantism, the nation's mainstream religion. To explain the decline of liberal "mainline" Protestant denominations and the rapid growth of conservative denominations, Dean Kelley offered an institutional explanation in his 1972 book. He argued that more-demanding religions tend to experience stronger growth compared with less-demanding ones.[19] This theory, known as Kelley's thesis, underscores the importance of a religion's institutional features—specifically, the durable attributes of its beliefs, practices, organizational structure, and network positions—in explaining its growth and strength.[20]

Insights from the sociology of conversion and Kelley's thesis have been incorporated into a grander theoretical framework known as the *rational choice theory of religion*, developed by Rodney Stark and his associates.[21] Introduced in the late 1980s, this theory has become highly influential in the field of sociology of religion. It represents a significant departure from the secularization theory; it rejected the latter's central claim that modernity inevitably leads to a decline of religion. Unlike secularization theorists, rational choice theorists made explaining variations in religiosity across different societies, as well as the differing growth and strength of religious organizations, central to their theory.[22]

Rational choice theorists highlight various institutional features of religious organizations in their efforts to explain the differing growth and strength of religions. They suggest that religions propagating monotheism, practicing exclusivism, imposing strict demands on followers, and maintaining a high degree of tension with the sociocultural environment are more likely to boost evangelistic activities, mitigate free-rider problems, strengthen bonds among followers, and increase followers' commitment, thereby fostering robust growth. Because the attributes identified as crucial to religious growth by rational choice scholars closely align with what I define as a religion's institutional features, the rational choice theory can thus be viewed as a variant of the institutional approach.

Rational choice theorists have applied their propositions to explain the growth and decline of religions across various historical contexts, including the rise of Christianity in the Roman Empire,[23] the emergence of the Methodists and Baptists as major denominations in nineteenth-century America,[24] the dominance of monotheistic religions in world history,[25] and the development of Mormonism into a vibrant world religion.[26] From these studies, it becomes clear that rational choice theorists maintain the position that the same institutional features would yield consistent impacts on the growth dynamics of religions, regardless of the broader contexts in which the religions are situated.[27]

In contrast to rational choice theorists, I maintain that the impact of institutional features on the growth dynamics of religions is not uniform across different contexts. The same institutional features that facilitate the growth of a religion in one context could hinder its growth in another. For instance, Stark and Finke suggest that a religion with higher tension with its surrounding environment tends to experience stronger growth, arguing that a higher level of tension demands greater commitment from members, enables the religion to screen out free riders, and pushes the religion to boost members' confidence in its otherworldly promises and provide more "public goods" to members.[28] However, they seem to have overlooked the possibility that in some environments, high tension with the surroundings could provoke animosity and opposition strong enough to endanger the very survival of the religion.

All this reminds us that to understand the growth dynamics of a religion, we must not only consider the institutional features of that religion but also the larger context in which it is embedded. I argue that among the various actors shaping a religion's environment, political actors, particularly the state, are usually of paramount importance because of the power they wield. In the following section, to maintain focus and brevity, I will outline the overarching theoretical framework of this book by concentrating exclusively on the context shaped by state actors. It is important to clarify that I am not proposing a theory that views the state as the sole determinant, but rather one in which the state plays a crucial role. I will begin by delineating the key tenets of the "institutions-in-context" theory that I advocate and explain how this theory is applied throughout the book.

MY INSTITUTIONS-IN-CONTEXT APPROACH

My approach is grounded in two key reflections. First, the impact of institutional features on the growth of a religion is inherently contingent upon its operating environment. This contingency implies, as mentioned earlier, that an institutional feature may drive a religion's growth in one context but hinder it in another. This contingency also means that, as circumstances change, the importance of specific institutional features may shift, with different features becoming more crucial to a religion's growth dynamics.[29]

Second, the state plays a central role in shaping the environment in which religious organizations operate, a role deeply rooted in the nature of the state itself. As an entity with coercive authority, the state often exercises clear priority, in many respects, over all other organizations, including religious institutions, in territories under its control.[30] This tendency to dominate has significantly intensified with the rise of modern states, which seek to monopolize law and coercion, expand their influence through sophisticated state machinery and advanced infrastructure, and assert control over various aspects of society, ranging from lawmaking and warfare to economic development, public education, and welfare provision. From this perspective, modern states potentially have far greater means and avenues to influence the growth dynamics of religions, both directly and indirectly, than their premodern counterparts.

Beyond its formidable power, however, there are other compelling reasons why the state should be regarded as paramount. Foremost among these is the state's need for ideologies to legitimize its authority. For premodern and some modern states, this legitimizing ideology takes the form of religion. Once a state establishes a particular religion as its official creed, its policies and actions—whether directly related to religious affairs or not—shape the religious ecology as a whole, affecting not only the state-endorsed religion but also the situations of other religions that do not enjoy official support.[31]

For modern secular states that do not base their political legitimacy on religion, the state is still by far the most important actor affecting the growth dynamics of religions. Modern nation-state building is usually concomitant with a demarcation of the religious and the secular.[32] The modern secular state defines what kinds of religions or religious forms are to be included in the category of religion and delineates the rights, benefits, and restrictions associated with the status of a recognized religion. Activities not admitted into the category of religion, such as the religious traditions of the aboriginal people in Indonesia,[33] Shinto and the popular practices of shamans in Meiji Japan (1868–1912),[34] and Confucianism and popular religion in Republican China from 1912 to 1949,[35] enter a different sphere of activities that presents different structuring orders. It must be added that modern states may also adopt radical secularism, by forcefully excluding religion from the political arena and actively seeking to limit or even eliminate religious space altogether.[36]

I would suggest that one of the major weaknesses with the institutional approach lies in its inability to fully incorporate and theorize the structuring role of the state in the analysis. Although the rational choice version of the institutional theory does touch upon the state, it does so in a limited way. According to this theory, the state's role can be summarized by two main propositions: (1) State sponsorship of a religion diminishes the motivation of religious professionals to produce high-quality religious products, leading to the weakening of religious organization;[37] (2) Reduced state regulation intensifies religious competition, compelling religious organizations to become more "energetic and efficient" in order to generate higher levels of religious commitment among members.[38] For rational choice scholars, the state is viewed primarily as an exogenous factor influencing religious dynamics by affecting the supply side of the "religious market."[39] This perspective overlooks the state's role as a resourceful and coercive actor, deeply intertwined with religions and religious actors in various ways.

Here are a few of the many scenarios in which the state could affect, directly or indirectly, the growth dynamics of religions: the state can suppress or support a religion; the state can designate a religion as the state religion; the state can carry out forced conversions, support missionary activities, or give special favor to a religion and thus create incentives for religious conversion;[40] the state can intervene in the internal operation of religious organizations, such as defining religious orthodoxy, appointing religious leaders, or launching reforms to "purify" religions;[41] the state's development of transportation, communications, and other infrastructures can be exploited by religions for their own transmission and dissemination;[42] the state can be a source of imageries and organizational models for religions;[43] and state policies and actions can introduce economic, demographic, cultural, and other transformations with far-reaching implications for religious development.[44] The list can go on and on.

Building upon the aforementioned insights, the approach adopted by this book for explaining the growth dynamics of religions consists of three crucial components. They are (1) an investigation into the institutional features of the religion in question; (2) an examination of the context, primarily the religious environment and the sociopolitical environment in which the religion is embedded; and (3) an analysis of how the identified institutional features of the religion play out in this context. Let me elaborate further.

1) *Institutional features of a religion*: In examining the institutional features of a religion, it is essential not just to consider how these aspects contribute to the religion's ability to attract, recruit, and retain followers. In my theory, institutional features play a crucial role in the growth dynamics of a religious organization in two significant ways: first, they shape the organization's drive and capacity to create, sustain, and expand the religious community; second, they influence how the organization interacts with other social actors, particularly other religious groups, state entities and major social institutions.

2) *The context*: This primarily involves investigating both the intended and unintended consequences of the policies and actions of political actors,

especially the state, in creating and shaping the sociopolitical environment and the religious ecology in which the religion is embedded.

Such an investigation of the context first requires a close look at the policies and actions of the state that directly impinge on religion. For premodern states and certain modern religious states, this analysis involves investigating the nature and extent of the state's alliance with the official religion and its treatment of nonstate religions. However, for most modern nation-states, understanding religious policies requires examining how the state conceptualizes and manages the category of *religion*.

The process of modern nation-state building entails introducing the concept of religion, a notion imported from the West, establishing a distinct religious sphere separate from the secular, and codifying constitutional rights related to individual religious liberty. Consequently, when exploring the religious policies of modern states, it is crucial to consider how the state defines the category of religion, which religious forms are recognized within this category, the legal rights and constraints imposed on these forms, and which religious practices are excluded from official recognition. Furthermore, even among religions that fall within the state-sanctioned category, there can be significant variations in how the state treats them.

The religious policies and actions of the state may have deep ideological roots, driven by the religious or secular ideology embraced by the political elite. However, they can also be shaped by practical considerations of state actors, including but not limited to geopolitical interests, concerns about regime stability, and the instrumental interests of various state actors that constitute the state machinery. Therefore, a thorough investigation of state religious policymaking must take into account both ideological motivations and the practical considerations that shape state policies and decisions.

It is important to emphasize that state policies and actions, even when not explicitly directed toward religion, can significantly affect religious dynamics. For example, the state's infrastructure-building projects may facilitate the growth of those religious groups that effectively leverage these developments. Likewise, the state's economic policies might drive urban expansion and rural-to-urban migration, potentially disadvantaging religions deeply rooted in rural communities and creating new opportunities for urban religious groups. Therefore, our analysis should carefully account for the relevance of state's nonreligious policies and actions.

The analysis of the context generated by the state also requires us to look at the gap between intended policy goals and their actual effects. The impact of state policies on religions depends on various factors, but above all, on the state's ability to penetrate society. This ability is in turn shaped by the state's infrastructural capacity, the incentive and efficiency of the bureaucracy, and the level of cooperation that the state can secure from nonstate actors.[45] Moreover, the implementation of the state's religious policies and actions can be diverted, or their effects offset, by the state's pursuit of other objectives. As we will see in subsequent chapters, the real impact of the post-Mao state's restrictive religious policies was significantly undermined by its prioritization of market-oriented economic development and the broader social changes that resulted from market-oriented reforms.

These complexities compel us to view the state as an actor with an incoherent agenda and conflicting interests, or even as a collection of different actors across various departments and levels, each driven by their own motivations, values, and network positions. It is therefore of vital importance that we closely examine the mindset, behavior, and power dynamics of the bureaucrats responsible for enforcing religious policies at the grassroots level.

3) *The interplay between religious institutions and the context*: This involves analyzing the patterned interactions between religious actors and the contexts shaped by the most relevant and effective state actors. How do the institutional features of the religion in question play out differently in specific sociopolitical and religious contexts, affecting its growth dynamics? How do religious actors, enabled and constrained by the institutional features of the religions, adapt to, exploit, and challenge the conditions shaped by the power of the state? These are critical questions that must be explored.

In summary, the institutions-in-context approach employed in this book emphasizes the interactions between two key actors—the state and religious organizations. It requires researchers to identify a set of institutional features of a religious organization that not only shape its internal growth mechanisms but also condition its relationship with other actors, including the state, other religious groups, and major social institutions. In addition, this approach entails an analysis of the state's role—how state actors, driven by ideological and practical concerns and constrained or enabled by state capacity, create an environment that religious organizations must navigate.

The first four empirical chapters of this book demonstrate how the institutional features of religions play out differently in various religious and sociopolitical environments, facilitating or impeding religious development.[46] However, I am concerned that this repeated emphasis might lead readers to perceive institutional features of a religion as immutable over time. Partly for the purpose of avoiding this potential misconception, chapter 5 shifts our attention to a comparison of the development of Chinese Buddhism in Republican China, in Taiwan under Chiang Kai-shek (1887–1975), and in post-Mao mainland China. By applying the same institutions-in-context perspective, this chapter highlights how the state shapes the social/political/religious contexts in ways that would either compel religious actors to modify the institutional features of their religion or discourage them from doing so.[47]

Overview of the Book

The extraordinary growth of Protestantism stands as one of the most remarkable religious changes in post-Mao China, drawing significant attention from scholars and the media alike. Chapter 1 builds on existing studies to shed light on the rapid rise of Protestantism. What sets my analysis apart is its situating of the post-Mao surge of Protestantism within a broader historical framework, contrasting it with the pre-1949 situation. The analysis centers on a compelling puzzle: Why did the rapid expansion of Protestantism occur in post-Mao China, even though the political environment appeared more favorable to the religion before 1949? To address this puzzle, this chapter identifies the institutional features of Protestantism vital to the religion's rapid growth and contends that each of these institutional features can facilitate or impede the spread of Protestantism, depending on the context. It argues that certain intended and unintended consequences of the Maoist policies, particularly those policies that dealt a severe blow to the lineage power in rural China, have rendered some of Protestantism's key institutional features no longer obstacles to the religion's expansion in Chinese society. The chapter further demonstrates the post-Mao state's market-oriented economic reform has given rise to an interstitial social space, which Protestantism, with the aid of its institutional features, was uniquely positioned to exploit for its own development.[48]

As I researched Protestantism, the ecological thinking led me to examine Catholicism, a religion similar to Protestantism in many ways. Chapter 2 compares the dynamic expansion of Protestantism with the notably lackluster growth of Catholicism in post-Mao China. When I compare the pre-1949 development of these two religions, an intriguing discovery emerged: before 1949, Catholicism actually maintained a significant lead in the number of Chinese converts over Protestantism. This prompted me to ask: Why has Catholicism, which enjoyed a substantial advantage over Protestantism before 1949, been eclipsed by Protestantism in terms of membership, vitality, geographic distribution, and other indicators? To unravel this puzzle, the chapter identifies three key differences in the institutional features of Catholicism and Protestantism consequential to their growth. It goes on to argue that the growth trajectories of Catholicism and Protestantism changed not so much because their institutional features had changed significantly but because their institutional features had played out differently in the pertinent political contexts of pre-1949 China, Mao's China, and post-Mao China.

Chapter 3 investigates the territorial cults, a major form of Chinese popular religion. In this chapter, I aim to move beyond the revival thesis, which emphasizes and celebrates the revitalization of popular religion in post-Mao China. Using the status of popular religion in the late Qing dynasty as the benchmark, I identify three trends accompanying the resurgence of the territorial cults in post-Mao China: feminization, bifurcation, and Buddhification. By exploring and explaining the changes, I unveil the profound crisis facing Chinese popular religion, beneath the surface of revival and prosperity. I argue that these changes and crises result from the weakening communal ties of the territorial cults due to the enduring legacies of the Maoist state and the market-oriented reforms of the post-Mao state.

Chapter 4 examines the development of NRMs in post-Mao China. It begins by advancing an argument that China's religious ecology is particularly conducive to the rise of syncretic NRMs. This potential was realized during Republican China, which can be seen as a "golden age" for NRMs. Analyzing this historical backdrop sets the stage for understanding the emergence of Falun Gong as the largest NRM in post-Mao China. The chapter analyzes the key institutional features of Falun Gong and explores how these features interact with the context, leading to its meteoric rise in popularity and subsequent swift downfall. This analysis aims to illuminate both the growth potential of NRMs and the political realities that confront them in China.

Chapters 1 through 4 focus on how institutional features have played out differently in different contexts, leading to the waxing and waning of religions. Chapter 5 uses Chinese Buddhism as a case to explore the conditions under which a religion would seek—or choose not to seek—to reform its core institutional features in response to pressures from without. The first part of this chapter examines why Chinese Buddhist actors in post-Mao mainland China, unlike their counterparts in Republican China and post-1949 Taiwan, did not feel compelled to adopt some institutional features of their competitors for self-strengthening purposes, despite the mounting pressure from the rise of Christianity. The second part analyzes why the Chinese Buddhist establishment in post-Mao mainland China chose not to emulate the organizational strengths of its challenger when confronted with a rapidly expanding lay sectarian Buddhist movement originating in Taiwan. The chapter concludes with a reflection on what "the path not taken" means for the development of Chinese Buddhism in mainland China, using Chinese Buddhism in Republican China and Taiwan as reference points.

The book's conclusion begins with a summary of the empirical findings and broader implications of the theoretical framework, followed by an assessment of whether policy shifts under President Xi Jinping since 2012 have significantly altered the religious ecology that emerged in the preceding era of post-Mao China. In the final part of the conclusion, I position the rise of Protestantism in post-Mao China within the broader context of the global expansion of Christianity since the fifteenth century and reflect on what the evolving religious ecology of post-Mao China signifies for China as a civilization.

Religious Ecology of Late Imperial China

The religious ecology of contemporary China has evolved from that of late imperial China. To understand how the religious ecology of contemporary China diverges from its historical roots, it is essential to have a basic grasp of the religious landscape of late imperial China. This section addresses two interconnected issues: the development of the religious ecology of late imperial China and some of its most noteworthy features. Due to space constraints, the overview below is highly stylized.

In many societies, the historical emergence of salvation religions such as Buddhism, Judaism, Christianity, and Islam led to a strong alliance between political power and religion, often resulting in these religions becoming established as state religions. This religious-political amalgamation elevated the salvation religion to the center of the religious ecology of that society. As a result, the once-prevalent pre–Axial Age religions,[49] which manifested in forms of shamanism, animism, ancestor worship, territorial cults, and others, were either assimilated into the dominant religious system, losing their distinct identity and coherence, or relegated to the fringes of the religious ecology.[50] These marginalized traditions became known as *popular religion* in the field of religious studies, a term that conveys not only a subordinate or peripheral status but also a perception of being less sophisticated or legitimate compared with the dominant salvation religions.

However, in late imperial China, it was popular religion—particularly its two most important forms, ancestor worship and territorial cults—that occupied a central position in the religious ecology, rather than a salvation religion. Salvation religions such as Buddhism, Daoism, or syncretic NRMs played second fiddle, assuming supplementary roles or being marginalized. This insightful observation was first introduced in C. K. Yang's now-classic *Religion in Chinese Society*,[51] and it was further highlighted and theorized in

Dingxin Zhao's magnum opus *The Confucian-Legalist State*.[52] However, my interpretation diverges somewhat from theirs. While both Yang and Zhao focus on the central importance of Chinese popular religion as a whole, I emphasize the significance of a major subset: ancestor worship and territorial cults. Below, I summarize the essence of my argument, which builds on Zhao's theory to better align with the focus of this book.

The centrality of popular religion in late imperial China's religious ecology can be attributed to the fact that Confucianism, rather than any salvation religion, firmly established itself as the state ideology.[53] Allow me to elaborate.

First, this can be largely attributed to the distinctive nature of Confucianism, which sets it apart from other world religions. Although it evolved over time, Confucianism remained, at its core, an ethical and political philosophy that prioritized moral conduct, social order, and good governance. It did not claim the ability to ward off misfortune, overcome crises, or bestow blessings through communication with superhuman powers, nor did it promise transcendental or otherworldly salvation.[54] As a result, the Confucian state was generally accepting of a wide range of religions, including popular religion, to meet the religious needs of the masses, provided they did not pose a threat to imperial rule or violate Confucian moral codes.

Yet despite its this-worldly orientation, Confucianism did possess a religious dimension. And its religious dimension was more closely aligned with popular religion than with any other tradition. Ancestor worship was an enactment of filial piety, the foundational principle of Confucianism, whereas the worship of deities continued the ancient Chinese practice of apotheosizing extraordinarily heroic and virtuous individuals—those who exemplified Confucian ideals and were believed to have performed miraculous deeds, as prescribed in Confucian classics such as the *Book of Rites*.[55] It was natural, then, for the Confucian state to espouse ancestor worship, bestow honorific titles on select deities, and incorporate the deities into state sacrificial ceremonies.[56]

However, I emphasize that ancestor worship and territorial cults could claim centrality in China's religious ecology because of pivotal historical transformations taking place during and after the Song Dynasty (960–1279), most notably the expansion of the civil service examination system and the rise of neo-Confucianism.

During the Northern Song dynasty (960–1127), to staff the officialdom with like-minded literati, the state significantly expanded the civil service examination and increasingly based it on mastery of Confucian classics.[57] The exam became a major channel for upward social mobility. In the same period, the neo-Confucian movement, which was aimed at reasserting Confucianism as the dominant ideological force in Chinese society in response to the growing influence of Buddhism, gained momentum under the leadership of prominent thinkers.[58] By the thirteenth century, neo-Confucianism began to gain official endorsement. In the early fourteenth century, the interpretation of the Confucian canon by neo-Confucian scholar Zhu Xi became the foundation of the civil service exam. The expanded use of the examination system, and the influence of neo-Confucianism on the system, solidified the alliance between the state and the Confucian elite.

Neo-Confucian scholars in the Song Dynasty also engaged in what China historians would call *society-making* activities, such as building private academies, reforming family rituals, and establishing communal granaries.[59] Central to their efforts was the creation of *lineage organizations*—patrilineal kin groups tracing their ancestry to a common forebear—in accordance with neo-Confucian principles.[60]

With neo-Confucianism becoming integral to the civil service examination curriculum, an increasing number of people were drawn to neo-Confucian learning. Village communities gradually came under the influence of retired officials and scholar-gentry who spent many years immersed in neo-Confucian studies but were unable to advance beyond the prefectural-level examination. These individuals emerged as leaders of local lineage organizations. During the Ming and Qing dynasties (1368–1911), lineage organizations also received significant state backing, cementing their position as a dominant institution organizing local society in late imperial China.[61]

The rising dominance of lineage organizations in late imperial China profoundly reshaped local religious life. Prior to the spread of neo-Confucianism into local society, ancestor worship in Chinese families typically consisted of private rituals worshipping deceased relatives whose memories were still vivid with the living. However, with the entrenchment of lineages, ancestor worship evolved to include lineage-based communal activities honoring common ancestors from generations past.[62] Moreover, although territorial cults had existed in China since antiquity, they now became increasingly intertwined with lineage organizations.[63]

One can thus conclude that the synergistic efforts between societal initiatives and state recognition and sponsorship since the Song Dynasty not only bolstered the presence of new forms of ancestor worship and territorial cults in local society but also secured their central role in the broader religious landscape.

Although the reality was complex, with significant local variations, the religious ecology that crystallized during late imperial China exhibited several key features.

Three major types of religions coexisted in local society: popular religion, established institutional religions, and syncretic NRMs. Chinese popular religion manifested in various forms, with ancestor worship and territorial cults being most important. Unlike institutional religions such as Buddhism and Daoism, which had professional clergy and organizational structures separate from other social institutions, ancestor worship and territorial cults lacked independent religious organizations or a formal clergy. Participation in ancestor worship and territorial cults was inherently tied to membership in social institutions such as family, lineage, village, town, guild, and hometown associations. These forms of popular religion played a central role in structuring the religious and social life of local communities, the building blocks of Chinese society.

In the religious ecology of late imperial China, Buddhism and Daoism were the two most prominent established institutional religions. Both possessed systematized teachings, liturgies, religious professionals, and organizational structures distinct from other social institutions. They catered to the religious needs of lay practitioners and also offered paths to salvation or a monastic lifestyle for the religious virtuosi. Although Buddhist and Daoist institutions commanded substantial resources and wielded considerable social influence, their role in structuring the religious life of the local communities was usually not as central as that of ancestor worship and territorial cults.

In the religious landscape of late imperial China, NRMs, also known as syncretic sects, were significant players. These movements synthesized elements from mainstream religious traditions to create their unique beliefs and practices, often centering on millenarian ideas. NRMs proliferated during late imperial China, yet their growth was inhibited time and again by harsh state suppression. Only a few managed to develop into large movements with nationwide influence. Typically, these movements gained traction during the late stages of a dynasty, coinciding with periods of state decay and social unrest.[64] Despite facing formidable obstacles, some NRMs were able to leave a lasting imprint on the religious landscape of late imperial China.

It is important to recognize that the religions mentioned above were not mutually exclusive. Instead, their boundaries were fluid, allowing for considerable overlap and interpenetration. Within this religious ecology, individuals often practiced multiple religions simultaneously, without necessarily distinguishing between them. Exclusive devotion to a single institutional religion could even invite punitive consequences, particularly if it led to withdrawal from ancestor worship and territorial cult activities—practices whose hegemonic and normative status was upheld by lineage organizations. This intricate religious landscape posed a unique challenge to Christianity upon its arrival in China in the nineteenth century.

Protestantism in Post-Mao China

A Phenomenal Rise

Protestantism has been the fastest-growing religion in China since 1978. The phenomenal rise of Protestantism is one of the most conspicuous and important religious changes taking place in post-Mao China. What makes it even more remarkable is that before 1949, Protestantism's growth in China was by no means impressive.

Protestant missionary work began in China in 1807.[1] The mission enterprise received a huge boost when China, under pressure from Western colonial powers, reluctantly granted foreign missionaries access and privileges through a series of unequal treaties signed between 1842 and 1860. In the period between 1867 and 1941, there were 170 different missionary bodies operating in China, representing a wide variety of Protestant denominations with headquarters in Europe and North America.[2] The number of Protestant missionaries in China reached a peak of 8,235 in 1926.[3] Yet despite the heavy investment of the Western mission enterprise, in 1949, or when the Communists came to power, the number of Chinese Protestants had barely reached one million, or 0.2 percent of the Chinese population.[4] Protestantism significantly weakened after 1949 and disappeared altogether from public view during the Cultural Revolution (1966–76), when the Chinese state strived to erase all religions from society. In the years following the end of Mao era in 1976, however, Protestantism began to grow exponentially. By 2010, the number of Protestants reached 58 million, or 4.3 percent of China's population.[5] This growth is even more impressive when we consider that it occurred widely across China, in both rural and urban areas,[6] and in a wide range of groups with different socioeconomic characteristics, including migrant workers,[7] entrepreneurs,[8] and college students.[9]

How should we account for the phenomenal growth of Protestantism in post-Mao China given that, as many have observed, China still had a highly restrictive religious regulatory regime?[10] A look at the history of Protestantism in China raises a related question. Up to the 1940s, Protestantism in China was supported by foreign missionaries who enjoyed extraterritorial rights.[11] During Republican China (1912–49), it also received support from the new political elite.[12] Under the religious policy of the Republican state, Protestantism not only was regarded as a legitimate religion and enjoyed the rights associated with that status (whereas Chinese religions were struggling for such a status),[13] but it was also treated as a model for other religions to emulate.[14] Hence we may ask: Why did the explosive growth of Protestantism take place in post-Mao China, not before 1949?

Existing explanations of the rapid growth of Protestantism in post-Mao China roughly follow two lines of reasoning, namely deprivation theory and the institutional approach. Fenggang Yang, for instance, argues that the rapid rise of a market economy in conjunction with post-Mao China's stifling political system created social dislocation and existential anxiety among urban youth, causing them to embrace Protestantism in massive numbers.[15] Similarly, scholars argue that economic reforms and the subsequent rapid social transformation led to the disintegration of rural communities, breakdown of traditional value systems, dissolution of the rural medical care system, and weakening of social support networks, creating conditions favorable for the spread of Protestantism in rural China.[16]

Another line of argument emphasizes the importance of institutional features of Protestantism, including its organizational structure, beliefs, practices, and networks, to its growth potential. Accordingly, the post-Mao rapid growth of Protestantism is attributed to Protestantism's fervent evangelistic drive, tightly bonded religious community, flexible organizational structure, and strong ties with the West.[17]

Neither deprivation nor institutional features of Protestantism, however, can explain the variations I have previously recounted. Deprivation theory cannot explain why Protestantism enjoyed much faster growth in post-Mao China than other religions; neither can it explain why Protestantism experienced little growth before 1949 but skyrocketed in post-Mao China, given that deprivation in Chinese society before 1949 was more rampant and severe due to social turmoil brought by the Republican Revolution, the Japanese invasion, and civil wars between the Nationalists and the Communists. Institutional theory can provide an explanation of the quick rise of Protestantism in post-Mao China. Yet it cannot tell us why Protestantism, with the same institutional features, was unable to achieve rapid development before 1949. The partial validity of the institutional argument compels me to develop the institutions-in-context approach presented in the introduction.

This chapter first provides a brief account of the history of development of Protestantism in River County in central Zhejiang Province, Southeast China, where my main field site is located.[18] It identifies six key institutional features of Protestantism and demonstrates how these institutions can become liabilities to the Protestant expansion under certain conditions. The chapter then examines the structural conditions generated by the actions of the Maoist and post-Mao states, and analyzes how leaders and followers of Protestantism, shaped by the institutional features of their religion, reacted to the structural conditions generated by the state, as well as how state actors, constrained by their own logics, interests, and capacity, responded to the actions of these religious actors. Finally, I will show how the growth of Protestant groups during the post-Mao era was shaped by the patterned interactions between state actors and religious actors.

Past and Present of Protestantism in River County

The development of Protestantism in River County is congruent with national trends. Foreign missionaries began surveying River County as early as 1858. The earliest recorded Protestant missionary activities—in the form of itinerant preaching—in River County date to 1867.[19] The China Inland Mission, a mission society established by Hudson Taylor (1832–1905) to bring the gospel to China's interior and to evangelize the entire country, was among the first to establish a presence in River County. It set up a missionary station in 1871 and a chapel in 1899 in the county seat. Missionaries and their Chinese assistants also went to towns and villages to spread the gospel. In 1910, they established a church school.[20] Among the other foreign mission societies that followed in the footsteps of the China Inland Mission, the most notable was the American Baptist Missionary Union, which established a church with some thirteen Chinese converts in River County in 1887.[21] Beginning in the 1920s, amid the rising nationalist tide in China following the May Fourth Movement of 1919, students and intellectuals denounced Christianity for its association with "Western imperialism."[22] Chinese Protestant leaders responded by launching indigenous church movements in which they sought to establish churches free from foreign finances, control, or leadership. A few well-educated Protestant converts in River County, under the influence of this move toward indigenization, broke away from mission-supported churches to start meetings of their own. In the process, they embraced the teachings and practices of the Local Church, a homegrown Chinese Protestant movement led by Watchman Nee (aka Ni Tuosheng, 1903–72) that gained tremendous momentum in China in this period.[23] Henceforward, the Local Church became active in evangelizing River County.[24] Even the Japanese invasion and occupation of River County from 1942 to 1945 did not stall its evangelizing efforts and expansion. After successfully bringing all church groups originally affiliated with the China Inland Mission into its fold, the Local Church came to dominate the Protestant community in River County, leaving an enduring imprint on its religious landscape.

By 1949, there were 10 Protestant churches in the county, with 966 members, or 0.27 percent of the county's population at the time. The Protestant community faced grave difficulties under the Maoist state. Shortly after the Communist victory, foreign missionaries were forced to leave the country. Those stationed in River County gathered in Shanghai before departing the country altogether. During the Land Reform of 1950–51, when the Communist government seized land and other property of landlords and redistributed them to the peasantry, small churches had their properties confiscated and were forced to merge into larger ones. The 1956 campaign to purge "hidden counterrevolutionaries" (*sufan yundong*) targeted the Local Church, leading to the arrest of many of its leaders across China. One of the prominent church leaders in River County was sent to a labor camp. In 1958, the largest church in River County was repurposed into a factory. When the Cultural Revolution began in 1966, all the churches were shut down, and religious activities vanished from the public scene.

However, when government relaxed its religious policy in the late 1970s, Protestantism resurfaced and began to experience rapid growth. The number of church members in River County reached 4,500 by 1987. By 2009, River County had at least twenty thousand Protestants (about 3.6 percent of the county's population), fifty-seven large church groups, and hundreds of small informal meeting groups spread all over the county, including in the county seat, towns, and villages. The demographic composition of church members has also become increasingly diverse over the years, revealing the vibrancy and the remarkable growth potential of this religious community. In the 1980s and early 1990s, church members were predominantly middle-aged and elderly women of low socioeconomic status. Since then, the gender ratio has become more balanced, and members have come from a wider age and class spectrum. During my intensive fieldwork phase from 2006 to 2009, males usually accounted for 15–25 percent of the congregants of Protestant communities.[25] Urban churches, in particular, have attracted a growing body

TABLE 1.1. Growth of Protestantism in River County and China

	River County Number of Protestants (percentage of the population)	China Number of Protestants (percentage of the population)
1949	966 (0.27%)	900,000–1 million (0.2%)*
1982	Unknown	3 million (0.3%)†
1987	4,500 (0.73%)	Unknown
2009/2010	20,000 (3.6%)	58 million (4.3%)‡

Sources:
* Bays (2012, p. 147)
† Document 19
‡ Pew Research Center

of young professionals, including physicians, teachers, white-collar workers, and businesspeople. Table 1.1 illustrates the development trajectory of Protestantism in River County and in China as a whole.

Let me further illustrate the robust growth of Protestantism by tracing the trajectory of two churches to whose development I have been an eyewitness. In 1992, I attended a church meeting held in a small, ramshackle house.[26] Most of the approximately thirty participants were middle-aged and elderly women who could barely read. They came from lower social strata, with a significant number working as peddlers or street cleaners. In 1998, this church split into two congregations. By 2009, their worship services were attended by approximately one hundred fifty and more than three hundred individuals, respectively. More than half the members of both churches were of urban, middle-class backgrounds.

In January 1995, I participated in a worship service at the newly established Rain of Grace Church.[27] Held in a private home, it was attended by about fifteen people. By 2009, the congregation had grown to around one hundred fifty regular attendees at its Sunday services, not including members of the four churches that the Rain of Grace Church had helped to nurture over the years.

Having depicted the rapid rise of Protestantism in River County during the post-Mao era, it is now time to explain what led to this phenomenon. The following section outlines six institutional features of Chinese Protestantism that I have identified as crucial to its rapid growth in post-Mao China. However, the central argument of this chapter is that it was the religious environment and the sociopolitical context established by the Maoist and post-Mao states that allowed these institutional features of Protestantism to flourish in ways conducive to its growth. Consequently, after the institutional analysis, I will shift my focus back to the role of the state.

FIGURE 1.1. Chinese New Year pictures (*nianhua*) sold at the market fair of a township in River County in January 2009. From left to right, the pictures feature a child-giving Guanyin (a Buddhist deity); a lamb-holding Jesus surrounded by grapevines and peony flowers, which symbolize prosperity in Chinese culture; and Mao Zedong proclaiming the founding of the People's Republic of China at Tiananmen Square in 1949. Only themes with huge popular appeal make it into nianhua, indicating the popularity that Christianity has come to enjoy. (Photograph by the author.)

Six Institutional Features of Chinese Protestantism

Protestant groups in River County exhibit a variety of differences, including, but not limited to, variations in church teachings and practices, differences and tensions between churches that have registered with the government and those that have not, and disparities between urban and rural congregations. Differences notwithstanding, Protestant groups share significant similarities, which can be encapsulated in six institutional features. It is important to emphasize that, although previous studies have addressed one or more of these institutional features of Chinese Protestantism, this is the first scholarship in which all six features are identified and presented together.

Zero-Sum Evangelism. Carrying the evangelistic imperative prescribed by the central tenet of the Great Commission, in which Christ commanded his disciples to spread his teachings to the world, Protestantism makes evangelism the duty of not just religious professionals but all members. One of the most frequent recurring themes in the sermons of the Protestant groups in River County was the call for members to share the gospel with others. Members used their personal networks to invite relatives, friends, and coworkers to church meetings, and also proselytized among strangers.[28]

The conversion of their families was of vital importance to church members and a constant focus in small-group prayer meetings. Family members' resistance and indifference was a persistent source of anguish. In church testimonies, I heard countless stories in which members struggled for years with their "obstinate" parents and eventually secured their deathbed conversions.

The evangelism of Protestantism is zero-sum in the sense that conversion to Protestantism entails abandoning one's previous beliefs and practices altogether. In a sermon, a preacher urged his congregation, "Once we come to accept Jesus, we must break with our past. We should put a period, not a comma, between this new life and the past." Church leaders demanded iconoclasm. For instance, a preacher instructed his congregants, "For all those images of questionable nature, the best solution is to cut them out and burn them. The Lord Jesus will compensate you for any losses." Testimonies of converts I heard were filled with stories of how they smashed the statues of the deities on their home altars and destroyed anything in their households featuring the image of a dragon—a common symbol with an auspicious meaning in Chinese culture but one deemed particularly "demonic" by these Protestant groups.[29] Converts were instructed to avoid Buddhist and popular religion temples as if they were anathema.

The Protestant faithful often attributed misfortune to lingering connections with other religious traditions. In one instance, when a new convert remained ill despite the church leader having destroyed all the "idols" in her home, the leader concluded that a statue the convert had donated to a popular religion temple years earlier was the source of the evil force causing her illness. He, along with his followers, made a special trip to demolish the statue.[30]

Practices of ancestor worship, such as having funerary rites performed by Daoist ritual specialists and visiting graves to offer sacrifices of food, drink, and paper money to the deceased, were strictly prohibited. Although some church groups—mostly those registered with the government—were more lax in this regard, allowing members to offer a bouquet of flowers at gravesites in lieu of a real sacrifice, the more conservative churches forbade this practice of remembrance. A preacher urged members to take an unwavering position by relating his own example: "My mother-in-law tempted us. She said, 'I understand you won't burn paper money for me [after I die], but could you at least come to visit my grave on Qingming Day?' To this, I said no. We cannot give her such illusory solace."[31]

The most conservative churches even required their members to give up celebrating traditional Chinese festivals, such as the Chinese New Year and the Dragon Boat Festival, altogether. The following is a testimony I heard in 2008 from a woman in her fifties:

> I grew up in a family steeped in superstition. During the Chinese New Year, my parents followed a custom—they invited our ancestors to come to the household to partake in feasts. They made the first sacrifice to them on the twenty-ninth day of the last lunar month and continued offering daily sacrifices until the third day of the first lunar month in the new year. But thanks to the Lord Jesus for freeing us from this bondage![32] After I became a believer in Jesus, an elder in the church told us, "As followers of Jesus, we can only worship the God in Heaven. We cannot worship anything else." So, I stopped visiting my parents during the Chinese New Year. I failed in my duty as a married daughter, but I had no choice, because the devils [referring to her ancestors] were present in my parents' household during the New Year celebrations. On the Dragon Boat Festival, my sisters brought me some *zongzi* they had made.[33] I refused to accept them, telling them that Dragon Boat Festival belonged to the Devil, and we Christians belonged to Heaven. The two must remain separate. My dad and my sisters were furious, accusing me of cutting ties with all my relatives [*duan liuqin*].

The testimony illustrates how the zero-sum practices mandated by the church can lead to tension between converts and their surrounding social environment and cause emotional anguish in familial relationships.

Congregational Structure. Protestantism is undergirded by a congregational structure. A *congregation* here refers to a body of people who regularly gather to worship at a particular place.[34] The congregation model helps ensure that Protestant groups retain their members. Forms of corporate worship, such as sermons, communion, prayer meetings, testimony sharing, and hymn singing, take place regularly and often, socializing members into the discourses and perspectives, beliefs, and practices of the religious community, building and cementing horizontal ties among members and enhancing a sense of belonging to a collective body with a shared faith and identity. Before his conversion, Chen (Informant No. 2) had been an avid religious seeker who had experimented with Buddhism, various forms of qigong, and Guanyin Famen (aka the Quan Yin Method).[35] He told me in 2009:

> When we were practicing Guanyin Famen, we only watched the recorded tapes of the master. There was no personal guidance, and very little communication

among the practitioners. The whole experience in the end didn't change me much. In the family of Christianity, we have fellowships, lots of them. Several brothers and sisters truly belong to the Spirit. I look up to them as my role models. You know, I need that. In a few months since I joined the church, my understanding of the word of God has deepened, through listening, studying the Bible together, learning how to give testimony, and praying. You know, praying is to have dialogue with God. Bit by bit, I've seen myself changing spiritually.

Various studies note that many converts in post-Mao China have been attracted to Protestantism by purported tangible benefits, especially supernatural healing.[36] I would argue that the congregation model of Protestantism sets in motion an intensive resocialization, transforming a great proportion of converts into ardent followers regardless of their initial motives for joining the church.

Moreover, the congregational model transforms the church into a community that offers a wide range of social services for its members, including paying home visits, assisting the poor, nursing the sick, and organizing funeral services. The following example is typical. A retiree diagnosed with terminal cancer was converted on her deathbed. Church members visited her in the hospital daily, nursing her and praying for her. After her death, her church organized her funeral, greatly easing the burden on her bereaved family. The turnout at the funeral, with several hundred attendees, drew the envy of neighbors. They remarked, "This is just like a funeral of a veteran cadre [*lao ganbu*]" (Informant No. 54); "Believing in Jesus really has its benefits—at the funeral, the church will help your family achieve *xing*" (Informant No. 55). The word *xing*, in the local dialect, means humming with activity and life. Events such as weddings or funerals with large turnouts are described to have the quality of *xing*, which is highly valued in local society, as it reflects a family's strong connections and extensive social networks. Hence, *xing* enhances the social status of the bereaved family.

Insistence on Church Autonomy. "Religion and politics are two separate realms" and "Jesus, not the government, is the head of the church" are examples of the kind of rhetoric I frequently heard in sermons and during interviews with Protestant leaders—particularly those from churches not registered with the government (we will return to them shortly)—in River County. This stance draws from New Testament teachings, particularly Jesus's words in Mark 12:17:"Render to Caesar the things that are Caesar's, and to God the things that are God's." Many Protestant leaders cited this passage to justify church-state separation. However, the insistence on autonomy from the state stems not only from Christian doctrine but also from the historical context of how Protestant missions established themselves in China. Protestant missionaries arrived in the country in the nineteenth century with the backing of Western colonial powers. Until the 1940s, the Protestant community largely succeeded in shielding itself from the control and interference of the Chinese state, operating outside the bounds of Chinese legal frameworks.[37] This emphasis on church autonomy remains a significant legacy even though Western colonial powers have long since departed. It distinguishes Protestant groups from the other religious communities, such as Buddhist groups, which have a longer history in China and, over time, have developed a state-oriented mentality, marked by a proclivity to seek state patronage and a willingness to submit to state control.[38]

A Polycephalous/Polycentric Structure. Compared with other religious communities such as Catholicism (discussed further in chapter 2), the Protestant community exhibits a distinct polycephalous or polycentric structure.[39] By this, I mean that Protestant groups are not unified under a single or few centralized authority structures. Within the highly diverse Chinese Protestant community, most churches function as independent congregations, subject to no higher ecclesiastical entities.[40]

The polycephalous structure is attributable to Protestantism's inherently fissiparous nature. Protestantism's insistence on the right of private interpretation of the Bible and believers' direct access to God lends legitimacy to dissenters setting up their own religious groups, leading to a proliferation of heterogeneous congregations and sects. Institutional diversity and fragmentation were features of the Chinese Protestant community before 1949, due to the multiplicity of mission societies and the proliferation of indigenous movements in the 1920s.[41] The Protestant groups in River County were also associated with various denominations, of both Western and indigenous origin.

The polycephaly of Protestantism was further intensified by the religion's experiences under Mao's regime. As mission-derived churches were forced to sever their ties with the West and the original denominational structure of Protestant groups was dismantled, Protestant groups that have resurfaced in the post-Mao era have become more localized and less tied to denominational structures than they were historically.[42] Even though the Local Church groups in River County since the 1980s have renewed contact with groups of the same denominational heritage outside the county, a nationwide ecclesiastic structure with headquarters and commonly recognized leadership has yet to be reestablished.

Without denominational authority to stave off fissiparous tendencies, Protestantism has been prone to schisms in the post-Mao years. The Protestant community in River County has undergone frequent splits, often triggered by disputes over doctrinal positions and church practices, alleged "moral failures" of church leaders, and personality clashes.

Glorification of Martyrdom. The discourse of persecution and martyrdom played a pivotal role in shaping Christian doctrines, institutions, and identity in the history of early Christianity,[43] and it continued to be an integral part of Christian self-understanding well into modern times.[44] The ultimate act of martyrdom is the voluntary offering of one's life, and lesser forms of martyrdom include perseverance in faith despite public humiliation or incarceration. Suffering for the sake of Christ is considered a special blessing and can significantly enhance the status and charisma of the persecuted in the religious community.

In River County, too, stories of how believers persevered in their faith in the darkest days of the Maoist era have been retold again and again to form a collective memory of the Protestant community, evoking the grand narrative of persecution and martyrdom. Although some of these stories are about nationally known Protestant leaders, most recount the experiences of ordinary local Protestants during the Cultural Revolution—how they continued daily rituals of singing hymns and praying, attended secret fellowships despite the danger of being discovered, and calmly endured public humiliation when being paraded as "a dangerous element who believes in Jesus" or "a lazy woman who relies on God for a livelihood" (Informants No. 6, 22, 23, 27). In contrast to Protestant groups, Buddhist, Daoist, and popular religion communities in River County did not develop a grand narrative of persecution and martyrdom, even though these groups faced similar suppression and had instances of individual practitioners secretly observing their faith during the Cultural Revolution.

Global Support Network. Chinese Protestants are embedded in the global networks of Protestantism and have strong Western connections. China was once a major field for Western missionaries, and although mission work ceased after the Communist victory in 1949, Western Protestant groups have maintained a special interest in China.[45] Since China reopened to the outside world in the late 1970s, evangelistic groups in the former mission-sending countries and Hong Kong have resumed missionary activities and established organizations to support Protestant groups in China.[46] This global support network gives Chinese Protestant groups what Tilly would call "influential allies," who could mobilize resources, including Western media and politicians, to pressure the Chinese government to ease repression.[47]

River County's connection to the global Protestant community was evident in several ways: Christian literature from outside China kept flowing in; church leaders of the Local Church tradition maintained strong ties with congregations of the same tradition in nearby cities such as Xiaoshan, Ningbo, and Shanghai, where they enjoyed closer foreign ties; the county was visited often by evangelists from other countries and regions; and one of the most active evangelists in River County was from Taiwan. This global network also shaped the self-understanding of local Protestant leaders and members, who viewed their religion as a true "world religion" and considered Americans as fellow believers.[48] Local officials in charge of religious affairs also recognized this global aspect of Protestantism.

Inadequacy of an Institutional Account

Each of the six institutional features could have a positive effect on the expansion of Protestantism in China. Zero-sum evangelism and the congregational structure drive and enable a religious community to recruit and retain followers. The insistence on church autonomy compels church groups to battle government-imposed restrictions. The polycephalous nature of Protestantism allows each independent congregation to adapt to local conditions, diversifies the niches of Protestant groups and complicates the state's ability to manage them. The enactment of the martyrdom discourse transforms repression into opportunities for mobilization and strengthens the solidarity of the Protestant community. The global support network facilitates an influx of resources and makes the Chinese state hesitant to adopt repressive measures against Protestant communities (table 1.2).

However, such an institutional argument is far from adequate, because the six institutional features are actually double-edged swords—they can facilitate or impede the growth of Protestant groups depending on the circumstances. For instance, a global support network can become a liability

TABLE 1.2. Six institutional features of Chinese Protestantism

	Defining character	Potential benefits for the religion's growth
Zero-sum evangelism	Fervent evangelism that condemns all other religions as false	Recruiting and retaining followers
Congregational structure	Regular corporate worship	Retaining followers
Insistence on church autonomy	Avoidance and/or rejection of state control	Fencing out political interference
A polycephalous structure	Highly decentralized authority structure of the religion	Niche diversification
Glorification of martyrdom	Self-explanatory	Endurance and mobilization in face of repression
Global support network	Self-explanatory	Inflow of resources; influential allies

when xenophobic nationalism rises in a country. Similarly, the martyrdom frame may lead mainstream society to perceive a religion as a dangerous cult, as seen in the case of the Peoples Temple.[49] In the following section, I will explore in greater detail how zero-sum evangelism—an institutional feature that rational choice theorists of religion consider crucial to the strong growth of religions—elicited antagonism in local society in pre-1949 China, which stalled the spread of Protestantism. I will then analyze how the Maoist state's social-engineering endeavors dismantled the organizational basis of the social forces that once blocked the expansion of Protestantism, paving the way for the religion's rapid growth in the post-Mao era.

ZERO-SUM EVANGELISM AS A LIABILITY

Compelled by zero-sum evangelism, Protestant groups require converts to withdraw from their existing religious networks, and they condemn other religious practices in local society as idolatrous and demonic. Before 1949, in River County and elsewhere in China, this approach backfired, making it difficult for Protestantism to gain a foothold in communities deeply entrenched in ancestor worship and communal temple cults (also known as territorial cults, a topic explored in chapter 3).

In River County, as in many other places of China, the abjuring of the practices of ancestor worship by Protestant converts was an even more significant cause of animosity.[50] In traditional China, ancestor worship was "literally the universal religion of China" and embodied "all the general characteristics of the Chinese approach to the supernatural."[51] As an expression of filial piety—the first principle in a society dominated by Confucian ethics—ancestor worship was the norm, a cultural imperative, and an "absolute obligation" for all Chinese.[52] As Hsu's 1948 anthropological study shows, ancestor worship continued to shape nearly every aspect of social life in market towns up to the Communist victory.

The most basic ritual required in ancestor worship consists of a proper mourning and burial ritual for parents, as well as regular sacrificial offerings to the deceased, so that they would be provided for in the nether world.[53] Accordingly, Chinese Protestants' renunciation of ancestor worship would be perceived as condemning their ancestors to a miserable existence as hungry ghosts,[54] and thus as unfilial and abominable.[55] In my interviews carried out around 2010, I found that elderly people, especially those in their eighties or older—that is, those who spent a substantial part of their lives before 1949—almost universally found "Jesus-believers" distasteful for this very reason. When an informant (No. 74) told his eighty-nine-year-old mother that he was ready to accept Jesus, she was overwhelmed with grief and said mournfully, "If you became a Jesus-believer, our ancestors would wail in their graves." Another informant (No. 71), an eighty-eight-year-old woman, told me, "Jesus-believers are without morals and conscience! They don't bring food, nor do they burn paper money [for their deceased parents]. Their [dead] parents are left with no food or money and would starve. These miserable ghosts would be forced to steal from their neighbors' supply and would be beaten until bruised all over." When I asked her opinion about the practice of more liberal Protestants offering flowers at the gravesite, she declared, "This is no use! Can flowers feed the stomach?" When I asked ninety-year-old Xu (Informant No. 66) what he thought of "Jesus-believers" in town, my otherwise amicable informant angrily blurted out, "I tell you, Jesus-believers are the most unworthy people! It must be that no one exercises authority in their family [so that they dare to convert]."

Before 1949, ancestor worship was reinforced by the lineage organization, the most powerful social organization in local society. The Chinese lineage organized people on the basis of patrilineal descent from a common ancestor. The critical period of its formation was the Song dynasty (960–1279), when neo-Confucian intellectuals advocated patrilineal descent-line ethics based on the ideas of kinship and Confucian filial piety, and took initiative in developing the organizational form and repertoire of activities that later coalesced to become the enduring features of lineage organization.[56] The Ming and Qing dynasties saw the emergence of a Confucianized "lineage society,"[57] as lineage organization became a major form of social organization thanks to the imperial state's efforts to advance the neo-Confucian agenda.[58]

Lineage organizations were allowed to play a major role in local self-governance, partly because the imperial state, with an insufficient bureaucracy and premodern technologies, had limited capacity to penetrate into local society.[59] Lineage organizations were the chief provider of public goods and welfare programs for villagers, maintaining irrigation systems, building bridges and roads, setting up schools for lineage youth, and providing aid to the needy in the lineage.[60] The organizations wielded a significant amount of judicial and policing power, resolving disputes among lineage members and punishing (sometimes severely) transgressors of lineage mores in the community.[61] Lineage organizations also assumed paramilitary functions, organizing both defensive and offensive collective action in the "common interests" of the lineage.[62] Usually, lineage groups in southern China, more than those in the North, were able to amass substantial corporate wealth and thus could provide more material benefits and exert more power over lineage members.[63]

It is impossible to overlook the religious aspect of lineage organizations. They took the initiative in constructing and maintaining ancestral halls and graves, orchestrating communal sacrificial rites to lineage ancestors, and overseeing the orthopraxy of death and sacrificial rituals in the community.[64] Moreover, lineage organizations often provided the leadership for the construction, renovation, and management of communal temples of popular religion and the organization of temple festivals.[65]

In short, lineage organizations reinforced the ideology and practices of ancestor worship as well as the communal aspect of territorial cults, helping them achieve a kind of hegemonic status in the local religious ecology of premodern China.[66] Other religious practices were allowed, but if they contradicted or challenged the norms and obligations of ancestor worship or communal temple cults, they would face censure from lineage organizations.

Lineage power was strong in River County. During the Ming and Qing dynasties, the county boasted the greatest number of ancestral halls in central Zhejiang Province.[67] Although lineage organizations were somewhat weakened during the Republican era, they still held significant influence and showed a remarkable ability to adapt to the new political context.[68] A 1934 survey of River County revealed that lineage organizations still owned 255 ancestral halls, 3,505 buildings, and 2,491.4 acres of land.[69]

Lineage organizations had an arresting effect on the growth of Protestantism. This is evident in the writings of a British author who visited River County in 1907 and 1912. She documented that an individual's conversion to Christianity would arouse the ire of other members of the same lineage, often leading to punitive measures. These included individuals having their names removed from the ancestral temple register and being forced to forfeit their rights to ancestral property.[70] This argument is further supported by the distribution of the Protestant population in River County before 1949. Out of the ten Protestant churches in the county around 1949, two were located in the county seat, and the remaining eight were scattered in rural areas. This indicates that missionary activities had already penetrated the countryside. However, as table 1.3 shows, by 1949, Protestants made up 1.11 percent of the population in the county seat but only 0.19 percent in the rural areas, where lineage power was stronger. Even this 0.19 percent was a highly inflated figure, because one village alone accounted for four hundred Protestant church members. Excluding this village, the percentage of rural Protestants drops to 0.07 percent. Further analysis of this 0.07 percent reveals that most of the converts were residents of market towns, where lineage organizations held relatively less power, or were rural residents on the margins of the lineage network, such as widows who had married into the village, young adults whose

TABLE 1.3. Urban and rural distribution of Protestant converts in River County around 1949

Locality	Number of Protestants	Percentage of Protestants in a given population	Number of churches	Average number of members per church
Entire county	966	0.27%	10	97
Urban (county seat)	350	1.11%	2	175
Rural	616	0.19%	8	77
Rural (excluding one anomalous village)	216	0.07%	7	31

Sources: Wenshi ziliao, Gazetteer Periodical of River County, River County Gazetteer, Gazetteer of the County Seat of River County

fathers had passed away, or members of a minor lineage. Even the anomalous case of one village where a great number of conversions took place is an exception that proves my point. The villagers joined the church *en masse* only after a powerful lineage elder converted in 1937. The successful "bloc mobilization" following the conversion of a lineage elder in one village versus the limited success of Protestant evangelism elsewhere in the rural areas underscores the argument that lineage organization was a major force that kept Protestantism at bay before 1949.[71]

In Protestant missionary reports from the late nineteenth and early twentieth centuries, I encountered numerous accounts of how lineage organizations obstructed mission work. These reports describe how potential converts feared losing their standing within the lineage, being deprived of property rights, being called disparaging names for abandoning their ancestors, and facing opposition from relatives as well as penalties and reprisals from their lineage. The documents note how lineage heads would take active measures to hinder missionary efforts, including prohibiting lineage members from renting property to missionaries. Some reports reveal the extreme lengths to which family members and lineage organizations would go to prevent conversions to Christianity. For instance, a missionary from Sichuan Province recounts how the mother and wife of a man who decided to get baptized attempted to prevent the act by locking him up and threatening to take their own lives if he persisted. At the same time, the lineage organization intervened, threatening to expel him from the community and even kill him.[72]

Frustration was obvious when Rev. J. W. Carlin and his wife claimed in their missionary report that lineage organization was "the mightiest hindrance to the success of the gospel."[73] Similarly, A. F. Groesbeck, a missionary with the American Baptist Missionary Union working in Guangdong Province, made an astute observation worth quoting at length: "Chinese civil, social and religious life cannot be separated. Hence, to become a Christian means for the believer to become an antagonist of Chinese religion and in consequence a more or less uncongenial element in both the social and the civil life of his people. . . . Now how can he preserve his social and civil relations without remaining a heathen? The moment he breaks with the religious life of clan or village he is considered the enemy of that clan or village and is ostracized."[74]

It should be noted that zero-sum evangelism and its ramifications were also behind the fate of Catholicism in China. In the seventeenth century, Dominican and Franciscan friars, who followed the Jesuits in coming to China to missionize, repudiated the Jesuits' accommodationist strategies toward local customs and condemned ancestral rituals and other Confucian rites as "idolatrous practices." The ensuing Chinese Rites Controversy, which embroiled both the Vatican and the Qing court, led Emperor Kangxi (reigned 1661–1722), who previously had showered favors on Jesuit missionaries, to proscribe Catholicism.[75] At the local level, the practices of zero-sum evangelism of the Dominicans and Franciscans aroused the animosity of lineage organizations and the Confucian gentry. They introduced lineage bylaws to forbid lineage members from converting to Catholicism, petitioned and pressured officials to take punitive action, and instigated riots against Catholic churches and their members.[76]

When Protestant missionaries demonstrated the same kind of inflexibility and intolerance toward local normative religious and cultural practices, they too faced the "continuous tension between Christian religious imperative and the social imperative of Chinese daily life."[77]

THE LEGACY OF THE MAOIST STATE

The radical actions of the Maoist state had many unintended consequences for religions. With regard to the growth of Protestantism, the most important legacy of the Maoist state was its destruction of the normative status of ancestor worship and territorial cults in Chinese society (more in chapter 3).

During the Republican era, particularly under the Nationalist regime from 1927 to 1937, the Chinese state implemented a religious policy that condemned these popular religion practices as "superstition" and launched antisuperstition campaigns.[78] However, the effectiveness of this policy was limited due to a weak bureaucracy, the prevalence of warlordism, ongoing civil wars, and the Japanese invasion from 1931 to 1945. In contrast, the Maoist state adopted a much more radical religious policy and was able to penetrate much more deeply into local society. Its attack on popular religion, therefore, was far more thoroughgoing and effective.[79]

In River County, for instance, while the majority of the communal temples still preserved their religious functions and continued hosting festivals during the Republican era, under Mao, these festivals were discontinued and temples were either repurposed or demolished. Unlike the Nationalist government, which did not categorize ancestor worship as superstition, the Maoist state branded it as such and sought its eradication. Still more importantly, the Maoist state dismantled lineage organizations, which had been powerful enforcers of the normative status of ancestor worship and territorial cults in local society, effectively weakening the societal structures that had long upheld these religious practices.

The Chinese Communist Party (CCP) had pursued a policy to break up lineage power even before it came to power in 1949. In his 1927 *Report of an Investigation into the Peasant Movement in Hunan*, Mao Zedong condemned lineage organizations as one of the four traditional authorities that oppressed the Chinese people, particularly the peasants. Between 1927 and 1934, in areas under Communist control, the CCP launched campaigns to confiscate lineage properties and redistribute them to peasants and to persecute lineage elders as "landlords."[80] After 1949, this policy was implemented nationwide. Economically, the Land Reform of 1951–52 dispossessed lineage organizations of their properties, and the ensuing collectivization of rural economy, first through agricultural production cooperatives and later through the establishment of people's communes, completely removed the economic foundation of lineage power.[81] Organizationally, the authority structure of lineage organizations was dismantled when lineage elders were persecuted as landlords and antirevolutionaries. Politically, for the first time in China, the state extended its power down to the village level with the establishment of village CCP branches and village administrative organs, thereby displacing self-governing bodies. Ideologically, the lineage system was condemned as a "feudal remnant" (*fengjian canyu*). Things associated with lineages, such as ancestral halls, tablets of ancestral spirits, and genealogy books, were subjected to massive vandalism. This destruction occurred more intensively at the hands of the Red Guards or by family members acting in self-protection during the campaign to smash the "Four Olds" (i.e., old customs, old culture, old habits, and old ideas) in 1966, which was an early stage of the Cultural Revolution.[82]

Since the late 1970s, in River County as elsewhere in China, activities traditionally associated with lineage organizations have reemerged, including the recompilation of lineage genealogy records, the restoration of ancestral halls, and the resuscitation of ancestor worship.[83] Kinship networks have also been reported to influence village elections,[84] boost entrepreneurship,[85] enhance accountability of village cadres,[86] and help villagers resist the draconian birth control policy.[87]

However, a closer examination reveals that the situation in River County (and many other places I have visited) does not support what some scholars have termed a "lineage revival."[88] Although many lineage genealogies have been updated, the recompilation in most cases was not initiated by lineage organizations but rather by a handful of elderly men, out of their fondness for "traditional culture." Although some ancestral halls repurposed during the Maoist era have been restored, a significant number of reconstruction projects were actually initiated and financed by the county government for the purpose of protecting cultural relics or attracting tourism, or by village cadres that turned ancestral halls into activity centers for the village elderly.

Of the sixty-four ancestral halls in River County that were completely destroyed in the Maoist years, only three had been rebuilt by 2015. The most grandiose of these new ancestral halls belonged to the Yao lineage, covering nearly twenty-eight thousand square feet. Yet even this case indicates the irrevocable loss of lineage power. The construction project was initiated not by lineage leaders, whose authority was never restored, but by an eighty-seven-year-old man, Yao, who left the village as a young man and made a fortune in Beijing. He initially pledged two million yuan (approximately US$293,000 according to the exchange rate in 2009). But as the construction costs spiraled out of control and no other lineage members stepped forward with significant donations, Yao had little choice but to contribute more and more. In the end, he donated a total of 4.5 million yuan (approximately US$659,000). Still, in an effort to make the ancestral hall a symbol of lineage solidarity, Yao suggested that every lineage member contribute at least sixty yuan (about US$9). Revealingly, although this was merely a token amount—worth no more than two packs of cigarettes—only 24 percent of the villagers were willing to contribute.

All in all, it must be emphasized that lineage organizations of the past—that is, the kind of organizations that commanded significant economic resources, provided a safety net for lineage members, wielded certain coercive power, and were able to enforce lineage bylaws by disciplining and punishing members—have not been revived in River County. In fact, this kind of lineage power has not reemerged anywhere in post-Mao China, not even in Jiangxi and Fujian provinces, where lineage activities have experienced arguably the strongest resurgence.[89]

Without being buttressed by lineage power, religious activities traditionally associated with lineage organizations no longer enjoy normative status. Participation has transitioned to being largely voluntary, with nonconformity rarely resulting in censure (this point will be revisited in chapter 3). In River County, it was a long-standing custom to hire Daoist ritual specialists for funerary rites, because it was believed that only through these rituals could ancestors pass into the netherworld and find peace.[90] Hiring Daoists was considered an act of filial piety. Christians, who deviated from this practice, were thus subjected to immense criticism from the local community. However, this has changed. A Daoist ritual specialist (Informant No. 391) told me, "Jesus-believers, of course, would not hire Daoists. In the past, villagers would say, how dare they not hire Daoists? These Jesus-believers have even abandoned their own ancestors [lian taigong dou buyao le]! They would be drowned in saliva.[91] But who nowadays would pass such judgment?"

As noted above, elderly parents typically objected to their children's conversion to Protestantism, because abandoning ancestor worship, a consequence of conversion, would deprive them of afterlife provisions. However, without backup from the authority of the patrilineal lineage organization, parental objections carry little weight today. It can be concluded that, by dismantling the power of lineages, the Maoist state unintentionally removed a major obstacle to the expansion of Protestantism.

The policy of the Maoist state also affected the growth of Protestantism in other unexpected ways. Maoist religious policy was shaped by both ideological and practical concerns. In line with the Marxist-Leninist assessment of religion as the opium of the people, a tool of the oppressors, and a reflection of a backward and distorted worldview, the Maoist state devised policies to systematically reduce the influence of religion in society. An even more radical line believed that all religions were in effect superstitions and advocated for the use of every available method, including administrative decrees and political campaigns, to consign religion to the dustbin of history.[92] At the same time, the religious policies formed in the early 1950s also reflected the need of the state to protect the fledgling Communist regime from its perceived enemies within and without; the latter mainly consisted of the Nationalist government, which had retreated to Taiwan, and its ally, the United States.

Out of concern for regime stability, the Maoist state, immediately after its establishment, launched a campaign against "reactionary secret societies" (fandong huidaomen), targeting the NRMs that had flourished during the Republican era. From another perspective, this campaign, which effectively removed the NRMs from the religious ecology, eliminated what could have been powerful rivals to Protestantism in the post-Mao era (chapter 4 will explore the fate of NRMs in greater detail).

Following a United Front policy framework, which sought to maintain alliances with various non-Communist groups to consolidate political power and maintain social stability, the Maoist state in the 1950s recognized five religions—Buddhism, Daoism, Protestantism, Catholicism, and Islam—as legitimate.[93] Nonetheless, it also imposed rigid control over them. All Protestant groups were pressured to sever their foreign ties and join the Three-Self Patriotic Movement, which was launched by CCP-aligned Protestant leaders in 1950 under the guidance of the Communist Party. The movement promoted the principles of "self-governance, self-support, and self-propagation" for church operations and, by 1954, had developed into a national umbrella organization for Protestant groups.[94] The Bureau of Religious Affairs under the State Council oversaw the national committee of the Three-Self church system. While the CCP used the carefully selected Three-Self church leaders to better control the Protestant community, it at the same time relentlessly quashed the noncompliant by incarcerating them or sending them to labor camps.[95] This divide-and-rule policy sparked internal discord within the Protestant community, with repercussions that continued into the post-Mao era and included the rise of the independent church movement, an issue I will explore later in this chapter.

From time to time, radicalism overtook the Maoist state's religious policy. During the Great Leap Forward from 1958 to 1961, when the nation was whipped into a frenzy of activities to reach the production targets of "surpassing the UK and catching up with the US," Protestant groups were forced to hold worship services together in a much-reduced number of churches and "donate" the remaining churches to the government to support "socialist construction."[96] It is against this backdrop that the biggest church in River County was "donated" and converted into a factory. The radical policies culminated in the Cultural Revolution, during which all forms of religions were targeted for eradication.[97] Across China, religious texts were seized and burned, religious sites were ransacked or converted to secular usage, religious professionals were defrocked or sent to labor camps, all religious activities were suspended, and even the supervisory state agencies and the semiofficial umbrella associations of religious organizations were disbanded.

This kind of indiscriminate repression, which lasted almost ten years and razed all religious institutions to the ground, had a leveling effect: it reduced the advantages of religions deeply seated in Chinese society, such as popular religion and Buddhism. Furthermore, in comparison with many other religions, such as popular religion, Chinese Buddhism, and Daoism, Protestantism was more able to endure the severe suppression. Protestantism's congregational model requires believers to worship together regularly, and its martyrdom discourse encourages believers to preserve their faith in difficult times. Even during the Cultural Revolution, small group meetings of Protestants continued in secret in about a dozen places in River County. When repression subsided in the late 1970s, Protestant groups were the first to emerge from underground to hold public gatherings and to petition the government for the return of church properties confiscated during the Maoist era. In response, local officials convened a meeting in 1981 attended by Protestant leaders for the purpose of restoring the Three-Self church system and returning church properties. In comparison, the reopening of the first three Buddhist temples to the public did not happen until 1988, and the first wave of rebuilding popular religion temples did not begin until the late 1980s. By the early 1980s, while the membership of Protestant groups in River County had already surpassed the 1949 benchmark, other religions had not yet emerged from dormancy. In short, the indiscriminate repression of religions by the Maoist state hurt popular religion and Chinese Buddhism more than it did Protestantism.

The Post-Mao Explosion of Protestantism

This section presents an account of how the post-Mao state gave rise to a set of structural conditions and how Protestant groups, by virtue of their institutional features, tapped into these structural conditions to attain vibrant growth.

THE RELIGIOUS REGULATIVE REGIME

To understand what was behind the rapid growth of Protestantism, we must also understand the structure of China's religious control agencies (figure 1.2) and the overall religious policy of post-Mao China.

The post-Mao state is more willing to tolerate religious activities than the Maoist state. This change was initiated under Deng Xiaoping (1904–97), who emerged as China's paramount leader not long after the death of Mao. Having personally fallen victim to Maoist radicalism, and in an effort to salvage the regime in the face of widespread popular discontent in the wake of Mao's death, Deng built a reform coalition by repudiating the "Leftist errors" committed under Mao.[98] Starting from 1978, the central government relaxed the repressive religious policy of the Maoist era—it reopened a selected number of religious sites to the public, exonerated persecuted religious professionals, and returned confiscated properties to religious organizations.[99] In 1982, the CCP Central Committee issued a circular titled "Basic Viewpoint on the Religious Question During Our Country's Socialist Period" (aka *Document 19*), which set the tone of the post-Mao state's religious policy, despite some later adjustments.[100] The

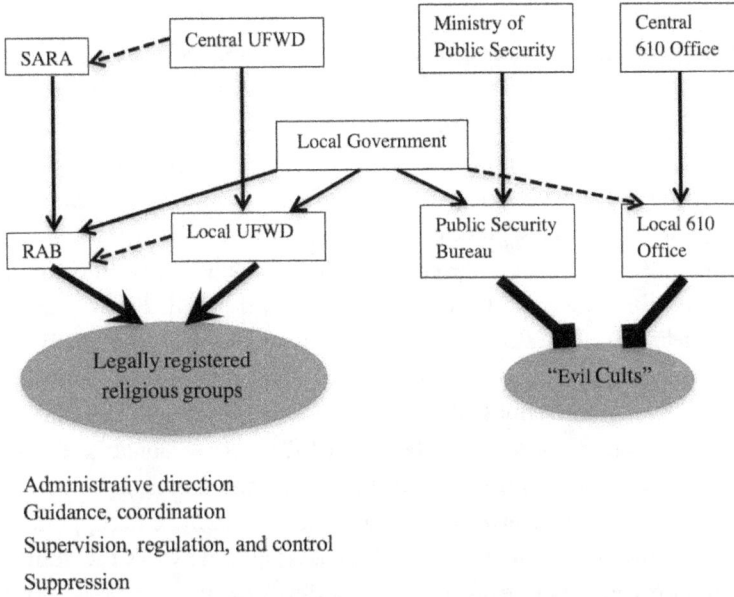

FIGURE 1.2. Relationships and jurisdictions of the main religious regulating/controlling apparatus in post-Mao China.

circular explicitly acknowledged that using force to wipe out religion entirely from society was "completely wrong and extremely harmful."

Nonetheless, the post-Mao state remains strongly inclined to exercise political control and has little intention of encouraging religious development. Well aware that religion is a mass phenomenon, has transregional connections, may constitute an alternative center of loyalty, and can be a basis for political mobilization, the post-Mao state has been alert to religious development and vigorous in trying to manage it.[101]

Like the Maoist state in the 1950s, the post-Mao state recognizes only five religions as proper religions, thus delegitimizing a wide array of religious forms. Moreover, the five state-sanctioned religions are all subject to the leadership of the Religious Affairs Bureau (RAB), a state agency installed at every administrative level to take charge of implementing and enforcing the state's religious policy and regulations. The RAB is under the direction of the United Front Work Department (UFWD), a party organ responsible for dealing with nonparty groups.[102] All religious groups are required to register with the RAB to obtain legal status. To retain administrative control over religious organizations, the RAB performs a wide range of responsibilities, including conducting inspections, monitoring religious activities, authorizing religious professionals, and appointing religious leaders. Umbrella associations for the five state-recognized

religions have also been established at every administrative level, with the purpose of channeling state directives and extending the RAB's control. All the
officially registered Protestant churches are affiliated with two umbrella associations: the Three-Self Patriotic Movement and the Chinese Christian Council. The state has also promulgated a wide range of regulations that set narrow
limits on the activities of sanctioned religious groups. Under the regulations,
religious activities are permitted to take place only within registered religious
venues; thus, public evangelism is outlawed. Only RAB-authorized personnel are allowed to preach, and must preach at designated sites; thus, itinerant
evangelism is illicit. Proselytization among people under eighteen is explicitly
prohibited; thus, religious groups are not allowed to hold Sunday schools and
evangelistic youth camps. The RAB also has a say in what can and cannot be
preached and practiced. For instance, the RAB in River County in the 1980s and
1990s discouraged sermons on millenarianism and exorcism.

The post-Mao state sometimes also resorted to force to suppress religion.
In 1983, the state condemned a religious group known as the Shouters as a
counterrevolutionary organization, making it the first major religious group
to be targeted in a nationwide crackdown in post-Mao China.[103] In 1995, the
Ministry of Public Security labeled the Shouters and several other religious
groups *evil cults (xiejiao)*. In 1999 and the ensuing years, to uproot Falun
Gong, the state reinforced the legislative and administrative framework of
defining and combating "evil cults." Once identified as evil cults, religions
are removed from the jurisdiction of the RAB and become targets of Public
Security forces and an even larger part of the state machinery (more on the
state's policy toward "evil cults" is found in chapter 4).

THE LIMITS OF THE RELIGIOUS REGULATORY REGIME

Given the presence of a restrictive religious regulatory regime in post-Mao
China, how were Protestant groups able to achieve rapid expansion? The answer lies beyond the analysis of religious policy. The following analyzes, first,
the limited capacity of the local state agencies responsible for implementing
religious policy, and second, the state's non-religion-oriented policies and actions that nonetheless had a significant impact on religious groups.

As a state agency responsible for routine management of local religious
affairs, the local RAB was supposed to follow directives from the State Administration for Religious Affairs (SARA), a functioning department under
the State Council in charge of religious affairs and issues.[104] However, because
local RAB officials were appointed and paid by local governments, they naturally were more under their sway. In the era of reform and opening-up,

particularly after 1992 when Deng Xiaoping pushed for the acceleration of market-oriented economic reforms, the central government, which prioritized economic development above everything else, increasingly linked the promotion of local officials to their contribution to developing the local economy. Under these circumstances, managing religious affairs became a minor issue on the agenda of local governments. The RAB occupied an insignificant position in the local administration, received few resources, was understaffed, and was often headed by unmotivated officials. This was exactly the situation in River County. From its establishment in 1981 until 2017, the River County RAB consistently operated with a staff of no more than three members (see the conclusion for an update). A retired River County RAB chief (Informant No. 89) told me in 2009: "Bureaus in charge of industry, agriculture, and commerce are valued as core departments, while the UFWD and the RAB are nonessential. UFWD and RAB cadres have little chance of promotion. Usually those close to the age of retirement would be appointed to head these departments. There is a saying here, 'Those who enter the UFWD are one step away from retirement' [ren jinle tongzhanbu, li tuixiu jiu cha yibu]. Or, cadres who are seen slack in work or mediocre would be assigned to the posts."

It is worth noting that River County has a population of more than half a million and occupies more than a thousand square kilometers, covering both urban and rural areas, basins and mountainous territory. It was virtually impossible for three unmotivated officials to monitor the activities of all the religious groups in the county, not to mention keeping them within the bounds dictated by the highly restrictive religious regulatory regime. Naturally, RAB officials were not inclined to initiate aggressive action, especially when higher-ups did not give them specific orders.

In Mao's time, local officials found surveillance and control much more manageable; first, people were fixed into work units or communes and their spatial movements tightly constrained by the rigid household registration system;[105] second, the Maoist state enjoyed wide support and could rely on mutual surveillance and voluntary informants among the populace.[106] In the post-Mao era, however, with the decline of the state's ideological legitimacy, such mutual surveillance was no longer effective.[107]

I also argue that the post-Mao state's prioritization of market-oriented economic development has resulted in consequences that have undercut the efficacy of political control, creating room for unauthorized religious groups and activities.

First of all, economic reforms of post-Mao China include, among others, decollectivization of agriculture, privatization of state-owned enterprises, and development of private homeownership.[108] As China's market economy advanced, people gained greater mobility and resources.[109] The reforms thus created opportunities and opened up spaces that religious groups could tap into.

Moreover, to attract much-needed capital, knowledge, and technological know-how to develop China's economy, the Chinese leadership launched an open-door policy and encouraged foreign trade and investment. Deng Xiaoping and his successors pursued better relationships with major Western countries, in particular the United States.[110] In the process, the Chinese government became more receptive to the normative pressure of the Western discourses of human rights and religious freedom,[111] and they became especially cautious in dealing with religious groups with strong Western ties.[112]

I suggest that the specified conditions of the post-Mao state led to the emergence and expansion of an "interstitial social space" where unsanctioned religious groups and activities could exist and thrive. This space can exist because it is outside the purview of any state agency and resides in the gaps between the jurisdictions of different state agencies. It can also arise when the state actors know certain activities are not legally sanctioned but nonetheless choose to acquiesce or remain indifferent due to a lack of motivation or capacity to enforce regulations rigorously and effectively.[113] The expansion of the interstitial social space was a widespread phenomenon in post-Mao China.[114] Although they did not explicitly employ the concept of interstitial social space, researchers highlighted analogous conditions produced by the post-Mao state to explain why unregistered grassroots nongovernmental organizations (NGOs) were able to survive and persist,[115] and why journalists could use and extend the "gray area" to make critical news reporting possible.[116]

In the next section, I will show that Protestantism could achieve explosive expansion in the post-Mao era precisely because its institutional features made Protestant groups uniquely positioned to exploit opportunities in the interstitial social space. I start my analysis with the development of the Protestant churches independent of the official Three-Self church system.[117] I refer to them as *independent Protestant churches* instead of *house churches* (*jiating jiaohui*)—their more common name—because many such churches I found in River County and elsewhere in China were not confined to private homes, were of impressive size, and operated quite openly. The following will show that independent churches were the early driving force behind the rapid growth of Protestantism in post-Mao China.

DEVELOPMENT OF INDEPENDENT CHURCHES

When River County officials tried to reinstate the Three-Self church system in 1981, the move was widely welcomed by members of the Protestant community, which had suffered severe persecution during the Cultural Revolution. Yet the Three-Self church system quickly earned their mistrust. At the Three-Self church system's inaugural meeting, local officials, through a manipulated election, made Lu the president. Through my interviews with leaders of independent churches, core members of Three-Self churches, and a former RAB official, I was able to construct the following profile of Lu. He developed a close relationship with the government as early as in the early 1950s. His absence from the underground fellowships during the Cultural Revolution was viewed by fellow Christians as a sign of weak faith. When he was the Three-Self church president, Lu made extensive efforts to confine church activities within the bounds set by official regulations. He did not permit evangelistic work by fellow church members, banned the circulation of Christian literature from outside sources in his own church, and duly informed the local authorities of the visits of itinerant evangelists. Lu's actions led more devoted members of the Protestant community to break away in 1987 from the Three-Self churches to form their own groups. The independent church movement in River County was thus launched.

The independent church movement in River County was also galvanized by what had happened in nearby Xiaoshan County, which has been a bastion of the Local Church movement since the 1930s. By 2009, Xiaoshan had estimated 140,000 Protestants (about 10 percent of Xiaoshan's population).[118] Between 90 and 95 percent followed the Local Church tradition.[119] Memory of the state's persecution in the 1950s has lived on in Xiaoshan's Local Church communities. As a result, these communities adopted an uncompromising attitude toward the state's co-optation, vehemently accusing churches that accepted the government's supervision of "committing adultery with the world." Invoking imagery from the Book of Revelation, they condemned the Three-Self churches as "the great Whore."[120] Since the 1980s, some Protestants in River County have attended revival meetings in Xiaoshan. Accepting the message of the Xiaoshan churches that "Three-Self churches cannot be saved" (*sanzi bu dejiu*) and that "Three-Self churches do not belong to the Spirit" (*sanzi bu shuling*), some church members in River County dropped out of the Three-Self system and joined the independent church movement.[121]

While these independent church groups rejected the Three-Self church system because it contradicted the church autonomy ideal, a smaller number of Protestant churches remained in the independent church sector because they were unable to join the Three-Self system. These groups in River County were associated mainly with Liang (Informant No. 12), a Taiwanese evangelist affiliated with a large charismatic church based in Taipei.[122] Liang arrived in River County in the early 1990s claiming to have money to invest in the local

cement industry; he was treated cordially by county officials who were trying every means to boost the local economy. When Liang sought permission
to hold religious gatherings in his own house, the officials acquiesced, even
though state regulations prohibited Taiwanese individuals from missionizing.
Within a few years, Liang's home became too small to accommodate the expanding congregation. He then purchased a two-story apartment building as
the site of the Rain of Grace Church, and the church's Sunday worship service
soon drew more than a hundred attendees. Liang did once try to register his
church with the RAB. However, after the RAB rejected his application on
the grounds that the head of the church could not be Taiwanese, Liang simply dropped the idea. He has also helped to found four other churches and
provided financial support to many other church groups. He told me that he
himself had baptized more than three thousand people in the county by 2009.
Because of Liang's connections with the charismatic church in Taipei, the
Rain of Grace Church has benefited from a continual inflow of preaching materials and frequent visits of evangelists from Taiwan. Adopting an exuberant
worship and prayer style, embracing prosperity theology, and emphasizing
faith healing and exorcism, the Rain of Grace Church has introduced ideas
and practices unlike those of the Local Church tradition and contributed to
the diversity of the independent church movement.

Not registered with the RAB, and outside of the Three-Self church system,
independent Protestant groups are by definition illegal under the post-Mao
religious regulatory regime. But with only a few exceptions, they not only es-
caped systematic suppression but also enjoyed robust development.[123] Why?

Despite their different stances toward the state, most independent churches
and Three-Self churches share the same origins, theology, and religious practices. Indeed, many independent churches started as breakaway groups from
Three-Self churches. This reduced the possibility of the Chinese government
labeling independent churches as "evil cults" based on their teachings and
practices.

In the post-Mao context, strong ties with the West have also protected
the independent church movement from outright suppression. Evangelical
groups in the West, which have maintained a strong interest in Christian-
izing China, are particularly enthusiastic about the development of independent Protestant groups. Likewise, Western media and human rights advocacy
groups have thrown their support behind independent churches.[124] Western
politicians also have paid close attention to the Chinese government's handling of independent churches, out of personal convictions, the necessity to
respond to lobbying, to appeal to voters and supporters, or to gain ground
in dealing with Beijing.[125] Since the mid-1990s, a rising political coalition in

the United States including Reaganite conservatives and evangelical Christians has pushed the worldwide promotion of religious freedom to be a top objective of US foreign policy.[126] The passing of the International Religious Freedom Act of 1998 signified their success.[127] Under this act, the US State Department established an agency to monitor religious freedom worldwide and issue an annual report.[128] Countries receiving low grades in the annual report could face economic sanctions and other punitive measures. With its economy tightly entwined with that of the West, the Chinese state had an interest in presenting a positive image to the international community.[129] Waging a systematic suppression campaign against independent Protestant groups, which would have jeopardized China's relations with the West, was not a good choice for the Chinese state.[130]

The independent church movement has also benefited from its polycephalous structure. The post-Mao state has been highly alert to the potential political threat posed by religious groups. In this context, the Chinese government has always been more wary of religions with a highly centralized authority structure, because such a structure facilitates quick and unified mobilization. The case of Falun Gong in China can illustrate this point. Falun Gong had a centralized authority structure, with a charismatic leader demanding allegiance from the national network of practice sites. This enabled frequent protests of Falun Gong practitioners, culminating in the Zhongnanhai protest on April 25, 1999. In response, the Chinese government perceived Falun Gong as an imminent threat to regime stability and decided to eliminate it by force (more on this history in chapter 4).

The state chose not to resort to systematic suppression to eliminate independent Protestant groups. Meanwhile, its institutional apparatus of managing the state-sanctioned religions also failed to contain the growth of independent churches.

For example, the Rain of Grace Church openly flouted the state's religious regulations on multiple fronts. Contrary to regulations prohibiting missionizing by foreigners and overseas Chinese, the church, founded and managed by a Taiwanese, regularly hosted preachers and faith healers from Taiwan and Singapore. Despite state rules against evangelism in public places, Liang, the church's figurehead, frequently conducted evangelistic activities and exorcisms in hospitals. Despite its illegal status, the church boldly displayed a conspicuous red cross and name plaque, impossible for passersby to overlook.

RAB officials admitted that Liang's persistent "unruly behavior" had long been a source of frustration for them (Informants No. 90, 91). Yet the RAB chiefs failed to curb the activities of Liang and his church. According to the incumbent RAB head at the time of my interview (Informant No. 90), they were unable to do anything because of Liang's overseas connections, afraid that "to touch him will cause negative international repercussions." What the informant did not mention, however, is that if the repressive measures against Liang's church provoked an international outcry, it would have been typical for higher-ups to take local officials to task for causing the uproar. Thus, inaction in cases such as the Rain of Grace Church becomes a rational move for local RAB officials. In the memorable words of a former RAB head (Informant No. 89), "Who is so foolish as to put a louse on his own head to cause itchiness?" A staff member of the RAB (Informant No. 91) described the handling of Liang and his church as typical of "passing the buck": "The RAB said this case was under the jurisdiction of the National Security Brigade of the Public Security Bureau. The [county] National Security Brigade said this case should be handled at the prefectural level. The prefectural level officials said it was up to the provincial-level authorities to make the decision. The provincial officials said this person has not endangered national security and they could not bypass all the local levels of government to arrest or deport him. In the end, nobody has touched Liang and his Rain of Grace Church has been growing bigger and bigger."

Neither targeted by the state as "evil cults" nor much constrained by the state's apparatus and regulations, independent churches gained an interstitial social space for their development. It needs to be emphasized that the emergence and expansion of this interstitial space came as a result of the boundary-expanding activities of independent church groups propelled by their evangelistic imperative and martyrdom complex, or more precisely, the contested negotiation between independent churches and state actors.

River County officials did try to contain the independent Protestant groups, especially in the earlier years when the strategy for dealing with them had not yet stabilized. However, these repressive actions tended to be sporadic and mild, taking the form of suspending an activity or reprimanding church leaders. Because of the polycephalous structure of independent churches, suspension of the activities of one group did not affect other groups.[131] More importantly, because of the martyrdom discourse entrenched in Protestantism, sporadic and mild repression by the local authorities only galvanized the Protestant community and produced heroes for them.

The following case was reconstructed on the basis of interviews with several informants, mainly No. 4 and No. 27. In 1996, Cai, a young leader in an independent church, the Christian Assembly Church, led church members in distributing gospel flyers on a busy street and attracted a crowd. The police came to break up the gathering and detained Cai for unauthorized religious activities in a public space. During the fifteen days of his detention, his church and the Protestant community at large (including members of Three-Self churches) demonstrated great solidarity. Numerous Protestants from churches across the county swarmed to the detention house to visit him. Every morning, a group of some twenty "sisters" from Cai's church climbed a hillock facing the window of his cell and called out, "Brother Cai, are you safe there?" Cai's father, head of another independent church, cheerfully visited the detention house as though his son's incarceration was to be celebrated. Another independent church leader went to the detention house to congratulate Cai and said with great envy, "Brother, God surely loves you more! Otherwise, why did He give you the entire blessing? If God let several of us divide up these fifteen days, I probably could have my share." Following Cai's release, he refused to visit the barber for some time. Fellow Christians viewed Cai's long hair with admiration, as a symbol of persecution and faith. Cai became the undisputed leader of his church, and under his leadership, it continued to seek autonomous development outside the government's regulatory framework. In subsequent years, the Christian Assembly Church grew to be the largest in the county, with its Sunday worship service regularly attended by more than three hundred people in 2009.

According to my informants, the reaction of the Protestant community to Cai's detention put the local authorities in an awkward position, and it taught them a lesson. Indeed, since this incident, the local government has not detained another Christian for unsanctioned evangelistic activities. Public evangelism by independent churches has become commonplace, and RAB officials almost never intervene. Reportedly, in 2006, the RAB head was riding a bicycle and saw a street gathering of an independent church group. Instead of confronting them, he rode in another direction to save himself from embarrassment (Informant No. 90).

THE POTENCY OF THE INDEPENDENT CHURCHES

Christians who opted out of the Three-Self church system were of the zealous type. They were eager to prove that their groups, rather than the Three-Self churches, were the embodiment of the "true faith." Thus, they devoted themselves to fervent evangelistic work with little regard for official regulations and restrictions.

In open defiance of state regulations, members of independent churches in River County carried out evangelism not only through personal networks but also in public. They distributed gospel tracts on streets and in parks. They also practiced hospital evangelism; using the occasion of visiting hospitalized fellow members, they preached to the patients' relatives, other patients, doctors, and nurses.

FIGURE 1.3. Members of an independent church hanging a banner on a rented bus that will transport them to a crematorium. The banner reads, "Believe in Jesus, and receive blessings forever." Funerals are occasions for Christians to engage in public proselytization, such as delivering sermons to participants and distributing gospel leaflets on the streets. (Photograph by the author.)

Disregarding state restrictions on interchurch exchanges and authorization of preachers, six independent churches in River County formed ministerial alliances, holding joint events and exchanging preachers. Evangelists were also brought in from outside the county. During my fieldwork, I attended revival meetings led by evangelists from nearby cities such as Shanghai, Ningbo, and Wenzhou, as well as faraway places such as Taiwan, the United States, and Singapore. Such revival meetings usually lasted for days and were attended by hundreds of Christians from churches across River County and even neighboring counties.

Independent churches also made great efforts, in violation of state regulations, to evangelize among youth. They organized Sunday schools and summer and winter youth camps. These camps were usually emotionally charged events during which many converted. At the end of each school semester, certain churches would organize a special event for the children of their members—typically high school and college students—during which church members would give encouragement, admonition, and instructions, and the youth were expected to provide updates on their spiritual progress.

In addition to devoting themselves to evangelism, independent churches invariably endeavored to establish strong congregations. Their commitment can be attributed to several factors. First, the early members of the independent churches were dissenters and faced pressure from the government when they withdrew from the Three-Self church system. They had a great incentive to stick together. Second, to prove themselves spiritually superior to the Three-Self churches, the independent churches tried to ensure that members stayed "fervent in spirit" (*ling li huore*). Finally, these groups were embedded in an extensive network of independent churches and were quick to emulate each other. Many independent churches sponsored activities throughout the week, such as Sunday worship, Bible study groups, prayer meetings, and hymn-singing evenings. They also organized their members into cells according to neighborhood. Some churches had early-morning prayer meetings throughout the year and organized fast and prayer (*jinshi daogao*) events from time to time. Over the years, churches added more programs and activities, such as brass bands and church gatherings on Chinese New Year's Eve. In the tightly knit communities of independent churches, members played the role of matchmaker for young adults in their community, and women members helped each other with household chores. The churches also provided new services to members and their families. Sunday schools and youth camps during school holidays were designed not just to pass faith onto the next generation but also to ease the burden of childcare for church members. To help church members deal with the challenge of caregiving for their aging parents, the Christian Assembly Church established an old-age home in 2005. The home, located in the same compound as the church buildings, had about sixty residents in 2009.

In summary, independent churches were able to carry out evangelism in ways much less constrained by state regulations than the officially authorized churches. Furthermore, fashioning themselves as a foil to the Three-Self churches, independent churches put greater emphasis on spreading the gospel and strengthening their congregations. As a result, the recruiting and retention mechanisms enabled by their institutional features operated more vigorously in independent churches.

ISOMORPHIC PRESSURE ON THE THREE-SELF CHURCHES

The extraordinary vitality of independent churches put great pressure on the Three-Self churches, whose development was constrained by the government's restrictive regulations.

FIGURE 1.4. Holy Communion at a Three-Self Protestant church in River County. Notice that most women are wearing black hair coverings, attributable to the lingering legacy of the Local Church, which cited passages from Corinthians 11 to mandate the practice. (Photograph by the author.)

The RAB tried to keep the Three-Self churches in line through conducting site inspections and organizing study sessions and training programs for church personnel. The Three-Self churches were required to seek approval from the RAB on many issues pertaining to church operations, such as the organization of religious events, the construction and expansion of church buildings, and the employment and transfer of church personnel. The RAB also manipulated the election of leaders of important churches and the Three-Self leadership.

Control over the Three-Self churches was achieved mostly through the compliance and self-censorship of church leaders. They chose to comply with government regulations not only out of their fear of the cost of not doing so—the loss of legal status and personal security—but also in exchange for officials' assistance and favors. Church leaders were often in need of the intercession of the RAB when dealing with other social actors and government officials. For instance, the RAB assisted the churches in River County in reclaiming church property expropriated during the Maoist years; it also helped in negotiations over the compensation and resettlement deals when old church buildings had to be relocated because of urban development. Church leaders on friendly terms with officials of the RAB and the UFWD were more likely to be selected as Three-Self leaders and recommended for positions in the Chinese People's Political Consultative Conference at the county or higher level. At the height of his career, Lu of River County was made not only the head of the Three-Self Church committee but also a member of the Political Consultative Conference both at the county and the prefectural level. These positions brought power and social status. Entrenchment in the networks that these positions entailed tended to push the mentality of the Three-Self leaders closer to that of the officials.

There is no way, however, for Three-Self churches to ignore the challenges posed by independent churches. When independent churches accused the Three-Self churches of allowing the government instead of Jesus to be the head of the church, or of embracing the world instead of the Spirit (*shushi bu shuling*), members of the Three-Self churches found it hard to formulate counterarguments. After all, the discourse of church autonomy from state interference has been ingrained in the Protestant community. Quite a few Three-Self church members with whom I talked held leaders of independent churches in higher regard than their own leaders. They expressed envy for the brass brands, large revival meetings, Sunday schools, and other activities organized by the independent churches. They believed that independent churches enjoyed a livelier spirit than their own churches. It is not uncommon for members of Three-Self churches to attend events of independent churches. For instance, in the revival meetings organized by independent churches, I often spotted members of the Three-Self churches in the audience. Some even switched to independent churches. A young leader of the Three-Self committee in River County candidly shared with me, "The Three-Self churches in the county seat are too soft and weak. That's why their most active members are attracted by Liang and his church, and their young people are drawn to Cai and his church" (Informant No. 34).

Some leaders and members of the Three-Self churches felt pressure to emulate the practices of the independent churches to stay relevant. In the biggest Three-Self church in the county seat, for instance, members tried to introduce new hymns that were circulating in the independent churches and to organize youth fellowships. However, Lu, head of this church and chair of the Three-Self committee, thwarted most of these initiatives, which in turn sparked complaints. On the other hand, Three-Self churches less controlled by Lu have become increasingly open-minded. For instance, farther away from urban centers and the grip of Lu and RAB officials, Three-Self churches in the townships and rural areas tended to be more responsive to pressure from independent churches. One after another, Three-Self churches in the villages and towns set up their own brass bands and added other activities pioneered by the independent churches. Two of them even established Sunday schools. In a nutshell, the entire Protestant community in River County has become invigorated as a result of organizational isomorphism.

Conclusion and Discussion

This chapter seeks to explain not only the explosive growth of Protestant Christianity in contemporary China but also why this upsurge took place in the post-Mao era and not before. Guided by the institutions-in-context approach, this chapter analyzes how the Maoist state unintentionally removed the cultural and institutional obstructions to the Protestant expansion in local society, and how the post-Mao state's pursuit of market-oriented economic development undercut the efficacy of political control, resulting in the rise of an interstitial social space, which Protestant groups were adept at exploiting. In other words, this chapter shows that the Maoist and post-Mao states have been crucial in facilitating Protestantism's phenomenal rise in China, albeit unintentionally.

Readers may question whether I have selected a case in which the Protestant population happened to enjoy stronger growth or if my findings can speak to the overall situation of the part of China with a predominant Han Chinese population. To address this question, let us recall that the Protestant population in River County was 0.27 percent in 1949, significantly higher than the national average of 0.2 percent. But in 2009/2010, the Protestant population in River County was 3.6 percent, significantly below the national average of 4.3 percent. In other words, if my study has a bias, the bias is toward underestimating the overall growth capacity of the Chinese Protestant population in the post-Mao era. Also, for the following reasons, I have a certain level of confidence in the representativeness of my findings.

First, the six institutional features of Protestantism apply to almost all Protestant groups in China, regardless of their location, denominational traditions, and other differences.

Second, Chinese popular religion, especially in the form of ancestor worship and territorial cults, had deep roots in local society across China and posed a significant obstacle to the development of Protestantism before 1949. But popular religion suffered an irrevocable loss from the onslaught of the Maoist state throughout China. In post-Mao China, popular religion has been revived to varying degrees in different regions, with central Zhejiang

Province, home to River County, witnessing a more robust resurgence than many other parts of the country.[132] Yet even in this part of China, it no longer wields the level of resources and power as before, nor does it regulate the most important aspects of people's lives. Furthermore, researchers found that Protestantism tended to experience stronger growth in places where Chinese popular religion had a weaker revival.[133] This finding also lends support to my argument.

Third, post-Mao China has seen greater variations in officials' behaviors than Maoist China. For instance, local officials in the southeast coastal regions of China, where River County is located, tended to be more lenient toward independent Protestant groups than local officials in the hinterland, such as Henan and Anhui provinces, but it is also true that everywhere in China, local RABs were understaffed and incapable of curbing unsanctioned religious activities within their jurisdictions.[134] The RAB of River County had three staff members in 2009. But the national average for a county-level RAB was only 1.07 in 1995 and 1.67 in 2012.[135] Moreover, even in Henan Province, where the local government's heavy-handed treatment of independent church groups sometimes resulted in detention and imprisonment of church leaders, such measures lacked sufficient severity and consistency to be effective. In the end, this kind of repression only energized independent churches in Henan, which has become a bastion of the independent church movement in China.[136]

Catholicism and Protestantism Compared

Reversal of Fortune

This chapter tackles a puzzle that arises when the growth trajectory of Catholicism is juxtaposed with that of Protestantism in modern China. Before 1949, Catholicism led the race of converting the Chinese by a wide margin. In the post-Mao era, however, Protestantism's exponential growth has dwarfed Catholicism, as indicated by both membership and religious vitality.

Catholic missions in China that had lasting impact were initiated earlier than their Protestant counterparts. Jesuit pioneers, including Matteo Ricci (1552–1610), set foot in China in the 1580s, whereas Robert Morrison (1782–1834) of the London Missionary Society began his mission in China in 1807. The Catholic missions came to a halt in the eighteenth century amid the Chinese Rites Controversy, which resulted in the imperial Qing government's prohibition of Catholicism and persecution of Catholics.[1] It was not until the 1840s, when the Qing government was forced to sign a series of treaties with Western powers following its defeat in the Opium War (1839–42) and in subsequent wars, that both Catholicism and Protestantism were able to launch missionary activities unimpeded by the previous proscription.[2] Because some Catholic communities had survived the century-long persecution, Catholic missionaries had a head start in proselytizing the Chinese.[3] On the other hand, because Protestantism started from a much smaller base, its growth rate appeared more impressive in the initial years. By the 1910s, however, the growth rates of Catholicism and Protestantism had more or less stabilized. In 1918, the number of Chinese Catholics was close to 2 million, about 3.3 times more adherents than Chinese Protestants.[4] This numerical gap between Catholicism and Protestantism continued until the time of the Communist victory in 1949. In 1950, Catholicism had more than 3 million followers, whereas

FIGURE 2.1. A stained-glass panel in the Cathedral of Our Lady of the Immaculate Conception in Hangzhou, featuring Matteo Ricci and Martino Martini, two Jesuit missionaries from the sixteenth and seventeenth centuries who played pivotal roles in the history of Catholicism in China. (Photograph by the author.)

Protestants numbered between 900,000 and 1 million.[5] Had this trend been sustained, there would be far more Catholics than Protestants in China today.

Both Catholicism and Protestantism suffered harsh suppression in Mao's China and even disappeared from public view during the Cultural Revolution, when Maoist radicals aimed to sweep away all religions in Chinese society. Both enjoyed a resurgence when the post-Mao state adopted a more

TABLE 2.1. Number of Catholics in Jinhua Prefecture, Zhejiang Province

City/County	Number of Catholics in 1955	Number of Catholics in 2016
Jinhua City	350	45
Lanxi City	280	30
Pujiang County	290	15
Dongyang City	397	50
Tangxi County	139	15
Yiwu City	100	150
Wuyi County	150	Unknown

Sources: The data for 1955 are from Guo (2011, p. 12). The data for 2016 were provided by the parish priest of Jinhua.

moderate religious policy. Nonetheless, in post-Mao China, Catholicism and Protestantism have displayed a significant disparity in growth rates. Protestantism has grown exponentially, whereas the growth of Catholicism has only kept pace with China's rate of population increase. By 2010, Protestants, at an estimated 58 million, outnumbered Catholics, estimated at 9 million, by 6.4 to 1.[6] Protestantism is widespread throughout China (see chapter 1), whereas Catholicism is confined largely to its traditional strongholds, such as Hebei, Shaanxi, Shanxi, Inner Mongolia, and Tianjin in the North, and Shanghai and Fujian in the South, where its roots can be traced to the late Qing dynasty or even earlier.

In many places where Catholicism had not developed into a self-contained strong community by 1949, the local Catholic population today is much smaller than in 1949. For example, in Jinhua Prefecture of Zhejiang Province, where River County is located, with the exception of the city of Yiwu there were fewer Catholics in all other cities and counties in 2016 than in 1955. At that point, the Catholic population had already shrunk considerably from the 1949 level due to government suppression (table 2.1). Only Yiwu seems to have enjoyed a slight increase in its Catholic population in the post-Mao years. This is because Yiwu, in its transformation in recent decades from a traditional agricultural county to the world's largest wholesale market, has attracted migrants from elsewhere in China, among whom there are some practicing Catholics. Few of the older-generation local Catholics of Yiwu have kept their faith or passed it down to their children (Informant No. 290).

Across China, in fact, there are signs of the faith fading even in its traditional urban strongholds. In Shanghai, one of the most important Catholic bastions during Republican China, the number of Catholics has not kept pace with the growth of the city's population. Although Shanghai's population soared from 5.4 million in 1949 to 24.2 million in 2016, its Catholic population rose from 110,000 to only 150,000 in the same period.[7] In post-Mao China, it is mostly in rural pockets where entire villages, or a substantial percentage of villagers, were already Catholics in the Republican era that Catholic communities have been able to maintain their strength.[8]

For more than a century, between the 1840s, when China was forced to grant foreign missionaries access to the country, and 1949, when the Communists came to power and would soon terminate foreign missions, Catholicism maintained a substantial advantage over Protestantism in the race to win converts. In Mao's China between 1949 and 1976, both were severely suppressed. Both have experienced a resurgence since China entered the post-Mao period. However, Catholicism has been eclipsed by Protestantism in terms of membership, vitality, geographic distribution, and other indicators. How, then, did Catholicism, which maintained a significant lead in the number of Chinese converts over Protestantism before 1949, come to lag so far behind?

The institutions-in-context theory developed in the introduction will be used to account for the "reversal of fortune" of the two religions. In what follows, I start by identifying three crucial differences in the institutional features of Catholicism and Protestantism in China that are consequential to their growth. But I will also argue, as I did in chapter 1, that an institutional argument alone is insufficient to explain the religions' different growth dynamics. I maintain that the fortunes of Catholicism and Protestantism were reversed less because their institutional features changed significantly than because the institutional features played out differently in the pertinent contexts. More specifically, in the environment before 1949, the institutional features of Catholicism did not greatly disadvantage it in its competition with Protestantism in winning converts. In fact, certain institutional features of Catholicism gave it a significant edge. However, under the Maoist regime, most of Catholicism's institutional features became liabilities, threatening its very survival. In the context of post-Mao China, while the institutional features of Protestantism became pivotal to the religion's rapid rise, certain institutional features of Catholicism continued to hamper its growth.

Institutional Features of Catholicism and Protestantism Compared

Catholicism and Protestantism in China share many similarities in their institutional features, particularly when compared with Chinese popular religion, Daoism, or Chinese Buddhism. Nonetheless, their apparent similarities conceal differences that that have significant implications for their growth dynamics. Table 2.2 highlights three key distinctions.

TABLE 2.2. Comparison of institutional features of Catholicism and Protestantism in China

	Catholicism	Protestantism
Recruiting members and maintaining a religious community	Reliance on the clergy	Lay activism and leadership
Authority structure	Centralized, hierarchical	Decentralized, polycephalous
Position in transnational networks	The pope's supremacy over the universal church	Not part of a universal church
	Strong links between the missions and Western colonial powers before 1949	Looser links between the missions and Western colonial powers before 1949

Both Catholicism and Protestantism are committed to creating and maintaining an expanding and robust religious community—that is, both have a strong drive to recruit and retain members. However, while spreading the gospel hinges on clerics for Catholicism, Protestantism mobilizes every member of the community to proselytize. This was acknowledged by a Catholic priest in Shanghai who expressed half amazement and half admiration: "Even an uneducated elderly woman of a Protestant group has full confidence in preaching to a nonbelieving university professor" (Informant No. 269). Indeed, every one of my Protestant informants with whom I discussed their proselytization activities told me they had tried to convert non-family members. Over the past decade or so, when traveling in China, I have had frequent encounters with proselytizing Protestants in various kinds of public places, but never have I met a proselytizing Catholic in public. A young Catholic in Hebei Province told me that, in her college, there were many Protestant students who actively proselytized among fellow students. She, however, did nothing of the kind, believing herself unqualified to talk to others about the gospel. The only thing she had done that was close to an evangelistic activity was helping to distribute gospel leaflets at the gate of her church, an activity organized by a priest (Informant No. 266).

Both Catholicism and Protestantism have tried to maintain strong religious communities through building congregations that gather the faithful to worship regularly and through socializing them into a world of specific discursive practices, morality, and values. Compared with Protestantism, Catholicism places more emphasis on sacramental observance, and Catholics' stages of life and transitions between them are intimately connected to the sacraments of the church, such as baptism, confirmation, confession, communion, marriage, and extreme unction. Catholicism places an even stronger focus on expanding and maintaining faith through familial ties. The practice of infant baptism incorporates the new generation into the Catholic faith. Marriages with non-Catholics can only take place with special permission from the parish priest, granted on the condition that the children born in the marriage will receive baptism and that the non-Catholic spouse will be open to the gospel. Thus, compared with Protestantism, Catholicism is equipped with more mechanisms to build self-sustaining communities. However, a more important difference between the two lies in the leadership of their religious communities. For Catholicism, well-functioning congregations depend on the leadership of priests, who alone have the prerogative to give sacraments. For Protestantism, the maintenance of a religious community involves more lay initiatives and leadership.

Leaders of Protestant communities can arise from the laity and do not necessarily require special training or a different lifestyle. Because the Catholic priesthood requires celibacy, a lengthy period of seminary training, and authorization from the church hierarchy, the leadership of Catholic communities cannot easily be substituted or reproduced. For this reason, the growth of Catholicism is more likely to be constrained by a shortage of personnel.

The second major difference between Catholicism and Protestantism lies in their authority structures. Protestant organizations, unlike the Catholic Church, are not subsumed under a unified ecclesiastical structure. Protestantism's polycephalous nature was clearly discernible in China before 1949 and thereafter has become even more pronounced. Before 1949, Protestant groups were affiliated with a great number of denominations. Most were foreign imports, but a few were indigenous. The latter include the True Jesus Church, the Jesus Family, and the Local Church, three of the most influential homegrown Protestant movements, all founded by charismatic leaders in the 1910s and the 1920s.[9] The Maoist state in the 1950s and 1960s forced members of different Protestant denominations and sects to worship together and effectively dismantled their hierarchical structure.[10] Consequently, the Protestant communities that reemerged in the post-Mao era were no longer under the control of denominations and sects, and hence were even more polycephalous than before. Moreover, because a central credo of Protestantism is that all believers have the right to interpret the Bible, there are few institutional barriers to Protestant groups splitting from the parent church. In other words, compared with Catholicism, Protestant communities have an inherent tendency toward a polycephalous authority structure.

In this respect, Catholicism is the antithesis of Protestantism. Ideally, practicing Catholics belong to a parish that supports the local church, staffed by one or more priests. Every parish priest answers to the local bishop, who presides over a diocese composed of a collection of parishes.[11] At the top of the church hierarchy is the Holy See, which oversees the Roman Catholic Church and its faithful from the Vatican. The Catholic hierarchy operates like a chain of command. Individual priests and bishops are not free to choose their stations but are assigned and transferred by their superiors.[12] A priest (Informant No. 259) explained:

> We priests are just like soldiers. We follow orders. A priest stays in a parish for five or six years, just long enough to familiarize himself with the local people and culture. Just when he feels at home and is up to accomplishing something, a transfer order comes and he is assigned to a new place. Everything has to start over again. Sometimes a priest doesn't get along well with the laity in his parish. Yet he has no choice but to remain there. This is distressful to both the priest and the laity. As for me, I serve all the Catholic faithful of an entire prefecture. In other words, I serve two municipal districts and seven counties. For years, I've been hoping that another priest could join me to share my burden. But he has to be assigned from the diocese. I can't possibly recruit another priest myself.

On the one hand, Protestantism's authority structure makes it a much less unified and coherent religion than Catholicism and more susceptible to the proliferation of dissenting sects and the eruption of NRMs. On the other hand, this institutional feature also promotes dynamic growth. Because Protestant groups have a freer rein to innovate, they tend to better adapt to local conditions and develop new niches. In comparison, Catholicism's bureaucratic centralism makes it less flexible. Nonetheless, this weakness of Catholicism can be mitigated to a great extent by the presence of religious orders: communities of individuals, who, bound by specific vows, dedicate themselves to spiritual pursuits and often engage in various ministries.[13] Because religious orders vary in their organizational forms and orientations, they can significantly enhance the internal variations within the Catholic Church and its capacity to explore different niches.[14]

Both the Catholic and the Protestant communities in China have strong connections with the West, yet they are embedded differently in transnational networks. This distinction is manifested chiefly in two aspects. First, characteristically, local Catholic churches are integral to a universal church and entirely subject to the supreme authority of the pope. This uniqueness in Catholicism stems from its doctrines, which assert that Christ himself instituted the papacy by giving Peter the Apostle "the keys to the Kingdom of Heaven" and proclaimed him to be the "rock" upon which the church would be built. The Catholic Church derives its spiritual authority from Peter and the succeeding popes, who are regarded as representatives of Christ on earth.

As the pope is the source and foundation of the unity of the Church, local churches cease to be "Catholic" if they do not acknowledge the highest moral and doctrinal authority vested in him.[15]

Second, in comparison with Protestant missions, Catholic missions in China were far more closely entangled with Western colonial powers that encroached on China from the 1840s well into the twentieth century. From the 1840s to the 1920s, France asserted itself as the protector of the Catholic missionary enterprise and Chinese Catholics, and the so-called French religious protectorate was largely supported by the Vatican.[16] Although it is true that predominantly Protestant countries, such as Britain and America, also insisted on the extraterritorial rights of their missionaries in China and offered them consular protection, this protection usually did not extend much beyond what was offered to other subjects or citizens. The British government, in particular, prioritized commerce and was concerned that the ill will excited by missionary activities might jeopardize its trade with China.[17] For France, trade with China was not large. Claiming guardianship over Catholic missions became its chief strategy to enhance its prominence and countervail the dominant British presence in China.[18] The religious protectorate was thus central to France's diplomacy.[19] The consular and diplomatic representatives of the French government were much more inclined than their British and American counterparts to press the Qing government to make religious concessions in treaty clauses and to use diplomacy or force to defend and advance the interests of missionaries and Chinese converts.[20]

Three Phases and Their Political Conditions

The institutional features of Catholicism and Protestantism delineated above have played out in different ways depending on the context, shaping the religious growth dynamics in various historical periods. According to the political conditions and their bearing on religions, particularly on Catholicism and Protestantism, we can roughly divide the history of China from 1842 to 2018 into three phases:[21] 1842 to 1949, 1949 to 1976, and 1976 to 2018.

The first period saw radical changes in China's political system: the Qing dynasty was overthrown in the 1911 Revolution and replaced by the Republic of China. Despite political upheaval, there was strong continuity in the political conditions that affected the fate of Catholicism and Protestantism. Under the treaties the Qing government was forced to sign with Western powers, missionaries were accorded extraterritorial rights as well as rights to purchase property, to proselytize, and to establish churches, hospitals, and schools. In the wake of the founding of the Republic, the political elite looked toward the West for a model to follow in building a nation-state. The elite rejected the idea of setting up a state religion,[22] and they declared religious freedom to be a constitutional right.[23] Under this new policy, "proper religions" that received state recognition enjoyed the legal right to congregate, proselytize, publish, and form associations; the properness of a religion was primarily determined by the extent it conformed to the normative model of Christianity.[24] Moreover, the Chinese governing elite was eager to avoid offending Western powers and even actively sought their support, for geopolitical and other reasons. The Nationalist government under Chiang Kai-shek's leadership (1928–49), in particular, favored Christianity—Chiang himself, his wife's family, and many members of his cabinet were Christians.[25] All in all, Christianity under Republican China continued to enjoy privileges as it had under the late Qing, until the establishment of the Communist government.[26]

The second period spans the time from the founding of the People's Republic of China in 1949 to the death of Mao Zedong in 1976. During this period, the Maoist state took drastic action to control and contain religion. Radical policies surged from time to time and culminated in the Cultural Revolution, when the state set out to wipe out all religions. China's international relations also dramatically changed after 1949. Hostility and enmity between Mao's China and the West ran deep.

In the third period, the post-Mao state abandoned ideological extremism, launched market-oriented reforms, and opened up China to the outside world. The state's religious policy also eased. Protestantism and Catholicism once again were allowed to operate, albeit under a strong regulatory regime.

The following discussion explores how the institutional features of Catholicism and Protestantism played out in the different contexts of the three historical periods (see table 2.3).

1842–1949

Reliance on clerics in recruiting members and maintaining the religious community makes Catholicism susceptible to shortages of key personnel. Between 1842 and 1949, however, this problem was mitigated by the presence of a large number of foreign missionaries who entered China after 1842 as a result of treaties between the Qing government and Western powers.[27] Neither did the Republican state pose obstacles to the entry of foreign missionaries. It did not want to defy Western powers over this issue. Moreover, many among the Republican political elite tended to be pro-West modernizers.

Being polycephalous, Protestant communities tend to be diverse and tap into a wider spectrum of niches than their Catholic counterparts. During this

TABLE 2.3. Institutional features of Catholicism and Protestantism playing out (1842–2018)

		1842–1949 (Late Qing and Republican China)	1949–76 (Mao's China)	1976–2018 (Post-Mao China)
Recruiting members and maintaining a religious community	CATHOLICISM Reliance on the clergy	Personnel shortage was alleviated by the presence of foreign missionaries	Repressive measures were more effective in damaging the Catholic community	Constrained by personnel shortages
	PROTESTANTISM Lay activism and leadership	Less constrained by personnel shortages	Repressive measures had less impact	Less constrained by personnel shortages
Authority structure	CATHOLICISM Centralized, hierarchical	Lack of flexibility and diversity was remedied by missionaries from different orders and nationalities	Regarded by the state as a menacing threat	Much more easily monitored and contained by the Chinese state; caught in bitter infighting between the open and underground churches, and other kinds of strife
	PROTESTANTISM Decentralized, polycephalous	Greater diversity; emergence of indigenous Protestant movements	Regarded by the state as a less menacing threat	More capable of evading state control for autonomous development; internal divisions lead to competition conducive to church growth
Position in transnational networks	CATHOLICISM Vatican supremacy; strong links between the missions and Western colonial powers before 1949	French religious protectorate allowed Catholicism to attract protection seekers who often converted collectively	The Maoist state suppressed Catholicism more severely in the 1950s	The Chinese state is more watchful and heavy-handed in handling Catholic groups
	PROTESTANTISM Not part of a universal church; looser links between the missions and Western colonial powers before 1949	Far fewer instances of mass conversion	Less severely persecuted in the 1950s	Less tension with the state than the Catholic counterpart

period, however, Catholicism's lack of flexibility and diversity was counter-
acted to a great extent by the presence of different religious orders, congregations, and societies.

The Protestant missions in China between 1842 and 1949 reveal a bewildering heterogeneity. Some missions were run by large denominations based
in the missionaries' home nations; others were interdenominational and international, such as the China Inland Mission; and still others were operated
by individual evangelists without a specific denominational affiliation.[28] Although many missionaries could be regarded as mainline Protestants, some
of the latecomers were fundamentalists or Pentecostals. The missionary activities of mainline Protestant denominations focused on educational, medical, and social work and were primarily centered in cities. Their investment
in higher education led to the creation of thirteen colleges and universities in
China in these decades, whereas Catholics founded only three.[29] The mainline
Protestants also founded six major medical colleges and a network of modern hospitals, greatly outnumbering Catholic institutions. This fostered the
emergence of a Protestant urban middle class, among whom were activists in
social and political reforms.[30] Unlike the mainline missions, the China Inland
Mission, founded by Hudson Taylor, was theologically conservative and focused on "faith" missions. Beginning in the 1860s, its missionaries trekked to
China's hinterland, untouched by prior Protestant missions, greatly extending the rural reach of Protestantism.[31] Moreover, Protestantism's decentralized authority structure facilitated the rise of indigenous Protestant movements in the 1910s and 1920s, which, with their strong Pentecostal coloration
and radical millenarian message, had wide appeal in rural society.[32]

Although Catholicism's centralized bureaucracy makes it less flexible
and less capable of tapping into diverse niches, this problem was partially
relieved by the presence of different religious orders during this period. Some
of the orders, such as the Foreign Missions of Paris, the Milan Foreign Missions, and Maryknoll, had members who came primarily from one country,
whereas other orders, such as the Lazarists, the Franciscans, and the Dis-
calced Carmelite Nuns, were international in membership. The Catholic religious societies operated with different focuses. Some were committed to education. The Salesians of Don Bosco, for instance, opened grammar schools
and vocational schools all over China. Some orders undertook a wide range
of apostolic work, including training catechists, caring for the aged, helping
the poor, and running orphanages and health clinics. A few other orders,
such as the Sisters Adorers of the Precious Blood, devoted themselves to a
cloistered, contemplative life.[33] It should be noted that the religious orders
and societies were able to play important roles in the growth of Catholicism

because the late Qing and Republican governments afforded ample opportunity for the formation of civic organizations and permitted religious groups to actively engage in social work. Because the majority of the religious societies were foreign imports and their members were primarily foreigners, their operations also owed much to the policy of the Chinese government of this period, which was receptive to foreign missionaries.[34]

The close amalgamation of the Catholic mission enterprise and the colonial French regime also helped Catholicism to gain converts during this period, particularly during the late Qing.[35] Not long after China was defeated in the Opium War in 1842, French representatives pressed the Qing authorities to return church properties confiscated during the long persecution after the Chinese Rites Controversy, to grant missionaries the right to rent and purchase property in China's hinterland, and to exempt Chinese Catholics from locally imposed contributions to village communal ritual activities.[36] French officials would also intercede when missionaries encountered obstructions in exercising their "treaty rights" and would exact substantial indemnities from the Qing government for the losses of missionaries and their Chinese converts in local conflicts and rebellions. With French naval forces stationed in Chinese waters and its warships ready to move into menacing positions at any time, the Qing government was forced to submit to the demands of the French diplomats.[37] Under the French protectorate, missionaries even enjoyed a "semiofficial" position in dealing with local Chinese officials.[38] They took advantage of this to intervene in local lawsuits to the advantage of Chinese converts, making the Catholic Church in China an "imperium in imperio" and a new source of power in local society. This made Catholicism especially attractive to two types of people in Chinese society.[39]

One type consisted of those living at the margins of Chinese society. For instance, the protection offered by the Catholic missionaries prompted mass conversion among the fishing community in southern Jiangsu Province,[40] and the Tanka, or boat people, in Fujian Province,[41] whom local society treated as outcasts.[42] Likewise, destitute Han Chinese migrating into the northwestern part of China, where Mongolian people predominated, were receptive to Catholic missions. With the active support of the French representatives, these missions were able to purchase large tracts of arable land and rent them to Han converts to cultivate.[43] Similarly, sectarian groups in Shandong embraced Catholicism hoping the protection of the Catholic Church would shield them from the ruthless persecution of sectarian religions by the Qing state.[44]

The Catholic churches' readiness to wade into the muddy waters of local politics also attracted groups of people who, trapped in long-standing and violent local conflicts, desperately sought any tipping point that would allow them to gain the upper hand over their foes. Catholic missionaries found a receptive audience in areas where violence, between migrant groups and natives as well as among different migrant groups struggling over scarce resources, frequently broke out,[45] and where feuding lineages, villages, or sectarian groups were ensnared in a history of mutual antagonism and violence.[46] The conversion of Donglü village in Hebei Province into a Catholic community is a case in point.[47]

Conversion in Donglü was triggered by a dispute in 1862 between the two major lineage groups: the impoverished Yangs and the better-off Cais. Convinced by a geomancer that their fortunes were adversely affected by a Buddhist pagoda the Cais erected to protect their own feng shui, the Yangs sent men to vandalize the pagoda.[48] The Cais seized the perpetrators and took them to the magistrate of Baoding Prefecture. Tipped off by a Chinese Catholic in a nearby village that conversion to Catholicism could bring them the church's protection in the litigation, the desperate Yangs sought out a Lazarist priest and received baptism from him. Their foe, the Cais, upon learning of the Yangs' conversion, found the same priest and converted *en masse* as well.

These converts were often called *rice Christians, litigation Christians,* or *feud Christians.*[49] Although some did leave the church when the church's protection was no longer needed, many of them were transformed into steadfast Catholics.[50] Donglü, for instance, became the locus of one of the highest concentrations of Catholics in the country and one of two Marian pilgrimage sites in China recognized by the pope.[51] Descendants of the fishermen in Jiangsu and Fujian and of the Han migrants in Inner Mongolia also stayed in the fold. Doubtless, the strength of Catholic churches in creating and maintaining a strong religious community through education and pastoral care had contributed to the transformation of protection seekers into pious devotees.[52] However, their transformation was also due to several processes set in motion following mass conversion. When the converts received the church's protection, they provoked more resentment and retaliation from their non-Christian foes.[53] To defend themselves, the converts came to rely even more on the church's protection. Moreover, when the converts, as enjoined by the church, abandoned the normative religious and cultural practices of Chinese society, withdrawing from ancestor worship and refusing to contribute to communal temple festivals, they became further stigmatized.[54] All this in turn induced them to remain within the Catholic community.[55]

Prior scholarship has emphasized how, under the religious protectorate, Catholic missionaries' meddling in local politics triggered anti-Christian incidents, culminating in the Boxer Uprising of 1899–1901.[56] But the religious

FIGURE 2.2. A wedding ceremony in the Catholic Cathedral of Donglü, Hebei Province, in 2016. Enshrined at the high altar of this cathedral is the painted image of Our Lady of China. The Marian shrine in Donglü was consecrated as the national shrine in 1937 by Pope Pius XI. (Photograph by the author.)

protectorate did enable the Catholic Church to tap into the structure of rural society to win converts through what social movement scholars have dubbed *bloc recruitment*.[57] Throughout rural northern China, the strategy of bloc recruitment won a large following for the Catholic missions.[58]

Missionaries and diplomats from Protestant countries often disdained, but were also jealous of, Catholic missionaries' exercise of temporal authority.[59] This is not to say that they themselves totally rejected intervention in local disputes. Nonetheless, such incidences were rare, and bloc recruitment was never a strength of the Protestant missions.[60]

To conclude, although Catholicism's centralized bureaucracy and reliance on the clergy could be a disadvantage in its competition with Protestantism, this problem was not salient during the late Qing and the Republican period. This is because the presence of a myriad of religious orders minimized the problem of organizational inflexibility associated with Catholicism's centralized bureaucracy, and because the inflow of a large number of foreign missionaries mitigated the personnel shortage problem associated with Catholicism's reliance on clergy. Furthermore, the Catholic Church's close alliance with colonial powers—primarily France from the 1840s to the 1920s—helped it to win mass conversion of protection seekers. All these mechanisms worked together to keep the growth rate of Catholicism comparable with that of Protestantism in pre-1949 China. And due to its earlier start, Catholicism was able to maintain a substantial numerical advantage over Protestantism by 1949.

1949–76: UNDER THE MAOIST REGIME

Through its radical and sweeping actions, the Maoist state decisively changed the effect of the institutional features of the religions. In contrast to the late Qing and the Republican states, the Maoist state, emerging triumphantly from the Chinese Civil War (1945–49), was able to build a massive state machinery and penetrate deeply into society. Yet at the same time, as a fledging regime, the state had a deep fear of sabotage and espionage. Its rival, the Nationalists, after losing the civil war and retreating to the island of Taiwan, was preparing to retake the mainland by force. And the Nationalists did have agents and supporters scattered across China, awaiting and preparing for an invasion in the initial years after their defeat. The United States and other Western nations were hostile to the new regime as well. Beijing's sense of crisis heightened after the outbreak of the Korean War (1950–53), particularly after China joined the fight against the US-led coalition. The new regime launched a nationwide "Resist America, Aid Korea" campaign to mobilize support for the war effort. Concurrently, it ordered a thorough investigation across the country of social organizations that received foreign funds. Western ties thus became the Achilles' heel of religious organizations.

Catholicism, with its centralized bureaucracy and loyalty to the pope, naturally became suspect to the Communist regime.[61] To make the situation worse, Pius XII (1876–1958), who served as pope from 1939 to 1958, was virulently anti-Communist. In 1949, the Vatican issued decrees forbidding Catholics to cooperate with Communists, or even to read Communist literature, under pain of excommunication.[62] Antonio Riberi (1897–1967), who served as the papal nuncio to China from 1946 until his expulsion in 1951, implemented the Vatican's policy zealously. He incited Catholics to use all kinds of methods to fight Communism. He also organized the Legion of Mary, an elite organization of Catholic activists, to thwart the goals of the new regime.[63] A showdown between the Communist regime and the Catholic Church became inevitable.

Starting in 1950, the Maoist regime tried to set up a mass organization called the Chinese Catholic Patriotic Association (hereafter the Catholic Patriotic Association) to cut the Chinese Catholic Church's ties with the Vatican and to place the Church under its control. However, most Catholics remained loyal to the pope and refused to cooperate. The regime responded with determined, swift, and severe suppression of Catholicism. Foreign missionaries were expelled, and Vatican loyalists were incarcerated.[64] In Shanghai alone, by the end of November 1955, 1,500 Catholics had been arrested, including several seminarians and about 50 priests.[65] Even under such duress, Catholic resistance persisted, and the national Catholic Patriotic Association could not be established until 1957.

The government's treatment of Protestantism in the 1950s was less severe. Even though it too had foreign connections, the polycephalous Protestant community was a diverse field, including indigenous sects that could claim they had no foreign ties and liberal Protestants who were critical of the complicity of missionaries in imperialism.[66] Moreover, because no authority could exercise the power of excommunication, it was much easier for Protestants to sever their foreign ties. Thus, unlike within Catholicism, there was a significant segment of the Protestant community ready to collaborate with the Communists. In 1951, Wu Yaozong (1893–1979), a liberal Protestant leader, published what is known as *The Christian Manifesto*. Promoting "self-governance, self-support, and self-propagation" of the Chinese Protestant community, this manifesto launched the Three-Self Patriotic Movement (hereafter the Three-Self Movement) to remove churches' foreign ties and to assure the government of Protestants' loyalty.[67] With a few notable exceptions, such as Wang Mingdao (1900–91) and Yuan Xiangchen (1914–2005), who insisted on the church's independence from politics even at the cost of their freedom, all Protestant groups joined the Three-Self Movement.[68]

The consequence was that, during the initial period of the Maoist era, Catholicism was hit much harder than Protestantism. Here, I will cite the case of River County to illustrate. In 1949, the county had 3 Catholic churches with 520 members, under the care of a Canadian priest of the Scarboro Mission Society.[69] In April 1950, the Canadian priest was forced to leave China, and a Chinese Lazarist priest was sent as his replacement. Within months, however, the Chinese priest was put under arrest, accused of assisting "the criminal special agents" (*feite*), an epithet used at the time for the Nationalists. His strong Western connections—receiving education from a Catholic elementary school, training at France-sponsored seminaries, and joining a Lazarist order—made his "crime" more egregious. Charged as a "counterrevolutionary," he ended up in a labor camp at a desolate farm in Qinghai Province until his release in 1980. Deprived of leadership, the Catholic community in River County was thrown into disarray. In contrast, the Protestants during this period were much less affected. Nine of the ten Protestant churches were founded by China Inland Mission. However, in 1935, the Chinese members decided to switch the church affiliation to the Local Church, an indigenous Chinese Protestant movement. Thus, for good reasons, these Protestant churches could avow that they had already acted on the "three-self" principles. When the Land Reform started in 1950, all religious sites in River County were ordered to suspend their activities so that the campaign could command people's full attention. But when the Land Reform was completed a year later, the county government was slow in issuing a decree to allow religious activities to resume. While other religious groups were reticent, Protestant leaders repeatedly petitioned. Eventually the county government acceded to their requests.

The political environment for both Catholicism and Protestantism deteriorated further as the Maoist regime grew increasingly radical. During the Great Leap Forward in 1958–61, a sweeping campaign to transform China into a socialist society through rapid industrialization and collectivization, religious organizations were forced to "donate" their sites to the government to "assist socialist construction." Radical religious policy culminated in the Cultural Revolution, during which all religions were targeted for eradication. The Red Guards, groups of zealous students encouraged by Mao to attack all traditional values and vestiges of imperialism, marched across China to wreak havoc on religions. Both Catholicism and Protestantism experienced outright oppression of unprecedented intensity and scale.

Yet the same kinds of severe oppression injured Catholicism more than Protestantism. Persecution targets leaders more. Because Catholicism relied heavily on clerics who cannot be easily replaced, the removal of priests inflicted indelible damage on the Catholic community. In many Catholic communities, after the arrest of priests, church functions were discontinued and followers dispersed. Across China, only in areas with a high density of Catholics, such as Catholic villages, was the community able to withstand the loss of priestly leadership and continue some religious activities, albeit secretly.[70] For Protestant communities, decapitation did much less damage because leadership was largely replaceable—when a leader was arrested, another individual could take on the mantle. Many Protestant communities were able to hold secret small-group meetings even during the Cultural Revolution (see chapter 1).

The religions' different experiences during the Mao era have had huge consequences for their post-Mao revival. As soon as repression subsided in the late 1970s, Protestant groups started the rebuilding of churches and congregations. The Catholic communities, on the other hand, had to wait for the return of the imprisoned priests to lead the rebuilding process. Because of the severe shortage of clergy created by the persecution, some Catholic communities did not have their priests restored until very late, and some never got them back. In River County, Protestant groups in the early 1980s not only congregated publicly but also managed to reclaim most of their church properties. Church membership grew from only a few hundred in the late 1970s to approximately 4,500 in 1987. In the case of the Catholics, their priest was not able to return to River County after his release from a labor camp in 1980. Without a priestly head, the Catholic community remained disintegrated, and its restoration has been impeded.[71] In 1986, the remaining Catholics in River County filed a petition to request the local government to return their church properties in accordance with the religious policy of the central government. The local government, however, denied the petition, citing the lack of a priest as the main reason.[72] The River County case might be an extreme one, but it is also telling, shedding light on why by 1982, the nationwide Protestant population, reaching roughly three million, was catching up with the number of Catholics.

1976–2018: UNDER THE POST-MAO STATE

After the death of Mao, Deng Xiaoping abandoned Maoism and ushered in a new era of "reform and opening-up." In this period, all sorts of religions, including Catholicism and Protestantism, experienced recovery and rejuvenation. It is in this era that the growth of Protestantism has far outpaced that of Catholicism.

Several conditions have defined the sociopolitical environment of religious groups in the post-Mao era. The state repudiated radicalism and adopted a more moderate religious policy. The principles of the policy were laid out in *Document 19* issued in 1982, which condemned radical policies that tried to eliminate religions through coercion and claimed that the state would protect the freedom of religious belief. With the implementation of this new policy, religious leaders were released from prison, some seized properties were returned, religious sites were reopened, and religious activities resumed.

To describe the government's religious policy as "moderate" does not mean it has surrendered control over religion. In fact, the post-Mao state still considers religions' transnational links and capacity for mass mobilization a challenge to national security and social stability.[73] To impose control over religious groups, the Chinese government installed the regulatory agency, RAB, at every administrative level and established umbrella associations for each of the five government-recognized religions (see chapter 1). Religious organizations are required to register with the RAB and join the umbrella associations. Restrictive regulations have also been put in place to define the boundaries of sanctioned religious activities. They outlaw itinerant and public evangelism, proselytization among minors, and missionary activities of foreign individuals and organizations.

Nonetheless, as chapter 1 argues, the efficacy of the religious regulatory regime in the post-Mao era was undermined, giving rise to an interstitial social space where unsanctioned religious groups and activities emerged. This occurred for three primary reasons: the society, as a result of the reforms, became more dynamic, with better access to the outside world and increasingly difficult for the state to rein in; the Chinese government, tied economically to the West, was compelled to engage, even if half-heartedly, in the Western discourse of religious freedom and human rights and restrain from outright suppression of religions, particularly world religions with strong Western connections; the agencies in charge of religious work, under a government that prioritized economic development, lacked the capacity and motivation to enforce rigorous rules on unsanctioned religious groups and activities.[74]

In sum, thanks to post-Mao China's more moderate religious policy, Protestantism and Catholicism experienced a revival. However, they were still subject to the state's surveillance, control, and restrictions. Yet, the emergent interstitial social spaces in the reform era gave religious groups ways to circumvent control and bypass restrictions. What did these political conditions mean for the two religious communities? I argue that Protestantism achieved faster growth in the post-Mao era than Catholicism largely because it was better equipped to explore and exploit the interstitial social spaces.

First, the lay activism of Protestantism helped its evangelistic activities to slip under the government's radar. Even though official regulations outlaw proselytization outside sanctioned religious sites, followers of Protestantism were able to spread the gospel through their personal networks. Taking advantage of an increasingly porous authoritarian regime, they also disseminated religious messages in the public space (e.g., campuses, busy streets).[75] Even though official regulations forbid foreigners from missionizing, Protestant missionaries circumvented the ban by working as, for example, English-language teachers or NGO volunteers as they missionized through ties developed during their stay in China.[76]

Due to their reliance on clerical leadership, Catholic groups were much more easily monitored and contained. Although foreign Protestant missionaries were able to circumvent, to some extent, the state ban by taking up a lay profession as camouflage, it was hard for foreign Catholic clerics to do the same. This was unfortunate for Catholicism because foreign clerics might otherwise provide some of the manpower needed to address the acute problem of professional personnel shortages that continued to be a great constraint on the Catholic Church in post-Mao China.[77] In recent years, the priest shortage has been aggravated as the number of young men willing to take the Catholic vocation has decreased, first in dioceses in major urban centers and coastal regions, then gradually in rural Catholic strongholds, partly due to rising economic opportunities and the implementation of the one-child policy.[78]

Another state ban also had a negative impact on the development of Catholicism. As noted previously, religious orders before 1949 had played an important role in the growth of the Church. In post-Mao China, although the Chinese government has permitted female religious societies affiliated with particular parishes to obtain legal status, it has not yet allowed male religious societies to reconstitute themselves.[79] Thus, only a few male religious orders, such as the Society of the Divine Word and the Franciscans, were active in the underground, but their influence was limited.[80] This means that religious orders have been unable to significantly contribute to Catholicism's revival in post-Mao China. One priest lamented, "Catholicism in China used to walk on two legs—diocesan priests and religious priests. Now, without the support from strong religious orders, we have to limp along" (Informant No. 259).

The polycephalous nature of Protestantism gave the religion some additional edge in exploring the new social space opened up in post-Mao China. Without a central authority to coordinate and command its diverse groups, Protestantism looked less menacing to the Chinese state. The heterogeneous Protestant groups, especially independent church groups, thwarted the monitoring and controlling efforts of those regulatory agencies (see chapter 1). Because of its hierarchical centralized structure, Catholicism was perceived as a greater threat. Moreover, because the Chinese government was in a constant battle with the Vatican for the allegiance of Chinese Catholics, Catholic groups were subject to tighter surveillance and control and had to maneuver in a more constrained social space than Protestant groups.[81]

Yet another stumbling block to the growth of Catholicism in the post-Mao years was internal conflict within the religious community. Just as they started to recover from the ravages wrought by Maoism, both Catholicism and Protestantism suffered a major division, but the consequences were different.

The division stems from the same root: the government's control bred discontent among believers, some of whom broke away from the government-controlled patriotic associations to create "underground" or independent groups. The breakaway Protestants found official restrictions on evangelism intolerable and criticized the Three-Self churches for being so compliant as to "allow the government, instead of Christ, to be the head of the church." The underground Catholics rejected the Catholic Patriotic Association because it denied the pope's supreme authority and, in turn, was not recognized by the Vatican. In Protestantism, the split led to the rise of the independent church movement (aka house-church movement), which drew inspiration from Wang Mingdao and other Protestant leaders who refused to join the Three-Self Movement and suffered the consequences in the 1950s. In Catholicism, a central figure who gave momentum to the underground churches is Bishop Fan Xueyan of Baoding Diocese in Hebei Province. Fan endured long prison terms for his unswerving loyalty to the pope and his criticism of the Catholic Patriotic Association. In 1981, without a mandate from Rome, Fan secretly consecrated three bishops, believing the dire situation of the Chinese Church warranted this extraordinary action. Pope John Paul II later not only approved Fan's action but also granted him permission to continue this practice without having to seek the approval of the Holy See.[82] With the pope's approval, Fan and the bishops he consecrated went on to consecrate dozens of bishops and ordain hundreds of priests in the next two decades,[83] creating a parallel network and authority structure of the underground churches that challenged the government-sanctioned open churches.[84] The underground church leaders denounced government collaborators as traitors, claimed the sacraments performed by Patriotic priests to be invalid, and urged the Catholic faithful to boycott the Masses said by Patriotic priests.[85] The young and zealous underground priests went to various provinces to mobilize the faithful against the open churches.[86] They sowed confusion, division, and antagonism in many places, and sometimes even paralyzed entire dioceses.[87]

Even though both the Protestant and Catholic communities were torn apart by the division between the official and the independent churches, the division had different ramifications. For Protestantism, although the independent churches condemned the official churches, their criticism was not sufficient to wreck the religious legitimacy of the official churches. With no ultimate authority to adjudicate and pass binding judgments, the Protestant community was already deeply fragmented. The division between the official and the independent sectors introduced just another fissure. Without the power to fundamentally damage each other's religious legitimacy, the independent and the official churches could part ways and work to strengthen and expand their own congregations. They became competitors on the level of recruiting and retaining followers. When independent churches opened Sunday schools, held revival meetings, and enthusiastically evangelized, the official churches were compelled to emulate them to stay competitive (see chapter 1). In short, the competition between the independent and official churches fueled the growth of Protestantism.

The same division has generated different dynamics for Catholicism. Due to the Catholic belief in the unity of the Church, the open and underground churches were unable to disentangle themselves from each other. In Catholicism, the papacy has the supreme and full authority over the universal church. It can denounce sacraments as invalid, condemn doctrines and practices as heretical, and wield ecclesiastical censure, including excommunication. That is why the underground church movement, backed by the Vatican, could fundamentally undermine the religious legitimacy of the open churches and why the infighting could turn so intense.[88]

Keenly aware that the source of their religious legitimacy can come only from the pope, and facing mounting challenges from underground churches, bishops of the open churches tried to reconcile with the pope. From 1989 and onward, the open churches started to include a prayer for the pope in their Masses, one by one.[89] The "illicit" bishops appointed by the Catholic Patriotic Association without prior approval of the pope also approached the Vatican in secrecy and asked for reconciliation.[90] In an attempt to regain oversight over the open churches, the Vatican agreed to pardon "illicit" bishops.[91] Furthermore, increasingly troubled by the growing rift in the Chinese Catholic Church and the development of underground churches,[92] in the 1990s the Vatican began to promote unity between the open and underground churches, encouraging leaders of the underground churches to take positions in the open churches.[93] This has eased the tension between the open and the underground churches to some degree, expanded the Vatican's control over the open churches, and diminished the influence of the underground churches in many places.[94] Yet these moves have left some underground church followers, who have paid a steep price for their loyalty to Rome and resistance to the Catholic Patriotic Association, feeling disturbed and betrayed. In fact, the Vatican's policy has introduced a new source of strife into some Catholic communities, especially in places where underground churches remain strong. When certain underground priests, encouraged by the new instructions of the Vatican, emerged from underground to join the open churches, they caused an uproar in the underground church community. This is what happened to An Shuxin (born 1949), who was consecrated as an underground auxiliary bishop of the Baoding Diocese in Hebei Province in 1993. Having served ten years in prison, he was widely regarded a hero in China's underground church community. However, after his release from prison in 2006, he decided to join the open churches and later the Catholic Patriotic Association. An's decision antagonized many in the underground community, who denounced him as a traitor. Consequently, the Baoding Diocese became even more bitterly divided.

In sum, while the division between official and independent churches gave rise to a kind of competition conducive to the overall growth of Protestantism, the same rift led to incessant and bitter infighting that wounded the Catholic community. When asked in an interview to assess the situation of Catholicism in Hebei Province, where a quarter of China's Catholics live, a priest from an open church in the Baoding Diocese lamented, "How can a church community with members quarreling all the time devote itself fully to the development of the church? How can a quarrelling household enjoy prosperity?" (Informant No. 265).

Alarmed by the chaos in the Chinese Catholic Church, the Vatican became eager to normalize diplomatic relations with the Chinese government. Secret negotiations between the two sides started in 1987. However, the nature of the papacy, with its claim to universal religious authority, has made it hard to reach a deal with the Chinese state, which is obsessed with its sovereign rights.[95] For decades, the negotiations were stalled over the nomination of bishops. Asserting that China's domestic religious affairs should not be subject to foreign interference, the Chinese government, from 1958 onward, used the Catholic Patriotic Association to nominate and consecrate bishops without reference to Rome. The Vatican insisted that the appointment of bishops was a papal prerogative and condemned the "self-consecration" of bishops staged by the Chinese government. What we witnessed was a modern-day rendition of the Investiture Controversy, in which the Catholic Church and states in medieval Europe clashed over who had the right to appoint bishops.

When negotiations were underway, the Vatican and Beijing reached a tacit understanding under which the bishops nominated by the Chinese government would also seek the Vatican's prior approval. However, there were breaches of this tacit agreement from time to time. Between 2000 and 2012, China consecrated sixteen bishops without seeking the prior approval of the pope. The Vatican responded by excommunicating these bishops and enjoining the faithful to avoid communion with them.

The contention between the two powers centering on the "illicit" bishops not only hindered the negotiations but also inflicted a deep wound in the Chinese Catholic community. Because these bishops were excommunicated by the pope, they could not perform their duties in their dioceses; priests refused to have communion with them, would-be priests avoided ordination officiated by them, the lay faithful refused to receive sacraments from them. This is what happened in the Hangzhou Diocese, whose bishop was consecrated without a papal mandate in 2000. The bishop later sought papal approbation and reconciled with the pope in 2008. Before that, the diocese was largely "leaderless" and "priests had to act on their own accord" (Informants No. 259 and 261).

In addition to unilaterally pushing ahead with the consecration of new bishops, the Chinese government has also attempted to deploy "illicit" bishops to "contaminate" the ordination ceremony of candidates who have obtained the prior approval of the Vatican. Such bishops were present at Ma Daqin's ordination as an auxiliary bishop for the Shanghai Diocese, which took place in July 2012. Ma tried to prevent the three "illicit" bishops present at the ceremony from performing the ritual of laying hands on him, and he refused to share the Eucharist with them. Furthermore, to everyone's surprise, Ma announced on the spot that he would resign from all his positions in the Catholic Patriotic Association. Shortly after his episcopal ordination, the Chinese government placed Ma under house arrest and stripped him of his title. It also went further to close down the diocesan publishing house and seminaries.[96] This was a terrible blow to the Shanghai Diocese. A priest I interviewed commented on this wryly: "Now, like the Hangzhou Diocese, our Shanghai Diocese has become paralyzed too! Yet for different reasons" (Informant No. 269).

In 2014, formal dialogues between the Vatican and Beijing were restarted. In 2018, the two sides signed a historic agreement on the appointment of bishops, overcoming the most daunting obstacle standing in the way of their rapprochement.[97] This deal was hailed with optimism that the fractured Chinese Catholic community would finally be reunited and that the Catholic Church could look forward to a new wave of evangelism in China.[98] Some church observers, however, urged caution.[99] We will explore this issue further in the conclusion. Yet even if the more optimistic prognosis becomes a reality, for Catholicism, four decades have already been lost. And it is during these decades that Catholicism has fallen far behind Protestantism.

Conclusion and Discussion

This chapter seeks to unravel the puzzle of why Catholicism, which maintained a significant lead in the number of Chinese converts over Protestantism before 1949, lags far behind Protestantism today. The answer to this puzzle lies in combining an institutional argument with a historical perspective that emphasizes the importance of sociopolitical conditions. More specifically, this chapter has identified three crucial differences in the institutional features of the two religious communities and analyzed how they have played out in the contexts of pre-1949 China, Mao's China, and post-Mao China.

Catholicism in China has been clergy-reliant, hierarchically organized, subject to a supranational religious authority, and for a time was closely associated with Western colonial powers. Centralized bureaucracy can lead to organizational inflexibility and reliance on the clergy can lead to priest shortages, both inimical to the dynamic growth of the religion. Yet during the late Qing and the Republican period, these problems were largely alleviated because political situations at the time made the operation of a large number of foreign missionaries from different religious orders and nationalities in China possible. Moreover, between the 1840s and the 1920s, Catholicism was able to take advantage of its close ties with colonial powers and a weak Chinese state to gain converts, particularly through mass conversion of protection seekers. All these enabled Catholicism to maintain a growth rate comparable with that of Protestantism in pre-1949 China. However, under the Maoist state, the Chinese Catholic Church's subordination to the supranational authority of the Vatican became a liability, leading to severe government suppression. Its reliance on clerics also made the suppression more effective. In the new sociopolitical environment of post-Mao China, Catholicism's reliance on clergy and centralized bureaucracy made it less able to take advantage of China's emergent interstitial social spaces. Finally, the unceasing conflict between the Chinese state and the papacy caused bitter divisions and infighting within the Chinese Catholic Church, which left church growth hamstrung.

In comparison, Protestantism in China mobilizes lay activism in sustaining and expanding its religious communities, is decentralized and heterogeneous, and is not subject to a single supranational religious authority. These institutional features allowed Protestant communities to weather the Maoist persecution better than Catholic communities. Under the post-Mao Chinese state, the decentralized authority structure and heterogeneity of Protestant groups helped them circumvent the state's surveillance and restrictions to seek autonomous development.

The major theoretical thrust of this book is that the effect of institutional features is contingent on the context, which is largely shaped by sociopolitical forces. From Richard Madsen's 1998 book *China's Catholics*, we can derive an alternative explanation to account for the differential growth dynamics of Catholicism and Protestantism in contemporary China: Catholicism, as a religion centered on tight-knit, self-contained communities, is less able than Protestantism to adapt to a Chinese society that has become increasingly individualistic under the market-oriented reforms. This argument is to a degree congruent with the theoretical framework adopted in this book, because it also recognizes the varying importance of the institutional features in a changing context. The major difference is that, while Madsen's analysis emphasizes the structural conditions shaped by societal forces such as modernization and urbanization, my theory points to more specific sociopolitical forces as consequences of the patterned activities of powerful political actors in the historical process. At a more empirical level, my response to this alternative argument is twofold: First, Protestants had already caught up with Catholics numerically in the early 1980s, well before China's market-oriented reform and urbanization gained momentum. Second, even if we concede that Protestantism, as a more individualist religion, suits better the increasingly individualist society of post-Mao China, we must ask: Why did Catholicism fail to meet the challenges? Why did it not initiate reforms, or emulate the practices of Protestantism, as it did after the Reformation,[100] and in Latin America in recent decades?[101] Had Catholicism taken such measures, it would not have lagged so far behind Protestantism in post-Mao China. The problem is that Catholicism, struggling with and often bogged down by personnel shortages, infighting, and state restrictions, lacked both the energy and the capacity to meet the competitive pressures of rival religions and the challenges of social change.[102] This brings us back to the drastic political changes that led to Catholicism's crippled state in the first place. Although this chapter emphasizes the role of political forces in shaping the context in which the institutional features of religion play out, it does not dismiss societal forces as irrelevant or unimportant. Nonetheless, this chapter has also shown that profound and abrupt social changes that affect religious dynamics are greatly shaped and often generated by political forces. This is another reason why my approach gives primacy to political contexts.

Readers may ask to what extent my institutions-in-context approach could shed light on the development of Catholicism and Protestantism in other places and times. By way of concluding this chapter, I shall offer my two cents on how the institutional features of Catholicism and Protestantism can play out in different kinds of contexts.

Under a more liberal political environment where different religious organizations all enjoy freedom to operate, Protestantism and Catholicism have their own respective strengths. Protestantism's lay activism makes its development less constrained by the personnel shortage problem, and its polycephalous structure makes the religion able to explore a wider range of niches and more flexible to adapt to the local conditions.[103] These strengths have helped Protestantism—especially its Pentecostal variants—to gain an edge in Latin America at the expense of the Catholic Church.[104] On the other hand, Catholicism's focus on building self-contained community makes it more capable of retaining the next generations. Perhaps this is a major reason that Catholicism has been better able to withstand the onslaught of secularizing forces than Protestantism in Europe.[105.]

However, if the two religions face an authoritarian regime hostile to both, Protestantism is more likely to fare better. This is not only because polycephalous Protestantism is more capable of evading the dragnet but also because an authoritarian state is more likely to take the more centralized and authoritarian Catholicism as a threat. If the regime is strongly authoritarian or nationalist, unless it is allied with Catholicism, there could be increased danger for the religion. In contrast to Protestantism, Catholics reserve allegiance to the pope, and the local Catholic Church is subject to the external religious authority. The Catholic Church thus could become the target of a state that wants to assert its sovereign rights, such as France during the French Revolution (1789–99), Zaire under the rule of Mobutu from 1965 to 1997, and Vietnam under Communism.[106]

In comparison with Protestantism, the international missionary movements of Catholicism historically were more directly supported and pushed forward by Western colonial powers. The establishment of Catholicism in Latin America and some parts of Africa was a product of the colonial rule of the Spanish, Portuguese, and Belgian empires.[107] Even though France under the Third Republic (1870–1940) launched aggressive anticlericalism and imposed secularization domestically, it made the French Catholic Church an integral part of its colonial expansion.[108] The fate of the Catholic expansion, therefore, has been more intimately associated with the fate of colonial powers. On the one hand, when colonial powers successfully established a lasting colony in the local society, then Catholicism made great inroads. On the other hand, when colonial forces encountered massive resistance and triggered nationalist movements, Catholicism could easily become a target of fury. Precisely because of their intricate ties with colonial powers, Catholic missions were attacked in the newly independent states of Africa such as Angola, Mozambique, and Zaire.[109] By contrast, the Protestant expansion did not directly gain as much from Western colonialism but neither was it so adversely affected by the collapse of the Western colonial powers.

Although the above preliminary observations require systematic scrutiny at the empirical level, the underlying logics behind them can provide a new understanding of the historical waxing and waning of Catholicism and Protestantism worldwide. Some of these logics will likely continue to shape the respective development of Protestantism and Catholicism for years to come.

3

Chinese Popular Religion

Feminization, Bifurcation, and Buddhification

After dealing with the two foreign religions that have contributed to the substantial changes in the religious ecology of China and brought new elements to Chinese society, it is time to turn to the indigenous, or more indigenized, religions of China to see how they have fared and how they responded to the rapid rise of Protestantism in post-Mao China. I start my analysis with Chinese popular religion because it occupied a central place in the religious ecology of late imperial China (see the introduction), and its fortunes best indicate how much the Chinese religious ecology has changed. In chapter 1, in my explanation of the rapid rise of Protestantism, I discussed the weakened significance of ancestor worship as a normative practice in post-Mao China. This chapter will bring territorial cults into the limelight. Because readers may not be familiar with Chinese popular religion and territorial cults, a brief introduction is in order.

An Overview

Also known by names such as *folk religion* or *diffused religion*,[1] *popular religion* refers to a wide range of religious forms practiced among the masses, which stand in contrast to a category of religions variously known as *salvation religion* or *world religion*,[2] *historic religion*,[3] or *institutional religion*.[4] Whereas promise of salvation is central to salvation religions, it is usually not a prominent feature of popular religion. Salvation religions have a community of adherents who have acquired a distinct identity and way of life through their religion; practitioners of popular religion usually do not form a religious community independent of other social communities or associations. Whereas salvation religions are highly developed institutions with

scripture, theology, liturgy, and religious professionals and organizations sep-
arable from the rest of the society, such institutional development is usually
rudimentary in popular religion.

Chinese popular religion consists of multifold beliefs and practices, including geomancy, divination, worship of household deities,[5] spirit medium-
ship, and vestiges of animism.[6] But two forms, namely ancestor worship and
territorial cults, were by far the most important because they were the cor-
nerstones of the Confucianized Chinese society of late imperial China (see
the introduction). The territorial cults are so named because territorial communities, in the units of village, village alliance, township, neighborhood, or
county, worshiped deities that protect the welfare of the community.

The fortunes of popular religion took a downward turn when the Qing—
China's last imperial dynasty—crumbled in 1912 and a new state, the Republic
of China, replaced it. Under the religious policy of Republican China, popular religion was excluded from the category of state-sanctioned religions and
was branded as superstition, subject to a series of antisuperstition campaigns.
Suppression of popular religion, however, culminated under Mao's China,
particularly during the Cultural Revolution. After the post-Mao state relaxed
its religious policy in the late 1970s, popular religion, including territorial
cults, reemerged.

The revival of popular religion in the form of territorial cults in post-Mao
China has attracted wide attention. Existing studies have explained the revival
by probing the role of its leaders and their tactics in a restrictive political climate,[7] interpreted the revival as an act of the local community to reclaim its
history and reassert its autonomy from the state,[8] or discussed the implications
of the revival for the development of civil society or provision of public goods.[9]

However, the post-Mao revival of territorial cults is not simply the resur-
rection of the tradition after a hiatus of suppression. It is thus imperative for
us to delve into the nature of this "revival" or "revitalization." This chapter argues that territorial cults have changed in character during the process of resurgence. The following pattern has been discerned in my fieldwork in River
County. First, there is a huge urban-rural discrepancy: while most rural popular religion temples have been rebuilt, urban temples, including most important cultic centers, have not. More importantly, where temples have been
rebuilt, three observable trends have accompanied the revitalization process:
(1) women have taken a much more prominent role in territorial cults than
before; (2) territorial cult temples have been experiencing what can be termed
a *bifurcation* (while a small number of have enjoyed ever-increasing popularity and prosperity, many have shown signs of decline years after the initial

revival); and (3) territorial cult temples have demonstrated a strong tendency to acquire Buddhist features.

The following introduces the territorial cults of the past and then analyzes the changes accompanying their post-Mao revitalization. The urban-rural discrepancy in the religion's revitalization will be examined, but the bulk of the analysis focuses on territorial cults' three trends of development: feminization, bifurcation, and Buddhification.

Territorial Cults of the Past

The first recorded popular religion temple in the history of River County was the Temple of the Marquis of Efficacious Response, built in 466. Most territorial cult temples in the county, however, were built between the twelfth and nineteenth centuries.

In late imperial China, neo-Confucianism had firmly established itself as the prevailing state ideology, and its influence permeated local society through the expansion and entrenchment of lineage organizations. The system of territorial cults developed in tandem with lineage organizations. Across River County, individual villages, village alliances, townships, and city districts all sponsored temples that protected the welfare of their respective communities.[10] Communal temples at the village or district level were known as *benbao dian* (literally, temple of our own community). In addition to each village having its own benbao dian, several neighboring villages could also jointly sponsor a multivillage communal temple.[11]

Each temple had a principal god, flanked by subsidiary deities. Lord Guan (Guan Gong), Lord Hu (Hu Gong), King Yan of Xu (Xuyan Wang), Guanyin, and the Dragon King were among the most popular choices as the principal god of village temples or village-alliance temples. Among all principal gods, only a few, such as Lord Guan and Guanyin, were worshipped across China. Lord Guan, a legendary warrior of the third century, came to be seen in late history as a paragon of valor, loyalty, and righteousness, and he was one of the most popular and influential gods in late imperial China.[12] Guanyin, a Buddhist bodhisattva transformed into the goddess of compassion in popular religion, reflected both the Buddhist influence on popular religion and the extent to which Buddhism had been Sinicized.[13] Some of the principal gods were popular regional gods in the midwestern part of Zhejiang, where River County is located.[14] For instance, Lord Hu was the Northern Song official Hu Ze (963–1039), who was credited with the exemption of the service tax levied on this region and deified by the local people after his death.[15] King Yan of

FIGURE 3.1. A territorial cult temple by a rice paddy. (Photograph by the author.)

Xu was ruler of the State of Xu during the Western Zhou dynasty (ca. 1045–771 BC), known for his pacifism and benevolence. His descendants, many of whom were concentrated in this region, were instrumental in his deification.[16] For some villages, the principal god of their communal temple was a hero specific to the village history or an ancestor of a dominant lineage group. Among the subsidiary deities in temples of territorial cults, the most common were fertility deities, agricultural deities, and rain deities. The Earth God and his wife, usually installed at a temple's entrance or housed in a separate small shrine, were an indispensable pair in the pantheon of a territorial cult temple.

In River County, a small number of these gods, such as the Marquis of the Accumulated Blessings, received imperial recognition and thus entered the official register of sacrifice.[17] These gods were entitled to receive sacrifice from the county magistrate, and the renovation of the gods' temples would receive some official support. For instance, the Temple of the Marquis of the Accumulated Blessings underwent major renovations many times throughout history, each time receiving state funding. The last renovation in the nineteenth century was funded by a special tax levied on fishing boats by the county magistrate for two years.[18] In other words, these territorial cults became an integral part of the state cult, by which I refer to official sacrificial rites performed by the emperor and local officials across the empire. It was an elaborate, hierarchical system that carefully stipulated who had the prerogative and duty to make sacrifice to which deities, according to which liturgical rules.[19] The state cult was based on the belief, rooted in China's antiquity and later blended with Confucian notions, that proper ritual conduct by rulers was essential to maintain harmony between cosmic forces and human society. It constituted an essential part of the foundation of political legitimacy for the imperial Chinese state.

Most gods of the territorial cults, however, were not included in the official register of sacrifice. During late imperial China, neo-Confucian domination of society was strong but not total, leaving room for the emergence of cults of dubious character as seen from the perspective of neo-Confucian orthodoxy. Sporadically, state actors would launch campaigns to curtail "immoral cults" that developed voluntary societies with supralocal networks or practices considered an aberration from neo-Confucian mores, particularly when

FIGURE 3.2. The principal god of this village communal temple is the deified Qian Liu (852–932), the founding king of the Wuyue kingdom, whose territory centered on today's Zhejiang Province. As is usually the case, the statue of the principal male god is accompanied by a statue of his female consort. (Photograph by the author.)

they involved the active participation of a large number of women.[20] In River County, as recorded in 1754, the magistrate took action to destroy a temple of a female deity because it attracted many female worshippers and gave rise to a devotional society.[21] Overall, it must be said that such repressive actions were rather infrequent and did not affect the dominance of territorial cults in the local society.

In the county seat—that is, the walled city of River County and its close vicinity—stood many temples. Most prominent were the City God Temple; the Temple of Confucius; the Temple of the Martial God, proverbially known as the Temple of Lord Guan; the Temple of the Eastern Peak, which enshrined the Emperor of the Eastern Peak; and the Wenchang Pavilion, which enshrined Wenchang, the patron god of literature, civil service examination, and scholars.[22] Among these temples mandated by the state cult, the Temple of Confucius was distinct.[23] Even though it was called a temple, Confucius was venerated as a sage rather than worshipped as a deity capable of supernatural intervention.[24] The rest of these temples, though part of the state cult, also elicited popular worship, because the gods enshrined in them provided divine assistance to the territory and its residents. The City God Temple, in particular, was central to both the state cult and the countywide popular devotion.[25]

The City God was seen as the counterpart, in the spiritual realm, of the magistrate. Upon assuming his post, the county magistrate would visit the City God Temple and pray for the god's assistance and guidance. In times of drought, flood, plagues, and other calamities, the magistrate would petition the god for intervention. The magistrate offered sacrifice to the god three times a year according to the ritual code prescribed by the state cult. Because the City God oversaw all the bereaved spirits in the territory, the god was invited to preside over the thrice-yearly ritual in which the magistrate made offerings to spirits of the unworshipped dead at a suburban altar. Zhu Yuanzhang (1328–98), founding emperor of the Ming dynasty, decreed in 1371 the installation of this altar throughout the empire and made the performance of the ritual an obligation for local officials.[26]

The City God Temple also held a special place in popular religion. Across the county, people came to the temple to beseech the god for protection and blessings. His birthday, designated the second day of the second lunar month, was an immensely popular festival.

As the gods bestowed blessings on the community, the community reciprocated by regularly making food offerings, renovating the temple, and staging an annual festival. The festival, held on the birthday of the principal god, was a grand communal event involving animal sacrifices, parade of the god(s), and theatrical performances. In particular, temple festivals of village alliances or market towns, which lasted for several days, drew tens of thousands of people from near and far. Some of these supralocal temples gave rise to large-scale trade fairs where buying and selling of all sorts of commodities took place.[27] Across River County, approximately thirty-three major trade fairs, found in almost every month and in different localities, formed a network of regional markets.

Because temples were suppliers of the common good, financial contributions toward their upkeep and festivals, as well as participation in communal ritual events, were obligatory for residents. Each household in a village contributed its share to the festivals of the communal temple. Lineage organizations played a prominent role in organizing the festivals of the village temples (more on this later). For village-alliance temple festivals, the participating villages took turns in organizing the event, with lineage organizations actively involved in mobilizing resources and allocating responsibilities in each village. For the City God Temple, the eight most powerful surname groups in the county seat financed the lion's share of the cost of staging its festival, with significant contributions from guilds and merchant associations. The strong communal aspect of the territorial cults is manifest.

In addition to the temple festival, the ritual of praying for rain was another major communal event. Most of the temples enshrined a deity to which the community could pray for rain. In River County, a handful of temples achieved more prominence in the rain ritual than others. By the nineteenth century or even earlier, there emerged an important rain ritual known as the cult of five temples, involving the City God Temple and four large village-alliance temples located in the county seat and its close outskirts.[28] The five temples were part of the state cult, as the gods were all on the official register of sacrifices and received imperial titles. At the same time, however, the gods were also the patron gods of powerful lineage-based territorial alliances. When a severe drought struck the county, one after another the statues of the principal gods of these five temples would be paraded through the thoroughfares before being placed in the sun until rain fell. As the male-only procession passed through the streets, all the shops were closed, and women were barred from sight. The county magistrate would take part in the ritual as well. If all five god statues were out and still there was no rain, the people of the county would petition the magistrate for relief from tariffs and rent. The demand was supported by a prevailing religious belief: because even the most powerful gods could not relieve the drought, extraordinary measures must be required. Anticipating this, the magistrate, in cahoots with the landlords, would try to hide the last god statue—the City God—before the villagers came to carry it out. It was a hide-and-seek game, with much at stake.

Focusing on River County, I have painted a picture of territorial cults in late imperial China to show their prevalence and centrality to local life. They could achieve this because, above all, the cults derived legitimacy from state orthodoxy. No less importantly, territorial cults were also fused with the lineage organizations that constituted the backbone of Chinese society in late imperial China. At that time, lineage organizations were simultaneously quasi-religious institutions and self-governing, secular institutions with socioeconomic and political functions. Following the 1911 Revolution, which overthrew the Qing and thus ended thousands of years of imperial rule, the Republican government embarked on a modern state-building project in emulation of the Western model. In this process, it introduced two seismic changes in policies toward religions, which would have huge ramifications for the reconfiguration of the religious field. First, it abolished the state cult and established the state as secular. Second, its religious policy came to hinge on the religion-superstition dichotomy. A narrow variety of religious forms were included in the category of state-sanctioned religion and allowed to enjoy "religious freedom," whereas a wide array of time-honored religious practices was dismissed as superstition. As a result of the changes, popular religion was deprived of the legitimacy and support imparted by the state. Further, it was labeled as superstition and, especially under the Nationalist government (1927–49), subject to antisuperstition campaigns.[29] However, these Republican-era campaigns were largely ineffective, especially in rural areas.[30]

In River County, territorial cult temples retained their grip on the local society. A 1934 survey covering a large part of the county recorded 341 territorial cult temples, which owned 3,015 buildings and 277.4 acres of land.[31] Dozens of temples were used as classrooms for modern education, but most also preserved their religious functions. People of the county continued to celebrate the City God's birthday until the Japanese occupation in 1942.[32] The grandeur and bustling festivity of the celebration left such an impression on some of my elderly informants that they recounted what they witnessed in their childhood to me with excitement and wistfulness. In 1946, the City God Temple was used as an elementary school, but the structure and god statues were left untouched. During the Republican period, the countywide rain ritual involving the five temples was held in 1929 and 1934, when River County suffered prolonged droughts. In the last rain ritual in the county's history, the crowd carried the god statues to the yamen and demanded the magistrate receive them. The magistrate, a university professor turned official, was compelled to offer sacrifices to the gods according to the prescribed ritual procedures.

Territorial cults suffered much more devastation in Mao's China. The Maoist regime shared the antisuperstition modernist agenda with the Nationalists but had a capacity far superior to the Nationalist government to push the campaign in every nook and cranny of society. A great number of god statues were destroyed during the antisuperstition campaigns of the early 1950s. During the Land Reform in 1950–51, temple land was seized and redistributed to the poor. The 1966 campaign against the Four Olds triggered massive waves of frenzied vandalism of religious icons and cultural relics by the Red Guards across China. The Red Guards in River County, mostly middle school students like elsewhere in China, answered the call to demolish the Four Olds. They broke into temples to smash the god statues. All the remaining religious icons were ravaged; all the remaining buildings were converted into granaries or pigsties, or torn down.

The City God Temple of River County, the cultic center of countywide popular religion, suffered this fate. In 1954, in an antisuperstition campaign, a plan was devised to destroy the god statue. Before this could take place, the statue was spirited away by some devotees at night and buried in a nearby field. In 1958, the main gate of the temple was dismantled. In 1966, the City God statue was dug up and smashed by the Red Guards. In 1975, the resting chamber of the god was demolished and turned into a school playground.

Post-Mao Revival

When China's religious policy turned more tolerant after 1978, territorial cults resurfaced almost immediately. It started when women went to the original sites of temple buildings to burn incense and light candles. The restoration of temples soon followed. The peak of reconstruction was from the mid-1990s to the first decade of the 2000s. According to a survey by the Religious Affairs Bureau, by 2009, around 660 temples had been restored in River County. Of the 124 villages I visited during 2006–9, none has left its communal temple unrestored.

There was clearly an urban-rural split in the restoration of territorial cult temples. The restoration mostly took place in villages and market towns. Most territorial cult temples in the county seat have not been restored. The county seat was no longer a sacred landscape where the cultic centers of popular religion were located and where the state cult and territorial cults converged. Of the temple cults revived in the rural and suburban areas of River County, the tendencies of feminization, bifurcation, and Buddhification have given them a different character compared with the past.

Middle-aged and older women, rather than men, played a pivotal role in the rebuilding of territorial cult temples in River County. They responded to the news of temple and statue building enthusiastically and often made donations to multiple building projects. It was common among women to pool money with relatives and friends to sponsor the cost of a god statue or a column in the temple so that their names could be inscribed on the donated objects. Seeking reputation was not the only motivation. For the female worshippers, temple building provided an opportunity to earn merit that could bring this-worldly and otherworldly benefits. The deeply entrenched notion and practice of merit-making was influenced by Buddhism, which was immensely popular in the county's history. Women often donated under the name of their husbands or sons with the hope that they also could receive gods' blessings.

Older women also served as indefatigable and effective fundraisers for temple rebuilding, often leveraging their personal networks or even embarking on fundraising tours, walking to neighboring villages and towns to solicit donations. As elderly women, they had a natural advantage: even though their methods were sometimes aggressive, the acts did not appear threatening, and it was harder for people to turn them down.

With the exception of temple festivals, which often involve the entire village, for all the other religious gatherings in the temples, such as consecration rituals, pilgrimages, and liturgical services, women usually constituted more than 95 percent of the participants. During temple festivals and the Spring Festival, when temples received an endless stream of worshippers, women volunteered in the kitchens cooking for visitors.[33] Old women were also most active in daily temple activities. They took care of cleaning the temple, made regular food offerings to the gods, and spent time there as though it were their second home. While women played a role as participants, patrons, donors, fundraisers, and volunteers before 1949, during the post-1978 revitalization, women in many instances were initiators and leaders of rebuilding projects and managers of temples—roles historically reserved for men. Of the 112 temples on which I have collected information, older women played a key role in initiating the rebuilding of 97 (87 percent). Restorations usually started in the following manner. Beginning in the early 1980s, older women would visit old temple sites to burn incense. They then made small, makeshift shrines dedicated to the gods, which attracted more women. When stories started to circulate of supernatural signs such as gods making their presence felt or appearing in dreams, the idea of restoring the original temples for gods was brought up.

I have encountered many stories of old women demonstrating admirable strength and tenacity in leading temple rebuilding. Many of them were already in their eighties or even nineties when I met them between 2006 and 2011. In 2008, I met eighty-three-year-old Dong (Informant No. 112) inside the communal temple of her village, of which she led the restoration. The temple was allocated to a family during the Land Reform. Dong started planning to restore the temple after the family moved out in 1999. She secured the help of a retired elementary school teacher who agreed to provide clerical assistance. The villagers, however, did not enthusiastically respond to her plan. Dong made the first donations, 1,000 yuan (US$146) in the name of her late husband and 40 yuan (US$6) in her own name.[34] Villagers followed with donations of 50 or 100 yuan (US$7 or US$15). Dong knocked on the doors of those who refused to pay their share and implored them to donate at least 30 yuan (US$4) per household. The restored temple has two halls with thirteen large statues and fifteen smaller ones made of clay. Red couplets were posted on the gate and every column in the building. The handwriting looked a bit unsophisticated to my eyes. I was told that all the couplets were handwritten by Dong herself, who had attended school for only two years before marrying into the village at fourteen.

Old female devotees like Dong played an instrumental role not only in restoring their own communal temples but also in reviving others. As mentioned above, all temples in the county seat were repurposed during the Mao years or even before, and none of them have been reclaimed from their occupants to restore their religious function. Only two, the City God Temple and the Temple of the Eastern Peak, found a way to continue their existence, mainly due to the efforts of female devotees. The City God Temple has been turned into an elementary school. Since the late 1970s, on the god's birthday, women would light incense and candles and burn joss paper at the school gate. In the mid-1980s, a tale circulated widely in the county that the City God was manifesting himself on the wall of the school, attracting women from all over the county to the site to worship. A petition was made to the county government to relocate the school and restore the City God Temple. After the petition was denied, six women in their sixties and seventies, in the village where the god statue was stashed by devotees and later destroyed by the Red Guards, built a small, makeshift temple for the martyred god. Finally, in 1993, the same group of women launched a project to build a much grander temple to replace the older one.

FIGURE 3.3. Dong and the village communal temple she helped restore. Behind her is the statue of the Earth Mother Goddess. The characters on the red couplets on the columns were written by Dong herself. (Photograph by the author.)

The Temple of the Eastern Peak has had a similar fate. The site was used as the office of the Nationalist Party during the Republican period, was later turned into the county Communist Party school, and is now part of a police station. According to a tale widely circulating among local female worshippers, the Emperor of the Eastern Peak, homeless for years, appeared in a dream of a woman in a village two kilometers from the original temple site, beseeching her to build a temple for him. In 2003, women in this village raised money and built a temple dedicated to the god, right next to their village communal temple, which they also helped to restore.

Among the temples whose rebuilding was led by women, some later were entrusted to a temple-management committee consisting mainly of men, and some temples have brought in a Buddhist monk or a lay Buddhist to help with management. In many cases, however, women continued to be in charge. Some temples, like the one under the care of Dong, never formed a formal management committee and continued to be managed by the women who led the restoration; some management committees were dominated by women with strong personalities and leadership.

In sum, in the post-Mao period, women have played an active and important role in reviving popular religion. Without them, territorial cult temples could not have been restored so quickly. In this process, women gained unprecedented influence. They moved to center stage, which was once only occupied by men. Male leadership tended to be more prominent in the restoration of village-alliance temples than of village communal temples, however. Yet even in these cases, the patrons, donors, and volunteers were also predominantly women.

FIGURE 3.4. Women worshipping in front of the substitute Temple of the Eastern Peak. (Photograph by Sun Jianguo.)

BIFURCATION

During the post-Mao revitalization of territorial cults, a process of bifurcation has taken place. Although a few have become more prosperous, most of the village temples have declined years after their restoration. This trend became more obvious after the turn of the twenty-first century.

In River County, a small number of temples have increased in prosperity since their restoration. For instance, the number of statues and buildings, as well as the floor space, of the complexes of the Temple of the Marquis of Efficacious Response and the Temple of Lord Zhao have surpassed previous records in their history. Both have undergone major renovation and expansion projects since their initial restoration. The scale of their festivals and the number of visitors on such occasions have also exceeded historical records. Several village temples have emerged from obscurity to become new pilgrimage centers. Attracting patrons from near and far, their influence reaches far beyond their village community.

Most small village temples in River County, however, have been much less fortunate, enjoying the enthusiasm of villagers for only a few years after restoration. Xu village was one of the first in the county to rebuild its communal temple. Afterward, the villagers celebrated the god's birthday by organizing

FIGURE 3.5. Temple festival of the Temple of Lord Zhao. (Photograph by the author.)

a wooden bench dragon dance, a traditional form of celebration and performance often seen in festive celebrations in the county. In the dance, several people would support the dragon head, and hundreds would carry decorated benches connected on both ends to form the dragon's body and tail. Traditionally, when the village decided to hold the wooden bench dragon dance, every household would contribute a bench. Between 2006 and 2009, however, it became more and more difficult for Xu village to organize the dragon dance because the number of households willing to contribute a bench dwindled. Between 2009 and 2011, no dragon dance was staged. The temple was open only on the first and fifteenth days of every lunar month. And, only once every other month, the temple would see some religious activities: about a dozen female devotees gathered to practice the *gengshen* ritual (an explanation of the ritual will follow).

The temple in Dong's village is another example. For the first few years after its restoration, the villagers organized celebrations of the god's birthday by carrying the statue of the god from the temple to the lineage hall, making communal sacrifices, and carrying it back. In 2007, however, communal celebrations were discontinued. On the god's birthday, only older women came to the temple, to make individual offerings. Dong would open the temple on the first and fifteenth days of every lunar month for villagers who wished to worship. It remained closed for the rest of the year except when Dong invited a nun from a nearby Buddhist temple to lead a ritual event called *chan liuli* (explained later in this chapter) in which older women in the vicinity participate. However, as Dong became more and more frail, she was no longer able to organize this event. Indeed, as the generation of female devotees who have the deepest attachment to the temples and associated practices are fading away, the future does not bode well for these small village temples.

Admittedly, in terms of the size of temples and the scale of their festivals, the premodern temples were also stratified. Nonetheless, the smaller ones were no less sustainable than larger ones in the past. Except when war intervened, annual celebration of the god's birthday was held, and temples were generally well maintained. In other words, there is little evidence to suggest that the kind of the bifurcation process described above was common in premodern times.

BUDDHIFICATION

Since their restoration, temples have displayed yet another tendency: a leaning toward Buddhism. It is true that Buddhism was historically influential in River County and that its influence could be identified in popular religion practices. For instance, deities of Buddhist origin had a presence in some territorial cult temples, and some hired Buddhist monks to perform liturgical services or look after the sites. Yet these practices affected little the deep structure of territorial cults. Buddhist deities incorporated into the pantheon of communal temples often assumed subsidiary roles; even in temples that adopted a deity of Buddhist origin (Guanyin in most cases) as their principal god, the organization of ritual events and relationship with the local community were the same as other territorial cult temples. Buddhist liturgies performed by the monks only supplemented the communal sacrifices and procession of the god(s), which were core to the celebration of temple festivals. Although Buddhist monks were hired to serve various functions, the temple-management committee, which consisted of local male elders, had ultimate control over assets and made important decisions.

During the post-Mao revival, however, a great number of territorial cult temples added Buddhist gods to their original pantheon or even Buddhist halls to their original structure. Among the 112 temples on which I obtained information by 2011, 23 invited monks or lay Buddhists to help with the temple management. Although at some temples the acquired Buddhist elements have not overridden their popular religion identity, a few have undergone a major transformation to become primarily Buddhist sites. It is the latter cases that reveal something distinct from the traditional pattern of territorial cult temples.

What follows are examples of territorial cult temples that display varying degrees of Buddhification. After its restoration in 1985, the Temple of the Marquis of Efficacious Response launched expansion projects, which included adding a Guanyin Pavilion and an Arhat Hall to the original temple complex. At the Temple of Lord Zhao, not long after its restoration in the early 1990s, some thirty women from nearby villages, who had formally gone through the ceremony of "taking refuge in the three jewels of Buddhism" (*san guiyi*) to become lay Buddhists, formed a group that met in the temple on the first and fifteenth day of every lunar month to recite Buddhist liturgy. In 2007, the temple-management committee kicked off a fundraising drive to build a Main Buddha Hall (Daxiong Baodian). In November 2008, the committee invited a Buddhist monk to reside in the temple and manage its routine work.

For temples like the Temple of the Marquis of Efficacious Response and the Temple of Lord Zhao, the management committee composed of villagers still has control over the coffers and major decision-making. Other temples, however, have yielded these powers to Buddhist leaders and allowed themselves to be thoroughly transformed into Buddhist sites. In these temples, Buddhist rituals replaced popular religion rituals, and their core patrons and participants have embraced the identity of lay Buddhists. One such example is Luminous Efficacy Temple, dedicated to the worship of Lord Hu and sponsored by four allied villages. Turned into a cowshed during the Cultural Revolution, it was restored to its religious functions in 1991. In 1997, a Buddhist monk was invited to reside in the temple. Under the management of the monk and his successors, the main hall, which originally enshrined Lord Hu, became the Main Buddha Hall, and two additional Buddhist halls were added to the flanks of the temple. Most original deities of territorial cults were relocated to the rear hall.

After Luminous Efficacy Temple was restored, on the birthday of Lord Hu villagers would organize a communal celebration that involved animal sacrifice and parading the statue of the god. As Buddhification developed, however, the event was discontinued. In September 2007, when I visited the temple on Lord Hu's birthday, I witnessed only a Buddhist repentance ritual taking place in the Main Buddha Hall. The ritual was administered by four monks joined by more than fifty female participants. About a third of the participants were dressed in black, long-sleeved robes, known as *haiqing*, which usually are worn only by those who have undergone the formal ceremony of becoming lay Buddhist disciples. From 9 a.m. to 2 p.m., I saw only about ten women going to the rear hall to light candles, and only one carried a tray of sacrificial meat for Lord Hu.

In still another example, Crystal Pond Temple, a temple of ten villages, was rebuilt during 1994–95. In 2004, the temple-management committee invited a young man, Shao (Informant No. 130), to take up residence and lead a group of some twenty female worshippers. Under his management, the temple was quickly transformed into a Buddhist site. Shao managed to raise some 210,000 yuan (US$307,000) to build, next to the original communal temple, a freestanding three-story building dedicated to Buddhist practice. The construction was completed in 2007. A devout lay Buddhist, Shao was deeply inspired by the teachings of Jingkong (1927–2022), a monk who was based overseas but nonetheless exerted tremendous influence over the Buddhist communities in mainland China since the mid-1980s through the free distribution of his lectures in printed and audiovisual format.[35] Shao organized the group of female worshippers to watch the lectures of Jingkong and took them on pilgrimage trips to Zhaoming Temple, some 250 miles away from River County, which was a national center promoting Pure Land Buddhist practices according to the teaching of Jingkong.[36] Shao's site, modeled closely on Zhaoming Temple in design and practice, organized regular Buddha recitation events. During my repeated visits to the temple during 2007–9, I observed that its regular events on average drew more than one hundred participants, of whom more than 95 percent were female. For special events when the Buddha Hall became overcrowded, Shao also made use of the space of the original territorial cult temple. On such occasions, the statues of deities would be covered with large paintings of the Buddha. Under Shao, the temple achieved a reputation among the county people as a site of Pure Land Buddhism. Those female devotees who originally patronized the territorial cult temples have converted to Buddhism and become the core members of Shao's Buddhist group. The communal celebration of the god's birthday by the villagers ceased in 2007.

Temples that have gone through the profound change of becoming predominantly Buddhist sites have had even their names altered to reflect the transformation. Usually, a temple name consists of two parts, the first part having at least two Chinese characters and the second being a term indicating the nature of the religious building.[37] In River County, temples in which Buddhification has gone deep, including Luminous Efficacy Temple and Crystal Pond Temple, have changed the second part of their names from *dian* or *miao*, which indicates a place that enshrines popular religion gods, to *si*, which is used to designate a place for practicing Buddhism.

To explain the feminization, bifurcation, and Buddhification of territorial cults, I examine their key institutional features, highlighting both the communal and individual dimensions. I then explain how Maoist political campaigns and post-Mao marketization have both intentionally and unintentionally undermined the communal foundation of territorial cults. Finally, I argue that all three changes in the post-Mao era resulted when territorial cult temples' individual aspect moved to the forefront and their bonds with territorial communities became attenuated.

The Two Faces of Territorial Cults

This chapter suggests that to account for the changes that territorial cults have experienced in post-Mao China, we must gain a better understanding of their institutional features than prior studies provide for us: that is, we must take full consideration of the two sides of territorial cults. In addition to the communal/mandatory dimension conventionally emphasized by students of Chinese popular religion, territorial cults have an often-overlooked individual/voluntary dimension largely associated with female devotees.

The communal dimension of territorial cults—that is, their function to protect the commonwealth of the local territorial community—has long been emphasized by scholars.[38] Scholars also point out the mandatory dimension associated with the communal dimension. Because the gods of territorial cults bestow "public goods" on the community, it is obligatory for residents to participate in and contribute to the temple festival celebrating the gods' birthday.[39]

In many parts of China, but especially in the southeast where River County is located, territorial cults had formed an intricate relationship with late imperial China's major local social institution—the lineage organizations.[40] Lineage leaders often led temple construction and served on temple-management committees. In multilineage villages, collecting dues and organizing ritual participation for festivals were often accomplished through lineage organizations. In single-lineage villages, lineage branches usually rotated the duty of staging the yearly temple festivals. An integral part of the celebration was carrying the statue of the god to the lineage ancestor hall or lineage branch ancestral halls to receive communal sacrifices. Hence, the communal and mandatory aspect of popular religion was reinforced by the authority and resources of lineage organizations.

In late imperial China, the communal aspect of territorial cults was also associated with male dominance. Temples were administered by a management committee, which usually was an all-male team of local notables. These leaders were designated as *toushou*, which was a position that brought significant prestige, especially in a supravillage-level temple. The *toushou* made major decisions regarding temple management and took responsibility for organizing festivals. Although women also participated in the communal sacrificial ritual, men always walked before them in the procession and carried important sacrificial objects. Moreover, women were excluded from certain important religious activities, such as the rain ritual.

Territorial cults, however, had yet another aspect. Although temples served communal interests, individuals also visited to pray for divine assistance, usually focusing on personal and familial concerns.[41] The communal and individual aspects of territorial cults reminds us of the distinction made by Mei-rong Lin between the sacrificial sphere (*jisi quan*), where sacrificial ritual to gods is organized by territorial communities, and the devotional sphere (*xinyang quan*) of translocal individual devotees in popular religion in Taiwan. While the former demands obligatory participation, participation in the latter is voluntary.[42] It should be noted that this voluntary aspect of territorial cults has been strongly associated with women.[43] Studies of late imperial China have acknowledged the significant role of women in territorial cults, noting that they were important donors,[44] active participants in voluntary religious associations,[45] and eager temple visitors, pilgrims, and festival participants.[46]

Research has also shown that women's biological attributes and social role, the structure of their life world, and their needs and desires shaped their distinctive views toward life and death,[47] their attachment to female deities,[48] and their participation in territorial-cult activities.[49] In River County before 1949, territorial cult temples often installed at least one statue that appealed particularly to the needs of women.[50] Many temples had fertility deities such as the child-bestowing goddess (Songzi Niangniang) or what the locals would call Zisun Tang (Hall of Prosperity) in the image of an idealized family of multiple generations with a dozen frolicking boys. But the most popular female deities in River County were Guanyin and the Earth Mother Goddess (Dimu Niangniang).[51]

A ballad type known as "small sutras" (xiaojing), usually with fewer than thirty verses, was widely popular among female devotees.[52] Although Buddhist influence is noticeable, because almost all the ballads end with the verse "Homage to Buddha, homage to the Amitābha Buddha," they form their own distinct tradition. The themes of these ballads are related to certain religious practices, such as lighting candles or burning incense; are about a religious object such as a lantern or a fan; are dedicated to deities such as earth gods, the bridge god, or Guanyin; or are to be chanted on occasions such as the gengshen ritual. Most of these small sutras take the perspective of married women and reflect their religious practices, life world, social relations, desires, and fears. Women chanted these ballads in the local dialect, sometimes drumming on a wooden fish to keep the rhythm. They treasured these ballads and eagerly learned them from one another.

A number of liturgical forms were particularly popular among this group of female devotees. They included the ritual of paying the debt for the next life (huan laisheng zhai), the repentance ritual of breaking the bloody pond (chan xuehu), and the "glaze repentance ritual" (chan liuli).[53] These rituals could be performed by Buddhist clerics, Daoist ritual specialists, or religious professionals known in the local society as "repentance ritual masters" (chansheng). Women also practiced rituals not mediated by religious specialists. For instance, it was popular among female worshippers to observe the gengshen days: the fifty-seventh day in the sixty-day cycle. On gengshen days, women would assemble in a local temple and stay awake throughout the night, reciting the "gengshen sutras," which belonged to the category of small sutras.[54] It was believed that keeping vigil on the gengshen days would reduce illness and prolong life. On the first year of a cycle, women observed the vigil for the well-being of their in-laws; the next year for their own parents; the third year for their husbands; and the fourth year, finally, for themselves.

Temple-visiting activities of women in River County are customs with a long history. An old-fashioned rhyme describes them with tongue-in-cheek humor: "On the third day of the third month, women worshippers go to temples to worship the bodhisattvas. Pluck, pluck, pluck, they plucked the rapeseed flowers from the field to decorate their hair. Oops, they slip and fall into the field. They blame it on the narrow ridge between fields. In fact, it is all because their feet are too wide!" A poem composed in 1754 depicts women from wealthy families dressing splendidly for the occasion, indicating that temple visiting was a custom among women across classes.[55]

Women on a temple-visiting trip could be identified by their appearance. A female pilgrim would usually wear her best attire and carry a yellow bag over her shoulder. The bag often had Buddhist symbols on it and contained incense, candles, joss paper, and offerings. Once female worshippers entered a temple, they followed several ritual procedures. They lighted two red candles and bowed to Heaven, the Earth, and the four directions before putting the candles on a stand. They placed a bag of fruit, candies, and pastries on the altar of the principal god. Then they prostrated themselves before the god images and placed incense in the incense burner. They burned yellow paper and paper ingots in the incinerator outside the temple gate. When these rituals were completed, they retrieved their bags of offerings blessed by the gods and moved on to the next temple. If a temple had cypress trees nearby, they would pluck a small twig as an auspicious memento to bring home.

It remains a custom in River County for women to visit as many temples as possible on the first day of the Chinese New Year. Women usually would kick off the pilgrimage by visiting their own communal temple, then visit some large popular religion temples. Female devotees were also eager to attend consecration rituals held when new buildings were completed or new icons installed. They followed the long-standing belief that the blessings one could receive from attending one moment of a consecration ritual were even greater than worshipping gods for a lifetime (*baifo yishi, kaiguang yishi*).

In sum, in pre-1949 local society, women constituted the main category of participants in voluntary activities associated with territorial cults and formed an enduring bond with them. In analyzing the female modes of practice in territorial cults, I would like to highlight three points. First, women participated in religious activities not only for the sake of their personal well-being but also for the welfare of the entire family.[56] Indeed, although men dominated the temple-management committee and the communal temple festivals, within each household, visiting temples and praying for divine protection on behalf of the family was women's business. This division of labor was universally practiced in River County.[57] Second, these women devotees were not bound exclusively to their own communal temples. Instead, they visited and patronized a variety of temples. Third, there was a deep affinity between these women devotees and Buddhism.[58] Female worshippers did not

TABLE 3.1. Two faces of territorial cults

	Communal aspect	Individual aspect
Manifestations	Temple festivals and rain rituals	Supplication, pilgrimages, participation in ritual services
The primary goal of religious practices	The common good of the territorial community	Individual or familial interest
Mode of participation	Mandatory	Voluntary
Gender role	Male precedence	Female predominance

distinguish between Buddhist deities and deities of territorial cults; they referred to temple-visiting activities as "lord worshipping" (*bai laoye*), "Buddha worshipping" (*bai fo*), or "bodhisattva worshipping" (*bai pusa*).[59]

Table 3.1 summarizes the two faces of territorial cults. In the past, the communal mode defined the main character of territorial cults, with the personal mode hiding underneath it. In post-Mao China, however, the personal mode has eclipsed the communal mode and has become more central to territorial cults. The three major trends that have occurred in the religion as highlighted in the prior section have been the result of this major change. What follows is an analysis of the sociopolitical forces that have contributed to the decline of the communal aspect of territorial cults.

The Attenuation of the Communal Dimension

The Maoist state has left two legacies with lasting impact on the development of territorial cults in the post-Mao era. The first was the various campaigns from the 1950s to 1970s to eradicate popular religion. Not only were icons and buildings destroyed, but propaganda campaigns were also organized to rid Chinese society of the influence of popular religion. In River County, exhibitions were orchestrated of "superstitious objects" and confessions of "superstitious professionals" (such as spirit mediums) that aimed to expose the ignorance and evils of popular religious beliefs and practices. Territorial cults, once a cornerstone of communal solidarity, were condemned as "feudal superstition." Association with territorial cults, once a source of power and prestige, brought stigma and persecution.

The second legacy left by the Maoist state was the disruption of lineage organizations and the traditional local elite. Because lineage power once was strong in River County, the campaigns against it were particularly severe. During the Land Reform and other political campaigns, lineage organizations were dispossessed of land and other properties and forcibly dismantled. Local notables who served as important *toushou* of temples were publicly humiliated and persecuted and some of them were even executed. The power structure that once buttressed communal temple religion suffered fatal damage.

In the post-Mao era, the state abandoned its radical policies, again recognized the legitimacy of five religions, and reinstalled the RAB at the county level and above to manage religious activities. But popular religion is not among the five. In the early reform era, stigma still attached to popular religion activities, and there were occasions of local cadres obstructing efforts to rebuild territorial cult temples. But as the political climate became more relaxed, even though popular religion had no granted legitimacy, the restoration and building of territorial cult temples encountered less and less official obstruction. Since the mid-1990s, officials in River County have adopted a largely noninterventionist stance toward territorial cults and other popular religious activities.

At the same time, the state's market-oriented reform policies have brought massive changes to rural China, which has a profound impact on the fortune of territorial cults. Beginning with the breakup of collective agriculture and the introduction of the Household Responsibility System in the early 1980s,[60] as well as the burgeoning of private entrepreneurship in nonfarm sectors during the 1980s, rural society has been shaped by unprecedented market forces.[61] Another major change is the massive outmigration of rural laborers to urban areas seeking employment. Between 1978 and 1999, an estimated 174 million people migrated from rural areas to cities in China, creating "history's largest flow of rural-urban migration."[62] The rural-urban migration has accelerated since the beginning of the 1990s as the expanding non-state-owned economy and newly created industrial parks in urban areas greatly increased the demand for labor, and the state relaxed restrictions on labor mobility.[63]

These changes have shaped the development of territorial cults in multiple ways. For one, as households and individuals have grappled with unprecedented opportunities and pressures brought by market forces, the rural community has become much less cohesive. In the process, the individualist orientation and materialist pursuits of villagers were reinforced.[64] The sudden swell of wealth could become a source of discord that further tears the community apart. For instance, villages, especially those on the outer rim of cities, often became embroiled in bitter disputes arising from the distribution of compensation for land sold during urban expansion.[65] Farmers who lost their land may complain that they did not receive a fair share of the compensation, and village cadres were often accused of reaping undue personal benefits. The grievances run so strong in some villages that residents became disinclined to contribute to communal causes such as hosting temple festivals, and instead expect the village committee, which retained a handsome portion of the land compensation fee, to cover the cost. Furthermore, outmigration of rural youth increasingly made the villages huge "empty nests." In many villages in River County, more than 60 percent of the households had young members working elsewhere in the early years of this century. Communal religious activities often lacked the participation of the younger generation. Even when they returned to their home villages for holidays, their schooling, which included atheist indoctrination, and their experience as migrant workers in urban centers ensured that they did not form the same attachment to the customs, beliefs, and practices of the past as the older generation did.

If the political campaigns of the Mao era swept away the traditional social foundations undergirding the communal dimension of territorial cults, it is the market forces unleashed by the economic reforms in the post-Mao era that have led to the disintegration of the village community and consequently the further attenuation of territorial cults' communal bond. The latter transformation appears less violent, but its impact is no less profound.

The Story of Multilayered Revitalization

It is in such a context that the resurgence of territorial cults has been taking place in rural society. Leading the temple-rebuilding projects supposedly was the responsibility of the male *toushou*, but, during the 1980s, when territorial cults were still stigmatized, even those who survived the political persecution in the Mao era were scared to do things that would suggest their association with them. At the time, across River County, it was the older women who initiated temple-restoration projects. They had the deepest personal bond with territorial cults and associated activities. Their marginal social position also worked to their advantage, because their religious activities were deemed harmless by the local cadres.

Hence, from the start, the rebuilding of temples in post-Mao China bore the imprint of the voluntary activities of female worshippers. In no position to impose the cost of rebuilding projects on fellow villagers, female worshippers were compelled to canvass outside their villages. Believing that contributions to temple building would bring blessings, women outside the territorial community were happy to donate. As a result, village-alliance temples and small village communal temples alike benefited from translocal donors. Fang, for instance, was a generous donor to a dozen of temples. Once she donated a handsome amount to a village communal temple to fund the statues of the Earth God and his wife, even though she was not from that village or connected with it through familial ties. To ask a stranger to fund the statues of earth deities would have been inconceivable in the past, because the earth deities were understood to protect the particular territorial community that worshipped them, not beyond.

Usually, after a temple was restored, it enjoyed the support of the villagers for a few years, but eventually enthusiasm waned, partially occasioned by accelerated rural-urban outmigration. As the bonds between temples and their village communities weakened, temples increasingly had to rely on resources from the outside. They were forced to become more entrepreneurial and compete for the attention and patronage of their main patrons—female worshippers. At the same time, the attenuation of the communal bond made temples less beholden to the village community. As a result, temple leadership has gained more latitude to explore diverse means of increasing revenues and expanding influence. In this process, they have become more receptive to outside influences.

Thus, temples found themselves increasingly operating in a field of mutual competition, and the competition has intensified because the number of restored temples has proliferated greatly. Now the question is: What kinds of temples are likely to be "winners" in such a competition?

Some temples have natural advantages. For example, village-alliance temples are in a better position than village temples, because the former can draw resources from a much wider catchment area. For the same reason, temples that historically established a countywide reputation are also likely to fare better. These two factors explain the continued prosperity of the Temple of the Marquis of Efficacious Response and the Temple of Lord Zhao. The former is the communal temple of five villages, and the latter is sponsored by eighteen villages. Both were historically an integral part of the cult of five temples that were the sites of countywide worship and pilgrimages.

Small village temples are underprivileged. Nonetheless, they still have a chance if they are adept at creating events to attract translocal female worshippers or can provide special services to them. Temple and icon building, and the consecration ritual following the completion of construction, are excellent occasions to draw support. Frequent ritual events help a temple to sustain the patronage of worshippers. The charismatic or liturgical services of spirit mediums or Buddhist clerics can also add to the appeal of a temple. It is little wonder, then, that Heavenly Mother Temple of Willow Mount Village could prosper, because it managed to make good use of all three means. Originally an obscure village temple that fell into disrepair during the Cultural Revolution, it was rebuilt in 1992 under the leadership of Lin, who claimed to have healing power given to her by Guanyin of the South Sea. Her reputation as a spirit medium spread across River County and even to neighboring counties. The walls of the room where she received clients were covered with testimonial banners praising her magical efficacy. With ample funds continuously flowing in, Lin launched expansion projects in 1996, 2003, 2005, and 2006. By 2011, the complex included five halls—the renovated and expanded territorial cult temple, the Jade Emperor Hall, the Heavenly King Hall, the Main Buddha Hall, and the Kṣitigarbha (Earth Womb) Bodhisattva Temple—and housed more than fifty statues. Monks or repentance ritual masters hired by Lin frequently performed liturgical services in the temple. It should be noted that the temple could not have achieved such success if its communal ties had not been broken. In the past, when the communal temple was controlled by the male leaders of the village community, Lin, a female spirit medium, would have had no chance to run the show.[66]

The prosperity of the "winners" in the competition has been boosted by modern transportation, which has made traveling to temples much easier for women, and by the economic boom in the reform era, which meant that female patrons had more money for religious undertakings. However, the number of temples that could turn the weakening of communal bonds into an opportunity for expansion was limited. When communal support waned, the majority of village temples became sites of occasional religious activities of a small group of village female worshippers. This is how the bifurcation among territorial cult temples came to pass.

How did Buddhification take place? Did temples acquire Buddhist features so that they might register as Buddhist temples to obtain official recognition? Did the RAB or the Buddhist Association then try to impose Buddhist standards on these popular religion temples registered as Buddhist temples? This kind of Buddhification prompted by the state's religious policy, which recognizes only Buddhism and the other four religions as legitimate, is plausible. Indeed, Goossaert and Palmer's study indicates this indeed has been occurring in some places in China.[67] My study in River County, however, provides a more complicated story. Before the mid-1990s, the restoration of temples still faced possible obstruction from village cadres and the RAB. Hence, temple leaders tried hard to secure official recognition. Between the mid-1990s and 2011, the local authorities grew lax toward popular religion (and toward religions in general). In this period, to register as a Buddhist venue became much easier, and temple leaders bribed RAB officials to do so. Between 1997 and 2011, twenty-one territorial cult temples obtained registered status as "Buddhist sites."[68] Yet even as local authorities became lax toward unregistered temples, those who controlled them increasingly felt less motivated to register.[69] After all, to gain registered status, a temple must pay a sizable amount of money (roughly 5,000 yuan or US$732) as an application fee, plus annual membership dues of 500 yuan (US$73) to the Buddhist Association.[70] What is more, during times of major calamities, the RAB would solicit donations from registered temples and take credit for providing the disaster-relief funds. Small temples with little financial means found these expenses a burden. In fact, quite a few on the list of registered temples did not initiate the application process for registered status themselves but were urged by the RAB to apply. And as the resources of some registered temples dwindled, at least three stopped paying the annual membership dues, relinquishing their registered status.

Between the mid-1990s and 2011, registered temples, as long as their representatives attended meetings organized by the Buddhist Association and the RAB, paid membership dues and other fees, and submitted annual financial reports in a timely fashion, were basically free from meddling by the RAB and the Buddhist Association in their internal management. In a rare instance, the Buddhist Association did dispatch a monk to take control of a popular religion temple following the eruption of a scandal, in which the monk whom the villagers invited to manage the temple absconded with its funds. However, in this case, Buddhification had occurred before the intervention of the association.

As I observed, factors other than seeking legitimacy through the official registration policy framework have been more significant in prompting Buddhification in River County. There were many advantages that a temple could gain by acquiring Buddhist features. Buddhist deities have a wider appeal than local deities. Buddhism also has highly sophisticated ways of attracting female worshippers and generating revenues through providing an extraordinarily rich assortment of liturgical services to the laity.[71] Hence, as the communal support of territorial cults weakened, temple managers were tempted by the obvious financial benefits of adopting or appropriating Buddhist features. When managers decided to add buildings or icons, they would give priority to the most popular Buddhist elements such as the Guanyin Pavilion, the Main Buddha Hall, or Buddhist icons such as the eighteen Arhats and the Maitreya Buddha. Even the Temple of the Marquis of Efficacious Response and the Temple of Lord Zhao resorted to this tactic to boost their popularity. In 1996, when the Temple of the Marquis of Efficacious Response was short of money to cover construction costs, its temple-management committee announced a plan to build a Guanyin Pavilion. Funds were raised shortly afterward, enough to pay off the debt and build the pavilion. This is also true for the Temple of Lord Zhao. As table 3.2 shows, the two biggest sources of its income between 2005 and 2009—donations to the construction of the Main Buddha Hall and payment for Buddhist ritual services—were directly related to the temple's adoption or appropriation of Buddhism.

TABLE 3.2. Revenue sources of the Temple of Lord Zhao, 2005–09

	2005	2006	2007	2008	2009
Donations for the Main Buddha Hall	47,183	89,760	119,706	56,159	55,244
construction project	50.6%	57.3%	64.0%	39.5%	39.0%
Buddhist ritual services	15,269	30,826	34,792	52,376	54,274
	16.4%	19.7%	18.6%	36.8%	38.3%
Recycling of red candles	14,156	17,263	15,701	16,207	15,618
	15.2%	11.0%	8.4%	11.4%	11.0%
Sales of incense and candles	3,979	2,842	4,218	3,372	3,592
	4.3%	1.8%	2.3%	2.4%	2.5%
Glaze repentance ritual	3,204	1,600			
	3.4%	1.0%			
Donation box	2,874	3,925	4,103	1,934	1,912
	3.1%	2.5%	2.2%	1.4%	1.3%
Sales of talismans	2,609	2,705	3,186	3,043	3,130
	2.8%	1.7%	1.7%	2.1%	2.2%
Divination services	2,193	3,594	4,450	7,727	7,400
	2.4%	2.3%	2.4%	5.4%	5.2%
Sales of tea	183	665	759	16	583
	0.2%	0.4%	0.4%	0.0%	0.4%
Miscellaneous	1,498	3,187		439	
	1.6%	2.0%		0.3%	
Interest earned on bank account	70	204	146	1,063	
	0.1%	0.1%	0.1%	0.7%	
Total	93,218	156,571	187,061	142,336	141,753

Source: Management Committee of the Temple of Lord Zhao

Note: Income figures in Chinese yuan

The sort of Buddhification arising from financial considerations could be superficial if a temple-management committee consisting of villagers retained ultimate control. Buddhification entailing more fundamental conversion to Buddhism and the dilution of the original territorial cult identity could only take place where a temple's communal foundation was in tatters and the village community was permissive toward such a development. Female worshippers were always among those most eager to invite Buddhist leaders to manage temples. Even though they played a key role in restoration, many female worshippers lacked self-confidence and felt more at ease if the task of management was entrusted to religious professionals. Furthermore, during the same period, Buddhism experienced resurgence in River County. Many women who were instrumental to temple reconstruction of territorial cults also patronized the restoration of Buddhist temples, participated in Buddhist ritual services, and even went through the refuge-taking ceremony to become formal disciples. Pilgrimages to large Buddhist temples in and outside the county, and intermingling with monks and lay Buddhists, could also be a transformative experience for women.

"I was told not taking refuges means that you haven't crossed the threshold to enter into the hall," the seventy-eight-year-old Bao said in 2008 (Informant No. 115). She had lived in the Temple of the Marquis of Efficacious Response for sixteen years and served as its janitor before retiring in 2000. She told me with pride that she had gone through the refuge-taking ceremony twice with two Buddhist monks in 1987 and 1992 and thus had two "masters." Before 1992, every time she visited a temple, she would try to learn three new small sutras from fellow female worshippers. Then her second refuge master asked her to discontinue reciting small sutras and study real Buddhist sutras instead. She told me in the interview, "Being unable to read, how could I understand those sophisticated Buddhist texts?" She then showed me a small jade image of Maitreya Buddha she was wearing as necklace pendant, saying this was her third master.[72] She continued with a smile: "In my next life, I wish I'd become educated so that I could learn Buddhist sutras from my third master."

For female worshippers like Bao, even though their understanding of Buddhism might not be much improved after the conversion ritual, their bond with Buddhism was nevertheless cemented. This gave them a strong inclination to allow Buddhist monks or lay Buddhist leaders to take up residence in their temple and assume leadership. The weakened communal control of the temples gave these female worshippers power in deciding whom they would like to invite. In quite a few cases, women met monks on pilgrimage trips and took the liberty of inviting them to their villages, an act unthinkable in the past. Under the management of Buddhist leaders, a territorial cult temple could then be transformed into a burgeoning local Buddhist center. The temple managed by the young Buddhist Shao is a notable example. Women affiliated with this temple were able to experience a more intensive and regular religious life and acquired a sense of belonging to a wider Buddhist community. Their strengthened piety and commitment in turn led to the stronger growth of the temple. On the other hand, there are cases in which women became gullible victims of swindler monks. Between 2006 and 2009, I encountered four cases in which Buddhist monks accepted into popular religion temples were of dubious character and eventually absconded with temple funds.

In sum, Buddhification of territorial cult temples in River County was less a result of the temples' need for official recognition under the constraints of the state's policies than an outcome of the benefits associated with Buddhification; another factor in play was the lack of resistance to Buddhist penetration. Both stemmed from the weakening of temples' communal support and ties.

Conclusion

Thus far, I have analyzed patterns that have emerged in the post-Mao resurgence of territorial cults based on fieldwork in River County. Can these patterns be observed elsewhere in China? The following will offer some thoughts.

First, the urban-rural divide is a universal phenomenon. Although rural revival is widespread, few urban temples of territorial cults have been restored to their former glory. Take City God Temples as an example. I selected seven provinces in different regions of China and checked the percentage of City God Temples that existed prior to 1911 and have been restored in recent years.[73] Table 3.3 shows that, by October 2022, only 20.3 percent of City God Temples in these provinces have preserved part of their original structure or have been (partially) restored. An even smaller percentage, 15.4 percent, have (partially) restored religious functions; some temples are now used as museums, recreation centers, libraries, or schools.

City God Temples that regained some religious functions no longer had connections with other territorial cult temples in the region. In other words, a territory-wide temple network, with urban temples such as the City God Temple and the Eastern Peak Temple at the center, had disappeared with little trace. In River County, the cult of five temples has never been restored. In Jiangsu Province, there was a custom known as *jie tianqiang* (collecting heavenly tax), according to which village temples collected money and grain from each household in their village and submitted them to the City God Temple as contributions to its festival.[74] This custom, however, has not been revived.[75] The centrality of the urban temples in the territorial cult networks was to a

TABLE 3.3. Percentage of City God Temples that have been (partially) restored in seven provinces by October 2022

	Hebei	Shanxi	Shaanxi	Anhui	Zhejiang	Jiangsu	Fujian	Total
The number of (partially) restored City God Temples	18	11	18	8	36	13	33	137
The original total number of City God Temples	138	114	97	67	117	63	78	674
Percentage	13.0%	9.6%	18.6%	11.9%	30.8%	20.6%	42.3%	20.3%

Sources: Relevant data from Wikipedia double-checked and updated by the author and research assistants

large extent due to their importance in the state cult. Thus, the loss of centrality of these urban cultic centers and the disintegration of the territory-wide territorial cult networks were inevitable following the destruction of the state cult with the demise of the Qing dynasty.

In rural areas where temples were massively rebuilt, the three tendencies of feminization, bifurcation, and Buddhification reveal the profoundly changed character of territorial cults in post-Mao China. My analysis attributes the changes to the waning of territorial cults' communal aspect. Ever since the end of imperial China, territorial cults' ties with the village community have been undermined by both political and economic forces. The revitalization of territorial cults in post-Mao China had to rely on voluntary participation and support. Put differently, popular religion has been acquiring more characteristics of a voluntary religion. For many small village temples, the weakening communal support was a curse. Admittedly, there are temples that have turned the decoupling from village communities into an opportunity for expansion. A few of the most successful temples even saw their leaders use temple wealth to gain social influence and political clout. River County, and Zhejiang Province where River County is located, have not yet produced notable cases of this sort, even though territorial cults in Zhejiang were quite strong in late imperial China. But such cases do exist within a country as big as China. For instance, the boss of Black Dragon Temple in Shaanxi Province was able to raise enough funds to finance a local primary school and reforestation project, which gained him fame and political clout—he won elections as the village head and was inducted into the county branch of the Chinese People's Political Consultative Conference.[76] Although the case reveals how far popular religion could travel in post-Mao China, its rarity is also telling. The empirical findings presented in this chapter, especially when we compare the development of territorial cults, a most important form of popular religion, with other religions such as Protestantism and Buddhism, warn against portraying popular religion's experience in post-Mao China as a simple revival story.

Have the three trends described in this chapter been taking place in other parts of China as well? Given that female piety in popular religion was a widespread phenomenon, that Maoist political campaigns and post-Mao marketization have had huge impacts across the country, and that Buddhism exercises strong influence over much of China, I venture to suggest that territorial cults in many other places in China may also have undergone similar processes as in River County, albeit to different degrees.[77] Other studies of territorial cults in Zhejiang, Jiangsu, Sichuan, and Hebei provinces render support to my argument, especially to the feminization and bifurcation theses.[78]

Yet what happened in central and southern Fujian, where territorial cult temples have not only experienced widespread revival but also retained communal bonds and male dominance, is an exception that begs to be explained.[79] I argue that at least three factors have been at work in the case of Fujian. First, Fujian, among all the regions of China, was known for exceptionally strong popular religion piety in late imperial China. The popular attachment to the gods in the territorial cult ran deep. Second, Fujian is a place where lineage organizations were highly organized, marshaled significant resources, and exercised extraordinary power in late imperial China,[80] continuing to hold sway well into the Republic.[81] Though suppression during the Mao era did deprive lineage organizations of the power and resources they once commanded, lineage-based networks were resurgent in the post-Mao era.[82]

The third and perhaps most important factor that contributes to the Fujian exceptionalism is its close ties with Taiwan.[83] More than 70 percent of Taiwan residents today are descendants of Fujian emigrants. The two sides of the Taiwan Strait share great similarities in terms of language, religion, and customs. When the emigrants settled on the island, they established branch temples for the gods from their hometowns. Once mainland China opened up in the late 1970s, the Taiwanese, eager to reconnect ties with their ancestral homeland, enthusiastically donated to temple (re)construction in Fujian, providing much-needed funds in the early stages of the restoration of territorial cult temples. They also pressured local officials on the mainland to adopt a more lenient approach to territorial cults early on, with great success. In addition, the Taiwan popular religion temple organizations organized frequent pilgrimage trips to ancestral temples in Fujian, with much fanfare.[84] The Taiwan factor was crucial, not only because the Taiwanese connections facilitated an earlier and stronger territorial cult revival in Fujian than elsewhere in China, but also because the vibrant territorial cults in Taiwan served as a model when religious actors in Fujian sought to reinvigorate their ritual life and rebuild temple organizations. Together, they have given the post-Mao development of territorial cult in Fujian some unique characteristics.

4

New Religious Movements

High Potential and Sporadic Outbursts

This chapter focuses on new religious movements (NRMs), which have teachings and practices significantly distinct from established religions and do not adhere to the authority of those religions. NRMs represent disruptive forces within a religious ecology. Their emergence reflects the prevailing ethos of their time, and the momentum they generate can lead to significant changes that shape the history of religion and, in some instances, even alter the course of world history.

Falun Gong, once widespread in post-Mao China, exemplifies a typical NRM. It was the largest NRM in post-Mao China and nearly became a prominent fixture on China's religious landscape. An examination of religious changes in the post-Mao era would be incomplete without addressing the rise and impact of Falun Gong. Researchers such as David Palmer, David Ownby, James Tong, and Benjamin Penny have produced excellent studies on various aspects of the Falun Gong movement.[1] Although it draws on existing studies, my analysis of the Falun Gong movement differs in several key ways. First, I focus on two fundamental questions regarding the movement: Why did Falun Gong experience such rapid growth? What led to its sudden demise? Second, my inquiry extends beyond Falun Gong to examine other NRMs in post-Mao China as a reference group. I aim to unravel a comparative puzzle: Why was Falun Gong able to attract tens of millions of followers even as other NRMs struggled to gain traction? Third, this study places Falun Gong within the broader historical context of Chinese syncretic NRMs, analyzing the niches and potentials of such NRMs in China's religious ecology. I propose a bold argument that the fundamental structure and nature of Chinese religious ecology have been conducive to the growth and flourishing of NRMs, with the primary obstacle to their expansion consistently originating from the state.

Potential for NRMs in Late Imperial China

Let me begin with an observation: humans desire individual distinction, and this desire naturally inclines certain individuals toward developing new religious interpretations, teachings, and practices. When endowed with charisma, these individuals have the ability to attract followers, leading to the emergence of NRMs. Most of the world's major religions today originated as NRMs. Take early Christian groups, for example. By centering their devotion on Jesus as the Messiah, the followers of the Jesus movement not only provided a radical reinterpretation of Judaism but also faced rejection from Jewish religious authorities.[2] Similarly, when followers of the Buddha formed a religious community to practice the salvational path revealed by him, they distanced themselves from the scriptural authority of the Vedas and the religious authority of the Brahmins. Early Buddhism thus emerged as an NRM in a religious environment where Vedic Brahminism was, more or less, the orthodoxy.[3] Islam, too, began as a monotheist NRM in the Arabian Peninsula, where polytheist worship was prevalent.[4]

These NRMs amalgamated with state powers, transforming into state religions. This new state-religion relationship gave rise to some of the most important world civilizations, reshaping religious landscapes and determining the fates of later-emerging NRMs within their respective religious ecologies.[5]

I argue that the state-religion relationship in late imperial China provided ample opportunity for the recurrent emergence of NRMs. A comparison with the niches of NRMs in medieval Europe (500–1500) helps to illuminate my point. Christianity had a zero-sum nature in the sense that it saw itself as the only and ultimate truth, condemning other religions and sects as fallacies that led people astray. As a religion aiming to provide universal salvation, it had a strong evangelistic drive to convert people from other religions or belief systems. The zero-sum evangelistic nature of Christianity meant that Christian states would not allow other religions to exist, with the only exception being Judaism, for the Jews were regarded as a living testimony to the authenticity of the scriptural events of the Bible.[6] Meanwhile, the Catholic Church, wielding supreme religious authority and permeating society through its network of parishes, had the capability to vigilantly monitor, identify, condemn, and, in collaboration with secular authorities, persecute heresies. In such an environment, NRMs had little chance to grow large.

In comparison with Christianity, advocates of Confucianism, the state ideology in late imperial China, did not claim it to be the only source of truth, nor were they interested in evangelizing.[7] Confucianism's chief concern was bringing order to this world, not propitiating gods or providing otherworldly salvation. As a result, other religions, including Buddhism, Daoism, and popular religion, could establish themselves and thrive, fulfilling people's religious needs. These religions, together with Confucianism, provided a rich array of sources from which the individuals I refer to as religious innovators could draw to form their own syncretic ideas and practices. Moreover, none of these established religions was zero-sum by nature; they were not keen on defining or persecuting heterodoxies or heresies. Although leaders of established religions sometimes criticized or attacked the teachings and practices of NRMs, the lack of an overarching and absolute religious authority—such as the papacy—meant that these religions simply lacked the power to enforce sanctions.[8] Furthermore, by the late imperial period, mainstream institutional religions like Buddhism and Daoism had lost much of their drive to spread salvational teachings or to integrate followers into tightly knit religious communities. This created ample room for NRMs, many endowed with messianic messages, proselytizing zeal, and strong bonds with followers, to grow. By tapping into the religious and social needs of the people, NRMs were able to build popular followings.

In late imperial China, the main force stalling the growth of NRMs was not the established religions, but the state—specifically, the Ming and Qing rulers, who, fearful of the high mobilization and subversive potential of NRMs, were intent on containing or suppressing them. The law codes of the Ming and Qing dynasties criminalized spreading heretical teachings to deceive or incite people and imposed severe punishments. Yet in most cases, NRMs—when small and local—were overlooked or even tolerated by local officials, in part because the premodern state's capacity at the local level was limited.[9] Typically, the emergence of an NRM would not prompt significant state action unless the movement gathered a massive following, forged translocal networks, and became a political threat. It should be noted that some of these political threats were perceived rather than real. In some instances, heightened state repression led adherents of NRMs to take up arms and revolt.[10] In addition, some NRMs, inspired by millenarian beliefs, transformed themselves into militant organizations and staged rebellions.[11] A few NRMs, such as the White Lotus sects and the Taiping Heavenly Kingdom Movement, brought about tremendous upheavals.[12] Although the insurgencies launched by these NRMs were eventually quelled, the state was unable to change the nature of the religious ecology, which remained conducive to the proliferation of NRMs. To its very end, late imperial China remained a fertile ground for NRMs.[13]

As argued above, in late imperial China, the primary obstacle to the development of NRMs was the state, which was chiefly concerned with the political mobilization potential of these movements, while the religious ecology itself offered ample niches for NRMs to exploit. One can easily imagine the surge of energy these movements would unleash once state suppression was lifted or eased. This is precisely why NRMs experienced explosive growth during the Republican period (1912–49).

Growth Potential of NRMs Realized in Republican China

The early Republican years (1912–27) under the Beiyang government of northern warlords was an era of bewildering changes and "unprecedented openness."[14] Institutions of the toppled Qing empire were swiftly abolished, and a novel governing structure emerged, modeled on the West and brimming with experimentation. Religion as conceptualized in the West and defined by certain Christian-centric criteria defined the religious policy of the Republican government. Religious liberty was written into the first constitution of the Republic.

Political disunity and fragmentation characterized this period. The absence of a strong central authority brought chaos but also fostered de facto freedom. Traditional ideas began to lose their grip, and new ones rose and faded with remarkable speed. The vibrant press and print culture facilitated spirited exchanges of ideas, fueling an iconoclastic new cultural movement that culminated in the epoch-making May Fourth Movement in 1919.[15] All sorts of civic associations and voluntary organizations flourished, ranging from chambers of commerce and student societies to workers' unions, professional associations, and even a beggars' union.[16]

It was in this new context that Chinese NRMs found great opportunity. During the early Republican era, a vast number of NRMs were allowed to register as religious, philanthropic, and public interest associations.[17] Prominent political figures openly practiced and supported NRMs of different kinds.[18] The NRMs of this period inherited the practice of religious syncretism, messages of universal salvation, and an emphasis on moral self-transformation from their predecessors in late imperial China. Hence, Duara coined the term "redemptive societies" to highlight their world-saving claims and projects.[19] Some NRMs, such as Tongshanshe, fashioned themselves into modern-style organizations with national headquarters and local chapters, and they displayed an eagerness to engage in charitable and social reform activities in response to the calls of the time.[20] In terms of the increase of membership and social influence, what the NRMs achieved in this period was unrivaled by other religions.[21] In contrast to Buddhism and Daoism, the NRMs' congregational structure and proselytization drive furnished them with a competitive edge for expansion in this new environment. Also, less burdened by institutional inertia, they were also much more adaptive to the rapid social changes of the age.

Throughout Republican China, the NRMs possessed three advantages that Christianity could not rival: Politically, the NRMs were adept at harnessing the burgeoning nationalist sentiment among the Chinese populace. Culturally, the NRMs' eclectic blending of messages from various deep-seated religious traditions resonated with the Chinese people.[22] Socially, NRM activists could take advantage of diverse networks that were inaccessible to Christians. These advantages allowed NRMs to continue growing under the Nationalists (1927–49) even though the regime's attitude toward NRMs soured.

Frowning upon the "superstitious" activities of NRMs and concerned about potential infiltration by enemy forces, the Nationalist government swiftly moved to ban several major NRMs after subduing the northern warlords in 1927. However, the regime was not rigidly ideological and was susceptible to lobbying efforts. Consequently, it was persuaded to permit the continued existence and development of NRMs under the guise of charitable organizations.[23] Furthermore, the Nationalist control measures were ineffective in regions governed by local strongmen or under Japanese occupation. Between 1931 and 1945, in Manchuria and other occupied territories, Japanese forces pursued a policy of using NRMs to advance their own interests, thereby encouraging their growth.[24] Meanwhile, both the Nationalists and the Communists also sought to co-opt and mobilize the NRMs for wartime objectives.[25] The rapid ascent of the Way of Unity (Yiguandao) to become the largest NRM of the Republican era can be attributed to its adept exploitation of opportunities during the Sino-Japanese War.[26]

The situation in River County shows a similar pattern. In the early years of the Republican era, NRMs such as Tongshanshe, Pududao, Wuweidao, and Changshengjiao all established branches and gained followings in the county. But they were all overtaken by the Way of Unity, which started its missionary activities in River County as late as 1943. The movement expanded so quickly that by 1949, 82 out of the total of 85 townships in River County had established chapters of the Way of Unity, functioning under the leadership of 1,035 religious specialists of different ranks. River County also developed into a regional bastion, sending out seventy-five missionaries to other counties and provinces. A head count of the Way of Unity in the county around 1952 reveals that it had 9,005 members. It is worth noting that there were only 966 Protestants and 520 Catholics in the county around the time. However, the reported figure of 9,005 members vastly underestimates the true membership of the Way of Unity in River County. The data were compiled from police reports during the CCP's 1952 campaign to suppress NRMs as "reactionary secret societies" (*fandong huidaomen*). It is understandable that a significant number of NRM followers managed to evade detection and were not included in the count.

Allow me to include my family's experience to further illustrate this point. The extended families of my maternal grandparents resided in a market town and its surrounding villages in River County. Within this family network, two individuals could be classified as missionary-adepts of the Way of Unity.[27] One of them held a high rank within the organization, having been appointed as an initiator at the age of thirty-five.[28] Together with another missionary-adepts in the town, they recruited through their network of acquaintances and successfully turned a significant number of my relatives and many townsfolk into followers of the Way of Unity. Altars were set up in the town, serving as places where followers would congregate, make offerings, and participate in other ritual activities. As far as I know, except for the two missionary-adepts who were later arrested and sentenced for their leadership roles in the Way of Unity, the rest of my family who were rank-and-file members of the NRMs avoided leaving any record that indicated their membership. In fact, my family' historical association with the NRMs was buried so deeply in the memories of my grandparents' generation that it was unknown to the younger generations, until I unearthed the past by interviewing my grandma in 2010.[29]

A national estimate puts the total number of NRM followers in 1949 at around thirteen million, approximately 2.4 percent of China's population at the time.[30] Drawing from my knowledge of the situation in River County and other cases, I would venture to assert that this figure is a significant underestimate. However, even if we accept this number, the membership of NRMs still surpassed both Protestantism (with approximately one million members) and Catholicism (around three million members) by a considerable margin. In any case, the Republican period demonstrates the immense energy NRMs could unleash if the state did not hinder their growth. McFarland likened the postwar period in Japan, when myriad NRMs proliferated and thrived, to the "rush hour of the gods."[31] Certainly, Republican China experienced a similar phenomenon. Had this trend continued, NRMs would likely have emerged as a significant and dynamic force in the religious ecology of contemporary mainland China, much like their counterparts in present-day Japan.

The NRMs suffered a devastating blow under the fledgling Maoist government, which harbored concerns that they were infiltrated by remnants of the Nationalist regime and could potentially engage in acts of sabotage. In response, the new government launched a nationwide campaign to eradicate them. Denounced as "reactionary secret societies" in 1952, NRMs were summarily banned and their leaders ordered to turn themselves in, and many of them later faced imprisonment or execution. Members were pressured to renounce their affiliation with NRMs. An intense propaganda campaign was orchestrated to "expose" the alleged crimes and evils of NRMs, and people were mobilized to report on NRM activities.[32] In River County, a regional bastion of the Way of Unity, diehard members persisted into the end of the 1960s. Their persistence led to two massive arrests, in 1954 and 1969. As a result, nine were executed, three received life sentences, sixty-two served prison terms, and dozens were placed under the supervision and surveillance of the communities where they labored and resided.[33]

Under the "iron fist" and harsh crackdown, the once-powerful Way of Unity, along with other NRMs, was subdued. Although movements resurfaced in the more open post-Mao environment, none could reclaim the level of influence they had wielded during the Republican era.[34] Although the early years of post-Mao China presented renewed opportunities for the growth of NRMs, Chinese society gravitated toward new trends and interests of a vastly different era.

The Anti-NRM Policy Regime in Post-Mao China

Having established that the nature of Chinese religious ecology could indeed provide NRMs with significant potential to become a major religious force, and having examined how this potential manifested itself during Republican China and Mao's China, I now turn to the development of NRMs in post-Mao China. As previous chapters have demonstrated, religions experienced a resurgence and flourished after the post-Mao state adopted a more moderate religious policy, relaxed control over society, and initiated market-oriented economic reforms. It is essential to explore how NRMs have fared in this new sociopolitical environment and to what extent they have realized their growth potential.

To address these questions, we must first recapitulate the state's bipartite system for managing religious groups in post-Mao China, as discussed in chapter 1. Under this system, the five state-sanctioned religions are overseen by the SARA and the UFWD along with their branches at various administrative levels. Conversely, religious groups labeled as "evil cults" fall under the jurisdiction of public security forces and are subjected to varying degrees of suppression (see figure 1.2 in chapter 1 for detail). In 1983, the Shouters, a Protestant sectarian group influenced by the teachings of Li Changshou (aka Witness Lee) and introduced to China in 1979 (as discussed in chapter 1), became the first religious group targeted for a nationwide crackdown in the post-Mao era. At that time, the campaign still employed the "reactionary

TABLE 4.1. 14 "Evil cults" publicly listed by the ministry of public security in 2000

New Religious Movements	Religious tradition(s) that were the main source of influence	Place of origin		Year it was labeled as an evil cult
		Outside mainland China	Homegrown	
Shouters and offshoots including Eastern Lightning	Christianity	United States		1995
All Ranges Church	Christianity		Yes	1995
Linglingjiao (Spirit Church)	Christianity		Yes	1995
Mentuhui (Three-Redemptive Christ sect)	Christianity		Yes	1995
New Testament Church	Christianity	Hong Kong		1995
Beili Wang (The Established King)	Christianity		Yes	1995
The Family International, identified as Children of God	Christianity	United States		1995
Dami Mission	Christianity	South Korea		1995
World Elijah Evangelical Mission	Christianity	South Korea		1996
Unification Church	Christianity	South Korea		1997
Zhushenjiao (Lord God's Teachings)	Christianity		Yes	1998
Sanban Puren Pai (Three Grades of Servant Church)	Christianity		Yes	1999
Guanyin Famen/Yuandun Famen	Buddhism	Taiwan		1995/1999
True Buddha School, identified as the Lingxian Zhenfozong	Buddhism	Taiwan		1995

Source: Notice of the Ministry of Public Security on Several Issues Concerning the Identification and Banning of Cult Organizations, issued by the Ministry of Public Security of the People's Republic of China on May 10, 2000 (https://www.china21.org/docs/CONFI-MPS-CHINESE.htm, accessed August 1, 2023)

secret society" discourse of the Mao era. However, by the mid-1990s, the Chinese state began adopting Western anticult discourse and started to use the epithet "evil cult" (*xiejiao*) or "cultic organization," following media coverage of tragedies involving groups such as the Branch Davidians, the Order of the Solar Temple, and Aum Shinrikyo.[35]

Table 4.1 shows that from 1995 to 1999, a total of fourteen NRM groups were identified by the Ministry of Public Security, the State Council, and the Central Committee of the CCP as evil cults. Among them, twelve were inspired by Christianity, and two mainly drew on Buddhism; eight were introduced from outside mainland China. Once branded as evil cults, NRMs became the target of campaigns that often entailed coordinated efforts from multiple government agencies. These agencies wielded the authority to detain NRM leaders and core members, subject them to labor camps or imprisonment, launch propaganda campaigns against them, and enlist the collaboration of work units and neighborhood communities to exert pressure on NRM adherents. Under this policy regime, targeted NRMs would often either dissolve or operate underground. However, I find it intriguing that Falun Gong, the largest syncretic NRM to emerge in post-Mao China, experienced explosive growth precisely during a period when the state had become highly vigilant concerning NRMs and had established apparatuses and institutions to suppress them. The puzzle that arises for me is: Why was Falun Gong able to achieve such a meteoric rise despite the stringent anticult policy in place? In the following sections, I will briefly introduce the movement before delving into this puzzle. Subsequently, I will explore the factors contributing to the movement's eventual downfall.

Explaining the Meteoric Rise of Falun Gong

Falun Gong was founded as a qigong movement by Li Hongzhi in 1992. Qigong, an ancient practice in China involving breathing and movement exercises, promises healing, the development of human potential, and spiritual enhancement. Throughout the 1980s and much of the 1990s, it was common to see people practicing qigong together in parks or public spaces in cities across China, with some gatherings attracting thousands of participants. Renowned qigong masters traveled extensively to give lectures and lead training sessions, establishing a nationwide network of practice sites. Falun Gong emerged during the latter period of this qigong fever. Initially following the path of other qigong groups, Falun Gong soon distinguished itself by acquiring a strong religious character. The publication of *Zhuan Falun* in 1994, the core text that presents the religious teachings of Li, marked the turning of Falun Gong into a full-fledged NRM.

After the mid-1990s, the voices of critics and detractors of qigong became increasingly heard in the Chinese media. In comparison with other qigong groups, however, Falun Gong groups responded to media criticism with less tolerance and more militancy. They organized letter-writing campaigns and staged demonstrations, demanding corrections and apologies from the media responsible. On April 25, 1999, some ten thousand Falun Gong practitioners gathered in Beijing and demonstrated outside Zhongnanhai, the residence compound of top Chinese leaders, following a clash between Tianjin police and local Falun Gong demonstrators. This event alarmed Chinese leaders, prompting them to launch a nationwide crackdown in July 1999, ultimately leading to the downfall of Falun Gong in mainland China.

I argue that under the vigilant and rigorous anti-NRM regime, only those NRMs that managed to evade the post-Mao state's scrutiny temporarily and capitalize on this brief period for rapid expansion were likely to emerge as large-scale movements. Falun Gong possesses several institutional features that, when considered together, distinguish it from other NRMs. They not only allowed Falun Gong to operate under the radar for several years but also enabled it to effectively seize this window of opportunity to achieve explosive growth.

A Qigong Group Turned NRM. In contrast to other NRMs active at the time, Falun Gong initially began as a typical qigong group.[36] Li Hongzhi, its founder, started as a qigong master, teaching a set of movements and claiming their superior health benefits. Even after its metamorphosis into an NRM, qigong exercises remained a crucial component of Falun Gong.

After 1994, Falun Gong's teachings started to acquire all the essential elements of a salvation religion.[37] Li claimed to possess the ultimate truth of the universe, asserting that truthfulness, compassion, and forbearance were fundamental characteristics and principles of the cosmos. According to Li, humanity was originally in harmony with these principles but deviated from them, descending to the level of ordinary humanity—a state characterized by unpleasantness, filthiness, and degradation. Salvation for Falun Gong practitioners entails "a return to the original state." Li purported to have revealed a path to salvation, or, in his parlance, "Consummation" (*yuanman*): practitioners were urged not only to practice the qigong exercise as taught but also to cultivate the qualities of truthfulness, compassion, and forbearance in their daily lives, as they studied Li's writings, in particular *Zhuan Falun*, as a sacred text. Falun Gong deified Li—or rather, Li deified himself. He was more than a qigong master with supernormal physical and healing powers; he was a godlike or Buddha-like figure capable of assuming countless incarnations to protect his followers and of installing a spinning wheel of energy in the abdomen of each Falun Gong practitioner, a savior holding the key to the secret of the cosmos and human salvation.

A Chinese Syncretic NRM. Compared with NRMs that primarily draw on religious traditions not yet widely resonant among people of China, such as Christianity, Falun Gong is a Chinese syncretic NRM, in the sense that its core ideas and practices borrowed heavily from preexisting Chinese religious/cultural traditions. In addition to the qigong tradition, Li Hongzhi extensively appropriated symbols, terminologies, and ideas of Buddhism and Daoism.[38] In particular, he borrowed heavily from the cosmology and soteriology of Buddhism but gave them his idiosyncratic interpretation. Here is an example of how Li used the Buddhist concept of karma. He sees karma as a black substance that accumulates in the body when a person commits an unwholesome deed. Accumulation of the black substance is identified as the root cause of diseases. Cultivating truthfulness, compassion, and forbearance, along with practicing the qigong exercise, will transform the black substance into white substance. This transformation is of vital importance to Falun Gong practitioners—it will eliminate the root cause of illness and lead to "Consummation." In the autobiographical account in the appendix of *Zhuan Falun*, Li depicted himself as having received instructions from various mysterious Buddhist and Daoist masters, beginning in his childhood.[39] In September 1994, Li managed to change his date of birth from July 7, 1952, to May 13, 1951, so that his birthday in the lunar calendar could fall on the same day of the birth of the founder of Buddhism. As much as he appropriated from Daoism and particularly from Buddhism, Li asserted that his teachings were far beyond them. In *Zhuan Falun*, he claimed that the teachings of Buddhism and Daoism were restricted within the Milky Way, whereas Falun Gong's teaching was in accordance with the principles of the universe and was thus of the highest order.[40] As a quintessential syncretic religion, Falun Gong also integrated into its teachings elements from parascience concerning prehistoric civilizations and extraterrestrials that were introduced from the West and became popular in China at the time.[41]

Proselytization Drive. Falun Gong was quite aggressive in proselytization. Li himself tirelessly promoted Falun Gong, giving lectures, training sessions, and workshops across China and abroad. The spread of Falun Gong was greatly facilitated through the dissemination of Falun Gong publications and audiovisual materials. He reminded practitioners that their obligation was "to use every favorable opportunity to spread Falun Gong, to prove its truthfulness,"[42] and that helping others to get to know Falun Gong was an integral part of self-cultivation.[43] He gave specific instructions to his followers on how to spread the practice (*chuangong*),[44] and propagate dharma (*hongfa* or *chuanfa*).[45] He encouraged practitioners to organize outdoor group practice sessions as a way to make Falun Gong publicly visible, or to set up a site where the practices could be taught free of charge. Practitioners also employed other ways to spread Falun Gong, such as one-on-one conversations about the movement's benefits. I first encountered Falun Gong when I was practicing martial arts in a park in Beijing in the spring of 1996. An elderly man stood nearby, watching. He approached me afterward and told me that there was a more advanced form of practice that I should know. He said he was willing to lend me a book for this purpose on the condition that I would tell him what I had learned from the reading when I returned it. That book was *Zhuan Falun*.

Dual Mobilization Structure. Based on the above analysis, I shall highlight another important institutional feature of Falun Gong—its dual mobilization structure. As a newly emerging religious movement, its founder, Li Hongzhi, could use his personal charisma in centralized proselytization. This distinguished Falun Gong from established religions. In addition, Li encouraged his followers to engage in decentralized proselytization efforts, linking such activities to their individual paths to salvation. This decentralized mobilization strategy makes Falun Gong similar to Protestantism, as both facilitate active participation of rank-and-file followers in spreading the religion. Yet Protestantism lacks a comparable form of mobilization centered on a charismatic leader.

Congregational Structure. Similar to Protestantism and Catholicism, Falun Gong had a congregational structure. The following outlines a typical daily routine of Falun Gong group practice that I constructed based on my interviews with former Falun Gong practitioners (Informants No. 302, 306, 311): Practitioners would rise every morning at 4:30 a.m. and convene at a practice site, typically an open space like a park, to collectively engage in morning exercises until 7 a.m. In the evenings, they would gather again, often at the private residence of a core member, to study Falun Gong texts or watch instructional videos featuring Li Hongzhi. These evening study sessions, referred to as "dharma learning" (*xuefa*), typically lasted from 7 p.m. to 9 p.m. Such an intensive schedule meant that an active practitioner of Falun Gong would dedicate more than four hours each day to Falun Gong–related activities in the company of fellow practitioners.

Centralized Hierarchy. Falun Gong had a centralized hierarchical organizational structure. Shortly after it was launched, Falun Gong adopted a structure that followed the standard of other major qigong groups at the time. At the grassroots level—that is, neighborhoods, work units, or towns—practice sites (*liangong dian*) were established. The practice site was the basic unit of Falun Gong. The practice site was managed by the councilor (*fudao yuan*). Councilors were seasoned Falun Gong practitioners and devoted followers of Li Hongzhi. Falun Gong would organize special training sessions for councilors, sometimes personally instructed by Li himself. Under the direction of a station chief (*zhanzhang*), a guidance station (*fudao zhan*) was established at the level of a county or an urban district to coordinate the activities of a group of practice sites. Above guidance stations were branch stations, established at the prefecture or city level. Main stations (*fudao zongzhan*) were set up at the level of a province or a municipality, overseeing guidance stations.[46] All the guidance stations were overseen by the China Falun Dafa Research Institute, an organization headquartered in Beijing and chaired by Li Hongzhi.

The centralized hierarchical structure ensured not only that information

FIGURE 4.1. A large-scale assembly of Falun Gong in mainland China. In Wuhan in 1998, more than 5,000 Falun Gong practitioners aligned themselves to form the shapes of the emblem of Falun Gong and the three Chinese characters meaning truthfulness, compassion, and forbearance—the core principles of the universe as proclaimed by Li Hongzhi. Organizing such large assemblies demonstrates the mobilization capacity of Falun Gong and further strengthens it. (Image from minghui.org.)

and orders could be swiftly, and sometimes secretly, passed from the top to the rank and file but also that practitioners could be efficiently mobilized for concerted actions. This hierarchical centralism also enabled Li to prevent the emergence of other charismatic figures within the movement. Only texts and videos authorized by Li could be disseminated within Falun Gong, and councilors were strictly limited to conveying Li's teachings without adding their own interpretations. Li repeatedly emphasized that councilors and station chiefs were merely ordinary practitioners, and all practitioners were disciples protected by his divine power.[47] In this way, Falun Gong was able to connect ordinary practitioners directly with the charismatic leadership of Li Hongzhi.

I will argue that on the one hand, these institutional features of Falun Gong helped it achieve explosive growth in early post-Mao years, and on the other hand, accelerated its head-on confrontation with the state. Before doing so, however, I will highlight a historically situated context of the early post-Mao years crucial to the swift rise of Falun Gong.

A FEVERISH NATION AND THE QIGONG FEVER

Fever (re) in the early post-Mao context refers to a trend that in a short period gains broad and enthusiastic following. A nation captivated by a bewildering array of fevers is a distinct condition that characterized Chinese society from

1978 and well into the 1990s. Fevers of traditional Chinese culture, Western philosophies, popular music from Taiwan, films and TV series from Hong Kong, fashion styles, and other fads swept across China.[48] The qigong fever was one of them. This peculiar condition is also one of the many unintended consequences of the Maoist state's radical policies. Under Mao, China had been a closed society, in which people were unable to access information outside a narrowly defined domain. In other words, the Maoist state policies had created a hugely homogenous population that was uninitiated and susceptive to influences. Thus, when China suddenly opened up only a few years after the death of Mao, the influx of "new" ideas and cultures immediately sparked fads and crazes that consumed the nation.

However, the qigong fever came into being and remained unbated for many years also because qigong was strongly supported by the state at the time.[49] Qigong, denounced and banned in the mid-1960s, was rehabilitated in 1979 because sympathizers, defenders, and advocates at the highest level pulled political strings. Among its most vigorous and influential advocates were prominent scientists such as Qian Xueshen and high-ranking officials including General Zhang Zhenhuan and Sports Minister Wu Shaozu. Qigong was officially recognized to be an integral component of Chinese medicine and to have healing benefits and significant scientific value.[50] Promoting qigong was therefore seen as serving the national interest. Under the official patronage, positive reporting on the miraculous effects of qigong appeared on state media; all sort of associations, research institutions, magazines, and conferences promoting qigong sprung up across China; qigong groups set up instruction stations, held training sessions, and rented stadiums for mass gatherings. Qigong masters who could demonstrate various "supernatural" abilities were pursued like movie stars during this time. They were invited to deliver talks and showcase their extraordinary capabilities at work units and college campuses, drawing audiences in the hundreds or even thousands.[51]

In the following, I will show that how the institutional features of Falun Gong played out in the specific context of the early post-Mao era, enabling its phenomenal rise.

Because Falun Gong started as a part of the qigong movement before it was transformed into a full-fledged NRM, its growth benefited from the state's support for qigong. At the outset, as a self-proclaimed qigong master, Li Hongzhi found sponsorship from the Changchun City Somatic Science Research Society to rent venues for workshops attended by hundreds in his hometown, Changchun. Soon, Falun Gong was accepted into the China Qigong Science Research Society, China's main national state-sponsored qigong association, with which most qigong groups were affiliated. Using the network and re-

FIGURE 4.2. In a qigong instruction session in Beijing in 1992, the audience raises their hands to receive qi emitted by the qigong master. (Photograph by Huang Xiaobing/VCG.)

sources provided by the association and its local branches, Li was able to organize fifty-six workshops in Beijing and other major cities across China between May 1992 and September 1994. Each of Li's workshops lasted seven to ten days and was attended by hundreds or thousands of practitioners.[52] On July 30, 1993, Li founded the China Falun Dafa Research Institute, with permission granted by the China Qigong Science Research Society. Li's first major publication, *China Falun Gong*, was published by a publishing house with military background in 1993; the bible of Falun Gong, *Zhuan Falun*, was published by China Radio and Television Publishing House, a press affiliated with the National Radio and Television Administration. No doubt, Falun Gong's rise rode on the qigong fever. Only three years after it was launched, Falun Gong had already gained millions of followers.[53] Had Falun Gong propagated its religious character from early on, it could not possibly have evaded detection by the state agencies that kept a watchful eye on NRMs. It might have ended up like the Shouters and the Guanyin Famen, which were struck down by the state before they could grow very large.

Falun Gong's syncretic nature and particularly its appropriation of Buddhism and Daoism helped the movement strike a chord with the masses, who had an affinity with general Buddhist and Daoist ideas but were unable to discern orthodoxy. In addition, Falun Gong's strong proselytization drive, assisted by its centralized and diffused modes of proselytization, its congregational structure, and its centralized hierarchical nature, allowed the movement to expand exponentially, retain its practitioners, and transform them into ardent followers ready to take coordinated actions on Li Hongzhi's orders and even to make sacrifices. These institutional features enabled Falun Gong to exploit the window of opportunity to achieve exponential growth and gave its founder, Li Hongzhi, leverage to mobilize his followers for actions.

Before dealing with the serious political implications of Falun Gong's institutional features, let us return to River County again, to illustrate how these features were working at a grassroots level to turn River County into a stronghold of Falun Gong in three short years.

Falun Gong was introduced into River County by Guo Yunshan, a retired schoolteacher, after she went to Beijing to attend a Falun Gong workshop by Li Hongzhi in 1992.[54] Guo went to Beijing seeking cures for her husband's illness. At the workshop, she was captivated by Li Hongzhi's charisma and the purported miraculous effects of Falun Gong and became an ardent follower. Guo introduced Falun Gong to a few friends and former colleagues in River County, one of whom was Zhao Guixiang, another retired schoolteacher, who would play a key role in the spread of Falun Gong in River County. Encouraged by Guo, Zhao also went to Beijing to attend Falun Gong workshops in 1993. Zhao, upon returning to River County, introduced Falun Gong to dozens of people and turned her home into a gathering point where they practiced together. Near the end of 1994, Zhao and a dozen practitioners went to Guangzhou to attend a Falun Gong workshop by Li Hongzhi. Galvanized by this experience, these early practitioners set up a practice site in a major public park of River County upon their return. Because the group was expanding quickly, Zhao petitioned the China Falun Dafa Research Institute for permission to establish a guidance station in River County. In 1996, with authorization from Falun Gong's top leadership, a guidance station was set up with Zhao appointed as the station chief. In this position, she established and oversaw Falun Gong practice sites in towns and villages across the county. In addition, Zhao played an instrumental role in disseminating Falun Gong to neighboring counties and cities. Soon, River County evolved into a regional stronghold of Falun Gong, reminiscent of its role within the Way of Unity in Republican China.

Previously, I have argued that NRMs, especially those with syncretic teachings that could resonate with the popular culture of Chinese society, strong proselytization drive, and congregational structure, have high growth potential in the Chinese religious ecology, so long as political forces do not suppress them too severely. From this perspective, the rise of Falun Gong should not be seen as too much of a surprise. It is one of the many instances of NRMs realizing some of their growth potential. What we need to explain is why the rigorous anticult policy and apparatus of the early post-Mao years did not pose an effective impediment, whereas they did keep many NRMs from growing. I maintain Falun Gong's taking the cover of qigong in its early stages allowed it not only to benefit enormously from the state's support for the qigong sector but also to ride on the fever that gripped Chinese society in the early post-Mao years. Consequently, millions were drawn to Falun Gong, a novel way of practicing qigong. At the same time, Falun Gong's emphasis on a salvational message and the associated power of the master, its prosely-tization drive and strong congregations, and its centralized hierarchical orga-nization enabled it to turn enthusiastic qigong practitioners into committed followers of Falun Gong and Li Hongzhi.

The Downfall of Falun Gong

As swift as the rise of Falun Gong was, the more sudden its downfall turned out to be. Falun Gong claimed in 1997 that it had a hundred million follow-ers, including twenty million regular practitioners, in China. Palmer, based on his observation and calculations, however, argues that ten million follow-ers would a more reasonable number.[55] Yet even this more realistic estimate bespeaks the astonishing ascendance of Falun Gong within a span of a few years. Followers of Falun Gong came from all social strata, and a considerable percentage were highly educated and among the social and political elite, in-cluding "Communist Party members, functionaries of state organs, military people, armed police, medical practitioners, teachers, and even diplomats."[56] Surely, had Falun Gong maintained its momentum or been able to consoli-date its growth, it would have become a major player in the religious ecology of post-Mao China. Yet this process ended abruptly after the government's crackdown in July 1999. In the following, I argue that the fall of Falun Gong was inevitable. More specifically, given its institutional features and the hard-line strategies adopted in the face of criticism, Falun Gong was bound to face suppression in the political context of post-Mao China.

First, in a political environment inimical to NRMs, Falun Gong's mov-ing out of the qigong field and metamorphosing into a full-fledged NRM made institutional legality and legitimacy difficult to achieve and rendered the movement susceptible to the charge of "evil cult." In 1996, Li Hongzhi and the China Qigong Science Research Society had a falling out.[57] In March of that year, Li decided to withdraw Falun Gong's membership, stating that he wanted to increase devotion to "Buddhist studies." On its side, in September the society issued a report on Falun Gong, condemning Li Hongzhi for deifying himself, propagating superstitions, and spreading political calumnies, thereby deviating from a proper qigong movement and the mission of the society. The following November, the society again issued a declaration that it had terminated Falun Gong's affiliation. Chinese law at the time required any social organization to be affiliated with a broadly related government agency or an official/semiofficial organization (*guakao danwei*) to maintain legally registered status. Hence, its disavowal by the society meant Falun Gong was deprived of both institutional affiliation and legal status. Falun Gong applied to several government agencies to register itself as an affiliated social organization, including the Ethnic Affairs Committee of the National People's Congress, the Buddhist Association of China, and the United Front Work Department, but was rejected in all cases.[58]

Moreover, Falun Gong's exponential expansion had made its presence felt strongly in society. Starting in 1996, various parties started to notice that Falun Gong was not just another qigong group. Critical voices began to surface. In June 1996, a major state-owned newspaper published an article accusing *Zhuan Falun* of "propagating feudal superstition and pseudo-science" and "producing pernicious influences on the spiritual life of the masses." It pointed out that Falun Gong was more "ideological" than other qigong groups and ridiculed Li's boastful claims and attempts to deify himself.[59] The State Press and Publication Administration issued a directive the following month banning the publication of all Falun Gong books, asserting they used the pretext of qigong to propagate superstition and pseudoscience.

Interestingly, the most vigorous attack on Falun Gong as an evil cult came from the Buddhist establishment, due to Li Hongzhi's excessive appropriation of Buddhist elements and the growing concern that many Buddhists were turning to Falun Gong. Starting in 1996, several Buddhist journals published indignant articles criticizing Falun Gong for appropriating, distorting, and slandering Buddhism. Chen Xingqiao, a lay Buddhist, penned a treatise declaring that Falun Gong by nature was "a novel popular heretical cult" with a qigong cover and the pretense of Buddhism; he linked Falun Gong with popular sectarian religions in Chinese history such as the White Lotus Sect.[60] With the approval of Zhao Puchu, then president of the Buddhist Association of China, Chen's article was published in the official journal of the association in 1998. Later the same year, Chen's various articles were assembled together and published as the first book-length criticism of Falun Gong. Zhao Puchu played an instrumental role in leading the Buddhist establishment's attack on Falun Gong, emphasizing the importance of refuting and debunking its teachings.[61]

It needs to be noted that in 1995, the entire qigong field was rocked by surging media criticisms, during which various qigong masters were criticized for practicing pseudoscience, swindling, and quackery. Yet compared with these charges, which could at most only discredit or criminalize some qigong masters, the charge of being an "evil cult" was far more damning—it meant that the entire movement should be under the purview of the Public Security forces. By transforming itself into an NRM, Falun Gong thus sailed into dangerous waters. In fact, the Ministry of Public Security in 1997 and 1998 launched three investigations into allegations that Falun Gong was carrying out "illegal religious activities" or was in fact an evil cult. Though the outcome of the investigations was inconclusive (probably because Falun Gong had followers and defenders in security circles), the possibility of Falun Gong being condemned as an evil cult still loomed large.

Some argue that Falun Gong might not have faced such a severe crackdown had it not launched repeated protests that culminated in the massive Zhongnanhai demonstration in April 1999. I agree only partially. Because Falun Gong had high-level supporters, harsh and widespread repression may have been avoidable. However, as long as the anti-NRM policy of the post-Mao state was in place, and with the kind of exponential growth that Falun Gong enjoyed thanks to its institutional features, I do not believe that the movement could have stayed out of trouble for long.

Nevertheless, as history unfolded, what eventually brought down Falun Gong in China was that it came to be seen as a grave political threat by the regime. Here, I would like to emphasize the double-edged nature of Falun Gong's institutional features in the political context of post-Mao China. Although Falun Gong's strong proselytizing drive, congregational structure, and centralized hierarchical organization were indeed crucial for it to quickly develop into a massive movement with committed core members, they also enabled Falun Gong to mobilize followers to stage repeated protests in an attempt to silence criticism. These protests, however, put Falun Gong's power and mobilization capacity in the spotlight and set it on a collision course with the mighty state power.

As previously mentioned, criticisms of the qigong movement had been mounting since 1995. Other qigong movements, lacking the mobilization capacity of Falun Gong, could only choose to ignore them or lay low. Falun Gong, however, responded to criticism with a rather militant approach.[62] Whenever critical voices emerged in the media, Falun Gong responded with letter-writing campaigns and public demonstrations. These protests demanded corrections, apologies, or even the dismissal of individuals responsible for specific articles. From 1996 to 1999, Falun Gong staged approximately three hundred protests, with the majority yielding favorable results.[63] These early successes encouraged Li Hongzhi and his followers to become more aggressive and eventually led to the large demonstration outside Zhongnanhai on April 25, 1999.

This was the turning point for Falun Gong in China. The place chosen for the demonstration was politically fraught, because Zhongnanhai is the residential compound of China's top leaders. The timing was also sensitive because it was close to the tenth anniversary of the 1989 Tiananmen student movement, which had almost toppled the regime—and Zhongnanhai is only a stone's throw from Tiananmen Square. The scale and the highly organized nature of the demonstration also alarmed government leaders; tens of thousands of participants arrived from different parts of the country, protested quietly, and dispersed with little trace. Even though Falun Gong followers insisted that the demonstration was apolitical in nature, the location and timing of the protest, and its sheer magnitude, suggested otherwise to the Chinese leadership.

Immediately after the demonstration, President Jiang Zemin reportedly characterized Falun Gong as the most serious political issue since the 1989 student movement.[64] In the wake of the Zhongnanhai demonstration, as the state was carrying out a nationwide investigation of the organization and preparing for a crackdown, Falun Gong followers, encouraged by Li Hongzhi, continued to mount rallies and protests, including another demonstration in Beijing.[65] The movement, with millions of followers and extraordinary mobilization capacity, susceptible to manipulation by a leader based in the United States beyond the reach of the Chinese state, was perceived as a nightmarish situation by Chinese leaders. Recognizing the political challenge posed by Falun Gong, they saw the campaign to crush it as crucial for upholding "the fundamental belief of the CCP members and the fundamental belief that propels the Chinese nation to strive together and move forward" and as "a political-ideological battle over the heart and mind of the masses."[66] The Chinese state decided to strike, and strike hard.

On July 22, 1999, the Chinese government, in a national televised broadcast, declared Falun Gong an illegal organization "engaging in illegal activities, propagating superstitious and fallacious beliefs, deceiving the masses, inciting and instigating disturbances, disrupting social stability" and officially banned it. A crackdown was launched, with the goal of wiping out Falun Gong. The state adopted their usual tactics for dealing with an evil cult. However, given the magnitude and influence of the movement, the state was compelled to mobilize much more resources to resolve the so-called Falun Gong problem. A special agency—the Central Leading Group on Preventing and Dealing with Cults—was created for this purpose. Its executive office was known as the 610 Office.[67] The 610 Office had branches established at every administrative level to coordinate multiple state agencies for the campaign. The campaign also involved various other actors, such as neighborhood committees and work units, in the surveillance and "deprogramming" of Falun Gong followers. The campaign to crush Falun Gong, in its intensity and duration, far surpassed the actions taken against any other labeled evil cults in the post-Mao era. It was an all-out war. In many aspects, it resembled the campaign to eliminate the Way of Unity in Mao's era.

The state ordered the dissolution of Falun Gong organization and the confiscation and destruction of publications and other materials. Leaders and activists were arrested and prosecuted, and rank-and-file followers were ordered to discontinue their association with the movement and to cease practicing Falun Gong. An intensive and multifaceted propaganda campaign painted Li Hongzhi as a swindler and charlatan with wild ambitions and pernicious intentions, denounced the absurdity of his teachings, exposed the political nature of the movement, and detailed the alleged harm that Falun Gong had inflicted on duped practitioners and their families.

Before the government's crackdown, several of Falun Gong's top leaders had already left China. Li Hongzhi, for instance, moved to the United States in 1996 with his family and in 1998 became a permanent resident. Falun Gong leaders established a headquarters in North America and, in response to the Chinese government's crackdown, launched a countercampaign. Through internet communications, they continued to influence Falun Gong followers inside China. Curiously, they adopted rhetoric similar to that of the Chinese state. Just as the state denounced Falun Gong an evil cult, Falun Gong declared the CCP an evil cult. Claiming that its struggle with the CCP amounted to a cosmic battle between good and evil, Falun Gong leadership prophesied that disaster would befall the CCP. Just as the Chinese state pressed the movement's followers to relinquish their association, Falun Gong called on Chinese citizens to renounce their affiliation with the CCP and its youth organizations—that is, the Communist Youth League and the Young Pioneers—lest they be damned along with the CCP in the coming catastrophes.[68] It enjoined followers in China to "tell the truth" (jiang zhenxiang). Li Hongzhi repeatedly emphasized that "telling the truth" was a paramount responsibility of Falun Gong followers and assured them that doing so would contribute to their own spiritual advancement toward "Consummation" and fulfill their roles in saving humanity.[69] For followers inside China, "telling the truth" primarily involved reproducing and distributing pamphlets and videos that exposed the persecution Falun Gong practitioners suffered at the hands of the Chinese government, debunked the official defamation of the movement, and attacked the legitimacy of the CCP.[70] Fully aware of the dire consequences for Falun Gong followers inside China, Li Hongzhi still persistently urged them to take such actions, in effect encouraging them to seek martyrdom.[71]

In face of the continued defiance of die-hard Falun Gong followers, the Chinese state sentenced them to labor reform institutions, where they were subject to conversion programs, which, in addition to law enforcement officials, involved the employers, Party cadres, colleagues, neighbors, and relatives of targeted subjects.[72] Many conversion programs allowed followers to study Buddhist writings and the Confucian primer *The Codes of Conduct for Students and Children*, in the hope that they would realize the fallacy of Falun Gong and switch to mainstream beliefs with which Falun Gong shares some affinity (Informants No. 329, 334).[73]

Although these measures succeeded to a considerable extent, for those most committed, neither coercion nor soft persuasion would break them. They would feign renunciation of the movement yet revert to Falun Gong practice after their release. An acquaintance of mine served prison terms for a total of five years for her role in producing and distributing Falun Gong materials. Months after her release, I met her in a private gathering. She told me that she endured the prison time by silently chanting "Falun Dafa is good" and "truthfulness, compassion, and forbearance" over and over again. She regretted that, overcome by a desire to reunite with her family, she had renounced Master Li Hongzhi. Although the renunciation was false, she thought that she had stepped down from her previous level of achievement on the Heavenly Ladder. Throughout our conversation, she urged me to renounce my affiliation with the Communist Youth League and the Young Pioneers to avoid damnation in the coming apocalypse, even after I repeatedly told her that these youth memberships had automatically expired a long time ago. For these die-hard Falun Gong followers, law enforcement agencies resorted to neighborhood committees for close monitoring of their activities and to assign community workers to regularly check up on them.

In River County, a regional stronghold of Falun Gong, committed Falun Gong practitioners persisted and engaged in acts of defiance and resistance. They wrote slogans such as "Falun Dafa is good" on Renminbi banknotes, distributed leaflets and pamphlets propagating the Falun Gong's version of "the truth," and sent birthday wishes to Li Hongzhi to show their loyalty. As of 2018, more than forty Falun Gong followers in the county were sentenced to prisons or sent to labor reform institutions. Many more have been sent to reeducation programs and were on the watch list of community-level surveillance for years. Because River County continued to be one of the "most plagued areas" (*zhongzaiqu*) of Falun Gong, the anti–Falun Gong campaign was the responsibility of the "number one in charge" (*yibashou*)—that is, the county CCP secretary himself.[74] Controlling and converting Falun Gong followers in their jurisdiction was also the assigned responsibility of the Party secretaries at the township and village level, and their success became part of their job performance evaluation criteria.

The campaign to eliminate Falun Gong lasted much longer and drained much more state resources than the top Chinese leaders might have expected. Nevertheless, under the iron fist and dragnet, Falun Gong did eventually disappear from the public scene in China. Except for the most recalcitrant, the majority of Falun Gong practitioners abandoned their practice. Some turned to alternative forms of calisthenics such as tai chi, and some switched to other belief systems. In my fieldwork, I have encountered a number of former Falun Gong followers who converted to Protestantism or Buddhism. They became core members of their new religious groups, respected by their coreligionists for their deep dedication and commitment. Perhaps the most significant achievement of the anti–Falun Gong campaign is that the Chinese state has effectively portrayed Li Hongzhi as crooked and evil, his teachings as absurd and injurious, and die-hard Falun Gong followers as delusional and fanatical. These notions persist and are widely accepted by people from all walks of life in China. Similar to the Way of Unity, which to this day still carries the bad reputation of "the Way of Persistently Harming People" (*yiguan hairen dao*) due to a pervasive propaganda campaign against the NRM in the 1950s and the 1960s, Falun Gong is likely to remain of ill repute in China for years to come.

Thus, I suggest that it is highly unlikely for Falun Gong to make a strong comeback, even if the state relaxed its repression (of which I see no sign). Again, the fate of the Way of Unity is instructive. In the post-Mao era, some members of the Way of Unity resumed their activities and connected with coreligionists in Taiwan. Some of their activities were not secret and became known to security forces, but the practitioners usually were not harassed.[75] Still, the movement has yet to gain substantial traction. The time for the Way of Unity seems to have passed, even though the soil for NRMs remains fertile.

After the crackdown on Falun Gong in July 1999, the government turned its eye to other popular qigong movements, imposing strict controls on the few qigong groups still permitted to exist.[76] As a result, qigong fever dissipated.

In the course of suppressing Falun Gong, the Chinese state has strengthened its anticult apparatus. Since 2003, the mission of the 610 Office has expanded to include targeting other designated "cultic groups." On October 30,

1999, the National People's Congress passed the *Resolution on Banning Evil Cults, Preventing and Punishing Cultic Activities*.[77] The Supreme People's Court and the Supreme People's Procuratorate issued a judicial interpretation, specifying how to apply existing criminal law to individuals involved in "evil-cult" activities. This interpretation defines *evil cults* as "illegal groups that are founded by using religion, qigong, or other pretenses; deify their leaders; produce and spread superstitious ideas and heretical teachings to deceive and swindle people; recruit and control their members; and pose a danger to society."[78] Even though the specific legal provisions have undergone revisions over time, these documents constitute the basic legal framework in China for dealing with NRMs deemed evil cults.

Conclusion

Suppose someone asked me: If we set aside political factors and look just at institutional features and the nature of the Chinese religious ecology, which specific religion or category of religions in Chinese society has the highest potential for rapid growth? I would respond: The NRMs that have a strong affinity with Chinese culture, namely the Chinese syncretic NRMs. These religious movements possess both a strong drive to spread their salvational messages and a congregational structure that fosters strong religious identity and commitment among members. In these aspects, they resemble Christianity. However, unlike Christianity, they are not that ideologically zero-sum—they do not require new recruits to abandon their other religious beliefs and practices entirely, which lowers the barriers to conversion in a highly pluralistic religious and cultural environment. Equally important, they are deeply rooted in the long-standing Chinese culture, unlike Christianity. This affinity gives Chinese syncretic NRMs an advantage for quick growth when conditions become opportune.

On the other hand, readers should not forget the key point I am making in the book. This chapter, much like the other chapters, further emphasizes the point that we can never disregard state-level political context when analyzing religious growth. Only by examining the institutional features of Falun Gong, along with the pattern of activities of the post-Mao state within a religious/cultural environment conducive to the rapid growth of NRMs, can we truly comprehend the forces leading to Falun Gong's meteoric rise and swift decline.

Chinese Buddhism

Competitive Isomorphism Arrested

This chapter turns to Chinese Buddhism.[1] A religion of Indian origin, Buddhism found its way to China around the first century AD. Through centuries of interaction with Chinese culture, a unique form of Buddhism known as Chinese Buddhism has taken shape. Although rooted in the tradition of Mahayana Buddhism, Chinese Buddhism established the authority of its own canon. Today, it is the dominant Buddhist tradition practiced in mainland China, Taiwan, Hong Kong, and Chinese diaspora communities.

Buddhism introduced to China a religion that deemed this world undesirable and offered teachings on how to achieve otherworldly salvation. It also introduced the institution of monasticism—a community of religious virtuosi living collectively and striving for enlightenment. With imperial patronage, and avid support and participation from both the elite and the commoners, Buddhism firmly established a foothold in China by the sixth century.[2]

During the Age of Disunion (220–580), the Sui dynasty (581–618), and the Tang dynasty (618–907), Buddhism flourished and spread its profound influence into all spheres of life. There were even attempts to establish Buddhism as a state religion.[3] Partly in response to the Buddhist challenge, neo-Confucianism, a Confucian revival movement, arose during the Song dynasty (960–1279).[4] In the ensuing centuries, particularly in late imperial China, Chinese society became more deeply structured by Confucian morals and institutions. In the "Confucian society" that was ushered in, Chinese popular religion, including ancestor worship and popular cults, forged tighter bonds with the mainstay institutions such as family, lineage organizations, and territorial communities, thereby securing its central position in the local religious ecology (see the introduction and chapter 3). Subsequently, the significance of Buddhist temples as "the foci of local organization" diminished in this transformed religious milieu.[5]

Nevertheless, until 1949 when the CCP took power, Buddhism was still by far the largest and most influential institutional religion in China, in terms of the number of religious professionals and religious sites.[6] Its otherworldly outlook and religious/ritual functions continued to have great appeal to Chinese society, and its symbols, terminologies, ideas, festivals, and practices have long become an integral part of Chinese culture.

There are myriad issues to explore regarding post-Mao Chinese Buddhism.[7] Researchers have studied the rebuilding of Chinese Buddhism,[8] the monastic institution,[9] lay Buddhism,[10] tourism and Buddhism,[11] the relationship between the state and Buddhist institutions,[12] Buddhist philanthropy,[13] and so on. This chapter chooses to focus on one issue: the change of Chinese Buddhism's institutional features, a key issue that has set the development of Chinese Buddhism in the post-Mao era on a path divergent from that in Republican China and Taiwan after 1949, and thus fundamentally shaped the growth dynamics and character of Buddhism in mainland China.

Previous chapters have explored how institutional features play out in different contexts, resulting in change in religious growth dynamics. This chapter explores the changes of institutional features themselves. Using the development of Chinese Buddhism as a case, it focuses on an important issue in the study of institutional changes—that is, how competitive pressure would spur organizations to launch reforms of their institutional features that would affect their development.

After a brief theoretical excursion, the subsequent two sections of the chapter tackle the following questions. In the first part, I juxtapose Chinese Buddhism's reactions to the rise of Christianity in post-Mao mainland China with the reactions in Republican China and in Taiwan during Chiang Kai-shek's rule (1949–75; Chiang's Taiwan hereafter).[14] I seek to understand why the Chinese Buddhist communities in Republican China and Chiang's Taiwan responded to the Christian challenge by initiating reforms to emulate certain features of its rival, whereas the Buddhist communities in post-Mao mainland China did not. In the second part, I introduce the Jingkong movement, arguably the most influential Buddhist sectarian movement in post-Mao China, inspired by the teachings of Jingkong (1927–2022). I then address the following inquiries: First, why did the Chinese Buddhist establishment in post-Mao China perceive the Jingkong movement as a more serious challenge than Christianity? Second, why did the Buddhist establishment refraining from adopting some isomorphic learning in the face of the challenge of the Jingkong movement?

Competitive Isomorphism as a Way to Religious Change

Examining the history of religions reveals that changes within a particular religious tradition often result from the isomorphic adoption of features from other religions.[15] For instance, Daoism, a native Chinese religion, borrowed a great number of terminological, conceptual, and liturgical elements from Buddhism, a foreign religion.[16] This borrowing was crucial in transforming Daoism in fifth-century southern China into "a complex and sophisticated organized religion."[17] In the nineteenth century, Buddhist activists in Sri Lanka, in an effort to revive Buddhism under British colonial rule, reformed the structure and content of the religion in close imitation of Protestant Christianity.[18] This reform was so profound that Obeyesekere in 1970 dubbed the transformed Buddhism "Protestant Buddhism."[19] Borrowing from the Christian model was a salient feature of the Buddhist self-renewal and self-reform movement in Meiji Japan and South Korea.[20] The modern global Buddhist missionary movement was also much influenced by the Christian model.[21] Isomorphic emulation has occurred among religions of immigrant communities, such as Catholicism, Buddhism, Islam, and Hinduism, when these religions were taking root in the United States. They adopted the "congregational model" and assumed features that made them resemble mainstream Protestant groups in organizational structure and ritual.[22] Isomorphic responses also emerged when the Catholic Church in Latin America faced the challenge of the rapid growth of Pentecostal Protestantism. One such response was the rise of the Catholic charismatic renewal movement, which involved the emulation of religious practices—including miraculous healing, a vibrant worship style, and speaking in tongues—of Pentecostal Protestantism.[23]

Two kinds of organizational isomorphism have been identified by DiMaggio and Powell.[24] *Competitive isomorphism* occurs when organizations emulate their competitors to improve efficiency and to maintain or increase their "market." *Institutional isomorphism* takes place when organizations are driven by the need to gain or enhance legitimacy. DiMaggio and Powell claim that the tendency toward homogeneity in the modern world of organizations is driven less by competition than by organizations' pursuit of legitimacy or conformity to cultural norms. In other words, they argue for the increasing importance of institutional isomorphism in organizational change. Their theory forms a bedrock of neoinstitutionalism and has reoriented the sociology of organization.[25] In the sociology of religion, neoinstitutional theory has inspired some noteworthy studies of religious change, such as Chaves's research on the diffusion of formal policy permitting women's ordination across Christian denominations in the United States, and Wilde's study of the voting behaviors of the cardinals at the Second Vatican Council, which resulted in reforms leading to seismic changes within the Roman Catholic Church.[26]

Even though they do not cite neoinstitutionalism literature, scholars of Chinese religions argue along a similar line—they emphasize how the introduction of the Western binary distinction between religion and superstition into state policies since the early twentieth century compelled religious groups in China to adapt organizational forms according to the state-sanctioned category of religion.[27] If we employ the terminology of neoinstitutionalism, these scholars essentially argue that normative and coercive isomorphisms were behind the aforementioned changes. However, the picture of religious change would be one-sided or incomplete if we do not acknowledge the importance of interreligious competition for strength and social influence and the associated isomorphic responses in shaping the development of religious organizations.

My analysis of the role of competitive isomorphism in religious change builds on two premises. First, what matters is not how strong competitors are according to *objective* measurements, but how threatened organizational actors feel when facing the competition. Unlike population ecology theory, which assumes that competition will automatically be kindled in a population of organizations that provide similar products or services, I maintain that it takes certain social processes for a religious organization to perceive others as competitors.[28] Accordingly, we need to investigate what makes the incumbent Chinese Buddhist organizations view a competing religious group as an imminent threat, or not.

Second, even if a religious organization perceives competitive pressure, it does not necessarily initiate institutional changes by emulating its competitor, especially when changes concern its core institutional features. In fact, religious organizations, especially established ones (the incumbents), are subject to organizational inertia because changes are likely to disrupt the power equilibrium within the organizations and undermine institutional claims and identities.[29] Only when the religious actors perceive the rivalry as posing a serious threat and have no other ways to neutralize it would they adopt competitive isomorphism. Therefore, in this chapter, we need to specify the conditions that compel or induce the incumbent Chinese Buddhist organizations to adopt, or not to adopt, an isomorphic response when they perceive competitive pressure.

In line with the overarching theory of this book, I see the great importance of contexts, particularly conditions created by the state, in shaping the nature and intensity of religious competition. In this chapter, I will show that the nature of Chinese state and its pattern of activities can alter the public visibility, social clout, and level of aggressiveness of the challenger in the religious field; give a sense of security or insecurity to an incumbent religion (i.e., the Chinese Buddhist establishment); and determine the extent of niche overlap between the incumbent and the challenger. Together, they shape the perception by an incumbent religious organization of the pressure of a rising religion and the type of response the incumbent will make.

Through juxtaposing the different responses of Chinese Buddhist communities toward the challenges posed by Christianity during Republican China, Chiang's Taiwan, and post-Mao mainland China, and through comparing the responses of the Chinese Buddhist establishment to the competitive pressures of rising Protestantism and the rapidly expanding Jingkong movement in post-Mao mainland China, I intend to underscore the importance of competition in religious development and the role of the state in shaping religious competition and to illuminate the logic of action of the Chinese Buddhist community in the political context of post-Mao China.

Chinese Buddhism in Face of the Christian Challenge

Since the early twentieth century, Chinese Buddhism has faced mounting challenges from Christianity. As shown in chapters 1 and 2, Republican China was a major mission field for the Catholic Church and a wide array of Protestant denominations from different countries. In addition, the 1920s witnessed the rise of indigenous Protestant movements, which considerably expanded the Chinese Christian population and indicated that Christianity had begun to enjoy some success in acculturation to Chinese society.[30] In Republican China, the Christian population grew from 1.46 million in 1910 to 3.95 million in 1949, its percentage of the total population increasing from 0.37 percent to 0.73 percent.[31] After 1949, with the regime change in mainland China, missionary resources and personnel, as well as Chinese Christians, flooded into Taiwan, giving a huge boost to the Christian presence in the island.[32] From 1950 to 1979, the Christian population in Chiang's Taiwan grew from approximately 87,000 (1.2 percent of the entire population) to 640,000 (3.7 percent).[33]

In post-Mao mainland China, Christianity soon recovered from the damage it suffered under the Maoist regime. Protestantism, in particular, experienced a meteoric rise from nearly three million followers in 1982 to fifty-eight million in 2010, making it the fastest-growing religion in the post-Mao period. The overall Christian population in mainland China grew from approximately six million in 1982 to sixty-seven million in 2010, increasing from

0.59 percent to 5 percent (see chapters 1 and 2). The numbers clearly show that the Christian population grew much faster in post-Mao mainland China than in Republican China and Chiang's Taiwan. Moreover, the growth of Christianity in post-Mao mainland China has been nationwide, occurring in both rural and urban areas and across wide-ranging sociodemographic groups. The phenomenal growth of Christianity in post-Mao mainland China did not go unnoticed. As early as the late 1980s, journalists and pundits in China began to use "Christianity fever" (*jidujiao re*) to portray the surge of Protestantism.[34]

In sum, in all three cases, Chinese Buddhism faced competitive pressure from a rising Christianity. In what follows, I show how the competitive pressure prompted significant isomorphic responses from the Chinese Buddhist establishment in both Republican China and Chiang's Taiwan, and how an even stronger competitive pressure was unable to trigger similar isomorphic responses from the Chinese Buddhist establishment in post-Mao mainland China, and then proceed to offer an explanation.

ISOMORPHIC RESPONSE DURING REPUBLICAN CHINA AND CHIANG'S TAIWAN

Isomorphic response, involving the emulation of institutional features of Christian groups to attract and retain followers, strengthen commitment, and enhance social influence, was prominent among incumbent Buddhist organizations in both Republican China and Chiang's Taiwan. This emulation mainly took three forms: adopting a more congregational structure, heightened proselytization, and engaging in charity, education, and other works inspired by Christian programs.

Moving Toward a Congregational Structure. In late imperial China, even though beliefs and practices of Chinese Buddhism were prevalent, Buddhist institutions generally had only a loose relationship with the laity. The majority of the laity visited temples only on Buddhist holidays, and requested ritual services from monastics only when the need arose. Most of the monastics made little attempt to organize the laity into a closely knit community that regularly and frequently met for religious activities, to give them religious instruction or spiritual counseling, or to provide them with pastoral care. In other words, they did little to nurture lay organizations that resemble a congregation like we see in Christianity.[35]

In Republican China, however, Buddhist organizations increasingly adopted the features of a congregation. They emphasized that it was important for the laity to take refuge vows to become formal members of the religious community and issued refuge certificates to those who did so.[36] They began to offer regular lectures and educational programs to the laity, set up temple-affiliated schools, and provided hospice care.[37] This development became full-fledged in Chiang's Taiwan. Beginning in the 1950s, Buddhist organizations in Taiwan provided a wide array of services to their followers, including kindergartens, schools, wedding ceremonies, hospice care, and burial sites.[38] Classes and retreats were offered on a regular basis, enabling followers to learn doctrine and receive training in Buddhist practices.[39] Lay members were organized into various volunteer groups, which were instrumental in keeping the Buddhist organizations running and expanding their social influence.[40]

Strengthening Proselytization. As Zürcher points out, Buddhism has scriptural foundation for "a missionary ideal"—its early texts depict the Buddha enjoining his disciples to go in different directions to preach.[41] Although not approaching the large-scale, organized missionary movement seen in Christianity, the efforts of individual traveling monks from India and Central Asia helped Buddhism establish a foothold in China.[42] From the third century to the ninth century, Buddhist monks and preachers dedicated themselves to translating scriptures, building monasteries, creating icons, employing storytelling, organizing public works and lay associations, and even performing wonders to propagate and popularize Buddhism in China.[43] However, by the time that Christianity made its inroads in China in the mid-nineteenth century, long-established Chinese Buddhism had clearly lost much of its missionary spirit.[44]

In Republican China, spurred by the ardent evangelism of Christian missionaries, Chinese Buddhist organizations began to rekindle their proselytizing zeal and adopt methods closely resembling those of Christian missionaries. For instance, they started offering public lectures to visitors and worshippers at temple sites,[45] preaching Buddhism in nonreligious venues such as hospitals, factories, and universities,[46] propagating Buddhism through popular literary works,[47] and conducting prison ministry.[48] Taking advantage of new print technologies, they published pamphlets, newspapers, periodicals, books, and dictionaries to disseminate Buddhism.[49] They also pioneered the use of radio to broadcast lectures.[50]

After the CCP took power in 1949, many Buddhist elites active in Republican China found their way to Taiwan.[51] They played an instrumental role in energizing and transforming Chinese Buddhism in Taiwan under Chiang's rule. Under their leadership, Taiwan's Buddhist organizations broadened and intensified proselytizing activities. One after another, they established research institutes of Buddhist studies, missionary stations, and libraries. Starting in 1958, mimicking Christian examples, they also began to offer scholarships to college students and facilitated the formation of Buddhist student study groups. By 1971, there were forty-one Buddhist student groups in ninety-six colleges and vocational schools in Taiwan.[52]

In addition, a variety of novel ways were adopted to propagate Buddhism, including organizing lecture tours, forming Buddhist choirs, offering summer camps, and employing modern media such as newspapers, radio, cassette tapes, CDs, and TV.[53] Venerable Xingyun (1927–2023), founder of Fo Guang Shan (Buddha's Light Mountain), which later grew to be one of the four largest Buddhist organizations in Taiwan, pioneered many of these programs.[54] He organized Buddhist choirs and led the first island-wide dharma propagation tour in the 1950s. Under his leadership, Fo Guang Shan launched its first summer camp for college students in 1969 and later organized summer camps for preschoolers, teenagers, and teachers.

Becoming Socially Engaged. Charity in traditional Chinese Buddhism followed certain conventional forms, including buying captured animals and releasing them and providing free medicine, tea, porridge, and coffins to the needy. During the Republican era, the charity works of Chinese Buddhist organizations, heavily influenced by Christian missionaries, expanded to new areas such as setting up orphanages, old-age homes, medical facilities, and schools, and organizing disaster and wartime relief.[55] Chinese Buddhist organizations in Chiang's Taiwan continued this practice of social engagement. Following the example of Christian groups, they concentrated on medical care and education. Li Bingnan (1891–1986), an influential lay Buddhist, founded the first modern Buddhist hospital in Taiwan in 1966.[56] Buddhist organizations in Taiwan also poured significant resources into education. Beginning in the 1950s, they established kindergartens, elementary schools, and vocational high schools throughout the island.[57]

These charity programs were made possible through mobilizing the support and participation of lay followers. In 1966, Zhengyan (born 1937), a Buddhist nun, launched the Buddhist Compassion Relief Tzu Chi Foundation.[58] A major source for its original fund came from thirty housewives who set aside the equivalent of fifty cents each day from their grocery money to support Zhengyan's cause. Knowing how to mobilize lay volunteers is the key to Zhengyan's success in turning Tzu Chi into by far the biggest philanthropic organization in Taiwan. It must be added that lay activism is in fact behind all the major Buddhist charity organizations in Taiwan.

It is worth noting that the above-mentioned efforts to refashion Buddhist institutions were launched by Buddhist elites of very different theological orientations. Students of modern Chinese Buddhism tend to highlight the pivotal role of Buddhist reformers or modernists such as Taixu (1890–1947) and his disciples in modernizing Chinese Buddhism in both Republican China and Chiang's Taiwan.[59] It is true that Taixu had outlined a vision and an agenda for reforming Chinese Buddhism unmatched in scope and depth in his time. It is also true that Taixu and his protégé Yinshun (1906–2005), who relocated to Taiwan in 1952 and had a profound influence on the development of Chinese Buddhism in Taiwan with his writings,[60] had articulated a new theology dubbed "Humanistic Buddhism," "Buddhism for the living," or "Buddhism for the human realm," which provided theological justification and inspiration for the this-worldly reorientation of modern Chinese Buddhism.[61] Yet Buddhist leaders of more traditionalist orientation also devoted themselves to reform efforts. For instance, Yuanying (1878–1953), widely regarded as a leader of the conservative camp in the late Republican years, opened orphanages, organized disaster relief, and went on public lecture tours.[62] Although Dixian (1858–1932), an eminent monk of the traditionalist stripe, opposed Taixu's reforms, many of his notable disciples, including Tanxu (1875–1963) and Changxing (1896–1938), were actively engaged in reforming Chinese Buddhism, and Changxing was a close collaborator of Taixu as well.[63] In Chiang's Taiwan, Li Bingnan, often regarded as a conservative because of his theological orientation, had pioneered in all three aspects of the organizational restructuring of Chinese Buddhism as outlined above. It is fair to say that Buddhist leaders of different stripes in Taiwan all espoused some forms of Humanistic Buddhism.[64]

The three forms of isomorphic responses made by Chinese Buddhist organizations in Republican China and Chiang's Taiwan elicited changes pertaining to the formal organizational structure, pattern of activity, and normative order. They concern how Chinese Buddhism restructures its relationship with followers, how it shifts the loci of its activities, and how it repositions itself in the world. A key motive behind these reforms is to build more robust Buddhist organizations through recruiting lay followers and strengthening their commitment, and to expand the social influence of Buddhism through mobilizing lay participation in social service works.

BUDDHISM'S RESPONSE IN POST-MAO MAINLAND CHINA

In comparison with Republican China and Chiang's Taiwan, post-Mao mainland China witnessed a more rapid growth of Christianity. Yet Chinese Buddhism showed few signs of isomorphic development. Due to the post-Mao state's restrictions on associational life and its control over religion's public role, Christian groups could not actively build hospitals and schools as they did in Republican China and Chiang's Taiwan. Thus, there is no point in discussing Chinese Buddhism's emulation of Christianity's charity programs. But post-Mao Chinese Buddhism did not emulate the other two core features of Christianity—avid evangelism and a congregational structure—even though they were crucial to the rapid rise of Protestantism in post-Mao China.

However, before I delve into the issue of competitive isomorphism of the Chinese Buddhist establishment, I shall first offer a general picture of Buddhism in post-Mao China. Like other religions, post-Mao Chinese Buddhism rebuilt itself from the ruins wrought by the Cultural Revolution.[65] According to the official statistics in 2012, there were more than 100,000 monastics and more than 28,000 temples affiliated with Chinese Buddhism, indicating that institutional Chinese Buddhism remains a major religious force in the post-Mao era.[66] On the other hand, these figures also reveal that the level of development still falls far short of the Republican era.[67] A survey conducted in 1930 shows there were more than 738,000 monastics in residence at more than 233,000 Chinese Buddhist temples.[68]

In the world of Chinese Buddhism in post-Mao China, several hundred temples stand out as the major nodes. They are large temples in the urban centers, Buddhist learning centers, ancestral temples of certain Buddhist schools, and transregional pilgrimage destinations. The restoration of these temples received the official green light and was aided by financial support from overseas Chinese.[69] After 1992, as China's market-oriented reforms accelerated, local officials were pressured to develop the economy by all possible means. In doing so, they tapped into Buddhism's potential to facilitate tourism. They allocated huge swaths of land for the rebuilding of temples, courted renowned monks to assume abbotships of important temples, erected giant Buddha statues, sponsored festivals, and even built Buddhist theme parks. Local officials' push for Buddhist tourism, on the one hand, brought increased revenue, improved infrastructure, and enhanced publicity to temples, and on the other hand often infringed on the autonomy of Buddhist organizations.[70] The monastic community, just reemerging from the devastation of the Cultural Revolution, was thrust into the corrosive environment of state-driven tourism. Disciplinary laxity of monastics was widespread.

Of the several hundred large Buddhist temples, only a small number have been able to establish not only a sizable monastic community but also a disciplined monastic life.[71] A handful, such as Pushou Temple of Shanxi Province, Pingxin Temple in Fujian Province, Zhenru Temple in Jiangxi Province, Yunmen Temple of Guangdong Province, Gaomin Temple in Jiangsu Province, and Wolong Temple in Shaanxi Province are held in high esteem precisely because the strict monastic life they cultivate is rare and admired in the Buddhist community.[72] Every day, the monks gather in the Buddha Hall for morning and evening chanting and in the dining hall for communal lunch in silence. Monastics in these temples work on their own enlightenment. According to the practice method of their school—mostly Chan or Pure Land Buddhism—they meditate in the meditation hall or engage in devotional acts to Amitābha Buddha.[73] In a few of these temples, monastics also dedicate their afternoons to manual labor, a practice rooted in the ancient Chan Buddhist tradition of "no work, no food." These few "model monasteries" represent in the post-Mao Chinese Buddhist world the closest approximation of the traditional ideal of a monastic community.

While Humanistic Buddhism rose to prominence and was practiced by elite Buddhists of different stripes in Chiang's Taiwan, in mainland China, traditional ascetic monasticism is widely aspired to by elite Buddhists.[74] It is no coincidence that Pingxing Temple and Pushou Temple, two of the most respected temples in mainland China, emphasized the utmost importance of upholding the Vinaya (precepts and monastic rules) and earned enormous respect for their rigorous discipline.

I do not imply that the Chinese Buddhist establishment did nothing to expand the influence of Buddhism. Some large temples did sponsor Buddhist studies conferences and cultural events, especially after the early years of the 2000s. However, many of such activities remained ceremonial and did not create a splash in terms of societal impact. One informant (No. 190), the abbot of a small temple in Zhejiang, called these events "face projects" (*mianzi gongcheng*) and lamented the wealthy monasteries spending large sums of money with little tangible outcome. The charity work of the Chinese Buddhist temples usually took the form of donations to disaster and poverty relief organized by the government rather than building and operating charitable programs of their own. That said, there are exceptions. For instance, Bailin Temple in Hebei Province has organized summer camps for college students since 1993, and Longquan Temple in Beijing operates an effective charity organization.[75] Interestingly, both temples received inspiration from the Taiwan model of Chinese Buddhism.[76] Though their practices have a knock-on effect and have gradually spread to the rest of the Buddhist establishment,[77] their proselytizing zeal and their social impact pale when compared with those organizations actively involved in Humanistic Buddhism in Taiwan. By and large, the Buddhist establishment in post-Mao mainland China still revolved around the monastic community, instead of reorienting itself toward missionizing and educating the laity, organizing them into congregations, providing them with pastoral care, or mobilizing them for charitable works or other forms of activism.

Large temples with a sizable sangha are few. According to 2012 official statistics, the average number of clerics stationed in a Chinese Buddhist temple is less than four. For a more balanced assessment of the development of Chinese Buddhism in the post-Mao era as a whole, we also need to look at the small temples, the majority. In this context, River County, a place dotted with small Buddhist temples but lacking big ones, comes back into focus.

Over its history dating to the fifth century, Buddhism has established wide and enduring influence in River County. According to the county gazetteer in 1889, there were approximately sixty Buddhist temples. In 2010, thirty-four temples were registered with the RAB as Buddhist sites in River County. Among them, sixteen could be identified as "true" Buddhist temples, and ten organized regular activities and attracted followers to a sizable lay community.[78]

At any given time between 2004 and 2023, no more than twenty clerics in total were stationed in River County. Two monks made key contributions to rebuilding Chinese Buddhism in River County and established themselves as local Buddhist leaders. Huixiu, a renowned master of Buddhist esoteric rituals, came to River County in 1985 at the invitation of the county RAB.[79] Huixiu invited a young monk, Kairen, to the county in 1998 to help him. In 2009, Huixiu presided over two major temples, and Kairen presided over three.

Even though majestic temples have been rebuilt in River County, no well-functioning, orderly, structured monastic community has been established. The monks residing in the temples under Huixiu were his tonsure disciples. They came and went with much frequency. Huixiu himself, despite his old age, traveled often to preside over ritual events at the invitation of other temples. The monks under Kairen, mostly coming from poor rural backgrounds with little education, were less mobile and more content with the stable income from performing ritual services. However, his temples did not adhere to the basic routines of Buddhist monastic life—not even the usual morning chanting.[80] For the other, even smaller temples in River County, each was managed by a single monk or nun, or by a lay Buddhist. These clerics typically came from impoverished family backgrounds or had faced significant hardships in their earlier lives. Poorly educated and equipped with little monastic or religious training, they occupied the lowest stratum of the monastic community. A few of these peripatetic monks managed to settle in one place, most continued to wander.

Except for one Buddhist community that, influenced by Jingkong's teachings, displayed a distinct pattern (discussed later in this chapter), the Buddhist temples in River County had a similar relationship with the laity. The laity, most middle-aged or elderly women, have spent years going to temples to worship, patronizing monks, and participating in ritual events. Temples provided the laity with different types of ritual services, each with a set price, and their operations revolved around the rituals.[81] The laity who patronized these hoped that the power of and merits generated by the rituals could deliver deceased relatives from a woeful state of existence, or avert bad fortune for the living. Charges for ritual services constituted the bulk of income for these small temples.[82] The seven-day rite for saving of sentient beings of water and land (*shuilu fahui*), involving the participation of dozens of monks,[83] is by far the most elaborate Buddhist ritual event.[84] *Shuilu fahui* performed in 2009 generated a total revenue of more than 800,000 yuan (US$117,000) for Huixiu's Cypress Shade Temple. In this monetized ritual economy, the laity assumes the role of clients, and their relationship with the service provider is highly transactional.

Senior monks in the county such as Huixiu and Kairen did take lay disciples, who went through the Buddhist refuge-taking rite. Even though some lay disciples formed close relationship with their masters or the temples, gave gifts to their masters from time to time, and volunteered labor, temples rarely provided religious teachings, guidance on practices, or advice on applying

FIGURE 5.1A. A ritual service performed at a small Buddhist temple by a monk. (Photograph by the author.)

FIGURE 5.1B. On the last day of *shuilu fahui*, all the paper images of gods and spirits on ships and horses are burned. The gods, ancestors, and spirits who were previously invited to attend the rite to receive the supernatural benefits of the rituals would be sent off, concluding the seven-day rite. (Photograph by the author.)

Buddhism in their daily life. Nor did the temples provide hospice care or death rituals for the bereaved families. If a family asked monks or nuns to conduct the mortuary rite, they were obliged to pay for it. None of these temples in River County actively engaged in spreading religious messages.

Allow me to summarize the picture I have just presented: in post-Mao mainland China, the challenge posed by the rapid rise of Protestantism has not prompted isomorphic responses from the Buddhist establishment, including the large Buddhist temples serving as major nodes and the majority of small Buddhist temples, as we have seen in River County. In other words, the emulation of institutional features of Christianity by Buddhist organizations, evident during Republican China and Chiang's Taiwan, was largely absent in post-Mao mainland China. But why? In the following, I address this question in three phases: First, I describe the divergent perceptions regarding the Christian challenge in the three respective periods. Second, I explain why the challenge was taken seriously in Republican China and Chiang's Taiwan but not in post-Mao mainland China. Third, I explore why Chinese Buddhists in Republican China and Chiang's Taiwan chose to respond to the perceived challenge through isomorphic competition.

Divergent Perceptions of the Christian Challenge

To assess how elite Buddhists understood the challenge of Christianity in Republican China, I relied heavily on the *Minguo Fojiao qikan wenxian jicheng* (*Collection of Republican-era Buddhist periodical literature*) and its supplement (together termed the Collection hereafter).[85] The 291-volume Collection contains reprints of numerous issues of 153 Buddhist periodicals published between 1923 and 1949. The Collection comprises approximately 140,000 articles, mostly theological expositions, transcripts of lectures, news reports, opinions, event announcements, stories, diaries, travelogues, correspondence, literary compositions, obituaries, and edicts of government, offering a key data source for understanding Chinese Buddhism in that era. The Dharma Drum Buddhist College in Taiwan has assembled a catalog database with title and author keyword search capacity.[86] By searching the database, we are able to locate the corresponding original texts in the Collection.

I first searched the database for titles possibly related to Christianity using a set of keywords, then located the corresponding full articles in the Collection to identify those focusing directly on the Christian expansion or making important reference to Christianity.[87] Because the authors who wrote these articles might also have penned similar ones in other publications, I used the author names to search for other Christianity-related works in the Collection. In total, I located 151 articles that explicitly mentioned Christianity. Because the Collection is not text-searchable, these may constitute only a portion of the articles that referred to Christianity. But what is revealed is still telling. Among the 151 articles,[88] 70 claimed Buddhism's superiority over Christianity or made direct doctrinal attacks on Christianity;[89] 24 presented stories of Christians taking an interest in, or converting to, Buddhism; 23 expressed outrage over Christians' aggressive proselytization targeting Buddhists, or indignation about Christian hostility toward Buddhism;[90] 11 discussed attitudes Buddhists should adopt to fend off the Christian incursion;[91] 4 were negative reports of Christianity;[92] and 19 mentioned Christianity but did not express a particular attitude. Overall, the articles demonstrated an acute awareness of and anxiety over the challenge posed by Christianity to the Buddhist community.

Yinshun, a leading reformist theologian, in an influential article titled "Crises of Buddhism and Its Remedies," explicitly warned that Christianity was among the most formidable foes of Buddhism.[93] Indeed, the agitation over Christian inroads ran especially strong in the reformist camp, because a large proportion of the 151 articles were published in reform-inclined Buddhist journals by Buddhists associated with Taixu. Nonetheless, this sentiment was

shared among Buddhists whose beliefs and practices were more traditionalist. For instance, Nie Qijie (1880–1953), a Christian turned Buddhist and
follower of the traditionalist master Yinguang (1862–1940), penned a series
of articles, later assembled into an anthology, repudiating Christian beliefs.[94]
In 1944, the traditionalist-leaning periodical *The Enlightenment* (*Jue youqing*) devoted a special issue to the testimonies of ex-Christians about their
conversion to Buddhism. Both Tanxu and Xuyun were prominent monks in
the traditionalist camp. In his memoirs, Tanxu recounted his encounter with
a Protestant evangelist on a train. Offended by the evangelist's contemptuous
remarks about Buddhism, Tanxu debated with him and refuted him point by
point.[95] Xuyun (1840?–1959), a much-revered Chan master, did not hesitate to
criticize Christianity when Chiang Kai-shek asked his opinion of Christianity
and Buddhism in 1943. Xuyun argued that Christianity resembled the Pure
Land school of Buddhism in many respects but was inferior.[96]

The sense that Christianity presented a threat was even more widespread
among the Buddhist elite in Chiang's Taiwan. Their anxiety was poignantly
expressed in an editorial in the magazine *Buddhist Today* published in 1958:
"At present, Catholic and Protestant churches are ubiquitous on the streets
and alleys [of Taiwan], and copies of the Old and New Testaments are widely
circulated. Christianity has almost superseded Chinese Buddhism in social
status. This has created a deep crisis and poses a big menace for Buddhism.
If we [Buddhists] do not try to remedy the situation, Buddhism in China
will not be able to sustain itself for long."[97] Buddhist authors in Taiwan including Yinshun, Li Bingnan, Shengyan (1931–2009),[98] and Zhuyun (1919–86)
engaged in heated debates with Christians, penned impassioned apologetic
tracts against Christians, or vehemently attacked Christianity in public lectures in the 1950s and 1960s.[99]

The Buddhist elite's acute sense of crisis in Republican China and Chiang's Taiwan contrasts sharply with the largely unperturbed attitude of the
Buddhist elite in post-Mao mainland China. My search of major Buddhist
publications in post-Mao China yields not a single article expressing concern
about the rapid expansion of Christianity. One may wonder if this silence
could be explained by the government's suppression of rhetoric that might
lead to religious discord. Yet my interviews with leaders of Buddhist temples
and young, enterprising monks and nuns in past decades suggest that the
lack of concern was genuine and widespread. When asked to appraise the
current situation of Chinese Buddhism, not one mentioned the Christian
challenge. When pressed to comment on the rise of Protestantism in China,
the responses were almost always nonchalant. The most memorable response
was from a well-read young monk in the famous Xiyuan Temple of Suzhou

in 2009, because his answer took me by surprise: "What's the problem with this? Why is it not a good thing for Protestantism to enjoy quick growth?" (Informant No. 255). I then probed further, telling the monk that while I admired his open-mindedness, I would still like to know whether he envied the success of Protestantism. His answer was again negative.

In River County, in spite of the growth of Protestantism (see chapter 1), leaders of the Buddhist establishment also did not perceive the challenge. Huixiu dismissed the Christian approach of proselytization: "Unlike the Jesus Religion, we Buddhists do not solicit people. We don't engage in self-promotion like Wangpo hawking melons (*wangpo maigua, zimai zikua*). We follow an approach similar to what Grand Duke Jiang did in fishing—let those who are willing come of their own volition (*Jiang Taigong diaoyu, yuanzhe shanggou*)" (Informant No. 95).[100] Local Buddhist leaders in general were unaware of the competitive pressure imposed by Protestantism. Kairen, abbot of three temples and secretary-general of the county Buddhist Association, when prompted by my questions about Christianity, replied, "Of course, we are more prosperous than Christianity. There is no way they can compare with us. We have more followers, and they do not even have capable leadership" (Informant No. 87).

Yet the jarring reality is, despite its long history and wide cultural influence, Buddhism has shown clear signs of weakness and has increasingly lagged behind the fast-growing Protestantism. For instance, in River County, only ten Buddhist temples had lay Buddhist communities with somewhat regular gatherings in 2009. By contrast, the number of Protestant groups amounted to fifty-seven, not including small meeting points. More importantly, whereas Buddhist followers were predominantly middle-aged and old women, Protestant communities had many more male and younger members.[101] Urban Protestant churches, in particular, attracted members from a wide social spectrum including young, educated professionals serving in leadership roles. Such people were missing in Buddhist circles. In all of River County in 2009, there were only two male lay adherents under the age of forty active in the Buddhist community. These indicators did not bode well for the future of Buddhism in River County, especially with Protestantism as a reference point.

Divergent Perceptions Explained

Why did the development of Christianity elicit a strong sense of crisis among Buddhists in Republican China and Chiang's Taiwan but not among their counterparts in post-Mao mainland China? I argue that even though

Christianity in Republican China and Chiang's Taiwan did not grow as fast as in post-Mao mainland China, it had a higher visibility, enjoyed greater social clout, and was more openly aggressive in proselytization and combative toward other religions (Buddhism being its main target).

First, the religious policy framework of Republican China and Chiang's Taiwan pivoted on Western ideas that draw a sharp line between "religion" and "superstition."[102] Whereas *superstition*, which referred to religious practices not grounded in "the spiritual and moral self-perfection delineated by the theological scriptures of a world religion," was to be suppressed, state-sanctioned religions were protected by the constitutional clause on religious freedom and allowed to carry out their activities.[103] Moreover, because the state elite of Republican China and Chiang's Taiwan were mostly modernizers who looked to the West for models of development, Christianity, the dominant religion of the West, was in their eyes the quintessential religion.[104] This belief, translated into policy, allowed Christian groups to carry out evangelistic work in public venues such as streets, factories, and prisons, publish newspapers and periodicals, broadcast sermons on the radio, engage in wide-ranging charity works and social activism, and set up medical and educational facilities. In higher education alone, for instance, sixteen Christian colleges were established in Republican China.[105] In Chiang's Taiwan, by 1970 ten Christian colleges and higher vocational schools were established. In short, Christianity in Republican China and Chiang's Taiwan was not only highly visible but also far more influential than the size of its membership would suggest.

Second, in Republican China and Chiang's Taiwan, even though the state was secular, Christianity was favored by political modernizers. Due to Christian institutions' preeminence in the field of modern education, a disproportionate percentage of the political elite were educated in Christian schools or exposed to Christian influence when they studied abroad.[106] Sun Yat-sen (1886–1925), the first president of the Republic of China, was a baptized Protestant. Sixty of the 274 members elected to the first national parliament of the Republic of China were Christians.[107] Chiang Kai-shek was a professed Methodist.[108] His conversion in 1930 was prompted by his wife's family, who were devout Protestants. Seven of the ten cabinet members in Chiang's Nationalist government in 1929 were Christians.[109] Throughout their years on the mainland and subsequently in Taiwan after the Nationalist retreat, Chiang and his wife maintained private chapels for their personal worship. Madame Chiang often invited high-ranking officers and their wives as well as foreign dignitaries to attend Sunday services together.[110]

Some Chinese political elites were also outspoken about their religious preferences. For instance, in a letter to the Chinese Buddhist Society in 1928, Xue Dubi, minister of the interior, lavishly praised Christianity:[111]

> The Christians went to great lengths—scaling mountains, crossing oceans, enduring countless hardships, and braving numerous dangers—to establish schools and hospitals wherever they set foot. Under Christian administration, even the most desolated place could be transformed into a pure land. Under the guidance of Christianity, even the most intractable customs could be reformed. Therefore, among the Christian followers in our country, women have learned to unbind their bound feet and children have been able to receive an education. All these are positive social effects of Christianity. What is particularly remarkable is that the organizational rigor of Christian groups, the staunch determination of the Christians, the scope of their endeavors, and the extent of their accomplishments have kept growing with time. The increasing strength of the Christianity has contributed to the increasing strength of the Christian nations.[112]

In the same letter, Xue did not hide his contempt for Buddhism. He claimed that Buddhist institutions were mere shelters of self-interested ascetics, parasites, and even criminals. Xue's opinion of Buddhism was representative among Western-educated modernizers, who considered Buddhism anachronistic. The prejudice of the political elite also seeped into policymaking, resulting in policies that discriminated against China's indigenous religions, including Buddhism.[113]

Arguably, no one among the political elite was more influential than Madame Chiang Kai-shek in promoting Christianity. She was an ardent advocate of Christianity in Republican China and assumed an even more active and assertive role in promoting Christianity in Taiwan. Soon after the Nationalist government's retreat to Taiwan in 1949, she started a prayer group whose participants initially consisted of wives of the dignitaries of the Nationalist Party. The prayer group grew quickly, and its branches sprung up all over Taiwan. During the Easter season, the prayer group led Good Friday services, which were broadcast on the radio. The group later expanded to include a score of full-time pastors who, with the government's permission, started evangelistic work in military hospitals, the army ranks, and settlements of military dependents.[114] The favor that the political powerful bestowed on Christianity further boosted Christians' confidence and sense of superiority; it encouraged audacious acts among Christians and aggravated Buddhists' sense of crisis, galvanizing their competitive consciousness, as is evident in their writings and speeches at the time.[115] Venerable Nanting (1900–82), an important leader in the Buddhist community in Chiang's Taiwan, summarized this state of anxiety in an article published in 1954: "All Buddhists, monastic and lay, should be fearful of the indifference and discrimination that Buddhism has suffered from the government, its oppression by a heretical and deviant religion, and the low regard in which it is held in the world."[116]

Because there were few political restrictions on the public display of their religion in Republican China and Chiang's Taiwan, Christians were able to openly exercise their zero-sum evangelistic zeal. Christian evangelists often carried out campaigns against Buddhism. In Republican China, the Women's Missionary Union in Shanghai in its publications included worshipping Buddha and burning incense in the category of "sinful acts" together with brothel visiting, gambling, and lying.[117] Taixu mentioned in his memoir that between 1933 and 1934 when he and his disciples lectured in a Buddhist temple on the famous Mount Lu in central China, Christians would sit in the audience and challenge them with questions.[118] When Jing'an Temple in Shanghai held an event celebrating Buddha's birthday in 1934, a group of Christians arrived and distributed gospel tracts.[119]

In Taiwan in the 1950s and 1960s, many Christian publications and pamphlets ridiculed and vilified Buddhism.[120] Christians often went to Buddhist sites to challenge Buddhists or distribute gospel literature. In 1953, the Buddhist community of Taiwan held a monastic ordination ceremony at Daxian Temple. While ordinations are always solemn occasions in Chinese Buddhism, this particular ceremony was especially significant as it marked the first ordination held in Taiwan after the island's restoration to Chinese sovereignty, following the end of Japanese rule in 1945. At this historic event for Chinese Buddhism, Christians, however, were present to proselytize.[121] In 1963, fifty-seven-year-old Yinshun, a revered Buddhist scholar monk, was visited by two Christians in his temple in Taipei. The visitors left him a copy of the Bible and urged him to study it.[122] Zhuyun, in his indignant public speech against Christianity in 1955, recounted many similar instances.[123] It is apparent that Christian groups' aggressive tactics played a crucial role in inducing Buddhists' acute sense of threat.

The case of post-Mao mainland China, in which the Buddhist elite did not take the threat of Christianity seriously despite its more rapid growth, offers a stark contrast. First, even though the post-Mao Chinese state allowed religions to reestablish themselves after the Cultural Revolution, it installed a regulatory regime that strictly limited their scope of activities. For instance, the state restrained groups from carrying out religious activities outside the state's sanctioned venues and imposed strict restrictions on religious organizations' involvement in the development of civic associations, hospitals, and educational institutions. Although these restrictions did not stem Protestant groups' evangelization efforts, they did compel them to devise ways to circumvent state regulations. Protestants, for instance, used various occasions—including wedding ceremonies, hospital visits, and funerals of church members—to proselytize, and tried to win recruits through networks of acquaintances. Such tactics certainly made the expansion of Protestantism in China much less conspicuous to outsiders.

In addition to its restrictions on the public display of religious activities, the post-Mao state placed a great emphasis on harmonious relations among religions. The administrations of President Jiang Zemin (1989–2002) and President Hu Jintao (2003–13) emphasized that maintaining interreligious harmony was the government's priority in handling religious affairs.[124] Protestants were compelled to restrain themselves from the kind of provocative behaviors frequently seen in Republican China and Chiang's Taiwan, such as disrupting Buddhist events, proselytizing at Buddhist sites, and openly publishing anti-Buddhist tracts. Therefore, despite its remarkable growth, Protestantism appeared much less invasive and aggressive in the eyes of the Buddhist elite of post-Mao mainland China.

Third, compared to Republican China and Chiang's Taiwan, in post-Mao mainland China, Christianity was less favored among the political elite. In contrast, Buddhist leaders often enjoyed a relatively amicable relationship with local officials. Since 1978, the mainland Chinese state has made market-oriented economic development its top priority. Particularly after 1992, officials were under enormous pressure to exploit every possible resource to develop the local economy. Buddhist temples' potential to boost tourism motivated local officials to seek a good relationship with resourceful Buddhist leaders and to readily support the construction and expansion of temples.[125] China's reform program has also led to decades-long explosive economic growth. The temple economy, as a result, profited from the booming tourism and an increase in donations. Content with the political and economic resources they enjoyed, Buddhist leaders were oblivious to the potential challenge posed by rapidly growing Christianity.

The state policies and actions of the post-Mao era did not diminish the evangelistic zeal of Protestant groups, but they restrained Protestant groups from openly attacking Buddhism and reduced their public visibility. In the end, despite Protestantism's rapid growth, the Buddhist elite has not considered it an imminent threat, and therefore it has not triggered any measurable isomorphic responses from Chinese Buddhist organizations.

In summary, if the state policies and actions in Republican China and Chiang's Taiwan served to amplify the competitive pressure of Christianity, the conditions created by the post-Mao state had the effect of dampening religious competition and diminishing the perceived competitive pressure experienced by the Buddhist community.

From Crisis Perception to Isomorphic Response

An organizational actor's response to perceived competitive pressure can take different courses, including coercion and avoidance. Many among the Buddhist elite in the Republican era, however, came to the understanding that Buddhism ought to emulate the organizational strength of Christianity to stay competitive. Taixu's attitude toward Christianity is representative. Although he criticized the central tenets of Christianity, he also urged Buddhists to learn from Christians the ability "to instill in individual believers . . . a remarkable oneness of mind and spirit that shaped their everyday lives and energized them for mission."[126]

This attitude is also evidenced in the articles I have selected from the Collection. Dozens of articles exhorted Buddhists to model themselves on Christians' proselytizing passion and methods, and their dedication to charity and social education.[127] One article reported on the ambitious plan of British missionaries to use radio broadcasting to bolster their evangelism in China, goading fellow Buddhists: "How can we Buddhists, with our religion's deep-seated roots and wide influence in Chinese society, not strengthen our efforts to propagate Buddhism?"[128] An author asserted that none in the Chinese Buddhist community had the same level of commitment to proselytization as Christians or Japanese Buddhists.[129] To change the situation, he recommended educating Chinese Buddhists in Western-style or Japanese-style schools to enable them to acquire profound knowledge of the religion, and equally importantly to have real passion in the propagation of Buddhism so they could "hold lectures, establish Buddhist youth organizations, publish Buddhist literatures, talk to anyone about Buddhism." An author named Shanyin pointed out that Christianity has gained worldwide dominance despite its uncommendable doctrines. He attributed Christian success to the religion's commitment to "building schools and hospitals everywhere" and exhorted Buddhists to emulate it.[130] Likewise, Liu Xianliang, a lay Buddhist leader in Beijing, called on fellow Chinese Buddhists to join the "game of proselytization," to learn from the Christian examples so as to "catch up with them, not to lag behind."[131] The editor of the journal commented on Liu's article: "While other religions are so dedicated and effective [in proselytization], Buddhism is rather indifferent and incompetent. How can we not feel any shame in the comparison?" He also expected the young generation of

Buddhists to answer the call by emulating Christian youth organizations.[132] In sum, these Buddhists shared the understanding that they should "compete for the survival" (Liu Xianliang's phrase) and advocated learning from the institutional features they thought made Christianity strong and influential, in particular its commitment to proselytization, education, and charity.

This trend of competitive isomorphism continued and was amplified in Chiang's Taiwan after 1949. In Taiwan, Zhuyun urged Buddhists to go deep into the countryside to missionize like Christian missionaries, and to set up their own kindergartens so as to "save children from the clutches of the Christians."[133] Establishing Buddhist scholarships and facilitating the formation of Buddhist study groups among college students were initiatives modeled after Christian practices.[134] The Buddhist nun Zhengyan's idea in 1966 of establishing a Buddhist foundation for charitable works was influenced by Christian charities and particularly stimulated by a conversation she had with Catholic nuns during which they commented that Buddhists, unlike Catholics, contributed little to social welfare.[135] Attributing Christianity's success to its dedication to education and charity, Nanting urged Buddhists to raise funds to build hospitals, schools, and orphanages with the same level of enthusiasm they had for temple construction. He himself was active in prison ministry and preaching on the radio, and in 1965 established a vocational school.[136] When Shengyan received his novitiate training from Dongchu (1908–77) in 1960,[137] he was instructed to emulate Christian evangelists by preaching Buddhism in public.[138]

Why did many among the Buddhist elites in Republican China and Chiang's Taiwan advocate or initiate massive isomorphic responses to the Christian challenge? First, they had no way to mobilize forces or appeal to the state to alleviate the competitive pressures posed by Christianity. In both cases, Christianity was a favored religion among the political elite, and its proselytization activities were protected by state policy. Buddhist organizations thus could not resort to state coercion to undercut the Christian rivalry. However, the Chinese Buddhist community still had dedicated and capable members passionate about defending the interests and glory of their religion. Rather than slinking away to find a smaller or different niche to survive the onslaught of rising Christianity, they met the Christian challenge head-on. Learning from the strengths of Christianity became part and parcel of their reform movement in a time of perceived crisis.

The process of reforming institutional features of Chinese Buddhism became full-blown in Chiang's Taiwan, giving rise to what can be called the Taiwan model of Chinese Buddhism. This model accords great importance to educating, organizing, and mobilizing lay practitioners, actively spreading the religion, and engaging with the broader society.[139] This energy manifested itself particularly after the lifting of martial law in 1987, leading to the proliferation of countless Buddhist associations, media outlets, and educational institutions. A number of gigantic Buddhist organizations such as Fo Guang Shan, Tzu Chi, Dharma Drum Mountain, and Chung Tai Shan emerged, serving as exemplary embodiments of the Taiwan model of Chinese Buddhism in action. They built extensive financial assets and drew millions of members. They not only established branches throughout Taiwan but also achieved a global presence. Chinese Buddhism in Taiwan effectively demonstrated its compatibility with modernity and offered a remedy to the challenges of modern life.[140] It has emerged as a dynamic and influential force in Taiwanese society, wielding significant influence in Taiwanese politics.[141]

As already indicated, Taiwanese Buddhists have left their mark on mainland China through various venues. However, it was through the dissemination of Jingkong's teachings that the Taiwan model of Chinese Buddhism was able to reach the broad Buddhist community and grassroots lay Buddhists on the mainland. Jingkong's teachings also played a pivotal role in generating what is arguably the most momentous Buddhist sectarian movement in post-Mao mainland China. In its process of expansion, the movement came to be perceived by the Buddhist establishment as a major challenge. Yet instead of meeting the challenge with isomorphic responses, the Chinese Buddhist establishment opted for an easier solution: to dissolve the challenge by resorting to state intervention and repression. Curiously enough, even though Jingkong started his preaching in Taiwan and other overseas Chinese communities, his teachings never much bothered these Buddhist communities. Therefore, probing Jingkong's success in China and the way the Buddhist elite responded to the rising movement sheds light not only on the deep logics behind competitive isomorphism but also on the deep-seated problems faced by the Buddhist community in mainland China.

The Jingkong Movement and Its Impact

Before discussing how the Jingkong movement affected the development of Chinese Buddhism on the mainland, a brief introduction of this charismatic preacher and his teachings is in order.[142] Jingkong was born in 1927 in Lujiang County, Anhui Province. In 1949, he relocated to Taiwan with the defeated Nationalist Army. He entered monastic life in 1959 and became an ordained Buddhist monk in 1961. His decade-long discipleship under Li Bingnan profoundly shaped his thinking and teaching methods.

The 1960s and 1970s were a critical period in the development of Chinese Buddhism in Taiwan. Established leaders such as Nanting and Dongchu were actively promoting the religion, and enterprising young leaders such as Xingyun and Zhengyan were making significant progress in building their organizations. Jingkong had an exceptional ability to communicate doctrinal messages plainly, and his skillful use of personal stories lent his teachings enormous persuasive power. He thus was able to carve out a niche of his own in this already crowded environment: he dedicated himself to preaching and pioneered the use of modern communication technologies to propagate his teachings. Since the late 1970s, Jingkong's lectures have been recorded and distributed through cassette tapes and later videocassettes, CDs, DVDs, and the internet. A satellite TV channel was founded in 2003 at Jingkong's suggestion, broadcasting his lectures from Taiwan twenty-four hours a day.

In 1997, Jingkong left Taiwan for Singapore, where he received patronage from the largest lay Buddhist society. Later he relocated himself again in Australia. However, he spent the last twenty years of his life primarily in Hong Kong. Wherever he was stationed, he devoted himself to lecturing on a daily basis. In a preaching career spanning almost six decades, his teachings gained influence in Chinese Buddhist communities around the world.

Several features make Jingkong's teachings distinct. First, it placed great emphasis on moral cultivation, seeing it as the foundation of a salvational path and the key to the improvement of one's personal fate. According to Jingkong, by practicing virtue and eschewing vice, one can change one's karma and effectively control one's own destiny. He lectured on Buddhist scriptures concerning karmic retribution and enthusiastically promoted Confucian classics, Daoist texts, and morality books that emphasize parallel themes. For instance, he made great efforts to repopularize *The Codes of Conduct for Students and Children (Dizigui)*, a popular primer used in the Qing and Republican eras to teach children to behave according to Confucian moral standards. Jingkong advocated using *Dizigui* to purify the human mind and harmonize human relationships to build a better society.

Second, for Jingkong, if moral cultivation lays the ethical foundation for salvation, then practicing Pure Land Buddhism provides the surest path to otherworldly salvation. Jingkong emphasized the importance of committing oneself single-mindedly to Pure Land Buddhism, allowing no distraction from other Buddhist schools. In the same spirit, he accentuated the importance of following one mentor and studying one sutra.

Third, according to Jingkong, whether one could achieve this-worldly goals and otherworldly salvation all hinges on the individual's own actions;

clerical mediation plays no role. He argued that lay Buddhists can attain even greater spiritual achievement than monastics and that it is totally legitimate for lay Buddhists to build and manage Buddhist temples, or even to teach the Buddha dharma to monks. He encouraged lay followers to organize themselves into Amitābha Buddhist societies, groups of lay practitioners who devote themselves to the practice of Pure Land Buddhism. Jingkong also promoted the building of Amitābha Villages, essentially Buddhist homes for elderly residents during the final phase of their lives as they prepare for rebirth in the Pure Land. Clearly, Jingkong's teachings, when institutionalized, would empower lay leadership and have the effect of erasing the lay-monastic hierarchy embedded in the more traditional teachings of Buddhism. Moreover, his teachings also tended to encourage the formation of lay Buddhist groups that separate themselves from the existing Buddhist milieu.

I should note that Jingkong's teachings are well within the Buddhist reform movement in Taiwan. This is evident in his enthusiastic promotion of Buddhism through modern media and his efforts in lay empowerment and mobilization. In his unique manner, he also showcased social engagement by advocating for the establishment of a virtuous society and the provision of hospice care to the elderly.

In the years following 1984, cassette tapes and CDs featuring Jingkong's lectures on Buddhism entered mainland China, and were embraced with great enthusiasm.[143] Buddhist institutions had suffered severe damage under Mao's radical policy. After the policy relaxed, there was a surge of demand for religious teachings among Buddhist followers. Yet the impoverished Buddhist institutions of mainland China, struggling to rebuild themselves, were unable to meet the demand. Under these circumstances, Jingkong's teachings, made available by modern communication technologies, were like "rain falling on long-parched land" (Informant No. 117). Among the numerous Buddhist devotees who regularly listened to his lectures and endeavored to live by his teachings, Jingkong attained rock star status. During his visits to the mainland, if his itinerary became known, massive crowds of enthusiastic devotees would come from all over China to pay homage. On one such occasion in 1996, for instance, his arrival in Shanghai unexpectedly drew more than three thousand people, causing a significant commotion at the airport. Jingkong found himself stuck in the crowd for more than twenty minutes before being extricated from the chaos.[144] The high demand and dire shortage that characterized the mainland Chinese Buddhist community in the early post-Mao years gave rise to what can be described as "Jingkong fever."[145]

Since the 1990s, the spread of Jingkong's teachings spawned the emergence of grassroots lay groups in China. The lay followers gathered in private homes to study his lectures, recite sutras, and chant Amitābha's name together. Capable and resourceful lay leaders also established large practice sites devoted to Jingkong's teachings.[146] Zhaoming Temple in the East Tianmu Mountains of Zhejiang Province, Jiangnan Amitābha Village in Jiangsu Province, the Ancient Dabei Temple in Liaoning Province, and Jinshan Temple in Gansu Province were among the most impressive and prominent sites. These sites were notable for their asceticism and group practice. Residents typically got up at three in the morning, circumambulated as they recited Amitābha Buddha's name until breakfast at six, then spent the rest of the day alternating between listening to recorded lectures of Jingkong, engaging in Buddha recitation (i.e., chanting the name of Amitābha Buddha), and volunteering labor for the site.

Lujiang Cultural Educational Center, funded by Jingkong's overseas disciples and located in his hometown in Anhui, was the only site on the mainland with which Jingkong was directly involved. With the help of local officials, it was registered as a nonprofit, private, educational institution, thus bypassing the state's proscription on the building of religious sites by overseas personnel. The Lujiang center operated with discretion, careful not to give any impression that it was promoting Buddhism. With promotion of Chinese tradition as its mission, the center offered courses to the public on how to discipline oneself and structure human relationships according to the ethical codes in the Confucian primer *Dizigui*.[147] It even initiated a social experiment, employing the Confucian primer to instill moral values in the residents of the town of Tangchi, with the objective of turning the town into a model for a "harmonious society."[148]

These large sites emerged as national practice centers and pilgrimage destinations among Buddhist practitioners who subscribed to Jingkong's teachings for years. When pilgrims returned home, they emulated the institution and practices of these large centers. Hence, the centers had the effect of standardizing the practices of Jingkong groups scattered across China.

Jingkong's teachings also found their way into River County. The most prominent lay group of Jingkong followers revolved around a charismatic young man, Shao, whom we met in chapter 3. Brought up by his grandmother, he was deeply influenced by her belief in popular religion and devotion to the Sect of Long Life Teaching (Changshengjiao).[149] Later, he became aware of the differences between Buddhism and popular religion and went through the rite of taking refuges, formally becoming a lay Buddhist. In 2000, the twenty-year-old Shao encountered Jingkong's lectures and fell under his spell. In 2002, upon learning of Jingkong's scheduled visit to Zhaoming Temple on his China tour, Shao and a few other followers in River County embarked on a pilgrimage to pay homage. This journey was transformative, leading Shao to fully immerse

FIGURE 5.2. The Buddha Recitation Hall of a lay Buddhist community. All the icons are of the Pure Land Buddhist school. In the corner stands a photo image of Jingkong, the revered master whose teaching inspired the lay Buddhist movement. The interior design of this hall is modeled after that of Zhaoming Temple. (Photograph by the author.)

himself in Jingkong's teachings and the networks of his followers. He extended his visits to other Jingkong centers, including the Singapore Lay Buddhist Lodge where Jingkong was stationed at the time. In 2006, Shao was entrusted by village cadres in River County with oversight of a village communal temple. Shao raised funds to construct a Buddha Recitation Hall, modeling its interior design and regulations after those of Zhaoming Temple, and to turn the place into what Shao called a temple of "true Buddhist followers" (Informant No. 130).

In 2008, Shao relocated his group to a hilltop for a more ambitious project. In just two years, he built a Buddhist complex, featuring a Buddha Recitation Hall capable of hosting more than three hundred people and a lodging facility with a capacity of up to seventy-two. Tapping into his connections within the broader Jingkong networks, he attracted donations from followers outside River County for his project. Shao's site emerged as a central gathering place for lay practitioners in the county who followed Jingkong's teachings.

Followers affiliated with Shao's group typically described their encounter with Jingkong's teachings as a conversion experience that elicited deep religious commitment. Deng Jianhua, a sixty-five-year-old lay Buddhist who played a notable role in the Buddhist temple restoration since the 1980s, told me in 2009 that if not for the teachings of "Old Dharma Master" (*lao fashi*)—as Jingkong was respectfully and affectionately referred to in this circle—she would still be fumbling in darkness, wasting time in making merits, learning chanting skills, and memorizing mantras (Informant No. 178). Fifty-eight-year-old Ren Zhaodi told me that her journey with Jingkong's teachings started with "superstition"—she spent years going to popular religion temples and Buddhist temples until 2003, when she received VCD copies of Jingkong lectures on *Sukhāvatīvyūha-sūtra* (*Wuliangshou jing*, *The Sutra on the Buddha of Eternal Life* or *The Infinite Life Sutra*).[150] She watched repeatedly, often with tears in her eyes. In the end, she felt she had found her way. Since then, she mainly stayed home watching Jingkong's VCDs and practicing Buddha recitation, her mind set on taking rebirth in the Pure Land of Amitābha (Informant No. 126). After Shao's temple was built, she became a regular. These Jingkong followers usually were highly critical of the Buddhist establishment in River County, claiming that the liturgical services provided by the monks were useless for spiritual attainment and that the monks were merely making a living rather than caring about others' salvation. With youthful bluntness, Shao once told Huixiu, the most senior monk of River County, that River County had "only temples but no teaching" (*you miao wu dao*).

In contrast to the networks of the Buddhist establishment in River County, Shao's group had a much stronger congregational structure. The group regularly gathered for Buddha recitation and spent time together watching Jingkong's videos. The group provided free hospice care according to the formula of Pure Land Buddhism to dying fellow devotees or their family members upon request.[151] Members of this group also displayed proselytization zeal. They earnestly shared ideas of karmic retribution and salvation in the Pure Land with acquaintances. They pooled funds to reproduce tracts of Jingkong's teachings and distributed them on the streets, in parks, and even at other Buddhist temples.

These sites and groups led by lay followers of Jingkong coalesced into a broad religious community. Increasingly, they developed a tendency toward exclusivism. Many of these sites committed themselves solely to Pure Land Buddhism, explicitly declaring their devotion to Jingkong and prohibiting the circulation of teachings of other Buddhist teachers within their premises. Zhaoming Temple went so far to erect a stone stele in its complex with the inscription:

> [We have] one master—the old Dharma Master Jingkong;
> [We study] one sutra—*The Infinite Life Sutra*;
> [We] chant Amitābha Buddha's name from the beginning to the end.

FIGURE 5.3. The stone stele inside Zhaoming Temple that proclaims its single-minded devotion. (Photograph by the author.)

As a result of their distinct identity and exclusivist tendencies, the Jingkong sites increasingly separated themselves from the Chinese Buddhist establishment. And with its evangelistic zeal, the Jingkong-inspired movement grew rapidly at the expense of the Buddhist establishment.

Perception of and Response to the Jingkong Movement

The Chinese Buddhist establishment in post-Mao mainland China came to view the quickly expanding Jingkong Buddhist movement as a threat. The same monk from Xiyuan Temple who was little perturbed by the quick rise of Protestantism was an active participant in an organized campaign to attack the Jingkong movement on theological grounds. This campaign, launched by Abbot Mingxue (1923–2016) of Lingyanshan Temple and his associates in 1997, shows that some elite Buddhists were already alarmed by the Jingkong movement in its incipient stage. In the following years, with the growing momentum of the Jingkong-inspired lay movement, criticisms of Jingkong became more strident and vociferous within Buddhist circles. An increasing number of leaders in the monastic community openly accused Jingkong of inciting lay usurpation of monastic authority and leading lay Buddhists astray. At a panel of the Second World Buddhist Forum in Wuxi in 2009 (for which I was in the audience), the abbot of Jile Temple in northeast China took the podium to slam Jingkong's followers, citing examples of their distributing teaching materials of Jingkong, proselytizing, and casting aspersions on the monastics at his temple.

What led leaders in the Chinese Buddhist establishment to become acutely aware of the Jingkong threat? Let me frame the question in a comparative perspective: Both Christianity and the Jingkong movement exhibited some form of exclusivism, so why did the Buddhist establishment have very different perceptions of the competitive pressure posed by the two? Here, an ecological mechanism of organizational competition—the greater the niche overlap of two organizations, the more intense their competition—is evoked to shed light on this question.[152]

From the perspective of niche overlap, the development of the Jingkong movement was perceived as much more threatening by the Buddhist establishment than the rapid rise of Protestantism for two reasons. First, in the early post-Mao era, both Protestantism and Chinese Buddhism were rebuilding themselves in a relatively open field. This openness allowed Protestantism and Buddhism to develop without their growth coming at the expense of each other, for the most part. In contrast, the Jingkong movement attracted followers from the exact same pool of patrons of the Buddhist establishment. Naturally, the practice of exclusive devotion to Jingkong would be detrimental to the interest of the Buddhist establishment and consequently piqued its leadership.

However, I want to highlight a more subtle aspect of niche overlap. From early on, the post-Mao state's policy against missionization by overseas groups compelled the dissemination of Jingkong's teachings to rely heavily on the existing network of the Buddhist establishment. Consequently, this same network fostered the formation of the sectarian movement. Therefore, it could be argued that the religious policy of the post-Mao state may have inadvertently enlarged the degree of niche overlap between the Jingkong movement and the Buddhist establishment.

Still, we can formulate yet another question: Why, in Taiwan and other Chinese societies, did Jingkong's teachings not elicited such strong reactions from Buddhist leaders and organizations as they did in mainland China? The reason lies in the fact that, essentially, it is in mainland China and not elsewhere that Jingkong's teachings commanded broad and enthusiastic followings and produced a nationally influential sectarian movement. In Taiwan, Jingkong was one of many enterprising Buddhist leaders vying for significance and influence. With no strong organizational base, Jingkong focused on teaching and expanding his influence through modern communication technologies. In terms of influence in Taiwan, he was no match for other prominent Buddhist leaders, including Xingyun, Zhengyan, Shengyan, and a few others who established massive organizations with island-wide branches, millions of members, and their own media outlets, educational institutions, and charitable programs. In contrast, during the 1980s and 1990s in mainland China, Buddhist institutions, devastated by the Cultural Revolution, were primarily engaged in reconstruction efforts. The shortage of religious teachers and teachings was an endemic problem. Therefore, Jingkong's use of modern media to propagate his teachings and the wide circulation of his audiovisual materials in mainland China uniquely positioned him to exploit this particular situation, allowing him to amass huge influence in a remarkably short period. In fact, until around 2010, Jingkong remained by far the most influential religious teacher among the grassroots lay Buddhist community in mainland China. In short, in the highly crowded and competitive environment of Taiwanese Buddhism, Jingkong could not exert significant pressure on other Buddhist groups; yet in mainland China, the devastating Cultural Revolution cleared the field, opening a niche for the momentous rise of the Jingkong movement. Here again, the state's structuring role in religious competition is apparent.

Despite their acute awareness of the threat posed by the Jingkong movement, the Chinese Buddhist establishment in mainland China did not launch a significant isomorphic response. This is because they had a variety of resources at their disposal to combat the Jingkong challenge. With temples, seminaries, and the Buddhist associations under their control, Jingkong's opponents could organize effective campaigns to denounce his teachings and ban his materials from their networks. More importantly, backed by the state's religious policy and enjoying close ties with the government, they could appeal to state agencies to curtail the movement. Because state policy explicitly prohibits missionizing activities by overseas individuals and organizations, leaders in the Buddhist establishment could attack Jingkong for using his teachings to "infiltrate China." Pointing out parallels between the Jingkong movement and Falun Gong, a NRM condemned by the Chinese government as an evil cult in 1999 (see chapter 4), Jingkong's critics called on the government to condemn his movement as another evil cult.[153]

Under pressure from the Buddhist establishment, and because of their own concerns with an overseas religious figure having enormous charismatic hold over a massive movement in China, state agencies in charge of religious affairs took a number of measures after 2008. Lujiang Cultural Educational Center was forced to close down, Buddhist sites promoting Jingkong's teachings were ordered to purge themselves of his influence, Jingkong himself was restricted from traveling to mainland China, and local affiliate groups were disbanded and Jingkong-related materials confiscated.

In River County, Shao's group encountered difficulties from the Buddhist establishment and the local RAB. Establishment leaders held grudges against Shao and his group for their exclusivist practices and contempt toward the monastics. Hence, the county Buddhist Association refused to endorse Shao's application to register his site as a state-sanctioned religious venue, blocking its legalization for years.[154] After 2008, the county RAB become even more watchful of Shao's group. The officials often came to inspect his site, ordering Shao to remove Jingkong materials and threatening to tear down the temple if their order was defied. Suspecting Shao of receiving funds from overseas, the local police once took Shao to their office for questioning and searched his home for Jingkong materials.

Although the Chinese state never officially declared the Jingkong movement an evil cult, they did take serious measures to suppress its development. These measures had the effect of undermining Jingkong's authority and popularity and curbed the movement. When pressured to purge Jingkong's influence, the affiliated sites and groups put up little resistance.[155] They removed disallowed materials from public view and shed their Jingkong identity, even though lay practitioners privately continued listening to his lectures. In River County, after Shao distanced from Jingkong influence, he was finally able to register the temple with the local RAB in 2018.

Around 2010, there emerged a number of emulators of Jingkong in mainland China, who also preached Pure Land Buddhism and used audiovisual media to popularize their teachings among lay Buddhists. The most influential one is Da'an, abbot of Donglin Temple in Jiangxi Province.[156] When the

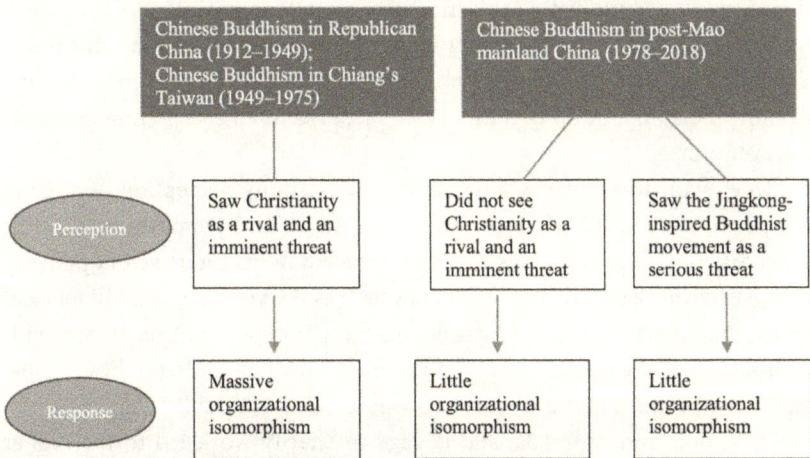

FIGURE 5.4. Chinese Buddhist organizations' perception and responses to competitive pressures in Republican China, Chiang Kai-shek's Taiwan, and post-Mao mainland China.

state blocked the circulation of Jingkong's teachings, it opened this niche to Da'an and others.[157] Hence, the Jingkong movement gradually lost its steam and coherence. As it was all too easy to use the state's coercive apparatus to undercut the movement, the Buddhist establishment had few incentives to launch competitive isomorphism by emulating the organizational strength of an otherwise forceful rival.

Conclusion and Discussion

The analysis presented in this chapter (see figure 5.4 for a summary) suggests that for a religious organization to launch competitive isomorphism, it must meet two prerequisites: first, it must perceive competitive pressure; second, it lacks the resources or means to neutralize the challenge but has the will and the capacity to (re)gain dominance by learning from the competitor's strengths. The Chinese Buddhist organizations in both Republican China and Chiang's Taiwan met these criteria. Many among the Buddhist elites perceived Christianity as a serious challenge, and Buddhist organizations did not possess the means to suppress their rivals but had committed and energetic members who strove to emulate certain institutional features of Christianity to strengthen Buddhism.

The case of post-Mao mainland China shows that the existence of strong rivalry does not necessarily lead to an acute perception of rivalry. Moreover, even if the organizational actor perceives rivalry, such a perception does not necessarily lead to isomorphic response because suppression of rivals and relocating to a different niche can be alternative ways to handle the situation. How the Buddhist establishment of post-Mao mainland China dealt with the challenge from the rising Jingkong movement illustrates this point: the Buddhist establishment had no incentive to meet the challenge through isomorphic competition because it had recourse to an easier strategy—state intervention.

To explain what shapes a religious organization's perception of and reactions to rivalry, this chapter reveals the major and pervasive role of the state. State policies and actions can influence how religious actors perceive competitive pressure by shaping factors such as the visibility and influence of rivals, the intensity of their engagement, the actors' sense of security or vulnerability, and the extent to which their niches overlap. In Republican China and Chiang's Taiwan, the greater freedom to carry out public evangelization, build schools and hospitals, and engage in charity work led to the higher visibility of Christianity in the public arena, made the Christian presence more imposing, and aroused the competitive energy of the Buddhist elite.

Furthermore, the fact that the state elite favored Christianity boosted the aggressiveness of Christians in denouncing other religions and converting their followers, leading Buddhists to acutely feel the Christian threat. In contrast, the religious policy of the post-Mao Chinese state restricted the public expression of religion, reduced the visibility of Christianity, and separated religions into different niches. Consequently, the Buddhist establishment did not perceive the meteoric rise of Christian groups' membership and grassroots social impact as a threat. Moreover, the congenial relationship between the state and the Chinese Buddhist establishment gave the latter a strong sense of security, making it even less likely to perceive potential rivalry unless its niche was infringed upon. On the other hand, under the restrictive religious policy of the post-Mao state, the spread of Jingkong's teachings and the rise of his movement had to develop by piggybacking on the resources and networks of the Buddhist establishment. The resultant significant niche overlap between the Jingkong movement and the Buddhist establishment prompted the latter to resort to state intervention to curb the challenge. It should be noted that it was also the post-Mao state's religious policy that allowed the Buddhist establishment to adopt such a course of action.

Although this chapter, in contrast to DiMaggio and Powell's argument, emphasizes the continued importance of competitive isomorphism in shaping institutional change and focuses on whether and how religious competition prompts isomorphism, let me note that competitive isomorphism and institutional isomorphism were to some degree confounded in my cases. Religious policy in the Republican era hinged on the introduced Western concept of "religion," which was heavily influenced by the model of Christianity. This notion of religion continued to inform religious policy in Chiang's Taiwan and post-Mao mainland China. Even though the political elite of post-Mao mainland China no longer held as favorable an opinion of Christianity as did the elite of Republican China and Chiang's Taiwan, the post-Mao regime's definition of religion and thus its religious policy retain a strong Christian bias. Hence, there were pressures from the state to compel Chinese Buddhism and other religions to conform to the normative model, or "reinvent" themselves accordingly. Nonetheless, the reforms of Chinese Buddhist organizations highlighted in this chapter—organizing the laity into a congregational organization, devoting energy to proselytization, and becoming socially engaged—were clearly not intended not only to obtain legitimacy but also to gain strength and social influence. Had their purpose been only to achieve legitimacy in the eyes of the state, Chinese Buddhism in the Republican era and Chiang's Taiwan would not have taken those reform measures that cut deeply into its core organizational structure and institutions. This point becomes clearer when we note that Chinese Buddhism did not adopt these restructuring measures in post-Mao mainland China, where forces pushing for institutional isomorphism were still in operation but forces pushing for competitive isomorphism were largely missing.

I hope this chapter does not convey the impression that I necessarily endorse the so-called Humanistic Buddhism. On the contrary, I fully understood the mainland Chinese monks I met in the field when they criticized the Taiwan model of Chinese Buddhism for "straying from Buddha's Path of Liberation (*jietuodao*),"[158] becoming too engrossed in charity work, and "losing the essence of Buddhism and becoming too Christianized."[159]

That said, their ability to voice such detached criticisms could arise precisely because they have not experienced the acute sense of crisis that Buddhist elites in Taiwan felt in the 1950s and 1960s. Had they been confronted with the same precarious circumstances, they might also have acknowledged the necessity of reform and renewal to make Buddhism more socially relevant and better equipped to face competition from Christianity.

Conclusion

A major change in the Chinese religious ecology in the post-Mao era is the extraordinary rise of Protestantism relative to other religions. This book argues that this phenomenon is an unintended consequence of state policies and actions. Conditions created by the state have prevented other religions from achieving growth comparable with Protestantism. For instance, Chinese popular religion, once central to China's religious ecology, could not reclaim its prominence due to the irrevocable loss of lineage power under Mao and the further disintegration of rural communities as a result of the post-Mao state's market reforms. New religious movements could have been strong contenders, as their explosive growth during Republican China attests. However, harsh suppression by the Maoist state and subsequent post-Mao campaigns against so-called evil cults stunted their potential, making any large-scale surge or resurgence unsustainable. Chinese Buddhism, historically the largest, most resource-rich, and most influential institutional religion in China, might have completely overshadowed Protestantism had Buddhists adopted strategies similar to those of their coreligionists in Taiwan, who emulated certain institutional features of Christian organizations to enhance religious competitiveness. However, under the post-Mao state, Buddhist institutions, benefiting from political security and economic prosperity, lacked a compelling incentive for competitive adaptation.

For Protestantism, on the other hand, the Maoist state inadvertently removed a significant barrier that had previously inhibited its spread in Chinese society. The post-Mao state, with its opening-up policies and market-oriented economic development, fostered an expanding interstitial social space where autonomous religious growth outside the state's oversight was possible. Protestant groups skillfully exploited this space, achieving rapid and robust growth.

Thus, it may not be an overstatement to suggest that the Maoist and post-Mao states, albeit unintentionally, acted as an "escort fleet" for Protestantism, creating structural conditions that fostered unprecedented and sustained growth, which was marked by a vigor unmatched by any other religion in the post-Mao era.

Astute readers may observe that the Chinese state's religious policies have undergone notable shifts since Xi Jinping (born 1953) assumed leadership in 2012. This prompts questions about whether these changes have influenced the growth dynamics of various religions, thereby reshaping the Chinese religious ecology. To address these concerns, the first part of this concluding chapter will explore the following questions: What are the defining characteristics of the new policies, and how have they been implemented? How have they affected each of the major religions examined in this book? And finally, do the policy shifts have potential to fundamentally alter the religious ecology that began to take shape during the earlier post-Mao period?

At this point, readers may wonder how my institutions-in-context theory, combined with historical-comparative methods and the religious ecology perspective, can contribute to understanding patterns of religious change beyond China. To address this, the second part of this chapter situates the Chinese case in a broader global historical context, attempting to explicate the logics behind the varied success of the worldwide expansion of Christianity in the past five hundred years.

Religious Policies Under Xi and Their Ramifications

China's religious policies have seen noticeable changes since 2016, four years after Xi Jinping assumed power. Certain developments in the policies have raised concerns among observers who claim that the Chinese state has increased its crackdown on religions and grown especially hostile to Christianity,[1] and that the new Chinese leadership's preference for traditional cultures would bring benefits to China's indigenous or long-indigenized religions.[2] I, however, do not take this view.

Before examining the policy changes under Xi Jinping and their implications, it is important to emphasize that the religious policies of the Xi administration show a significant degree of continuity and consistency with those of the preceding post-Mao era. Like previous administrations, the Xi administration remains committed to upholding the principle of secularism, but has no intent to return to the kind of radical secularism of the Mao era, which sought the eradication of all religions. Continuing to recognize and allow the existence and growth of religions, the Xi administration still follows the principles outlined in *Document 19*, published in 1982. State-sanctioned religions, including Protestantism and Catholicism, continue to enjoy legal protection under this administration. To be clear, the religious policies of the Xi administration are not intended, as some Western politicians insist, to wage a "war on religions."[3] Nor, contrary to an even more widespread belief, are they specifically aimed at pursuing a war on Christianity.[4]

The changes in religious policy under Xi are in line with the general trends of the Xi era. The Xi era features three persistent, major political changes: heightened disciplinary actions toward officials, particularly on the issues of corruption, job performance, and political commitment; more control of Chinese society by legal and administrative means, with the assistance of advanced technologies; and increased pursuit of ideology, centering on the notions of the "Four Confidences" and the "Chinese Dream."[5] The policy changes in religious oversight since 2016 reflect all three of these shifts. In the following, I will first highlight the changes directed from the central state level. However, because previous chapters have already demonstrated the wide gap between policy intention and its effect, I will also look at how the bureaucracy responsible for implementing these policies works and what patterns emerge in its activities.

The central state intends to enhance bureaucratic control over religious organizations and activities. It has formulated and passed administrative regulations, rules, and measures at an unprecedented pace to provide guidance for the bureaucracy in charge of religious work and religious organizations. China's State Council also passed a revised *Regulations on Religious Affairs* in 2017 (which became effective in February 2018), replacing the older version promulgated in 2005.[6] Compared with the old regulations, the new version has greatly expanded the scope of administrative oversight. Following this, the SARA issued a flurry of new administrative measures that encompass a broad range of issues, including management of religious personnel, religious organizations, and religious schools; financial oversight of religious organizations; and regulation of religion-related content online.

The central state also intends to put those religions formerly existing in the legal gray area, including Protestant independent churches, Catholic underground churches, and popular religion, on a shorter leash. It has devised ways to incorporate some of these organizations into the officially sanctioned system and exerted pressure on those who are reluctant to follow.

As detailed in chapter 1, the Religious Affairs Bureaus, in the preceding post-Mao period, were ill-equipped to effectively monitor and supervise religious organizations and activities within their jurisdictions. In 2018, as part of the *Plan on Deepening Reform of Party and State Institutions*, the State

Administration for Religious Affairs (SARA) was merged into the United Front Work Department of the CCP Central Committee, while retaining SARA's name externally. This structural change was replicated across different administrative levels, with religious affairs offices throughout the system similarly incorporated into United Front Work Departments. The institutional change marked a significant move to centralize and reinforce the CCP's direct leadership over religious work at all levels.

To address persistent capacity constraints, measures were also taken to bolster the manpower of county-level RABs. In River County, for example, the RAB has doubled its personnel from three to six since 2017. Still, for six people to oversee religious affairs of a county covering more than a thousand square kilometers with more than half a million people is a stretch. Therefore, the state has also employed village- and street-level control mechanisms, used digital technologies, and sought to reinforce self-compliance among religious organizations through repeated meetings and "thought education."

One important change involves the installation of a United Front commissar (*tongzhan weiyuan*) at each of the county's sixteen subdivisions of townships, towns, and subdistricts. This apparatus is tasked with assisting the RAB in gathering information, monitoring activities of religious sites, and enforcing policies in their respective jurisdictions. The creation of this position has greatly extended the reach of the religious regulatory regime at the grassroots level, as the United Front commissar is not only well connected but also wields considerable resources and clout in his/her local society.[7] In addition, the task of keeping a watchful eye on religious groups has also become part of the job of grid managers (*wangge yuan*), another position "in the trenches." The system divides a county into many smaller zones called grids, assigning each to a manager who is required to regularly report activities under his/her watch to the upper-level government. The system can be traced back to 2004; however, under the Xi administration the grid system has been implemented nationwide.

The Xi era is contemporaneous with the advent of new digital technologies. The widespread adoption of mobile apps, e-commerce platforms, and social media has not only transformed daily life in China, enhancing efficiency and connectivity, but has also provided a means for unprecedented levels of bureaucratic control. Local governments have extended the use of digital technologies to manage religious affairs. This includes the creation of WeChat groups for immediate information exchange and coordinated actions among different governmental agencies, the implementation of apps for religious work management,[8] and the installation of surveillance cameras at religious sites.[9]

Since 2016, the state has been carrying out a campaign to Sinicize religions—that is, to demand religions, especially those perceived to have strong foreign roots and connections, to align their teachings, customs, and morality with Chinese culture.[10] Religious organizations have also been urged to better integrate the core socialist values (*shehui zhuyi hexin jiazhi guan*) and reinterpret their teachings in line with the sets of values advocated by the CCP.[11]

In addition to the increased control, another notable shift in religious policy orientation is a heightened effort to cultivate and fortify what the Chinese state perceives as the cultural core of China. This endeavor aims to counter the influence of foreign cultures and foster a "spiritual home" for the people of China.[12] Under Xi, the central state no longer regards popular religion as superstition and instead has endorsed the legalization and registration of popular religion temples, considering them part of traditional culture.[13] Among the state-recognized religions, Chinese Buddhism and Daoism have been integrated into the state's strategy to revitalize traditional culture and enhance the global influence of China's soft power.[14] The state has called for the "healthy development" of Chinese Buddhism and Daoism and has implemented policies for this purpose. Specifically, the state has banned profit-making activities by the two religions with the hope that the measure would serve to "purify" and set them on a more righteous path.

More will be discussed concerning this in the next section, where I will examine the state's specific policies toward different religions. First, however, we must look at how these policies have been implemented at the ground level. This requires, as usual, a close examination of the responsible bureaucracy. I offer four observations.[15]

First, given the paramount importance assigned to political alignment (*zhengzhi zhanwei*) and proactive dedication in evaluating the performance of local officials, it becomes important for officials in charge of religious affairs to manifest commitment to their work.[16] Especially on certain hardcore issues defined by the state, such as pushing religious groups out of the legal gray area, some local officials have made persistent efforts. The endeavors not only involved the religious regulatory agencies but also a larger part of the bureaucracy. For instance, the Public Security Bureau, township and village officials (including the United Front commissar), neighborhood committees, and other government agencies could all get involved to persuade or push Protestant house churches to get registered.

The bureaucratic pressure from above sometimes led local officials to overperform. Yet overperformance could cause backlash. Should overly aggressive performance incite widespread protest or even violent conflict, the responsible official could be perceived as lacking competence and sidelined by superiors.[17] In today's China, the job of the RAB chief has become "much more demanding and more likely to antagonize," as a recently retired RAB official commented (Informant No. 377).

Second, tasks such as the routine supervision of registered religious groups, campaigns to Sinicize religions, and efforts to align religions with core socialist values remain primarily within the purview of the local RAB, which, however, operates with limited tools at its disposal. Its repertoire usually includes devising more complicated rules and bureaucratic procedures, decorating religious venues with political symbols, and organizing meetings, study sessions, contests, and tours to historical sites deemed significant to the history of the CCP. For instance, to show their effort to infuse religious groups with core socialist values, RAB officials required religious sites to fly the national flag and adorn their premises with posters promoting the values. To demonstrate engagement in the Sinicization campaign, River County's RAB officials orchestrated two major activities. For Buddhist groups, they arranged a speech contest where participants gave speeches on topics such as "How Buddhism can align with core socialist values" and "Lessons from the Sinicization of Buddhism in Chinese history." Concerning Protestant groups, the RAB invited a college professor to deliver lectures concerning "Why history favored the CCP" and "How to strengthen cultural self-confidence." In addition, they organized a tour for Protestant representatives to "red tourism" sites in Jiangxi Province for patriotic education.[18]

These acts, staged by the RAB with the collaboration from the religious groups, remain at a superficial level, however. They did not penetrate, in the sense that they elicited no substantive behavioral changes by the religious actors. In short, even though the Sinicization campaign has been criticized by China scholars as an effort in "political domestication,"[19] its actual effect often echoed a situation expressed by a Chinese idiom: "Loud thunder but little rain."[20]

Third, under Xi, the local officials, including those in charge of religious work, in the face of dramatically increased rules, regulations, campaigns, inspection tours, and directives, are compelled to meet the flood of demands with bureaucratic formalism, striving to demonstrate their compliance to prescribed forms as they make little effort to tackle the substantive issues. Higher-ups create endless targets, tasks, meetings, and excessive paperwork to demonstrate their political adherence, and overwhelmed subordinates are forced to feign compliance to get along. As one township-level CCP secretary told me, "If I do not deal with orders with some kind of formalism, either my career ends right here or I will have to work myself to death" (Informant

No. 381). Hence, during the urban renewal campaign launched by the Zhejiang provincial government between 2013 and 2015 to demolish illegally constructed buildings, including religious sites built without prior legal permission, officials in one county I visited decided to tear down only those popular
religion temples located in conspicuous places, such as by the roadside or in
the middle of rice paddies, as these could be easily spotted by inspection officials from higher up.

In most cases, as long as religious actors complied with the necessary
formalities, bureaucrats would not press further. Often, it seemed that RAB
officials and religious leaders were tacitly cooperating to cope with the tightening control measures. For instance, RAB officials would alert religious site
leaders in advance of inspection tours from higher authorities, allowing them
to prepare.

Suspecting that their subordinates might feign compliance, the higher-
ups order inspections to be conducted by different agencies and adopt so-
called trace management (*henji guanli*), which demands recording of work
done at every step and providing photographic proof. These bureaucratic
procedures are highly redundant, time-consuming, and demoralizing, causing many grassroots bureaucrats to resent their jobs.

Bureaucratic formalism has been a problem for preceding administrations.
In fact, such a tendency is inherent in any bureaucratic institution, an issue
that Mao wanted to combat but failed.[21] However, obsession with formalities
and the pursuit of workarounds, rather than focusing on the substantive, have
dramatically escalated in recent years.[22] Perhaps this surge can be explained
by both the increased political demand and a careerist bureaucracy that has
lost value-based commitment and is driven mainly by self-preservation and
advancement. In the Xi era, formalism has become the prevailing culture and
mentality of the bureaucracy. Of this phenomenon, my informant, the leader
of an official religious association, gave a pithy characterization: "Everybody
has been trapped in this weird circle of formalism. Everybody has been busy
with box-ticking, but nobody knows or even cares why we are doing it" (Informant No. 379).

Across the board, religious leaders whom I interviewed in 2023 found the
unending paperwork, evaluations, inspections, meetings, and study sessions
vexing. Nonetheless, it is precisely the widespread formalism that renders the
seemingly stringent rules hollow in practice, leaving room for religious actors
to maneuver.

The fourth and last observation concerns street-level bureaucrats such
as grid managers and United Front commissars tasked with strengthening

oversight of religious sites. These grassroots functionaries are closely embedded in local networks. Local variations notwithstanding, these agents tend not to enforce rules too rigidly, wary of provoking complaints or, worse, an outcry from the local community. Consequently, despite the ban on minors attending religious services being emphasized since the revised *Regulations on Religious Affairs* took effect in 2018, United Front commissars in many areas continued to turn a blind eye to parents taking their children to Sunday schools, as this practice is commonplace in local communities.

The policy shifts mentioned above, along with new trends in the practices and culture of the bureaucracy, have led to changes in the environment in which religious groups operate. In short, the interstitial social space for autonomous religious growth seems to have diminished, as religious groups in the legal gray area have been pushed to register and join the official sector and as the government has enforced stricter regulations on religious activities. However, the interstitial social space has by no means withered away. After more than four decades of reform and opening-up, China has become a dynamic society with countless actors willing to explore new interstitial spaces and resourceful enough to find and create them, even when existing ones have been closed off.

The religious groups operating in the officially sanctioned space have become subject to strengthened bureaucratic control in recent years. A soulless bureaucracy implementing control measures leads to prevalent formalism. This practice has created onerous burdens that religious groups struggle to cope with. The grievances are palpable among religious leaders, many of whom lived through the reform era and experienced decades of political relaxation, until recently being thrust into this new reality. Still, competent leaders who learn to navigate increasing red tape and maintain their focus on strengthening and expanding their religious communities can still find room for growth.

For religious groups labeled evil cults and targeted by the state for suppression, the space for operation has become even more constrained, given the entrenchment of the grid management system and an enhanced surveillance capacity enabled by digital technology over the past decade.

Let us now discuss the impact of the new political environment on the growth potential of different religions. This analysis is necessary because the state has specific policies toward different religions, and each religion has distinctive institutional features and thus responds to the new political environment differently. In the following, I will examine the dynamics of these religions under the new political conditions, beginning with popular religion and concluding with Protestantism, the fastest-growing religion in the preceding period of post-Mao China.

Varied Impacts of Policy Shifts

POPULAR RELIGION

During the Xi era, a milestone policy shift regarding popular religion has been its recognition by the state as a legitimate form of religious practice.[23]

In 2015, the UFWD and SARA issued a directive titled "Some Views on Managing Folk Beliefs," offering a framework and instructions for local authorities to advance the "legalization" of popular religion. Currently, although the state, on paper, does not exactly equate popular religion with the five major officially sanctioned religions, categorizing it instead as "folk beliefs," it is accorded official endorsement. Furthermore, popular religion has been increasingly acknowledged by the state as an integral part of the traditional culture it endeavors to promote.

I call this policy change a milestone because ever since the beginning of the twentieth century, popular religion has been branded by the state as superstition and consequently suffered stigmatization, discrimination, and suppression. In the preceding period of post-Mao China, even though popular religion was tolerated, it still largely survived in the legal gray area. A question naturally arises: Could this favorable turn of policy from 2015 on bring significant advancement in the development of popular religion?

To be sure, the policy shift brings some positive developments. Previously, only a small number of popular religion temples were able to gain legal status, by registering as Buddhist or Daoist sites. Under the new policy, popular religion temples can be registered as "folk belief activities sites" (*minjian xinyang huodong changsuo*).[24] In Zhejiang Province, 10,606 popular religion temples were granted legal status by 2017. This number surpasses the number of sites of all five state-sanctioned religions in Zhejiang combined.

With legal recognition, popular religion temples can enjoy strengthened property rights and other forms of state protection like those of state-sanctioned religions. This legalization and the state's inclusion of popular religion as part and parcel of Chinese traditional culture have also effectively removed the stigma associated with popular religion. This encourages participation of both the elite strata and youth in popular religion rituals.

Nevertheless, based on my field observations, it appears that the new policies have brought to popular religion some negative consequences, due to the intricate and, at times, counterproductive bureaucratic practices discussed earlier in this chapter.

First, the local bureaucracy, in registering folk belief activities sites, established eligibility criteria, which include the size of the temple and the number of participants.[25] This excluded many popular religion temples from obtaining legal status. In River County, where the registration of popular religion temples began in 2015 and was nearly concluded by 2017, less than half of existing temples have obtained registered status. Previously, almost all popular religion temples existed in a state of legal ambiguity, and the local officials were usually permissive to them all. Now, with some having obtained legal status, the illegality of remaining temples stands out.

For those popular religion temples without legal standing, local governments adopt different strategies to deal with them. Zhejiang Province's strategy has developed on the basis of the practice of officials in the city of Taizhou, who merged unregistered temples together, repurposed some, and demolished the rest.[26] Local authorities in Hunan Province adopted a similar approach, targeting for demolition temples built after the revised *Regulations on Religious Affairs* took effect on February 1, 2018, and temples that were deemed to lack historical significance, cultural heritage, or proper approval procedures.[27] Consequently, the registration system for popular religion temples has effectively diminished the legal gray zone for the religion, making the existence of unregistered popular religion more precarious and hindering the emergence of new temples.

The bureaucratic oversight and intervention following the registration may also stifle the dynamic development of popular religion. In the past, when popular religion operated in a legally ambiguous space, renovations and expansions of temples could actually be carried out more easily—once village cadres gave the green light, they could proceed. Now, for renovations and expansions, temple management must go through cumbersome bureaucratic procedures. Previously, no prior official approval was needed for fairs and consecration ceremonies. Now, organizing religious events of a certain scale requires a complex application and approval process. The act of applying can be burdensome, especially for temples run by elderly individuals with limited education, not to mention the risk of the application being rejected by the risk-averse bureaucracy.

In addition, for the registered temples, the bureaucracy took initiatives to "enhance the quality of folk beliefs." Local officials, under the lingering influence of the dichotomy between religion and superstition, moved to cleanse the registered popular temples of what they deemed "backward elements." For instance, authorities in Hunan prohibited practices like exorcism, possession, and trance dance from taking place at registered temple sites.[28] Officials have also striven to align the values of popular religion temples with what they perceive as "excellent values of Chinese traditional culture" and "core socialist values" and to press the temples to take up a political role in "transmitting positive energies (*zheng nengliang*) to society."[29] In this spirit, officials in Taizhou initiated a project known as "One Temple, One Story" in which cultural workers were dispatched to gather folklore from temples and compile them to highlight values such as harmony, loyalty, and integrity. Furthermore, the local officials moved to decorate popular religion temples with posters and exhibitions displaying political slogans, traditional values, and sanitized stories or legends associated with the temple that could illuminate the values deemed as "positive energies."[30] The Taizhou practice has been emulated by officials in and outside Zhejiang Province. The state's efforts to "elevate and transform" popular religion in today's China has followed a top-down, campaign-style approach. Orchestrated by bureaucrats who have no deep-seated value commitment but aim to score political credit, these efforts remain largely at the formalistic and superficial level. In fact, the official imposition might have produced an alienating effect.

In chapter 3, I argue that the collective bond between popular religion temples and the local community has been deeply eroded by the sweeping changes in rural social life, particularly those brought about by political campaigns in the Mao era and economic reforms in the post-Mao era, compelling popular religion temples to rely on the patronage of individual believers, especially middle-aged and elderly women. This reliance has resulted in a series of significant transformations of popular religion temples, which I describe as feminization, Buddhification, and bifurcation. The legalization of popular religion temples has not changed the structural conditions leading to the weakened communal bonds of territorial cults. To exacerbate the situation, the elderly women—who have been the most devoted patrons of these temples— have steadily declined in number. During my field visits between 2017 and 2024, I was repeatedly told that many of the elderly female worshippers I previously met had passed away.[31] Meanwhile, few younger people have stepped in to take their place. This demographic change raises questions about the long-term sustainability and vitality of many popular religion temples.

It is too early to make an accurate assessment of the impact of the legalization of popular religion temples. Still, it appears that it would increase their bifurcation. Registration has favored big temples over small ones. Furthermore, by tapping into state resources and gaining elite support, managers of large temples would be more capable of exploiting the new political opportunities presented to them. All in all, the new policy cannot change the fate of many small popular religion temples, which have been succumbing to the forces leading to their decline.

President Xi Jinping seems to exhibit more goodwill toward Buddhism than any other religion. He has shown affirmation of Buddhism in his speech to the United Nations Educational, Scientific and Cultural Organization and during meetings with Venerable Xingyun, an influential monk from Taiwan.[32] In any event, under the current administration, Buddhism has been given an important role in the state's project to rejuvenate traditional Chinese culture and build China's soft power. Meanwhile, the state was aware of the problems Chinese Buddhism has been facing and, in particular, recognized the harm wrought by overcommercialization, referring to various profit-making activities during the post-Mao years in which many Buddhist temples have engaged. To tackle this problem, in November 2017, SARA and eleven other departments, including the Ministry of Public Security, issued a directive. This directive set forth ten guidelines aiming to prevent local governments and business interests from exploiting Buddhism and Daoism for commercial gain. It also forbade Buddhist and Daoist temples from seeking profit in the name of religion, enjoining them to "continuously improve the quality of religious personnel and rectify the problems of weak faith and lax discipline."[33]

The role assumed by the state that this document demonstrates is reminiscent of China's imperial past, in which state leadership believed it was responsible for employing government power to uphold the purity of the religions it endorsed. However, as demonstrated earlier, many policies implemented by the bureaucratic apparatus today have led to unintended, even counterproductive, effects. This phenomenon is also pertinent to this case. When implementing the policy to curb the commercialization of Buddhism and Daoism, some local officials—particularly in China's hinterland—have demonstrated rigid conformity or overzealousness, demanding that temples cease all business activities, including selling Buddhist souvenirs or charging accommodation fees to visiting lay Buddhists who stay overnight in temple hostels. Already, elite figures in Chinese Buddhist circles have expressed concerns about this trend, fearing that the policy, if implemented rigidly and excessively, may lead to "economic difficulties for Buddhist temples" (Informant No. 390).

The intent behind the state's efforts to curb commercialization was to foster "healthy development" of Chinese Buddhism and Daoism. However, the reinvigoration of Chinese Buddhism is certainly not something that can be achieved simply by state orders such as those prohibiting commercial activities. Chapter 5 demonstrated how religious competition in Taiwan spurred Buddhist organizations to reform their institutional features and achieve tremendous growth. In post-Mao mainland China, the Buddhist establishment was mostly indifferent to the competitive pressure posed by the rapid expansion of Christianity and was content to use the state's power to combat the challenge from the largest lay sectarian movement inspired by Jingkong's teachings. Consequently, the Buddhist establishment had little incentive to reform its modus operandi to become more akin to the Taiwan model of Chinese Buddhism.

The Chinese Buddhist establishment today still does not recognize the significant competitive pressure from Christianity. As a matter of fact, because the new religious policies and Sinicization campaign appear to be unfavorable toward Christianity, and because the Jingkong movement that posed a strong challenge to the Buddhist establishment has experienced further disintegration, the Buddhist leadership seems to feel even more secure than in the past.

Much more than Christianity, the Chinese Buddhist establishment tends to operate within the parameters set by the state. As a result, the tightening of political control in recent years has led to a surge in self-imposed restraints among Buddhist organizations. For instance, since the revised *Regulations on Religious Affairs* took effect in February 2018, bureaucrats have intensified their crackdown on activities that contravene the regulations. Through various search strategies on the Chinese internet, I discovered that Buddhist temples have essentially ceased hosting summer camps for adolescents. Even the number of Buddhist summer camps for college students has significantly decreased. This finding has been corroborated through conversations with my informants in the Buddhist communities.

Since 2008, the Chinese government has taken measures to curb Jingkong's influence on Buddhist communities in China. After Xi's rise to power, Jingkong openly praised him, even calling him a bodhisattva incarnate.[34] However, this adulation did not prompt the government to lift its restrictions. On the contrary, with heightened concerns over national security and foreign religious infiltration, efforts to suppress Jingkong's influence intensified, ultimately leading to the movement's decline well before his death in July 2022.

However, as with the aftermath of the Shouters' ban, Jingkong's suppression created opportunities for new leaders to emerge. In his absence, preachers mimicking Jingkong's style began competing for followers and influence among lay Buddhists. Lacking formal Buddhist training, some veered into developing teachings far more heterodox than Jingkong's, by the standards of the Buddhist establishment. This highlights how the suppression of one major movement can inadvertently incubate the emergence of new religious movements.

In 2014, following a highly publicized homicide, the Chinese state launched a new wave of campaigns to crack down on "evil cults." Aggressively proselytizing cult followers beat a woman to death in public when she refused to give them her phone number. This horrific crime took place at a McDonald's in the city of Zhaoyuan, Shandong Province, and became known as the Zhaoyuan McDonald's murder case.

Video of the killing, recorded by onlookers with mobile phones, went viral and caused a national uproar. The government claimed the culprits to be followers of the Eastern Lightning (aka the Church of Almighty God), a Christianity-inspired religious movement preaching that Jesus has returned as a Chinese woman and that the righteous are engaged in an apocalyptic struggle against the CCP, which they refer to as the "great red dragon."[35] The Eastern Lightning trains its members to infiltrate Protestant communities by building trust with existing members, slowly revealing doctrines, and converting them. Protestant house churches have been their main targets. In response, many house-church leaders have persistently attacked the Eastern Lightning and actively helped the state to rid their communities of the sect's elements.

From testimonies and journalist interviews of the culprits in the Zhaoyuan murder case, however, it appears likely that they belonged to an offshoot group. The Eastern Lightning follows a pattern typical of NRMs under severe suppression, including adopting the tactics of secrecy and constant fissions. An offshoot group of the Shouters, the Eastern Lightning has generated splinter groups itself. Following the widely publicized murder case, massive arrests of Eastern Lightning members were made across the country.

Fighting against evil cults has been a state policy since 1995, and the Xi administration did not make any major modifications in this regard. If there is any change, it should be attributed to the increased control and surveillance capacity of the state. As a result, it has become even more difficult for NRMs to sustain themselves. The rise of a massive NRM has become highly unlikely at present. For NRMs to have any chance of experiencing substantial growth in such a political environment, the case of Falun Gong suggests that this growth would likely occur in areas where the state remains either oblivious or even inadvertently facilitates their rise. Nevertheless, once NRMs attain substantial growth, they would inevitably attract the state's attention and face suppression.

Overall, state policies toward NRMs, supported by the grid management system and digital surveillance technologies, have forced these groups to operate with even greater secrecy. At the same time, the growing prevalence of bureaucratic formalism in China has redirected the focus of local officials toward formalistic activities, leaving small niches little attended to. Most of the "evil cults" have adapted to this new environment. Although their operations are more restricted than before, they remain active in certain areas.

Moreover, the Chinese religious ecology still offers significant growth potential for NRMs, particularly Chinese syncretic ones. Buddhism and Daoism lack a competitive spirit and strong proselytizing drive. And although Protestantism has been experiencing rapid growth, plenty of niches remain open for NRMs to claim. If opportunities arise, as they did in Republican China or the early reform years of post-Mao China, I would not be surprised by how swiftly these NRMs could rise and spread like wildfire.

CATHOLICISM

For Catholics in China today, the most consequential event for the religion's growth dynamics has to be the China-Vatican deal on the appointment of Catholic bishops in China, signed in September 2018.

Compared with Chinese leaders since Deng Xiaoping, Xi dares more to break with precedent and make bold moves. It so happened that his contemporary, Pope Francis, was also a leader who took big strides. Since his inauguration in 2013, Pope Francis (1936–2025) tirelessly pushed for a thaw in Sino-Vatican relations. In February 2017, China and the Vatican reached a groundbreaking agreement, despite opposition and criticism within the Catholic Church, on the appointment of bishops, overcoming the most daunting obstacle in the way of their rapprochement.[36] Although details of the document remain undisclosed to this day, it has been revealed that a joint China-Vatican commission on bishop appointment was set up; the Chinese side would recommend episcopal candidates, and the Vatican would have veto power.[37] Valid for two years, the agreement was twice renewed, in October 2020 and October 2022. In October 2024, the agreement was again extended, this time for four years. Between 2017, when the deal was first reached, and 2024, when the deal had been thrice renewed, ten new bishops were appointed and consecrated, and the Chinese government officially recognized the public role of several previously unrecognized bishops.[38]

Would the making of the deal, as some within the Church hoped, heal the rift between the underground sector and the official Patriotic sector of the Chinese Catholic communities? Such an eventuality could allow the Catholic Church in China to focus its efforts on pastoral and evangelistic work, ultimately rescuing the institution from its state of stagnation and charting a course toward a brighter future.

The faithful in the Patriotic sector of Chinese Catholicism, to which the majority belong, tend to see more the positive side of the deal because they could finally live openly in full communion with the Roman Catholic Church. For the underground churches, however, the signing of the agreement has pretty much sealed their fate. This is because, unlike in Protestantism, the sole source of religious legitimacy of the Catholic Church is the pope. When some members of Protestant groups are unwilling to be officially registered, they can form their own groups and continue to exist. However, for the underground Catholic Church, the pope explicitly called for unity and urged it to join the official Church, removing any legitimate reason for Chinese Catholics to remain underground. This also cleared the way for government officials to push the defiant priests to submit to the will of the pope.[39] The underground Catholic Church in China has drastically declined as a result.

So far, it seems that the merger of the underground and the official Catholic churches has not brought substantial advancement of Catholicism in China as a whole. First, while Protestantism is decentralized and polycephalous, Catholicism has a centralized hierarchical authority structure. If a Protestant house church is large enough and owns its own properties, the government allows them to be registered as a separate church, and the original church leaders can retain their positions. However, in Catholicism, normally a parish can only have one church. This means that underground churches have no other options except to merge into the Patriotic sector. Second, in a diocese, there can only be one bishop. This means that in situations where both official and underground bishops coexist, a zero-sum game ensues. This made the merger process fraught with conflicts and power struggles. Though reaching the agreement in itself shows goodwill on both sides, it should be recognized that the Vatican and the Chinese state were not on equal footing; the Vatican has fewer bargaining chips but a stronger desire to forge a unified and properly functioning Chinese church in full communion with the pope. Although the deal could help the Chinese government to bring the underground Church under its oversight, a divided and stagnant Catholic Church in China did little harm to its rule. Therefore, the Vatican chose to stick to the deal even after protesting violations committed by the other side.[40]

Let me pose another question: With tightening political control, how much room truly remains for the Catholic Church in China, which has largely absorbed the underground communities, to grow? My short answer is: not that much, especially when compared with Protestant groups. Because of Catholicism's centralized structure, the Chinese government needs to monitor only a small number of priests and bishops to exert control, a task that has become easier following the merger. In contrast, Protestantism's decentralized and polycephalous structure enables widespread evangelism and diverse activities across various church groups. This makes it much harder for the government to effectively control Protestant groups. Therefore, the Chinese state's tightening political control does not help Catholicism close the gap with Protestantism.

PROTESTANTISM

Because of its institutional features, Protestantism, more than China's indigenous or long-indigenized religions, has been experiencing pressure and tension under the new policy. The house/independent churches, in particular, faced increased pressure to register with the government. Although under the Hu Jintao–Wen Jiabao administration (2002–13) the state already began to register independent churches, the current administration has pushed for it with greater rigor.

Under persuasion and pressure, some independent churches chose to register and join the Three-Self sector, whereas others splintered into smaller house-church groups. Similar situations occurred in River County. By 2017, two major independent churches in the county seat—the Rain of Grace Church and the Christian Assembly Church—have become officially registered. Those who did not want to join the registered churches formed their own groups.

Previously, under the Hu–Wen administration, as shown in chapter 1, the independent churches could operate rather openly. Their services drew hundreds of attendees; they were able to rent spaces or even build churches large enough for their sizable congregations and to display crosses and name plaques in conspicuous places. In fact, house churches and government-registered churches became increasingly indistinguishable in their outer appearance. That is why, in chapter 1, I suggested that *independent churches* rather than *house churches* or *underground churches* might be a more fitting name for them. Today, however, it is increasingly difficult for independent churches to openly rent spaces. In many cases, they have been forced to confine themselves to private settings and break into smaller groups. The reality of "house church" has again become closer to its name. Nevertheless, fragmentation into smaller groups is not necessarily bad for the development of Protestantism, because smaller groups can tap into more diversified niches and have even stronger congregational structure.

In chapter 1, I pointed out that independent churches' more dynamic development created pressures on their Three-Self counterparts, galvanizing the latter to emulate their practices. The isomorphic process has considerably animated the Three-Self sector and contributed to the overall development of Protestantism. Now with independent churches joining the Three-Self sector *en masse*, the Three-Self sector has become even more dynamic. In River County, when the Christian Assembly Church, once the largest independent church, merged with the largest Three-Self church, they brought a sizable fund, various other assets, more than a hundred members, competent leaders, and energetic preachers. The effect was noticeable. On a Sunday in June 2019 when I visited the merged church, their Sunday service was attended by more than five hundred people. In addition to Sunday services, the church also held faith training classes for beginners on Wednesdays and Bible study group on Fridays. The church has become active in reaching out to other vibrant Three-Self churches. For instance, every Sunday at 6 a.m., the church dispatched a bus sending around thirty people to attend the Sunday service at the Chongyi Church in Hangzhou, one of China's largest churches. During the Chinese Labor Day in 2019, the church organized a three-day revival meeting, presided over by two pastors from other cities in Zhejiang Province.

My revisits to other Three-Self churches in River County affirm that this sector has been growing in today's China. The church ministered by Qiu, who is in her forties, is a case in point. In 2008–9, their Sunday service was regularly attended by eighty to ninety people. In 2019, the attendance increased to 120–130 people, with one-fourth of them under the age of 50. Along with the membership growth, the church has become more dynamic, with activities almost every day. In addition to a brass band established in 2008, an electronic band was formed in 2017, with investment in musical instruments amounting to 30,000 yuan.[41] Their Christmas celebration has become a public cultural event that in 2018 drew approximately seven hundred participants, including many non-Christians, showing that Christianity has been gaining influence beyond the faithful. Qiu's church is not alone. In fact, the other four Three-Self churches in neighboring towns that I visited in recent years have all enjoyed significant growth. This led Qiu to comment, "Now is the great time for churches to develop. I do not see the need to engage in underground activities" (Informant No. 41).

I queried two other leaders of Three-Self churches about their views of the tightened political control in recent years. Although they admitted it has indeed brought nuisances from time to time, they also emphasized that "things could be managed" (Informant No. 363). They told me that they had no qualms about flying the national flag at their church sites and were not bothered by frequent inspection tours, because they "have nothing to fear or hide" (Informant No. 361). They told me they did have some discomfort about surveillance cameras installed inside the churches but added that they have learned to act as if they were "nonexistent" (Informant No. 361). They also told me that the increasing rules and regulations were not substantive barriers as long as they have their mind set on church growth. And, as the older-generation leaders are passing away, members of the younger generation who have taken the helm of Three-Self churches are more open-minded, energetic, and daring. In fact, they think and behave more like independent church leaders of yesteryear. They openly acknowledged the contribution independent churches had made, calling them "trailblazers" (Informant No. 363). They noted that, without independent churches pushing the envelope in the past, Sunday schools, brass bands, praying for the sick in hospitals, and holding Christian funerals in public spaces would not have been accepted or acquiesced to by the local officials. Now, however, with independent churches hamstrung, it is time for the Three-Self churches to take up the mantle.

Recently, with the ban on public proselytization being more rigorously enforced, activities such as disseminating gospel leaflets on streets or engaging in evangelistic outreach in hospitals and on campuses have visibly decreased. Yet this only drove committed Protestants to carry out proselytization more discreetly. For example, they would visit old-age homes owned and managed by fellow Christians to sing hymns and pray for the residents. Moreover, the ban could not prevent the Protestants from spreading their message through personal networks and one-on-one interactions, which are more effective tactics than public proselytization anyway.

Last but not least, the alarming political environment gave rise to a sense of uneasiness among the Protestants. Especially for house-church members, martyrdom discourse has been more frequently invoked in their meetings, further reinforcing their feelings of precariousness. This heightened pressure turns out to be healthy for the religion. It helps the Protestant community fight against the secularizing tendencies introduced by an affluent society and mitigates the free-rider problem, which has been growing with the increasing attraction of church resources. In addition, the tightened ban on minors attending church services has served to remind the Protestants of the importance and urgency of passing faith on to their children.[42]

In summary, although the regime's policy has forced many independent churches to break into smaller groups, it did not make them disappear. Moreover, the Three-Self church sector has been strengthened and invigorated considerably by those independent churches that have chosen to join it. The increased regulations and restrictions have not dampened the spirit of the Protestant community, nor stalled its growth. On the contrary, the challenges have instilled a sense of crisis, which proves, as it has time and again in history, highly beneficial to the development of Christianity as a whole.

After examining the shifts of religious policy under the Xi administration, it becomes apparent that the current policies still remain broadly consistent with those of previous administrations. The state continues to adhere to the principle of secularism and recognizes the legal status of the five state-sanctioned religions. The intensified bureaucratic control applies to all of the religions, rather than singling out a specific one. However, this does not mean that the expanded control has affected all religions equally. The state has varying strategic considerations for different religions and each religion has its own distinct institutional features. As a result, adherents of each religion have been responding to the changing political environment differently and entering into particularized relationships with the state, giving rise to different growth dynamics.

In my observation, the new policy regime appears to add greater constraints on Chinese Buddhism and Catholicism than on Protestantism. The Chinese Buddhist establishment tends to exercise greater self-restraint in face of tightening control. Catholicism's institutional features allow government bureaucrats to have more effective control over the religion. Protestantism continues to lead in dynamic growth.

Perhaps one of the most important policy overhauls under Xi is the legal recognition of popular religion. This might invite an expectation for rejuvenation of popular religion in China. The reality, however, is more complicated. With official recognition comes stringent oversight and active intervention, which could stifle autonomous development. Moreover, despite the legalization, the underlying issues affecting the vitality of popular religion, in particular the disintegration of communal bonds and the demographic attrition of its most dedicated patron population, remain unchanged.

As for the NRMs, the government's consistent harsh stance, in conjunction with the heightened bureaucratic control, has made them almost entirely disappear from public view. Yet ample evidence suggests that they are still operating covertly but actively in various ways. The current political environment offers little possibility for NRMs to experience the kind of dramatic growth, as seen with the Way of Unity during Republican China and Falun Gong in the 1990s. On the other hand, because the nature of Chinese religious ecology is congenial to the emergence and development of NRMs, their potential should not be underestimated.

Overall, I would suggest that the Xi administration's tightened bureaucratic control and promotion of traditional culture have not stalled the growth momentum of Protestantism, nor have they altered in any significant manner the Chinese religious ecology that crystallized in the preceding post-Mao period.

In the following, I will place the case of China in a broader context of the worldwide expansion of Christianity since the fifteenth century. This contextualization will enhance our understanding of the Chinese experience and demonstrate the broad applicability of my theory and the insights of my perspective.

Expansion of Christianity in a Global Context

The Age of Exploration and Colonization paved the way for the intercontinental movement of Christian missionaries to evangelize the world. The Catholic Church and, later, Protestant denominations dispatched missionaries, intending to convert indigenous populations and establish Christian communities worldwide. However, the reception of Christianity varied significantly across different societies, resulting in widespread success in some and failure in others.[43]

In a hypothetical environment devoid of preexisting social institutions, where all religions engage in open competition, the zero-sum evangelism and congregational structure that are central institutional traits of Christianity would confer a significant advantage to any religion seeking growth and social impact, because these two features generate multiple mechanisms crucial in recruiting and retaining followers. However, such a hypothetical world does not exist—Christianity always enters an environment with preexisting religions and power networks.

The zero-sum evangelism and congregational structure of the Christianity would naturally provoke strong antagonistic reactions not only from the preexisting religious organizations but also from states and social groups closely intertwined with them. Moreover, these institutional features of Christianity may stimulate competitive isomorphism among existing religious actors. Given their social embeddedness and cultural resonance, the indigenous religions, once they strengthen their own proselytization efforts and congregational structures, can often outcompete Christianity in the respective societies.

Thus, understanding the varying receptions of Christianity in different parts of the world and the consequent changes the faith brings to preexisting religious ecologies requires us to analyze the specific religious and sociopolitical contexts, and how the institutional features of Christianity play out in them.

Christianity triumphed in societies in sub-Saharan Africa, the Americas, Oceania, and the Philippines, where weak or very weak local state traditions allowed complete political domination by colonial powers, where the social fabric supporting the preexisting and prevailing religious systems—usually in the form of pre–Axial Age religion or popular religion as defined in this book—was torn apart by the same colonial powers, and where no strong institutional religions capable of adapting and competing with the missionizing Christianity existed. In these societies, Christianity rose to become the single most important religion in the local religious ecology. Even after decolonization, Christianity continued to thrive and assert its predominance in these regions.

In societies where an institutional religion, such as Islam or Buddhism, held a dominant position prior to Western colonization, the outcome was quite different, even though these societies similarly faced the onslaught of colonialism and extensive Christian missionary efforts. Although the local state was dismantled by Western colonial powers, the bond between the major social institutions and the dominant religion, while weakened, did not entirely disintegrate. Moreover, the indigenous religion often played a pivotal role in the anticolonial movement, fostering religious nationalism, and it was often established as the official religion after independence. The newly independent nation-state granted it privileged status and imposed limitations on other religions. In essence, the state reestablished a barrier against Christian missionary activities. As a result, Christianity has not been able to attain a dominant position in the religious ecology of these societies.

In societies such as Turkey, Japan, India, Indonesia, and the Republic of China, the principles of secularism were established as part of the pursuit of a modern nation-state. Although Christianity was allowed to operate, it found itself overshadowed by resurgent native religions and emergent syncretic NRMs rooted in indigenous culture, as the latter, by emulating the institutional features of Christianity, enhanced their competitive edge. Demonstrating remarkable resilience and adaptability in new conditions, they retained their central role within mainstream society. As a result, Christianity has failed to eclipse the indigenous religious systems to secure a prominent place in the religious ecology of these societies.

This broad historical survey demonstrates the wide applicability of my institutions-in-context theory. At the same time, it underscores that to gain a profound understanding of religious change in the contemporary world, we, as sociologists, must fully mobilize our historical imagination by situating our research within a *longue durée* perspective and engaging in historical comparative studies. It also highlights the necessity of adopting a religious ecology perspective to analyze religious change—that is, to juxtapose the development of one religion with others in the field, examine this development through its interreligious relations, and study how the differentiated growth dynamics of major religions might alter the nature of the overall religious ecology. Together, the institutions-in-context theory, historical comparison, and religious ecology perspective form the theoretical and methodological foundation of this book, distinguishing my work from other sociological studies of religion developed since Max Weber.

This broad survey also enables us to discern the unique and challenging situation that China, as a world civilization, faces in modern times. In other world civilizations defined by transcendental world religions, despite the grave challenges brought about by the onslaught of Western colonialism, Christian missions, revolutions, rebellions, wars, regime changes, and tumultuous social upheaval in the modern age, the preexisting dominant religion and its associated institutions managed to survive, adapt to new conditions, and retain predominance within its respective religious ecology. In China, however, the religious ecology that had crystallized in late imperial times—a pluralistic composition with popular religion at the center and other world religions such as Buddhism and Daoism in secondary roles—was unable to remain intact. This was largely because this religious ecology depended heavily on the support of the Confucian state and the backing of Confucian social institutions. When the Confucian scaffolding collapsed during China's coerced modernization process beginning in the early nineteenth century—with the abolition of the civil service examination in 1905, followed by the fall of the Confucian state in the Republican Revolution of 1911, and finally the dismantling of lineage organizations during Maoist China—this religious ecology has lost the institutional foundation necessary to sustain itself.

Viewed from this perspective, we might gain a more nuanced understanding of certain religious policies in present-day China, particularly the state's recognition of Chinese popular religion as a legitimate form of religious expression and its efforts to promote traditional Chinese culture. However, the irony is that these initiatives are being carried out by a rigid, soulless, and formalistic bureaucracy with no deep-seated value commitment, rather than by a combination of genuine societal initiative and state coordination, as seen in the neo-Confucian movement of the Song dynasty. This presents an intractable challenge for China's top policymakers today and serves as a major source of both opportunities and constraints for all religions in China. Ultimately, this sociopolitical context will shape the trajectory of religious development and the nature of Chinese religious ecology in the years to come.

Acknowledgments

Researching and writing about religious change in China has been a long journey for me.

It began in the summer of 2004, when, as a sociology PhD student at the University of Chicago, I joined an expedition team led by Peter Bol of Harvard University to explore the cultural history and religious life in the rural areas of Jinhua Prefecture. This trip changed the course of my academic life. Soon after, I decided to change my dissertation topic from environmental movements in China, on which I had nearly completed fieldwork, to the study of religions in China. Over the years, Peter generously shared his collected materials, deep knowledge, and passion for local history with me. In 2016, he invited me to Harvard as a visiting associate professor to teach two courses on Chinese religions, showing his continued recognition and support of my work.

Since I made the decision to study Chinese religions, I have greatly benefited from the guidance and support of Rob Weller at Boston University. I vividly recall a semester when he offered a weekly reading class on Chinese religions for me, Alison Denton Jones, and Wu Hsin-Chao—three graduate students, none of whom were affiliated with Boston University. Rob's kindness and generosity were matched only by his sharp intellectual discernment. He has always provided thoughtful critiques of my papers, delivered in the most constructive and encouraging manner—a mentoring style I strive to emulate, though I still have much to learn.

I was fortunate that my journey in studying Chinese religions was accompanied by kindred fellow travelers. I was enriched by yet another reading and discussion group formed with Kuo Ya-pei and Lin Wei-pin, occasionally joined by Lee Fong-Mao, Liu Yuan-ju, and Rebecca Nedostup. Ya-pei, teaching at Tufts University at the time, graciously hosted our meetings in her apartment and delighted us with tea, beer, and barley wine. From these anthropologists, historians, and scholars of religious studies, I gained invaluable insights. It was with shock and profound sadness that I learned of Ya-pei's sudden passing in 2023. A person with a big heart, noble character, and infectious laughter, she will forever hold a special place in my memory.

During a project that took so long, I endured one personal loss after another. My mentor at the University of Chicago, Martin Riesebrodt, passed away in 2014. Martin gave his students the utmost freedom to pursue their interests and urged them not to confine themselves to the conventional empirical foci and theories of American sociology of religion. His sociology of conversion class began with a discussion of *The Golden Ass*. His scholarship was grounded in broad historical comparisons, and he defied prevailing trends by arguing that a universal definition of religion was not only possible but also necessary. After I defended my dissertation, Martin congratulated me and encouraged me to turn it into a book right away. However, I wasn't satisfied with my theoretical framework at the time and felt that I needed to include in my study new religious movements and Catholicism in China. I promised him that I would continue my research and improve the writing. Little did I expect that it would take another fifteen years for the book to see the light of day—and that Martin would not be able to see it.

At the University of Chicago, Bruce Lincoln was another professor whose approach to religious studies has been deeply influential to me. I remember one moment in the last class of Theories of Religion, a course he cotaught with Martin. A student asked whether it was possible for an insider of a religion to conduct good research on that religion, and Bruce gave a resounding one-word answer: "No!" This punchy response has stayed with me ever since. It has compelled me to be unrelentingly self-reflexive, reminded me not to fall into the "insider" trap, and spurred me to produce work that balances my intimate understanding of the subject with a necessary critical distance.

I would also like to express my gratitude to Richard Madsen, Ji Zhe, David Palmer, Vincent Goossaert, Chen Jinguo, Philip Clart, Michael Szonyi, Mayfair Yang, and Gareth Fisher, who provided valuable feedback on my papers and presentations and shared their insights on Chinese religions in communications. Many scholars have provided help of various kinds in the late stage of this project. Here I can only mention a few: David Stark, John Hall, Peter van der Veer, Krishan Kumar, and Peter Bang. My appreciation also goes to Feng Shizheng and Zhang Yang. For multiple years, we planned together the Chinese Political Sociology workshops, during which I have learned much from both.

I have been privileged to receive institutional support throughout this journey. In particular, I would like to thank the Society of Fellows at Columbia University for three years of support. At the University of Chicago, the writing group organized by Jenny Trinitapoli provided an atmosphere of undivided attention to writing. The one-year fellowship at the Wissenschaftskolleg zu Berlin (Wiko) was instrumental in helping me to complete and revise the manuscript. Wiko, under Barbara Stollberg-Rilinger and Daniel Schönpflug, provided me with an ideal academic environment as I was trying to push my project to the finish line. My thanks also extend to the members of the writing group we formed there—Barbara Prainsack, Hendrik Wagenaar, Michal Kravel-Tovi, Harry Willekens, Kirsten Scheiwe, and Xu Bin—for their suggestions on how to improve my concluding chapter. My short-term fellowship at The New Institute at Hamburg allowed me to put the finishing touches on the book.

I would like to thank the editors and publishers of *American Journal of Sociology*, *Theory and Society*, *Modern China*, and *Comparative Sociology* for granting me permission to use substantial portions of my previously published articles "The Rise of Protestantism in Post-Mao China: State and Religion in Historical Perspective" (*American Journal of Sociology*, 2017); "Reversal of Fortune: Growth Trajectories of Catholicism and Protestantism in Modern China" (*Theory and Society*, 2019); "Popular Religion in Zhejiang, Southeast China: Feminization, Bifurcation and Buddhification" (*Modern China*, 2014); and "Competition and Isomorphism: Institutional Change of Buddhist Organizations in Chinese Societies" (*Comparative Sociology*, 2025).

This book would not have been possible if the people I encountered in the field had not opened themselves up to me. Their generosity, sincerity, curiosity, and passion have never failed to move me. With many of them, I have formed enduring bonds. It is a regret that their names must remain anonymous. But I am happy to be able to thank a few by name: Venerable Yanzhen, Lee Tsuku, Lei Lei, and Bao Shengyong for their assistance in expanding my access to the Buddhist world; Li Guozhong, Alice Yeh, and Zhang Youguo for their help during my fieldwork on Catholicism; and Hu Zixiang for sharing his expertise on Daoism and popular religion.

Throughout my research, Qiu Min has provided countless forms of assistance—he has been an unfailing friend. My parents, Sun Jianguo and Xu Yuhua, and my brother, Sun Ningfei, have been witnesses to this project from its inception to its completion. They have offered whatever support they could give during my academic journey, and I am grateful for their love and understanding. Now is the time to express my deepest thanks to them all.

My grandmother, Hu Xiuying, an illiterate woman with a strong personality, remarkable memory, and exceptional intelligence, was an endless source of local knowledge for me. In 2001, as I prepared to leave for Chicago to pursue my PhD studies, she took me to the communal temple that safeguards the welfare of the village where I, as a child, lived together with my grandparents. She offered prayers to Guanyin, the main deity. Then, underneath the large camphor tree behind the temple, she scooped up a small handful of soil, wrapped it in red cloth, and asked me to carry it with me wherever I traveled. This pouch of soil embodied her hopes: she sought the protection of our home village's deities for me and wished that, as a sojourner, I would never forget my roots.

When Grandma passed away in 2024 at the age of 96, I felt that the last vestige of her generation—those whose formative years were before 1949—had left us. Over the years, many elderly women and men of her generation, whom I once interviewed, have also faded away. With their passing, a piece of history has vanished. In many ways, I feel I owe them this book—a book that captures the religious world they grew up in and the transformation it underwent during their lifetimes.

In 2016, I returned to China and joined the Sociology Department at Zhejiang University. Overall, the experience has been far from ideal. Shortly after joining, I was "advised" by an authority figure in the department to abandon my interest in the sociology of religion entirely. It also took two years of persistent efforts just to gain departmental approval to offer a course on the sociology of religion. These and other obstacles significantly hindered my work. That said, there were bright moments during my time at Zhejiang University. Under the leadership of Zhao Dingxin, a former University of Chicago professor, the department welcomed a group of like-minded young scholars and the sociology program flourished, giving us all a sense of hope. Unfortunately, this was ephemeral. Everything changed after Dingxin's retirement in spring 2024—a story too painful to recount. Through all of this, it was the aspirations instilled in me during my years at the University of Chicago that sustained me and gave me the determination to complete this book against all odds.

Hence, it is especially meaningful to me that my journey has come full circle with the University of Chicago Press. I thank Elizabeth Branch Dyson for her trust and encouragement in making this book possible and Mollie McFee for her great assistance in the production phase of the book.

If there is one person to whom I owe my deepest gratitude, it is Dingxin. He believed in me and in the value of this project, even when my own confidence wavered. He pushed me forward when my determination faltered.

He has been both my most steadfast supporter and my fiercest critic. His sharp empirical sensibility, unparalleled theoretical imagination, deep understanding of social science methodology, and profound wisdom, alongside his unflinching courage and selfless dedication, have inspired me at every step. Above all, he has, more often than not, placed my work before his own with immense generosity. It would be impossible to detail how Dingxin has helped me along the way, but it is enough to say that this book would not have been completed without his love and support. I dedicate this book to him.

Appendix I: Doing Fieldwork on Religions in China

This appendix outlines my research methods and fieldwork experiences, and offers some reflections.

This book is the product of two decades of fieldwork and research on post-Mao Chinese religions, starting in 2004. The purpose of my project was to map and analyze the changes in the religious ecology in a large part of China predominantly inhabited by the ethnic Han Chinese population. For this purpose, selecting a suitable base for conducting focused fieldwork is crucial. River County, covering more than a thousand square kilometers with a population of more than half a million in central Zhejiang Province in southeast China, was chosen as the site.

The choice of a county rather than a neighborhood, village, township, municipality, prefecture, or province as the base of fieldwork was guided by several considerations. First, unlike a neighborhood, village, township, or municipality, a county in China covers a sufficiently large territory to contain both rural and urban populations and significant religious diversity. Consequently, findings from a county-based study are more likely to offer insights that reflect the broader nationwide situation. Second, a county's size allows for a feasible ethnographic study, essential for a contextualized understanding, whereas a prefecture or province is too vast for in-depth ethnographic work. Third, a Chinese county stands as the lowest level of administration that has nearly all the branches of the functionary departments of the central government, making it ideal for scrutinizing the patterns of interactions between state actors and religious groups.

Although fieldwork in River County laid the foundation for understanding all the religions discussed in this book, there are differences in the scope of fieldwork and the primary data sources chosen for each religion. These distinctions stem from considerations regarding the representativeness of each religion's situation in River County and the specific research questions formulated. For Protestantism, Chinese popular religion, and NRMs, ethnographic and archival data collected in River County constitute the primary source, even though I also undertook field trips outside River County to situate my findings in the national context. However, for Catholicism and Chinese Buddhism, River County is only one of the major field sites, even though work in River County was the starting point. This move was prompted not only by the realization that the River County case no longer adequately illuminates the national situation for these two religions but also by the need to address the research questions crucial to understanding their growth patterns.

The research inquiry for Protestantism focuses on understanding its extraordinary rise in post-Mao China. The experience of Protestantism in River County mirrors the national trend; much like elsewhere, its rapid expansion occurred across both rural and urban areas, encompassing different genders, age groups, and social strata. Notably, the growth rate of Protestantism in River County during the post-Mao period was below the national average. In 1949, Protestants in River County accounted for 0.27 percent of the population, surpassing the national average of 0.2 percent. However, by 2009/2010, the Protestant population in River County reached 3.6 percent, whereas the national average was 4.3 percent. Therefore, if I make an argument about the rapid rise of Protestantism in post-Mao China based on the River County study, my argument will actually be strengthened by the fact that the growth of Protestant population in River County is below the national average. Still, to position my findings about Protestantism in River County within a national context, I conducted fieldwork with church groups in the cities of Beijing, Shanghai, Hangzhou, and Guangzhou as well as in rural areas in Anhui, Fujian, Gansu, Hubei, Liaoning, and Zhejiang provinces, along with the Ningxia Hui Autonomous Region. These research expeditions gave me further confidence that the analysis of Protestantism's growth dynamics in River County offers substantial insights into its nationwide development.

Similar to my examination of Protestantism, my analysis of popular religion relies on my fieldwork in River County, albeit for a different reason. In the case of popular religion, the central research question is to unravel why, in post-Mao China, it could not restore its former grandeur. Although the revitalized popular religion in River County may not exhibit the same vibrancy as seen in places like Fujian and Guangdong provinces, overall, it still far surpasses the national average. A majority of villages in River County have reconstructed their village temples, and many ancestral halls have also been restored. This puts River County way above most places in North China, northeast China, central China, West China, northwest China, and the northern part of Zhejiang Province. Explaining why popular religion in River County, a place with development significantly above the national average, cannot reclaim its past glory, thus sheds considerable light on why, in the post-Mao era, popular religion has been unable to replicate its former prominence nationwide.

River County provides a crucial case study for NRMs. My inquiry revolves around why, despite having numerous advantages, NRMs ultimately failed to establish themselves as a formidable force in the religious ecology of post-Mao China. The two NRMs with the most significant impact in modern Chinese history during their respective periods—the Way of Unity and Falun Gong—thrived in the county which was a significant regional stronghold for both. If we can explain why powerful NRMs eventually dissipated in River County, we can address the question of why they faced a similar fate at the national level.

For Catholicism and Buddhism, I made adjustments to the research methods. The regional variations for the development of the two religions are such that relying solely on research based on River County could lead to biased assessments. Although Catholicism had a sizable following in River County before 1949, with several hundred believers, by the first years of the twenty-first century only a few dozen remained. Although this situation may represent the development of Catholicism in certain regions, there are still areas in China where large Catholic communities concentrate. Thus, in addition to research on the history and current state of Catholicism in River County, I also undertook field trips outside the county. I first extended my research to other areas of Jinhua Prefecture, where the county is located. I then conducted interviews in a Catholic church in the city of Hangzhou, undertook field trips to two Catholic villages in Hebei and Zhejiang provinces, and visited seminaries and churches in Shanghai, Jilin and Guangdong provinces, and Ningxia. This expanded fieldwork allowed me to gain a more comprehensive understanding of the development of Catholicism in China.

Much like Catholicism, Chinese Buddhism exhibits pronounced regional disparities. River County boasts no Buddhist temple with influence extending beyond the county and no well-ordered, sizable monastic community. However, elsewhere there are Buddhist temples serving as renowned pilgrimage destinations and temples hosting large monastic communities. They serve as the major nodes in the nationwide, interconnected network of Chinese Buddhism. Therefore, in addition to researching the past and present of Buddhism in River County, I travelled to other provinces to visit these nodes. In particular, I spent time at influential temples in Jiangxi, Jiangsu, Hunan,

Hebei, and Shanxi provinces. Altogether, I visited sixty-six Buddhist temples and three Buddhist seminaries. The post-Mao era has witnessed the rise of a massive lay Buddhist movement inspired by the teachings of Jingkong. A picture of Chinese Buddhism would be incomplete without properly considering the influence of this movement. I thus conducted fieldwork in five major sites associated with the movement, in Zhejiang, Liaoning, Jiangsu, Anhui, and Gansu provinces and in its Hong Kong headquarters. As I pieced together a more comprehensive picture of the state of Chinese Buddhism, I couldn't help but notice the distinct differences between Chinese Buddhism in the post-Mao era and the religion in the Republic of China and Taiwan. Specifically, while Buddhist organizations in the Republic of China and Taiwan actively sought to reform the institutional features of Buddhism, the Buddhist organization in post-Mao mainland China showed little enthusiasm for such reforms. This divergence is fundamental to understanding the divergent paths taken by Chinese Buddhism in mainland China and Taiwan. Identifying this as a core question in my research on Chinese Buddhism, I delved deeper into investigations of Chinese Buddhism in the Republic of China era and Taiwan. Beyond consulting existing studies, I used primary sources, including memoirs, biographies, and chronicles of prominent figures in the Chinese Buddhist world, along with Buddhist periodicals, to comprehend the situation of Chinese Buddhism in the Republican era. In addition, I made field trips to major Buddhist organizations in Taiwan, including Fo Guang Shan, Tzu Chi, Dharma Drum Mountain, and Chung Tai Chan Monastery, and visited their overseas branches in Boston and New York.

The most intensive phase of fieldwork in River County was carried out between 2006 and 2009. After 2009, I returned frequently to track religious developments, except in the years of 2014, 2017, 2018, and 2020. Several of my key informants, with whom I have formed lasting friendships, have kept me updated on new developments. My fieldwork on Catholicism outside River County was carried out mainly in 2011, 2015–16, and 2018. For Chinese Buddhism outside River County, the most intensive phase of fieldwork was conducted in 2007, 2009, 2010, and 2013.

Participant observation and interviews are the two main methods I have employed in the field. The purpose of participant observation was not only to gather information, reach a contextualized understanding, establish acquaintance and trust, and verify what was learned from the interviews, but also to immerse myself in the religious community to learn their knowledges, languages, ways, and ethos. I participated in a wide range of activities organized by religious groups, including Sunday worship services, Catholic Mass, Buddhist repentance rituals, temple festivals of popular religion, qigong practices, religious holiday celebrations, Bible study groups, interchurch revival meetings, youth camps, sutra chanting, meditation retreats, funerals and weddings, home visitations, pilgrimage trips, inauguration ceremonies, consecration rituals, closed-door meetings, and conferences (including the World Buddhist Forum in Wuxi in 2009). I took every opportunity available to immerse myself as much as I could in the field. For instance, as many Buddhist temples provide accommodations for the laity, I chose to stay in a temple rather than a hotel when doing fieldwork on Chinese Buddhism. Hence, I had the experience of staying in sixteen different Buddhist monasteries. During the stays, which lasted from two days to several months, I lived by the rigorous schedule of the monastery, participated in the religious life, volunteered labor, and mingled with people.

I conducted a total of 405 semistructured interviews during the fieldwork. Among my interviewees are rank-and-file religious practitioners and their coworkers, relatives, and neighbors; religious leaders (including some of national prominence); officials and retired officials in charge of religious affairs at different administrative levels; and local cadres working at the township and village levels. I took time to prepare and refine interview guides. Preparation and further development of the interview guides provided an opportunity to reflect on what had already been learned and what needed further exploration, to contemplate the theoretical framework and research questions, and to consider strategies for asking questions during interviews. Although the interview guide kept me focused and enabled me to cover every major aspect, in real practice, I was inclined to let the interview flow like an open-ended conversation rather than a rigid Q&A session. I was alert during the interviews to cues that would prompt me to reformulate the next questions or even change the direction of the interview entirely.

Much information, including serendipitous discoveries and enlightening insights, also arose from the numerous casual conversations I struck up. On occasion, I also employed focus-group interviews when the opportunity presented itself.

My fieldwork experience was, overall, very fruitful and rewarding. Over the course of two decades of immersion in the field, I have acquired the ability to communicate effectively with practitioners of each religion, using their respective jargons; built up extensive knowledge of the history, teachings, and practices of each religion and the organizations, institutions, networks, and power dynamics of the religious world; developed rapport with many of my informants and formed enduring bonds with some; developed an empathetic understanding of my informants, both religious actors and bureaucrats; and gained insight into their concerns, fears, and hopes.

The depth of my knowledge allows me to pick up crucial clues and subtle nuances, sometimes leading to important discoveries. For instance, I immediately realized that two young women who attempted to proselytize me on the street were associated with the Eastern Lightning, a Christian-related NRM, rather than Protestantism when they said that "the Lord has returned to China to work."[1] Followers of the Eastern Lightning, demonized by both the Chinese government and Protestant groups, act secretively and hide themselves from public view. Before this encounter, I had no access to the group. I thus decided to take advantage of the occasion. Pretending that I was unfamiliar with their religion but curious enough to learn a little, and showing my appreciation for their religious commitment, I struck up a long conversation in which I inquired into their family background, their conversion experience, and their journey as devoted missionaries. Sometimes, serendipitous discoveries came from casual conversations with acquaintances. One day my mother-in-law was recounting to me her devotion to Buddhism when she was a teenager living in the Republican period. She mentioned that everyone in the assembly wore a blue robe and chanted *King Gao's Sutra on Avalokiteśvara* (*Gaowang guanyin jing*).[2] The details caught my attention and prompted me to suspect that the religion she was practicing might not be Buddhism but one of the NRMs that existed in the Republican period. Upon further probing, it turned out that she was indeed a follower of a Chinese syncretic NRM called the Moral Society of the Middle Way (Zhongjiao Daoyi Hui), along with many of her relatives. This discovery, surprising to the family who have always thought she was a Buddhist, allowed me to gain a vivid understanding of how pervasive NRMs were in Shanghai in the Republican era.

With this level of insight and understanding, I was able to win respect from my informants, who gradually became more forthright with me. Admittedly, some interviewees accepted my interview requests only out of courtesy or because of some ties we shared. They could act impatiently or dismissively. This often happened, for instance, when I interviewed government officials—at the start of the conversation, they wanted only to rush to the end. Yet after I demonstrated solid knowledge about the subject matter, casually dropping a few insights unknown to the interviewees, and showed my understanding of the difficulties entailed in their position, they changed their attitude. One retired RAB official who maintained high vigilance in the beginning of the interview was amazed by how much I knew and began to answer my questions in a much more candid manner. In fact, he explained the reason behind his behavioral change using a Chinese idiom: "One won't lie in front of a person who knows the truth (*zhenren mianqian bushuo jiahua*)." My research experiences over the years have made one thing clear to me: although many interview manuals emphasize the importance of building trust, they often overlook the power dynamics at play between interviewer and interviewee. In this game, it is knowledge and understanding more than anything else that empowers the interviewer.

I have also encountered numerous difficulties in the field, with each religion presenting its unique set of challenges. Foremost among these is the issue of access. This issue was most pronounced for fieldwork on Protestant house churches, NRMs, and underground Catholic church communities. Due to legal barriers that the people of these religious groups were facing, it is understandable that they wanted to remain low key and harbored suspicions about an outsider like me.

In River County, my ability to speak the local dialects and my rootedness in local networks were assets. My connections led me to leaders of house churches and former Falun Gong practitioners and played a crucial role in their acceptance of my fieldwork requests. The most formidable access challenge arose in finding underground priests in Hebei Province, a stronghold of the underground Catholic Church, where I had no known ties. Undeterred, I decided to place faith in the theory of six degrees of separation, which posits that any two individuals on the planet can be connected by a chain of acquaintances roughly six links long. I asked around among my acquaintances about their Hebei connections. One day I had luck! A visiting scholar at the University of Chicago disclosed that he had relatives residing in a town in Hebei Province who were well acquainted with some underground priests. Thanks to the kindness of his relatives, who contacted the priests on my behalf, I was able to meet with them. They graciously agreed to interview requests and even introduced additional interviewees to me. The power of weak ties has clearly proven itself in my fieldwork.

Getting interviewees to speak candidly during interviews can be another significant challenge because they often have their own agendas and concerns. This challenge was particularly pronounced when, for instance, interviewing devout members of Protestant house churches. In such cases, interviewees are often more eager to convert me than to be interviewed. I often had to work diligently to redirect their evangelistic persuasions toward questions of my concern rather than letting the interview slide into an occasion for personal testimony. Employing interview skills, such as building the life history of the interviewees rather than directly asking the reasons for their conversion, can be helpful, but it may not always be effective, especially when facing strong-willed evangelists. On one such occasion, before I could even pose any questions, the leader of a house church placed his hands on my head and began to pray enthusiastically for me, asking God to bless me and open my heart. On another occasion, at the beginning of an interview, a leader of a house church straightforwardly asked whether I was a fellow Christian. When my answer was not affirmative, he chastised me for wasting time on a meaningless, worldly research project instead of seeking the eternal truth. Occasions such as these did bring me moments of discomfort, but they were highly valuable because they allowed me to get a visceral sense of how individual followers' behaviors could be profoundly shaped by their religion's institutional features.

As a religious outsider to Protestantism, I also encountered suspicion and mistrust when interviewing some Protestant house-church leaders. On one occasion, when I was interviewing such a leader in his home, his wife, also a core member of the church, came in, sat by his side, and frequently kicked him under the table, signaling that she did not want him to speak with me too candidly.

There were also occasions when I faced suspicion during interviews with Buddhists. In 2013, I tried to interview a leader of the Jingkong movement in northwest China when the movement was under scrutiny from the state. Initially, she rejected my request, suspecting me of being an undercover journalist. She only agreed, reluctantly, when I demonstrated in-depth knowledge of Jingkong's teachings and her role in the movement. However, she did not ask me to sit down; the interview took place with both of us standing awkwardly in a reception room. Her responses to my questions were terse, her face looked stern, and her assistant continually urged me to wrap up quickly. In this interview, I managed to ask only ten questions.

When candid formal interviews were hard to come by, I devoted more time to participant observation and gleaning information from casual chats. For instance, to understand the network structure, organizational features, and ground-level activities of the Jingkong movement, I took research trips to five major sites inside China, spending days in each one of them. As for the Protestant house-church groups, frequent attendance at their meetings and other activities turned me into a familiar face. Over time, even avid evangelists began to ease up when interacting with me. They were no longer acutely mindful of my nonbeliever status, and, in casual conversations, let down their guard.

Although my outsider status sometimes stood in the way during my fieldwork on Protestant house churches, my somewhat insider status in Buddhism became a double-edged sword. My preexisting knowledge of Buddhism and my connections within the broader Buddhist community allowed me to quickly gain trust and respect. This proved highly advantageous. However, it also came at a cost; my prior understanding of Buddhism at times hindered me from delving deeper, as I assumed I already knew enough. And I found myself strongly committed to certain values and biases without realizing it. Only upon reviewing my notes, and particularly during the writing and re-writing processes, did I begin to acknowledge my blind spots. I asked myself again and again: Has my appreciation of certain values entailed in "Human-istic Buddhism," a modernist Buddhist movement that believes Buddhism should become more engaged with this world, led to a biased understanding of Buddhism that takes other forms? It took a considerable amount of time for me to cultivate detachment and become mindful of my bias. To be sure, during fieldwork, it is imperative for a researcher to scrutinize one's research agendas, hypotheses, positions, and hidden assumptions. However, when it came to Buddhism, peeling away my own biases proved to be particularly challenging.

Among all the religions examined, popular religion was most accessible to me. Research on it requires minimal prior connection. Participants of this religious community, typically consisting of middle-aged and elderly women, were easygoing and accepting. I could mingle and chat with them when they were preparing a meal in the temple kitchen or folding joss-paper ingots.

Reflecting on the challenges that emerged during my fieldwork for popu-lar religion, I cannot help but recall two major health-related scares I experi-enced. During one of the incidents, I was visiting a temple located by a vast rice paddy. The manager warmly welcomed me, opening every hall for me to visit. However, upon stepping into a hall that had been locked for nearly a year, I was hit by an overwhelming mildew smell. Instantly, I felt acute pain in my throat. Even the slightest movement brought unbearable pain. I fled the site, leaving the friendly elderly lady bewildered. I took a taxi to the county hospital for urgent care and was diagnosed with acute pharyngitis.

In another instance, I attended a consecration ritual for a newly built popular religion temple, a bustling event attended by thousands. Following a communal meal, I experienced sharp abdominal cramps and had to rush to a makeshift toilet. Succumbing to constant urges, I found myself unable to leave the toilet. In the end, I became dehydrated. It was already midnight. The temple was in the middle of nowhere. And no medication was available. The worried people brought a spirit medium to treat me—as it turned out, there were quite a few spirit mediums in the crowd! In a low yet powerful voice, the spirit medium commanded various spirits to leave my body, her hands gently massaging me. The exorcism ritual drew a big crowd of observers. The researcher became part of the spectacle.

Reflecting on these two incidents occurring only a month apart, it dawned on me that they may not be unrelated. Popular religion temples in rural China usually were not well maintained, with little attention paid to hygiene. Even though I grew up in the rural part of River County as a child, speak local dialects, have close and extensive relationship ties, can interact with different people with ease, and would very much like to see myself as one of the locals, my body, hypersensitive to the environment, suggested otherwise. Such em-bodied experiences led me to realize, with some sadness, that after all I was no longer one of them, and that a sojourner can never truly return home. Nevertheless, I also became aware that this simultaneous insider-outsider identity is a blessing to me as a researcher.

Appendix II: Primary Sources Consulted for the Religions Analyzed in the Book

I have consulted primary sources when researching religions analyzed in the book. Below are some common sources for all religions:

Wenshi ziliao (*The cultural and historical documents*), a collection of oral histories and historical documents published annually since the 1980s by the Committee of the Chinese People's Political Consultative Conference of River County;

The periodical *Local Gazetteers of River County* published by the River County Gazetteers Office since the early 2000s;

The Gazetteers of River County, published in 1983 and 2013.

The following table lists the materials I consulted for each specific religion.

TABLE A.1. Primary Sources Consulted for Studying Each Religion

	Primary sources
Protestantism	Missionary reports from *Baptist Missionary Magazine* published by the American Baptist Missionary Union
	Reports by missionaries of China Inland Mission
	Changkai de men (*The Open Door*), the 19-issue publication of internal correspondence of the Local Church 1938–39
	Archival materials of Protestant groups in the Bureau of Archives of River County
Catholicism	Materials compiled by church historians such as *Zhejiang Tianzhujiao shilue* (*Brief History of Catholicism in Zhejiang*) and *Zhejiang sheng zongjiao zhi ziliao huibian* (*A Collection of Materials on the Religious History of Zhejiang Province*)
	Memoirs of Bishop Jin Luxian and Celso Costantini, who served as apostolic delegate to China 1922–33
	Archival materials of the Catholic community in the Bureau of Archives of River County

(continues)

TABLE A.1. *(continued)*

	Primary sources
Chinese popular religion	Local gazetteers of River County composed in late imperial China, the first in 1510 and the last in 1889. Each gazetteer includes a section describing temples and shrines in the locality, a section on local customs, and a section on official rituals and altars
	During the Republican era, River County was an experimental county (*shiyan xian*) designated by the government and subjected to county-wide social investigations, producing valuable information about popular religion temples and lineage organizations
	Record of Local Culture (*Wenhua zhi*) of all 50 townships and towns in River County published 1987–88
	Record of Local Customs (*Fengsu zhi*) of River County
	Gazetteers of several towns and villages of River County
	Leaflets or gazetteers of several large temples
	Inscriptions on stone steles for the popular religion temples
	Genealogy records of several lineages
New Religious Movements	Archival materials of the Way of Unity in the Bureau of Archives of River County and other localities
	Works by Li Hongzhi
	Falun Gong publications and information on its websites
	Chinese media reports on Falun Gong
Chinese Buddhism	*Minguo Fojiao qikan wenxian jicheng* (*Collection of Republican-era Buddhist Periodical Literature*), published 2006, and its supplement, compiled by Huang Xianian and associates, published 2007
	Memoirs, biographies, chronicles, and writings of prominent figures in the Chinese Buddhist world
	Fayin, the official journal of the Buddhist Association of China, and other Buddhist periodicals
	Transcripts and audiovisual materials of the teaching of Jingkong and his disciples
	Inscriptions on stone steles at Buddhist temples

Notes

Introduction

1. The book does not include a separate chapter on Daoism, though it comes up frequently in different places.

2. The ethnic Han people constituted about 91 percent of the Chinese population according to the 2021 census. Regions in China's northwest and southwest as well as Tibet, which are significantly populated by non-Han ethnic groups, have religious ecologies with distinct features and histories. Therefore, these regions merit separate treatment.

3. 1949 marked the establishment of the People's Republic of China by the Chinese Communist Party (CCP). This event ushered in the Mao era, characterized by the leadership of Mao Zedong (1893–1976), who was China's paramount leader at the time. Mao's death in 1976 signaled the end of this era. Following Mao's death, Deng Xiaoping (1904–97) ascended to power. After 1978, Deng initiated a series of reforms that propelled China toward economic development and greater integration with the global economy. This period, known as the post-Mao era, is also referred to as the era of reform and opening-up.

4. See Clart (2013) for an overview of the religious ecology perspective and its application in studying Chinese religions.

5. Following the convention of most historians, I designate the beginning of the Ming dynasty (1368–1644) as the commencement of late imperial China. This decision is grounded in the observation that although numerous characteristics now recognized as indicative of late imperial China emerged during the Song dynasty (960–1279), they truly flourished only during the Ming dynasty. For more details, please refer to the section on the religious ecology of late imperial China later in this chapter. The period came to its end when China's last imperial dynasty, the Qing (1644–1912), was overthrown in a revolution, which led to the establishment of the Republic of China (1911–49).

6. The switchman metaphor is from Weber ([1915] 1946, p. 280), and the tracklayer metaphor is from Mann (1986, p. 341). Both are employed to underscore the role of world religions in guiding societies along distinct paths and contributing to the divergence of world civilizations.

7. This methodological choice is influenced by Dingxin Zhao's insights. He argues that research based on a single or very limited number of questions often faces the problem of overdetermination—when a question can be answered in multiple, if not endless, coherent and plausible ways. To mitigate this, Zhao advocates for a research strategy that raises as many

research questions—or questions containing as much information—as possible and answers them through a theory or analytical framework that is parsimonious, employing "as little explanatory apparatus as possible" (Zhao 2015, p. 5). The empirical validity of such a theory can then be assessed by the range of variations it is capable of addressing (Zhao 2015, pp. 24–25).

8. Notable exceptions are Goossaert and Palmer (2011) and Dubois (2005), which also examine wide-ranging religious practices. Goossaert and Palmer also explicitly adopt the term *religious ecology* in their important book. What distinguishes the present book from these works is its greater focus on the post-Mao period and on analyzing changes in the religious ecology through posing sociological puzzles and providing a theoretical framework that can be consistently used to explain these puzzles and has broad applications beyond the case of China.

9. The following are some examples: Hunter and Chan (1993), Cao (2010), Reny (2018), and Vala (2018) for Protestantism; Madsen (1998) and Lozada (2001) for Catholicism; Fisher (2014) for Chinese Buddhism; Dean (1995) and Chau (2006) for Chinese popular religion; Jones (2017) for Daoism; Palmer (2007), Ownby (2008), Tong (2009), and Dunn (2015) for NRMs.

10. See chapter 3 for details of the popular religion revival thesis.

11. See https://www.pewresearch.org/religion/2011/12/19/table-christian-population-as-percentages-of-total-population-by-country (accessed October 1, 2023).

12. This functionalist view of religion was most elaborately expounded in Durkheim's *The Elementary Forms of Religious Life* ([1912] 1955), but can also be seen in his *Suicide* ([1897] 1951) and *The Division of Labor in Society* ([1893] 1964).

13. Weber's ([1922] 1963) *The Sociology of Religion* also explores the formation of distinct religious ethics in different world religions.

14. The lack of attention to the strength and growth dynamics of religions could become problematic for Weber's followers, who tried hard to identify functional equivalents to the "Protestant ethic" in non-Western societies and argued for their relevance to modern industrialization. Bellah (1957), for example, suggested that Shingaku in Tokugawa Japan (1603–1867) provided one of the cultural foundations that allowed Japan to rapidly transform into a modern industrial society. However, this argument was made without conducting a solid investigation into "the place of this sect in Japanese society, its organizational forms, and its relationships with established religion" (Bell 1959).

15. For the original formulation of the secularization theory, please refer to Berger (1967), Wilson (1979), and Dobbelaere (1981). For later significant synthesis or adaptation, see Bruce (2002), Norris and Inglehart (2004), and Casanova (2011). See also Gorski (2000).

16. See Glock (1964) and Glock and Stark (1965) for the formulation of the deprivation theory. According to Glock and Stark (1965, p. 246), deprivation is "any and all of the ways that an individual or group may be, or feel, disadvantaged, in comparison to other individuals or groups, or to an internalized set of standards."

17. See Durkheim's ([1897] 1951) book and Merton's (1938, 1957) work.

18. Some examples are Lofland and Stark (1965); Lofland (1966); Beckford (1978); Greil and Rudy (1984); Snow and Machalek (1984).

19. Kelley (1972).

20. The institutional argument is also widely employed in disciplines outside sociology to explain the growth dynamics of religions. For instance, the explosive spread of Pentecostalism in Latin America and Africa is often attributed to various institutional features that enable the religion to attract converts. These features include the resonance between Pentecostalism and local religious practices, the church's provision of supernatural healing, its role as a surrogate family,

and its emphasis on family-oriented values (Burdick 1993; Brusco 1995; Miller and Yamamori 2007, pp. 22–25). This suggests that attributing a religion's success or failure to its institutional features is a not uncommon perspective.

21. For significant developments and comprehensive presentation of the rational choice theory of religion, see Stark and Bainbridge (1987); Iannaccone (1991); Stark and Iannaccone (1994); Stark and Finke (2000). For important critique of this theory, see Bruce (1999); Bryant (2000); Jerolmack and Porpora (2004); Sharot (2012); van der Veer (2012); McKinnon (2013); Sun (2017a).

22. The rational choice theorists claim that their entire theoretical framework is derived from a single basic axiom: human beings are utility maximizers who weigh cost and benefits when making decisions. They also assume that people always desire otherworldly rewards and have constant religious need. Consequently, according to the theory, individuals' choice of and commitment to religion are influenced by the quality of religious goods provided by religious organizations. Religions that offer higher-quality goods tend to attract more committed followers, allowing the religions to grow stronger and outcompete others. As we can see, central to the theory is the supply-and-demand dynamics of the "religious market." Hence, the rational choice theory of religion is also known as the theory of religious economy. And, due to its emphasis on the supply side, it is also known as the supply-side theory.

23. Stark (1996).

24. Finke and Stark (1992).

25. Stark (2001).

26. Stark and Neilson (2012).

27. The rational choice theorists regard their propositions as constituting a "general theory" of religion with universal applicability.

28. Stark and Finke (2000).

29. My institutions-in-context approach can also be understood as an "institutions-in-time" theory because the significance as well as the causal directions of the institutional features of a given organization are conditioned by sociopolitical and/or geopolitical circumstances of a specific historical moment in which the organization is situated.

30. Tilly (1992, p. 1).

31. For analyses of how major premodern empires in Eurasia, after adopting a state religion, were compelled or enabled by the nature of that religion to pursue policies toward nonstate religions or manage religious diversity within their territories, leading to varying religious ecologies and even the divergence of civilizations, see Sun and Zhao (2019) and Sun (2019b).

32. See Asad's (2003) critical examination of secularism's assumptions and implications.

33. Schiller (1996).

34. See Josephson's (2012) book on the introduction of the Western concept of religion to Meiji Japan and its wide-ranging and far-reaching implications.

35. See Chen (1999) and Sun (2013) on Confucianism, and Nedostup (2009), Goossaert and Palmer (2011), and Poon (2011) on temple cults.

36. *Secularism* here refers to a way of structuring the state-religion relationship that emerged historically in the West in the eighteenth century. It is an institutional arrangement designed to keep religion out of state affairs. In a secular state, political legitimacy is not based on religion, no religion is established as the state or official religion, and the government's operations—including legislation, jurisdiction, and administration—are free from religious control. Secular states could adopt different approaches to religion. For example, some states, like the United

States of America, practice what Ahmet Kuru (2009) calls *passive secularism*, where the state adopts a passive stance on a religion's role in the public sphere, allowing the public visibility of religion. In contrast, some states, such as France, practice *assertive secularism*, where the state plays an assertive role in excluding religion from the public sphere. Despite their differences, both passive and assertive secular states refrain from intervening in religion within the private sphere. In addition, some secular states may adopt what is sometimes referred to as *radical secularism*, aiming to contain, control, or suppress religion in both public and private spheres, often in pursuit of what they consider to be the greater good of society.

37. Finke and Stark (1992, pp. 230–31).

38. Stark and Finke (2000, p. 219).

39. Gorski (2003, p. 115).

40. For instance, Islamic empires' differential treatment of Muslims and non-Muslims had induced non-Muslims' conversion to Islam for economic and political benefits (Lapidus 2002, p. 271).

41. For instance, the Byzantine emperor presided over ecumenical councils, wielded decisive power in appointing patriarchs, and determined territorial boundaries for their jurisdiction. See "Caesaropapism," *Encyclopaedia Britannica*, https://www.britannica.com/topic/caesaropapism (accessed August 17, 2024); and Hussey (2010).

42. For instance, the early spread of Christianity piggybacked on the communication channels of the Roman Empire (Mann 1986, pp. 310–17). Similarly, Christian missionaries in the Age of Exploration took advantage of military advances and the infrastructures built by the colonial powers (Hastings 1994, p. 404).

43. For example, in Chinese popular religion, many deities were envisioned as celestial counterparts to imperial bureaucrats, organized in a hierarchical pantheon led by the Jade Emperor. Their status was subject to promotion and demotion based on their performance, similar to bureaucratic appointments (Wolf 1974). Similarly, the organizational structure of the early Christian Church was significantly influenced by Roman administrative systems and political institutions. See "History of Early Christianity," *Encyclopaedia Britannica*, https://www.britannica.com/topic/history-of-early-Christianity (accessed August 17, 2024); and Strand (1992).

44. For instance, the US Immigration and Nationality Act of 1965, which ended racially restrictive immigration quotas, led to a sharp increase in immigrants from Latin America and Asia. This influx triggered significant religious changes in American society: the European foundations of American Christianity were reshaped, world religions other than Protestantism, Catholicism, and Judaism began to take hold, and NRMs inspired by Asian religions emerged (Finke 2006).

45. Mann (1984); Zhao (2001, p. 18).

46. This would be the overarching scheme that guides my analysis of Protestantism, Catholicism, popular religion, and NRMs.

47. To maintain concision in my presentation within this book, I sometimes employ a practice commonly found in historical comparative studies. This involves resorting to *reification*, wherein I attribute "a unity of unitary interest, rationale, capacity, and action" to both the state and religions (Tilly 1992, p. 34). It is important to note that this does not imply a disregard for the inherent complexity of reality.

48. I have adapted Mann's (1986) concept of *interstitial development* into the term *interstitial social space*, which I have used on several occasions (e.g., Sun 2017a). In my understanding, *interstitial social space* denotes social spaces not effectively controlled by or lying outside the control of the state. Although this concept is important, it is not the foundation of my theory.

Instead, it represents just one of many sociopolitical contexts created by the activities of the post-Mao state. Understanding the complex and varied patterns of religious development in post-Mao China requires more than just this concept. For works that have used *interstitial space* or its sister *gray area* as the core analytical concept to analyze post-Mao Chinese society, see Lin (2008) and Zhou (2023).

49. *Axial Age religions* refers to the major religious and philosophical systems that emerged between 800–200 BCE, along with their key derivatives. These traditions introduced individual spirituality, universal ethics, transcendence, and shifting from tribal or local practices to broader, abstract, and universal concepts. Emphasizing salvation, enlightenment, and philosophical inquiry, they laid the foundation for many of the world's major religious traditions. Notable examples include Zoroastrianism, Judaism, Buddhism, Confucianism, Daoism, Greek philosophy, and later developments such as Christianity and Islam. They continue to shape spiritual and intellectual thought today. In many ways, we still live under the enduring influence of Axial Age religions (see Jaspers [1949] 1953; Armstrong 2006; Bellah and Joas 2012).

50. *Territorial cult* refers to a form of religious practice organized around the worship of deities or spirits associated with specific geographic areas, such as villages, towns, or regions. These cults are deeply ingrained in the local community's social and cultural life, and they typically focus on the protection, prosperity, and well-being of the area and its inhabitants. See chapter 3 for a more detailed introduction.

51. Yang (1961).

52. Zhao (2015).

53. Zhao (2015, pp. 342–46).

54. Here I use Martin Riesebrodt's definition of religion (Riesebrodt 2010, p. 72).

55. Regarding the standard of apotheosis, the most relevant passage from the *Book of Rites* reads: "According to the institutes of the sage kings regarding sacrifices, offerings should be made to those who have enacted beneficial laws for the people, who have labored to the point of death in their duties, who have strengthened the state through their tireless efforts, who have successfully managed major calamities, and who have averted great evils" (Book XX: The Law of Sacrifice). This English translation has been slightly modified from Legge's 1885 translation.

56. Hansen (1990, pp. 88–89).

57. The civil service examination before the Song dynasty was much smaller in scale. During the Northern Song dynasty (960–1127), it was much expanded. For instance, in 977 only about 5,200 candidates participated in the capital examination; by 992, the figure rose to 17,300. For the prefecture-level examination, the number of candidates rose from 80,000 in the eleventh century to 400,000 by the thirteenth century (Ge 2001, p. 271). See Zhao (2015, pp. 331–46) for an account of the roles of civil service examination in the Confucianization process of Chinese society during and after the Song.

58. See Kasoff (1984), Bol (1992), Yu (2004), and Zhao (2015, pp. 331–46) for the differences between the traditional Confucian classics and the neo-Confucianism canon.

59. See Brook (2005, p. 8) for this concept, and Rankin (1986), von Glahn (1993), Schirokauer and Hymes (1993), and Bol (2008) among others for this view.

60. On the neo-Confucian institution-creating and community-building projects, see also De Bary and Chaffee (1989); Ebrey (1991); Bol (2008).

61. Bol (2008, pp. 256–61); Chang (1988, 2001, 2003).

62. David Faure (2007) documents how the lineages became the dominant institutional form by which the local society was organized in the Pearl River Delta from the sixteenth to the

eighteenth century. He shows that this process was associated with the building of ancestral halls where collective sacrifice to common ancestors took place.

63. In the works of Zhenman Zheng (2001), Michael Szonyi (2002), and Yonghua Liu (2013), it becomes evident that in the Ming and Qing dynasties, the expansion of the lineage organizations, the proliferation of ancestral halls, the institutionalization of ancestral rituals, and the establishment of the territorial cults were deeply intertwined and mutually reinforcing.

64. The White Lotus Rebellion (1796–1804) and the Taiping Rebellion (1851–64) are two of the most significant examples.

Chapter 1

1. Bays (2012, p. 37).

2. Dunch (2001, p. 198).

3. Stockwell (2002, p. 100).

4. Bays (2012, p. 147).

5. Estimates of the Protestant population in China around 2010 vary widely, from a low of 23.05 million, provided by the Chinese Academy of Social Sciences (CASS) based on a national survey (Research Group from the Institute of World Religions, CASS, 2010), to a high of 130 million reported by *Christian Today* in 2010 (http://www.christiantoday.com/article/church.in .china.experiencing.tremendous.growth/26420.htm, accessed July 7, 2015). The CASS survey has been criticized for vastly underestimating the number of Protestants affiliated with independent churches that are not officially registered (Liu 2014), and the *Christian Today* figure has not been substantiated. The estimate of fifty-eight million Protestants in 2010, which is adopted in this chapter, comes from the Pew Research Center's Forum on Religion and Public Life and has been well received by scholars in both the United States and China. For details on the methodology behind this estimate, see https://www.pewresearch.org/wp-content/uploads/sites/7/2011/12 /ChristianityAppendixC.pdf (accessed July 7, 2015). The Pew estimate is further supported by a national survey carried out in 2007 by Horizon, a reputable polling firm in China. Based on a sample of 7,021 individuals, the Horizon survey initially estimated 28 million Protestants in China. However, after facing similar criticisms for not accounting for the high percentage of Christians who refused to be interviewed or concealed their religious identity due to concerns over political risks, a follow-up study was conducted. This adjustment revised the estimate to slightly more than sixty million (Stark and Wang 2015).

6. Hunter and Chan (1993); Leung (1999); Aikman (2003); Huang and Yang (2005); Yang (2005); Huang (2012).

7. Huang (2013; 2014).

8. Chen and Huang (2004); Cao (2007, 2010).

9. Hua (2008); Xie (2010).

10. Potter (2003); Leung (2005).

11. Bays (2012, pp. 48, 75–76, 108).

12. Sun Yat-sen (1866–1925), founding president of the Republic of China, and his successor Chiang Kai-shek (1887–1975), leader of the Nationalist government from 1928 to 1949, were both Protestant Christians. The inaugural 1913 Republican parliament included 60 Christians among 274 members, while Chiang's 1929 cabinet had seven Christians in a ten-member lineup (Goossaert and Palmer 2011, pp. 70–72). For more detailed discussions on the political elite's support for Christianity, particularly Protestantism, during the Republican era, see chapter 5.

13. Nedostup (2009, pp. 36–37).

14. Goossaert and Palmer (2011, pp. 73–79).

15. Yang (2005).

16. Liu (2007, pp. 242–57); Yang and Tian (2010); Du (2011).

17. Hunter and Chan (1993, pp. 170–73); Bays (2003, p. 502); Chen (2012); Koesel (2013).

18. See appendix I for an introduction of River County as the field site.

19. The history of Protestant missions in River County is reconstructed on the basis of articles in the county's *Wenshi ziliao* collection, which document the local history of Protestantism, and missionary reports from the *Baptist Missionary Magazine* published by the American Baptist Missionary Union, as well as reports by missionaries of the China Inland Mission. For further details, see appendix II.

20. It is worth mentioning that woman missionaries played an instrumental role in the China Inland Mission's work in River County, as in many other places. One such missionary served for twenty-one years in River County, continuing her work until her death in 1917. For much of her time there, she was the sole missionary from the China Inland Mission stationed in the area. She earned widespread respect from the local community, including non-Christians, particularly for the medical services she provided.

21. The American Baptist Missionary Union set up a mission house in the prefecture seat in 1888, where it also established a hospital, a dispensary, and a girls' boarding school. Medical mission work was important to both the China Inland Mission and American Baptist Missionary Union. The American Baptist Missionary Union also had women mission workers, some of whom were wives of missionaries, while others were single women. But unlike in the China Inland Mission, they tended to work under the leadership of a male missionary, engaging in teaching and working among women. Both the China Inland Mission and American Baptist Missionary Union employed Chinese preachers. In 1887, the yearly salary for a Chinese preacher was US$36.

22. For an account of the anti-Christian movements in the 1920s, see Lutz (1988). For analyses of the Chinese Protestant Indigenization Movements, see Chao (1986) and Bays (1996).

23. The Local Church, aka the Christian Assemblies (*Jidutu jühuichu*) or the Little Flock (*xiaoqun jiaohui*), emerged in the 1920s as one of the most influential indigenous Chinese Christian movements that was truly "independent of foreign missions, autonomous in operations, and indigenous in ideas and leadership" (Bays 1996b, p. 309). Strongly influenced by Watchman Nee's theology, which carried a "millenarian vision of the spiritual victory over the evils and trials of the world through identification with Christ's death" (Bays 2012, p. 133), the Local Church emphasized spiritual purity and separation from the world. Rejecting denominationalism, the movement insisted that there should be only one church in any place, undivided by denominational differences. It also disavowed a clergy-laity distinction, entrusting church leadership to "co-workers." Watchman Nee was arrested in 1952 and died in prison in 1972. For more on the history of the Local Church and the life of Watchman Nee, see Bays (1996), Ying (2005) and Lian (2010).

24. To reconstruct the history of the Local Church in River County, I consulted articles on the history of Protestantism in the *Wenshi ziliao* collection of the county and the Local Church's own publication *Changkai de men* (The open door). During 1938–39, when Japan invaded China, Local Church members in coastal provinces were forced to move inland. To maintain cohesion within the dispersed religious community and keep the ministry alive, Watchman Nee initiated *Changkai de men*, a newsletter that published correspondence from coworkers across China. These letters provided updates on the correspondents' locations, safety concerns, and the evangelistic work they were carrying out as they moved from place to place. A total of nineteen

issues were published. The letters offer a glimpse into the Local Church's situation and its missionary activities in River County during this tumultuous period.

25. In contrast, women older than sixty constituted the vast majority of lay participants at Buddhist ritual events in River County, with men making up less than 5 percent.

26. A family friend who converted to Protestantism in 1991 invited me to this gathering with the intention of "sharing the Good News" with me. At the time, I was a college student. She also brought my mom to a few of their gatherings.

27. This time, I went to the church meeting with a friend, at the invitation of his colleague who was active in proselytizing.

28. Vala and O'Brien (2007) analyze how Protestant evangelists recruited nonnetworked individuals in public spaces in China.

29. See also Cao (2010, pp. 20–21, 71–72).

30. These exclusivist religious practices of Protestantism are distinct from the more inclusive and eclectic practices of other major religions in China (Hansen 1990, pp. 29–47), which can peacefully coexist within the same locality and even in the same household. It is by no means unusual for Daoist priests, Buddhist monks, and professional wailers to perform their respective rituals and complement one another at funerals.

31. The Qingming Festival, which falls in early April, is a traditional Chinese holiday to remember and honor ancestors at their gravesites.

32. This woman was the first in her family to convert to Protestantism, followed by her mother several years later. Both converted because they received "healing from Jesus." Her father converted on his deathbed.

33. *Zongzi* is a traditional Chinese rice dish typically enjoyed during the Dragon Boat Festival. It is made of glutinous rice stuffed with fillings and wrapped in bamboo leaves.

34. Wind and Lewis (1994, pp. 1–2).

35. Guanyin Famen is an NRM with a strong Buddhist leaning founded by Ching Hai, an ethnic Chinese Vietnamese, in Taiwan in 1988. It instructs followers to discover and awaken "the Divine Presence within" through the practice of vegetarianism, daily meditation on the Inner Light and the Inner Sound, and observing Five Precepts: injunctions against killing, lying, stealing, sexual misconduct, and using intoxicants. Introduced to mainland China in 1989, it was proscribed by the Chinese government as an "evil cult" in 1995 (Thornton 2008).

36. Hunter and Chan (1993, pp. 145–55); Bays (2003).

37. Brook (1996); Yip (2003); Nedostup (2009, pp. 34–37).

38. Ch'en (1964); Brook (2005, pp. 132–58).

39. Oblau (2005, p. 416).

40. It must be emphasized that a polycephalous structure characterizes interorganizational relations in Protestantism. The fact that the leadership of some Protestant churches is authoritarian and a few groups have developed multiple branches does not contradict my assessment, because these groups have not coalesced into a unified ecclesiastical organization.

41. Dunch (2001).

42. Denominations with stronger authority structures were subject to more severe persecution under Mao. Another important step in eliminating denominationalism was the introduction of "united worship" in 1958. Smaller churches were closed and people of different denominational backgrounds were ordered to attend joint worship services held in a greatly reduced number of churches (Keating 2012, pp. 117–24).

43. Castelli (2004).

44. Leemans (2005).

45. Bays (2012, pp. 203–4).

46. Bays (2012, p. 204).

47. Tilly (1978).

48. During my fieldwork from 2004 to 2010, I was a graduate student from the University of Chicago. When local Protestants in River County learned this, they became more welcoming and comfortable with my presence. In church sermons, the United States was often referred to as "a Christian nation."

49. The Peoples Temple, led by Jim Jones, was an NRM founded in the 1950s in the United States. Jones called for "revolutionary suicide," leading to mass suicide of his followers in Jonestown, Guyana, in 1978.

50. Ying (1997).

51. Hsu (1953, p. 248).

52. Wolf (1976, pp. 361–62).

53. Freedman (1979, p. 296); Thompson (1988).

54. In the Chinese religious imagination, ancestors who are unprovided for will turn into hungry ghosts who roam in the world and cause havoc among the living. They thus need to be propitiated. The Ghost Festival, which falls in the seventh lunar month, is a traditional observance when offerings are made to pacify hungry ghosts. Weller (1987) analyzes the Ghost Festival in modern-day Taiwan. Teiser (1996) traces the Buddhist origin of this festival.

55. Ying (1997, p. 91); Li (2010).

56. Twitchett (1959); Ebrey (1986, 1991); Bol (2008).

57. Szonyi (2001, p. 1).

58. Chow (1994); Chang (2001, 2006).

59. See Zheng (2001, pp. 287–308); Faure (2007). At the county level, only the magistrate was officially appointed and subject to the administrative authority of the imperial center. His assistants, including clerks, runners, servants, and private secretaries, were not. This led to limited state penetration into local society (Chu 1962).

60. Zheng (2001, p. 23).

61. Potter and Potter (1990, pp. 9–10); Xiao (2010, pp. 55–56).

62. Most commonly, these collective actions involved feuding with neighboring lineage-based villages. But lineages also provided a basic organizational structure for local militarization in response to large-scale military threats (Kuhn 1970). During the Taiping Rebellion (1851–64), lineage organizations in River County formed local militias and fought both the invading Taiping forces and the pillaging Qing army (Jiang 1991; Zhou, Lin, and Chen 2001, pp. 45–47).

63. Huang (1985, pp. 233–37); Cohen (1990).

64. Watson (1988); Zhou, Lin, and Chen (2001); Zhou (2005).

65. Siu (1990); Zhou (2005, pp. 116–21). See chapter 3 for more on this point.

66. Yang (1961).

67. Shao (2011, pp. 66–67).

68. See Chen and Li (2010, p. 57); Shao (2011, pp. 68–70).

69. Feng (1935).

70. This observation is noted in the travelogue of A. S. Roe (1920, pp. 77–78). Roe spent a week in River County on her visit to China in 1907. During her second sojourn in China, in 1912, she spent almost a year in River County, living with a missionary from the China Inland Mission (Shen 2010). In her book, she provides a rich and detailed account of the local society.

71. By 1949, with only 10.6 percent of its population living in cities, China remained by and large an agrarian society (Chan, Henderson, and Tsui 2008, p. 787). Hence, social and religious norms tied to ancestor worship and other forms of popular religion prevailed in society and constituted a major obstacle to the nationwide expansion of Protestantism.

72. Beanman (1901).

73. This assertion comes from an 1892 missionary report by Rev. J. W. Carlin and his wife, who were stationed in Ungkung (that is, Huanggang), Guangdong Province.

74. Groesbeck (1900).

75. Mungello (1994); Brockey (2009). See also chapter 2, note 1.

76. Menegon (2009, pp. 61, 89–90); Fan (2015).

77. Menegon (2009, p. 91).

78. Nedostup (2009); Goossaert and Palmer (2011).

79. Chan, Madsen, and Unger (1984, pp. 87–89).

80. Feng (2011, pp. 144–50).

81. Agricultural production cooperatives and the people's communes were implemented by the Maoist state in its endeavor to collectivize agriculture in the 1950s. Farmers in the cooperatives pooled their land, tools, draft animals, and labor, and earned income based on shares of land they owned and later their labor contributions. Introduced in 1958 in China, communes were large rural organizations that comprised multiple cooperatives. They were designed to manage all economic and social activities within rural communities.

82. Red Guards were primarily composed of young students who fervently supported Mao Zedong's ideology. Formed in 1966 in response to Mao's mobilization and with his blessings, they made it their mission to assist Mao in combating CCP leaders whom Mao deemed insufficiently revolutionary and to eradicate remnants of traditional Chinese culture, so as to enable a political and social transformation of Chinese society. The Red Guards' distinct role as protagonists in the mass movement to dismantle the Four Olds distinguishes the movement from earlier state-launched political campaigns. Across the country, Red Guards wreaked havoc on cultural objects and historical sites. Even state leaders sometimes found their methods problematic and intervened to curb their excessive violence and destruction. See Li (1995, pp. 426–28); Kraus (2012, pp. 44–49).

83. Tan (2006); Szonyi (2015).

84. Kelliher (1997).

85. Peng (2004).

86. Tsai (2007).

87. Peng (2010).

88. Ma (2000); Pan (2006).

89. See Xiao (2001). Lineage networks have further disintegrated since the mid-1980s as a result of the migration of rural laborers to the cities, the much-increased general mobility of rural residents, and rapid urbanization.

90. Household-based Daoism functioned as a profession, with Daoists offering ritual services, especially funerary rites, for residents in their communities in exchange for payment to sustain their livelihoods. In late imperial China, Daoist lineages emerged in River County, scattered in market towns and villages. Within the lineage, training and knowledge were usually transmitted from father to son only. Household-based Daoism faced severe suppression during the Cultural Revolution; religious texts and ritual paraphernalia were destroyed, and ritual services largely ceased. After 1978, Daoist ritual services resurged. The economic boom spurred by

post-Mao reforms led to a growing demand for such services, which continued into the early years of the 2000s, allowing Daoist ritual specialists to enjoy a period of economic prosperity.

91. It is a figurative expression often used in an exaggerated way to indicate that someone is overwhelmed with criticism, negative comments, or complaints.

92. MacInnis (1972).

93. The United Front policy, based on the principle of uniting to combat the primary enemy, is one of the most important traditions in the history of the CCP.

94. Bays (2012, pp. 159–66).

95. Xu (2004).

96. Teiwes and Sun (1999).

97. Bush (1970).

98. See Vogel's (2011) biographical account of Deng Xiaoping. See also Baum (1994).

99. Leung (2005).

100. The text of *Document 19* can be found at http://www.mzb.com.cn/html/folder/290171 .htm (accessed October 5, 2015). See Morrison (1984) for an introduction of the circular.

101. Morrison (1984); Potter (2003); Leung (2005).

102. In 1981, the River County government established an Ethnic and Religious Affairs Department in charge of affairs related to ethnic minorities and religious groups. The department shared an office and staff with the county UFWD. In 1991, the Ethnic and Religious Affairs Bureau was formally established and acquired office and staff separate from the UFWD. Although the bureau also supervises ethnic affairs, for the sake of convenience, it is referred to as an RAB in the book. The UFWD is an organ of the CCP, whereas the RAB is a government agency. As the CCP assumes control over the government, the UFWD directs the work of the RAB. However, there is also a division of labor between the two agencies. The UFWD is responsible for dealing with religious leaders as individuals and the RAB with religious associations as corporate entities (Goossaert and Palmer 2011, p. 329).

103. The *Shouters* is a derogatory nickname for sectarian groups in China that are influenced by the teachings of Li Changshou (Witness Lee, 1905–97). Witness Lee was an acolyte of Watchman Nee and thus associated with the Local Church movement. In 1949, he relocated to Taiwan. In 1962, he moved to the United States. He founded the Living Stream Ministry, currently based in Anaheim, California. He played a key role in the expansion of the Local Church movement internationally. Teachings and practices advocated by Witness Lee's followers were introduced to China in the late 1970s. Because the followers continually shout "Lord!" "Amen!" and "Hallelujah!" as part of their service, its critics gave it the epithet "Shouters." The Chinese government and the Three-Self churches accused the Shouters of creating civil disturbances, disrupting Three-Self church activities, and organizing protests against the government. Mainstream Protestant groups in and outside China largely view the Shouters as heretical. The Shouters spawned a number of offshoot groups such as the Established King and Eastern Lightning. These groups further generated their own offshoots. A number are on the Chinese government's list of "evil cults" (Lian 2010, pp. 216–32; Dunn 2015, pp. 31–32). See also chapter 4 on NRMs.

104. The predecessor of the SARA is the Bureau of Religious Affairs under the State Council. It was first installed in 1954 and then disbanded during the Cultural Revolution. It was reinstated in 1979 and changed its name to SARA in 1998.

105. Walder (1986); Cheng and Selden (1994).

106. Shaw (1996).

107. Zhao (2001, pp. 107–9).

108. Howe, Kueh, and Ash (2003); Brandt and Rawski (2008).

109. Davis (1995); Saich (2000).

110. Vogel (2011, pp. 294–348).

111. Leung (2005); C. Wang (2015).

112. Y. Wang (2015).

113. My analytical concept of *interstitial social space* should not be confused with Fenggang Yang's concept of *gray market*. In Yang's (2012) theory of "triple religious markets," heavy state regulations will not change the religious demand but will change the structure of religious supply, leading to the rise of three markets of religion: a *red market* containing all officially sanctioned religious organizations, activities, and believers; a *black market* with all officially banned religious organizations, activities, and believers; and a *gray market* consisting of religious organizations, activities, and believers of ambiguous legal status. Because religious organizations in the red market have to comply with restrictions imposed by political authorities, their religious goods tend to be "sanitized" or "watered-down." In response, a black market emerges to meet the need of the zealous, who are "willing to pay a higher price for their religion, even to the extent of life sacrifice." Then, "when people cannot find satisfaction in the red market and are unwilling to risk black-market penalties, a gray market fills the gap or the niche." Yang's "gray market" emerges as a response to strong state regulations. In contrast, my interstitial social space is the outcome of the state's incapacity to regulate unsanctioned religious activities and of the intricate contests between state and religious actors in the post-Mao reform environment. Moreover, Yang never specifies and explains what kind of religion is more capable of exploring of this interstitial social space in China today and why, but this is precisely what I aim to do. Yang's (2012) overarching theory in explaining religious growth dynamics in post-Mao China closely follows the rational choice theory of religion. Therefore, my criticisms of how rational choice theory of religion has treated the state also apply to his work. In other words, Yang's work also treats the state as an exogenous and secondary factor, relevant only when the state's religious regulations change the supply-and-demand dynamics of the religious market; it also limits the analysis of the state to a few static propositions. For my more detailed critique of Yang's theory, please refer to Sun (2017a).

114. Scholars, to explain why the authoritarian post-Mao state has allowed space for autonomy, introduced the concept of *fragmented authoritarianism* (Lieberthal and Oksenberg 1988; Mertha 2009), which suggests a disjointed, decentralized authority structure behind policymaking. Their analysis aligns well with discussion of the emergence and expansion of the interstitial social space in post-Mao China.

115. In Spires's (2011) study of NGOs in post-Mao China, he coined the term *contingent symbiosis* to characterize the relationships between NGOs and the state.

116. See Lin's (2008) dissertation on liberal-leaning media in post-Mao China.

117. Hunter and Chan (1993, p. 3); Bays (2012, p. 177).

118. Zhang (2010).

119. Sun (2009).

120. For an account of a confrontation between independent churches and the government in Xiaoshan, see Lian (2010, pp. 1–2).

121. The quotes in this paragraph are standard discourse of Xiaoshan Protestant groups, but I was informed in this context by Informant No. 9, leader of a major independent church in River County.

122. In the summer of 2009, I visited this large charismatic church in Taiwan and interviewed one of the church leaders (Informant No. 200). He told me that strictly speaking, Liang

was not a missionary dispatched by the church but operated on his own initiative. Nevertheless, the church readily provided assistance when Liang requested it.

123. A major exception is the All Ranges Church (aka the Born Again Movement), founded by Xu Yongze in 1968. Despite some recognition that this group received from a few independent church leaders in China and international advocacy groups, it was still labeled by the Chinese government as an "evil cult," primarily for two reasons. First, because it developed into an extensive national network with a tight organizational and hierarchical authority structure, it was perceived by the Chinese government as politically threatening. Second, the movement has not gained institutional legitimacy because of what organizational ecologists would call the *liability of newness*. And its emphasis on copious weeping as a requirement for a dramatic conversion experience has reinforced the perception of leaders from both the Three-Self and independent church sectors that this group is unorthodox. Hence, when the Chinese government suppressed the movement, mainstream Protestant groups in China hardly came to its defense.

124. Since the late 1980s, major newspapers in the United States such as the *Washington Post* and *New York Times* have frequently reported on the Chinese government's persecution of independent Protestant churches.

125. For instance, during Deng Xiaoping's official visit to the United States in 1979, President Carter tried to persuade him to permit the reopening of churches, the printing of the Bible, and the return of foreign missionaries (Wehrfritz and Clemetson 1998). President George W. Bush received representatives of independent Protestant churches in the White House in 2006 to show his support (https://chinaaid.org/news/bush-meets-chinese-christian-activists/, accessed October 1, 2015).

126. Smith (2001); Wald and Calhoun-Brown (2011); Wilcox and Robinson (2011).

127. Goldberg (1997).

128. Sider and Knippers (2005, pp. 59–60).

129. Kindopp (2004b).

130. The Political Prisoner Database of the Congressional-Executive Commission on China shows that arrests of Protestants by the Chinese government evidently dropped after the year 2000 (Y. Wang 2016). Although I am unable to establish a direct causal linkage here, it is reasonable to speculate that the drop might have been related to increasing pressure from the US government.

131. For instance, in the summer of 2009, out of concern over a potential SARS epidemic, the Ministry of Education ordered the suspension of students' group activities. Accordingly, in River County, the Education Bureau, with the collaboration of the RAB and other state agencies, shut down a summer camp at the site of an independent church. But this did not affect two summer camps concurrently held by other independent churches, because the RAB officials did not know of their existence.

132. Dean (2003); Tan (2006); Fan, Chen, and Madsen (2015).

133. See Chen (2009); Duan (2010); Li (2010); H. Yang (2014).

134. Aikman (2003); Kindopp (2004a).

135. According to a SARA report, in 1995, 1,551 out of 2,861 counties in China had installed agencies in charge of religious affairs, with a total of 3,053 staff members (http://www1.umn.edu/humanrts/research/CHsara.html, accessed October 5, 2015). The 2012 figure was from a Shanghai UFWD official (Informant No. 93).

136. See Aikman (2003) for an account of independent churches in Henan.

Chapter 2

1. The Chinese Rites Controversy (ca. 1630–1715) was a drawn-out dispute among Catholic Catholic missionaries over the nature of certain Confucian rites practiced in China. Jesuit missionaries defended the position of Matteo Ricci that the rites did not have religious content and were compatible with the Catholic belief, whereas missionaries of other religious orders strongly disagreed. After the Vatican sided with the Jesuits' opponents and condemned the Chinese rites as idolatry, the Qing emperors proscribed Catholicism, expelled Catholic missionaries, confiscated church properties, and persecuted Catholics (Mungello 1994). In the following years, Catholicism was further labeled an "heterodox teaching" and was persecuted along with other heterodox religious societies until 1842.

2. As the first unequal treaty that foreign powers imposed on China, the Nanjing Treaty in 1842 opened up five coastal cities as ports for British trade. The supplementary Bogue Treaty in 1843 specifies that the British could buy property and take residence in the treaty ports and were granted extraterritorial privileges. In the Treaty of Wangxia with the United States and the Treaty of Whampoa with France in 1844, Christian missionaries were granted the right to buy land in the five treaty ports to erect churches and hospitals. In 1845, under pressure from France, the Qing government formally lifted the ban on Catholicism, which had been in force since 1724. In the Tianjin Treaties signed in 1858 following the Qing's defeat by British and French troops in the Arrow War, foreign missionaries gained the privilege to travel in China's vast hinterland and preach Christianity. By way of the most-favored-nation clause in the treaties that foreign powers imposed on the Qing, these missionary privileges granted to one power were extended to all other powers.

3. The century-long proscription and persecution of Catholicism severely set back its growth in China. Catholic communities that had once thrived in urban centers dispersed, and Catholicism no longer attracted elite converts. It was in places remote from the centers of power, such as rural Fujian, Shanxi, and Sichuan, where persecution was not carried out rigorously and consistently that Catholic communities were able to sustain themselves. After experiencing some steep drops, by the early years of the 1800s, the number of Chinese Catholics reached two hundred thousand, close to the level a century earlier (Bays 2012, p. 31).

4. The original data are from Milton Stauffer's *The Christian Occupation of China*, first published in Shanghai in 1922. In 1918, there were more Catholics than Protestant converts in all Chinese provinces except two (see also Stark and Wang 2015, pp. 25–26).

5. The estimates of the Catholic and Protestant populations in China around 1950 are from Bays (2012, p. 169) and Bays (2012, p. 147), respectively.

6. For the estimate of the Protestant population in China, see chapter 1. This chapter also uses the widely adopted data of the Pew Research Center (2011) to estimate China's Catholic population. That 9 million estimate is close to the estimate of 9–10.5 million made by the Holy Spirit Study Center in 2015, a Hong Kong-based Catholic organization committed to gathering information on the Chinese Catholic Church.

7. The number of Catholics in Shanghai in 1949 is from Bays (2012, p. 169). For the 2016 estimate, the figure of 150,000 was provided by a priest in Shanghai Diocese in December 2016 (Informant No. 264). The Shanghai municipal government's figure for the Shanghai Catholic population was 138,800 by 2014 and 116,280 by 2024 (https://mzzj.sh.gov.cn/2021tzj_shtjzgk/in dex.html, accessed April 12, 202).

8. Madsen (1998, pp. 50–71; 2003); Kang (2006); Wang (2006); Harrison (2013); He (2013).

9. Bays (1996); Tao (2004); Lian (2010). See also chapter 1 for information about the Local Church.

10. Tao (2004); Bays (2012).

11. Between 1856 and 1946, China was divided into different apostolic vicariates. In 1946, these apostolic vicariates were promoted to dioceses. This change notwithstanding, clerics were always organized into a chain of ecclesiastic authority.

12. Bays (2012, pp. 141).

13. Finke and Wittberg (2000).

14. Wittberg (1994).

15. Mariani (2011, p. 20).

16. See Latourette (1929, pp. 307–13) on the history of the French religious protectorate in China. It was not officially abandoned until the French government negotiated away its old treaty rights in China in 1946 (Young 2013, p. 34). But after the violent antiforeign and anti-Christian Boxer Uprising of 1899–1901, and especially after the anti-Catholic Nanchang incident in 1906, France was no longer keen to play the protector role (Young 1996). Meanwhile, the Vatican began to seek direct control over missionary societies in China (Bays 2012, pp. 113–14; Li 2012, pp. 96–109; Young 2013, pp. 211–32). The effect of the French religious protectorate, however, lingered into the 1920s.

17. Latourette (1929, pp. 473–75); Tiedemann (2010a, pp. 326–27).

18. Latourette (1929, p. 306); Tiedemann (2010a, p. 302).

19. Despite of the surge of anticlericalism at home during the Third Republic (1870–1940), and despite of the Law of Separation—which separated church and state—adopted by the National Assembly in 1905, the French government was convinced that an alliance with Catholic missions served the national interest (Young 2013, pp. 88–92).

20. See Esherick (1988, pp. 79, 84); Tiedemann (2010a, pp. 296–331); Li (2012); Young (2013, p. 41); Lee (2014). It shall be noted that the French religious protectorate was transnational, affording protection to all Catholic missionaries regardless of their nationality (Young 2013, pp. 29–30). The French sought to prove the effectiveness of their protection in order to influence Catholic missionaries of different nationalities to rely on France for protection rather than other alternatives, such as Germany or Italy.

21. The year 2018 was chosen as the endpoint of the third period because I completed data collection for the analysis presented in this chapter that year. More importantly, significant changes occurred in Sino-Vatican relationship in 2018, which had major implications for the development of Catholicism in China. This topic is explored in the conclusion.

22. Chen (1999) has detailed the failure of the campaigns to make Confucianism the state religion during the Republican period.

23. Goossaert and Palmer (2011, pp. 56–58).

24. Goossaert and Palmer (2011, pp. 73–74).

25. Goossaert and Palmer (2011, p. 72).

26. Extraterritorial rights were abolished in 1943.

27. In 1948, China had 5,788 Catholic priests, of which 2,676 were foreign missionaries (Leung 2010, p. 794).

28. Tiedemann (2010b).

29. Lutz (1971); Bays and Widmer (2009).

30. Dunch (2014).

31. Bays (2012).

32. Lian (2010); Bays (2012).

33. Tiedemann (2016).

34. According to the database on Catholic religious communities in China 1800–1950 compiled by Tiedemann (2016), only five of the fifty-seven male religious communities were constituted by Chinese. And even they were founded by foreign missionaries.

35. L. Guo (2012, pp. 249–50); X. Li (2012, pp. 52, 56).

36. Young (2013, pp. 24–34).

37. Young (2013, p. 48).

38. Tiedemann (2010a, pp. 316–17).

39. Esherick (1988, p. 84).

40. Y. Li and Chi (2006).

41. Anderson (1970); Fan (2005).

42. Hansson (1996).

43. Taveirne (2004); Zhang (2006).

44. Esherick (1988, pp. 88–89); X. Li (2012, p. 256).

45. Weng (1985); Ge (2009).

46. Tiedemann (2011); Lee (2014).

47. Charbonnier (1992, pp. 239–40).

48. Feng shui feuds were common in premodern China (Coggins 2003, pp. 211, 309).

49. Lee (2014, p. 78).

50. Latourette (1929, p. 311).

51. Clarke (2013, pp. 83–110).

52. Latourette (1929, pp. 331–38).

53. X. Li (2012).

54. Litzinger (1996).

55. Zhang and Guo (2005); L. Guo (2012, pp. 189–91).

56. Cohen (1963); Esherick (1988).

57. Oberschall (1993, p. 24).

58. Zhang (2006); Tiedemann (2011); X. Li (2012).

59. Groesbeck, a missionary from the American Baptist Missionary Union, clearly expressed this complicated feeling in his report in 1900. See also Esherick (1988, pp. 83, 94).

60. Latourette (1929, pp. 473–75).

61. J. Liu (2012, p. 81).

62. Mariani (2011, p. 21); Jin (2012, p. 165).

63. Madsen (1998, pp. 34–35); Mariani (2011, p. 47).

64. Mariani (2011); Jin (2012).

65. Tang and Weist (2013, p. 11).

66. Bays (2012, p. 161).

67. J. Liu (2012, pp. 90–116).

68. Wang was incarcerated from 1955 to 1980, Yuan from 1958 to 1979.

69. The history of Catholicism in River County can be traced back to 1643, when the Jesuit missionary Martino Martini (1614–61) arrived and started missionary activities. He founded a church in River County in 1646 and baptized as many as 250 converts in the year of 1648 alone (Guo 1993, p. 87). This was partly because a local scholar gentry became a convert and his key supporter (Guo 1993, pp. 17–18; Li 2022, p. 49). Following the footsteps of the Jesuits, the Dominicans also began their mission in River County. They built a church in 1656 and made River County an important outpost for their mission (Zhao 2002). At the time, Jesuit and Dominican missionaries in China were fighting over the issue of Chinese rites. In 1645, the Congregation for

the Propagation of the Faith sided with the Dominicans and condemned the rites. The Jesuits dispatched Martini to Rome in 1651 to defend their position. Martini successfully persuaded the Congregation to lift the ban in 1656. In 1658, he returned to China with the favorable decree. In reaction to the change of Vatican policy, the Dominican missionaries in China gathered in River County for a conference in 1661. The conference reaffirmed the Dominican policy on Chinese rites, insisting Chinese converts should renounce all sacrificial rituals to Confucius and the ancestors (Menegon 2009, pp. 286–87). In the early eighteenth century, the papacy adopted the hard-line position and banned the rites. This in turn caused the proscription of Catholicism by the Qing court. The proscription and subsequent persecution seriously damaged the missionary enterprise in River County. The Dominican missionaries were arrested, and their church was converted into a Confucian memorial hall in the 1720s (Guo 1993, p. 88). Over time, the local Catholic population seemed to disappear. Catholic mission was reintroduced to the county when China was forced to open to Western missionary activities after the signing of a series of treaties with Western powers in the 1840s. In 1909, Catholic missionaries erected a church in River County (Guo 1993, p. 49). In 1939, the Catholic community of River County came under the jurisdiction of the Prefecture Apostolic of Lishui (Zhejiang), entrusted to Canadian missionaries of the Scarboro Foreign Mission Society (Guo 1993, pp. 123–4).

70. Madsen (1998, p. 57); Wang (2006).

71. The church property in the county seat of River County was confiscated in 1957 and turned into a factory. In 1986, the remaining Catholics in River County filed a petition requesting the local government to return the church property in accordance with the religious policy. The local government denied the petition, citing the nonpresence of a priest as the main reason.

72. In the ensuing years, the Catholics were still thwarted in their efforts to reclaim the confiscated church properties. With the old generation of Catholics, who acquired their faith prior to 1949, withering away, the number of Catholics in River County further dwindled. It seemed that the faith of the old generation did not pass down to their children very well. Four or five families even went to see their priest in Jinhua, returning their Bibles and requesting to be disaffiliated from the Catholic Church. The priest was heartbroken (Informant No. 259) and stopped visiting River County regularly.

73. Potter (2003).

74. Hamrin (2004); Wang (2015).

75. Vala and O'Brien (2007).

76. Forney (2001).

77. According to the data of the Hong Kong-based Holy Spirit Study Center, the total of 2,650 priests in China in 2002, which includes both the open and underground churches, was less than half the number in 1948.

78. There has been a substantial and steady drop in the number of seminarians in China—from 2,250 in 2004 to 1,260 in 2014 (Lam 2016).

79. The Chinese government allowed female religious orders to operate only within their parish, prohibiting cross-regional or national organizations. According to figures from the Catholic information website xinde.org, as of 2009, there were 106 female religious orders, consisting of 5,451 women who had pronounced vows. In contrast, there were just over 350 members of male religious orders (https://xinde.org/show/13349, accessed October 5, 2015).

80. The Franciscan order in Fengxiang Diocese of Shaanxi is an exception. It was reestablished in the early 1980s and remained underground for many years. After the underground

church changed its status to an open church in 2004, the Franciscan priests obtained legal status by association (Chan 2012b).

81. Madsen (2001).

82. Tong (2013).

83. More than eighty bishops were consecrated secretly by Fan and his associates between 1981 and 1993 (Lam 2011).

84. Here, *underground Catholic churches* refers to those that are not registered with the RAB and do not have legal status. Yet similar to independent Protestant churches, the underground Catholic churches in the post-Mao era did not necessarily operate secretly. In some areas, they organized religious activities openly.

85. Madsen (1998, pp. 45–48).

86. Tang (1993, p. 34).

87. Charbonnier (1993, p. 65); Tang (1993, pp. 34–35).

88. Madsen (2003, p. 470).

89. The inclusion of the prayer was largely pushed by Jin Luxian (1916–2013), one of the most prominent personalities of the Catholic Church in China (Clark 2010). A Rome-educated Jesuit, Jin was in prison and labor camps from 1955 to 1982. In 1985, he accepted an appointment by the Catholic Patriotic Association to serve as the auxiliary bishop of the Shanghai Diocese, without papal approval, and in 1988 was made the official bishop. Due to his efforts, the Shanghai Diocese became the first among Patriotic dioceses in China to include a prayer for the pope at Mass. In 2005, Jin reconciled with the pope.

90. Mariani (2011, p. 223).

91. By February 2017, only seven such bishops remained to be pardoned by the pope (Fraze 2017).

92. The underground bishops ordained priests and bishops, some of whom were poorly qualified. In some dioceses, more than one underground bishop was ordained, with chaotic results (Madsen 1998, pp. 44–48; Tang 1993, p. 35). Because of a lack of training, many of the underground priests have an inadequate understanding of the Church's doctrines and history. Indeed, while I was often impressed by the knowledge of the Patriotic priests I encountered in the field, I was surprised by the lack of knowledge among some of the underground priests I interviewed.

93. Pope Benedict XVI's 2007 pastoral letter to bishops, priests, and lay Catholics in China, in particular, signified a sea change of the Vatican's policy toward the Chinese Church.

94. There is a huge variation in the relationship between the open and underground churches. Some dioceses were rife with antagonism, whereas others enjoyed limited collaboration (Chan 2012a). In Fengxiang Diocese in Shaanxi Province, there was no underground church sector; instead, the open churches resisted the Catholic Patriotic Association and were in communion with the pope (Chan 2012b).

95. Leung and Wang (2016).

96. As of October 2016, only four students remained in the Sheshan Seminary, once the best Catholic seminary in post-Mao China. It has trained a great number of seminarians and contributed significantly to the revival of Catholicism in China.

97. Fraze (2017).

98. Gaetan (2017).

99. For instance, Mariani (2018).

100. Bireley (1999).

101. Chesnut (2003).

102. I should note that although Catholic communities in post-Mao China were generally not vigorous in evangelism, especially compared to Protestantism, there were exceptions. A few urban churches, such as Xikai Church (St. Joseph's Cathedral) in Tianjin, Xishiku Church (Church of the Savior) in Beijing, and Shengxin Church (Sacred Heart Cathedral) in Guangzhou, have been notably active in evangelistic activities.

103. Stoll (1990, p. 29).

104. Burdick (1993); Chesnut (1997).

105. Martin (1978); McLeod (2000).

106. On the case of France, see Chartier (2015, pp. 92–110). On Zaire, see Hastings (1979, p. 191). On Vietnam, see Nguyen (1983).

107. Barnadas (1984); Hoornaert (1984); Hastings (1996).

108. See Daughton (2008); Young (2013).

109. On Angola, see Hastings (1979, pp. 143–44). On Mozambique, see Hastings (1979, pp. 210–13). On Zaire, see Hastings (1979, pp. 135–36) and Stanley (1990, p. 19).

Chapter 3

1. Yang (1961).

2. Weber ([1915] 1946, [1922] 1963).

3. Bellah (1970).

4. Yang (1961).

5. Such as the door gods and the stove god.

6. Such as the worship of tree gods.

7. Feuchtwang and Wang (2001); Fan (2003); Chau (2005, 2006).

8. Anagnost (1994); Jing (1996); Yang (2004a).

9. Dean (1997, 2003); Tsai (2007).

10. As is often the case, a village formed alliance with neighboring ones because it participated in a common irrigation system or joined in defense against outsiders.

11. Brim (1974); Sangren (1987); Lin (2008); Dean and Zheng (2010).

12. See ter Haar's (2017) study on the cult of Lord Guan.

13. See Yü's (2001) study on the cult of Guanyin.

14. Zhu (2011) divides Zhejiang into three regions. The geography, climate, economy, transportation, and history of each region have given rise to the distinct characteristics of its popular religion gods.

15. Zhu (2009).

16. Han (2015).

17. The county gazetteer of 1889 listed sixty-four such temples.

18. As recorded by the 1889 county gazetteer.

19. Thompson (1995) provides a good and concise overview of the state cult. Feuchtwang (1977) provides a detailed account of the sacrificial rituals in late Qing. Zito's (1997) book is an anthropological and cultural study of the grand sacrifice performed by the imperial court in eighteenth-century China.

20. Goossaert (2008a).

21. Such an incident was recorded in one of Wang Qishu's poems. Wang (1728–99) was a salt merchant from Anhui when he visited River County in 1753–54. During his stay, he composed

a hundred annotated poems about the local sites and customs, a valuable source of the religious history of River County. Wang was known as a collector of Chinese seals among his contemporaries.

22. Emperor of the Eastern Peak was originally the god of Mount Tai but evolved to be the god governing the dead and the hells, as well as births.

23. Taylor (1997) outlines the history of the official altars, temples, and shrines established by law in the counties during the Ming and Qing dynasties.

24. The temple consisted of shrines devoted to Confucius, his disciples, and sages in the Confucian traditions, and a government school where local students who passed the lowest-level examination signed up to receive government subsidies and periodically received instruction in Confucian classics.

25. Feuchtwang (1977).

26. The purpose of the ritual was to show compassion to those wondering spirits and to placate them so they would not harm the human realm (Meulenbeld 2015, pp. 139–40).

27. Cooper (2013).

28. The following reconstruction is based on the gazetteer of the Temple of Lord Zhao and my interviews with Informant No. 113, who chaired the management committee of the temple and is the composer of the temple gazetteer, and with Informants No. 50, 115, and 116.

29. Duara (1991); Nedostup (2009); Poon (2011).

30. Goossaert and Palmer (2011).

31. Feng (1935).

32. See Poon (2004, 2008) on the temple festival of the City God in Guangzhou during Republican China.

33. See Kang (2009) for similar observations in Sichuan.

34. Dong lived a frugal life. She told me in 2008 that her overall expenses for the entire year did not exceed 300 yuan (approximately US$44).

35. Chapter 5 will discuss in detail Jingkong's teachings and the lay Buddhist movement they inspired.

36. Pure Land Buddhism, a school of Mahayana Buddhism, is one of the most widely practiced Buddhist traditions in Chinese societies. It holds that, by practicing devotional acts to Amitābha Buddha, such as the repeated invocation of his name, one can be reborn in the Western Pure Land of Great Bliss.

37. Naquin (2000, pp. 19–21).

38. Yang (1961); Shi (1975); Lin (1987). For this reason, Dean (2003) simply calls territorial cults the local communal religion.

39. Yang (1961); Lin (1987); Litzinger (1996); Goossaert and Palmer (2011, pp. 24–25).

40. Siu (1990); Szonyi (2000); Liu (2013).

41. This rather personal relationship between the devotees and gods is highlighted in Hymes (2002).

42. Lin (1988).

43. For exceptions, see DuBois (2005, pp. 48–51); Chau (2006, pp. 62–73).

44. Naquin (2000, pp. 161, 227–32).

45. Duara (1988, p. 115); Naquin (2000, pp. 237–38).

46. Dudbridge (1992); Zhao (2002).

47. Martin (1988).

48. Sangren (1983).

49. See Zhao (2002, pp. 259–96). Huang, Valussi, and Palmer (2011) and Kang (2016) discuss how gender is generally related to Chinese religious life.

50. Sangren (1983) offers a perceptive discussion about how the meaning of female deities is best understood with reference to the demands, roles, and needs of women in the structure and culture of Chinese families.

51. The Earth Mother Goddess has the image of a white-haired elderly lady in a yellow robe, holding a whisk in her hand and riding on a mysterious animal with a dragon's head and a fish's body.

52. The longest ballad in my collection has seventy-five verses.

53. The ritual of paying the debt for the next life is based on an originally Daoist belief that life is a loan that has to be repaid. Participants in this ritual would have ritual specialists calculate the debts they and their family members owe, and through the ritual services would repay the debts to the underworld treasury to ensure they would not suffer hell or misfortune in the next life (Berezkin 2018). The repentance ritual of breaking the bloody pond is for the redemption of women who, having committed sins of female blood pollution, are condemned to fall into the bloody pond, a most dreadful prison of hell (Seaman 1981; Mollier 2008, pp. 183–84). The "glaze repentance ritual" is popular among female worshippers and is believed to have the effect of improving eyesight or curing eye diseases. Both Daoist ritual specialists and Buddhist masters perform this ritual, but they use different texts—Daoists use the text for the water repentance ritual (*Taishang cibei daochang sanyuan miezui shuichan*), while Buddhists use the text for the Medicine Buddha repentance ritual (*Yaoshi baochan*). The name "glaze repentance ritual" likely derives from the Medicine Buddha, or Bhaiṣajyaguru, who is traditionally depicted with a radiant, glazed blue body.

54. A Daoist belief holds that there are three worms dwelling in the human body. On the night of the *gengshen* day, these worms leave the body while the person is asleep to ascend to Heaven to report to the Celestial Emperor about their host's wrongdoings. The Celestial Emperor would then punish the person with illness or reduce his lifespan accordingly. To prevent this from happening, Daoism believed that people should try to remain awake throughout this night so the worms cannot leave the body (Yamada 2008).

55. The poet is again Wang Qishu.

56. Zhao (2002, pp. 270–71).

57. Gan (2007, p. 125) observed similar gender division in Fujian.

58. Sangren (1983, p. 19).

59. Even female spirit mediums would call the spirit that possessed them "Buddha."

60. Under the household responsibility system, the household replaced the production team as the unit of production and income distribution. Each household was allocated a parcel of land and agricultural implements, given limited autonomy over land-use decisions and crop selection, and could keep what they produced after fulfillment of the state quotas (Putterman 1993).

61. Huang (2008).

62. Zhang and Song (2003).

63. Meng (2000).

64. Yan (2003).

65. Zhou (2009).

66. For a recent study on the role of female spirit mediums in popular religion in southeast China, see Cline (2010).

67. Goossaert and Palmer (2011, pp. 247, 249, 347).

68. In 2010, there were thirty-four temples registered as Buddhist sites in River County.

69. Managers of the unregistered popular religion temples told me that only district police would occasionally visit their temples and "they don't care whether you are registered or not; they only care about fire safety."

70. A third of the sum was transferred to the RAB.

71. Welch (1967, pp. 178–207).

72. According to the Mahayana Buddhist tradition, Maitreya Buddha is the future Buddha of this world. When the teachings of Gautama Buddha become completely decayed, Maitreya Buddha will descend to earth to preach the dharma.

73. For each of these provinces, Wikipedia entries list the names of all the City God Temples that existed prior to 1911 and highlight those restored in recent years (e.g., https://zh.m.wikipedia.org/zh-hans/Template:河北省境内的城隍庙). With the help of my research assistants, we meticulously cross-checked this information. Because the restoration of a City God Temple is typically a notable event, often reported in local news or featured on websites, we were able to search the name of each City God Temple to verify whether it had been restored. As a result, we compiled an updated list of all the City God Temples restored by October 2022 in these seven provinces.

74. Wu (2004); Goossaert (2015).

75. Goossaert (2015); Tao and Goossaert (2015).

76. Chau (2006, pp. 184–86).

77. Zhao (2002, pp. 259–96); Goossaert (2008a).

78. Fan (2003); Luo (2010); Kang (2009); Qu (2015); Tao and Goossaert (2015); Wu (2015). To obtain state-sanctioned status, some popular religion temples, especially in places such as Fujian where Daoism's influence on local popular religion is strong, were inclined to register as Daoist rather than Buddhist sites because of the natural affinity and compatibility between their beliefs and practices (Gan 2007). However, conversion to Daoism did not occur in these temples.

79. Dean (2003); Wang et al. (2006); Dean and Zheng (2010).

80. Zheng (2001).

81. Lin (1947).

82. Wang et al. (2006); Gan (2007).

83. Gan (2007, pp. 92, 256–57); Stewart and Strathern (2009).

84. Yang (2004b); Stewart and Strathern (2009).

Chapter 4

1. Palmer (2007); Ownby (2008); Tong (2009); and Penny (2012).

2. Regev (2016).

3. Harvey (2013).

4. Berkey (2003).

5. Sun (2019b); Sun and Zhao (2019).

6. Lipton (1999, p. 56); Rist (2016, pp. 73–74).

7. Even though the form of Confucianism installed as the state ideology during the Ming and Qing dynasties—namely, the neo-Confucianism expounded by Zhu Xi (1126–1271)—placed greater emphasis on orthodoxy, this general characterization of Confucianism remains applicable.

8. Overmyer (1976, pp. 35–37).

9. There was no formal government below the county level in premodern China. The county government itself was hamstrung by insufficient staff, lack of funds, and the short terms of officials. All this made it difficult for officials to keep the county population, which averaged 100,000–250,000, under close surveillance (Overmyer 1976, pp. 199–200).

10. See Perry and Chang's (1980) study of the Yellow Cliff sect for an example.

11. Naquin (1976, 1981); Liu (2004).

12. On the White Lotus Rebellion, see Naquin (1976, 1981); Liu (2004); Dai (2019). On the Taiping Rebellion, see Wagner (1982); Weller (1994).

13. See Ma and Han (1992). The myriad of NRMs that proliferated in late imperial China influenced and intertwined with one another, giving rise to even newer movements. Most of these NRMs venerated the Eternal Venerable Mother (Wusheng Laomu) as the supreme deity—the creator and savior of humanity. According to their teachings, the human race, once created, became estranged from the Mother and was endangered by calamities. In response, the Mother dispatched various deities to save her children from the apocalypse and reunite them with her. These NRMs produced popular scriptures and established hierarchical structures, each led by a patriarch (Lu 2008, p. 3). Major NRMs active during the Republican era, such as Tongshanshe and the Way of Unity, can trace their origins to these earlier movements.

14. Dikötter (2008).

15. Chow (1967).

16. See Zhang et al. (1979); Dirlik (1993); Xu (2001); Dikötter (2008).

17. Goossaert and Palmer (2011, p. 93).

18. Chen (2014).

19. Duara (2001).

20. Palmer (2011).

21. Palmer (2011).

22. Duara (2001, p. 119).

23. Chen (2014).

24. Duara (2001).

25. Goossaert and Palmer (2011, p. 106).

26. For instance, in Shanghai alone, the Way of Unity had 1,144 altars, more than 6,200 religious specialists, and around 300,000 adherents in 1949 (*Shanghai gongan zhi* [Gazetteer of Shanghai Public Security] 1997); Shanxi Province had 1.47 million followers of the Way of Unity prior to 1949 (B. Li 2017).

27. Missionary-adepts not only work on self-cultivation but are active in bringing others to the path of salvation. See Billioud (2020).

28. Like many other NRMs at the time, the Way of Unity had a multilevel hierarchy structure. At the top was the patriarch, below whom are the leaders of the way (*daozhang*), the initiators (*dianchuan shi*), and the masters of the altars (*tanzhu*). See Lu (2008, p. 32); Billioud (2020).

29. My husband's family in Shanghai had a parallel experience. Many of them, including my mother-in-law, who was a young girl at the time, joined the Moral Society of the Middle Way (Zhongdao Jiaoyi Hui), an NRM founded in 1932 and headquartered in Shanghai. Registered as a religious association with the Shanghai Bureau of Social Affairs in 1936, it grew quickly in the Yangtze River Delta and gained a membership of more than two hundred thousand people in ten years (Han 2015). After the NRM was suppressed in the early 1950s, the family's association with it became a secret. Even my husband had no knowledge of it—he had always thought his mother was a Buddhist until I picked up a clue from the conversation with my mother-in-law.

Both of our families' experiences are indicative of how pervasive the NRM's influence was prior to 1949.

30. Palmer (2011).

31. McFarland (1967).

32. See Lu (2008, pp. 39–41) for strategies adopted by the Maoist state in the campaign.

33. Information is from 1969 police reports in the county's Archive Bureau.

34. In the early 1980s, several NRMs that had been repressed during the Mao era resurfaced on a small scale in River County. For instance, a group of a dozen or so middle-aged and elderly women revived Changshengjiao and made a few new initiates. However, by the early 1990s, the group dissolved as many of its followers joined lay Buddhist communities. As for the Way of Unity, I found no evidence suggesting its revival in River County during the post-Mao period. However, in another city in China in the early years of the 2000s, I encountered two missionary-adepts of the Way of Unity. At the time, they were both in their late eighties. Both had endured long prison terms during the Mao era, and together with their daughter, they actively recruited followers and reconnected with the Way of Unity in Taiwan.

In Taiwan, the Way of Unity gained legitimacy and societal acceptance after the lifting of martial law in 1987. Amassing millions of followers and substantial resources in Taiwan, it has also achieved notable success in overseas missionary work. The Way of Unity's promotion of traditional Chinese culture and sympathetic stance toward closer Taiwan-mainland relations made it appealing to mainland authorities. The mainland Chinese government, interested in fostering connections with individuals and organizations in Taiwan as part of its United Front work, saw the Way of Unity as a useful partner. This alignment allowed the group to foster a cooperative relationship with the mainland Chinese government, leading to tacit permission for its activities in mainland China, provided they remain discreet, even though the Way of Unity remains officially classified as a "reactionary secret society." See Billioud (2020).

Fayi Chongde, one of the largest and most dynamic branches of the Way of Unity, is particularly active on the mainland. It has established altars in every province of mainland China, according to private communication with a scholar in mainland China who has followed the development of the organization for decades and gained access to its internal documents. However, in recent years on the mainland, there have been sporadic cases of Way of Unity missionaries from Taiwan being detained and its gathering place being raided by local authorities. See https://www.guancha.cn/society/2018_06_07_459221.shtml (accessed November 1, 2024) and https://www.zaobao.com.sg/realtime/china/story20241204-5489286 (accessed December 5, 2024). This indicates that the permissive environment has come under strain, as the mainland Chinese government has heightened its scrutiny due to perceived foreign religious infiltration. See also the conclusion.

35. Palmer (2008).

36. At the time, there were qigong movements also founded by charismatic leaders that had massive followings. These movements, such as Zhonggong, exhibited a centralized hierarchy and some form of congregational structure. The key difference between these movements and Falun Gong is that, although some of the former began incorporating religious elements, they had not yet become full-fledged religions at the time when Falun Gong transformed into an NRM. See Palmer's (2007) book for an examination of other large qigong groups.

37. Penny (2012) offers the most systematic and comprehensive scholarly treatment of Falun Gong's teachings to date. Also see Palmer (2007, pp. 225–35) and Ownby (2008, pp. 93–123) for analysis of Falun Gong's religious messages.

38. Penny (2012, pp. 113–35).

39. H. Li (1994, pp. 333–45).

40. H. Li (1994, p. 35).

41. Penny (2012, pp. 90–92, 131–33).

42. Li's speech on January 8, 1996, https://big5.falundafa.org/chibig5/jjyz_26.htm (accessed October 1, 2023).

43. Li's speech on February 21–22, 1999, https://big5.falundafa.org/chibig5/uswest.htm (accessed October 1, 2023).

44. For instance, H. Li (1994, pp. 121–24).

45. For instance, Li's speech on September 4–5, 1998, https://gb.falundafa.org/chigb/swiss.htm (accessed October 1, 2023).

46. By the time Falun Gong was suppressed in July 1999, it had 39 main stations, 1,900 guidance stations and 28,000 practice sites in China (Tong 2009, p. 9).

47. For instance, Li Hongzhi's speech on January 6, 1996, https://gb.falundafa.org/chigb/jjyz_25.htm (accessed October 1, 2023).

48. On social fevers in the Deng Xiaoping era, see Wang (1996); Zhao (2001, pp. 42–45).

49. Palmer (2007, pp. 46–85) meticulously documented how political patronage enabled the formation of the qigong sector.

50. Palmer (2007, p. 55).

51. I personally witnessed the qigong boom and participated in it. Every evening, when the music started to play, my neighbors and I, then a high-school student, would gather in the open space in the neighborhood to practice the Aromatic Gong (Xianggong). When the master of Soaring Crane Qigong (Hexiang Zhuang) came to my hometown in 1990 to give instructions to practitioners in the stadium, the event was attended by thousands. Qigong masters were also invited to give talks at universities. At one such lecture I attended at my university in 1993, the audience, including students and professors, all raised their hands high to receive the "external qi" (*waiqi*) that the qigong master supposedly emitted.

52. See https://package.minghui.org/mh/center/chuanfa.htm#1 (accessed October 1, 2023).

53. Palmer (2007, p. 223).

54. All names are pseudonyms.

55. Palmer (2007, pp. 260–61).

56. Penny (2012, p. 59).

57. Palmer (2007).

58. Palmer (2007, p. 248).

59. Xin (1996).

60. X. Chen (1998).

61. See http://www.xjsmgq.gov.cn/zdl/fxjzl/13109.htm (accessed August 1, 2023).

62. Hence, Palmer (2007) calls Falun Gong a "militant qigong."

63. See http://www.scio.gov.cn/xwfb/gwyxwbgsxwfbh/wqfbh_2284/2001n_13621/2001n02y27r/202207/t20220715_158526.html (accessed August 1, 2023).

64. Ownby (2008, p. 175).

65. Palmer (2007, pp. 273–74).

66. These verdicts on the gravity of the political threat posed by Falun Gong adopt primarily the same rhetoric across different official media. See, for example, the commentary of the *People's Daily* with the title "Enhance Awareness, Recognize the Harm: Revisiting the Urgency of Resolving the 'Falun Gong' Issue" (July 27, 1999) and the commentary published by *Qiushi*,

the leading official theoretical journal of the CCP—"There Has Never Been a Savior: Refuting Li Hongzhi's Millenarianism" (July 27, 1999).

67. It was thus named because the date of its creation was June 10.

68. In a campaign launched in 2005, Falun Gong declared that all those who have participated in the CCP or its youth organizations, such as the Communist Youth League or Young Pioneers, bore the "mark of the beast" and should promptly renounce their association to erase it. Readers may find its rhetoric strongly echoing the apocalyptic imagery of the Book of Revelation. As Falun Gong moved its base to North America, it started to appropriate more elements from Christianity, befitting its syncretic nature.

69. See for examples https://gb.falundafa.org/chigb/jjyz3_76.htm; https://gb.falundafa.org/chigb/jiangfa2_1.htm and https://gb.falundafa.org/chigb/na2002.htm (accessed August 1, 2023).

70. In 2004, *Epoch Times*, Falun Gong's media outlet, published a series of editorials in the form of nine articles attacking the CCP under the title "The Nine Commentaries on the Communist Party." See Ownby (2008, pp. 221–22).

71. This is precisely what Lewis argues in his 2018 book.

72. See Tong (2009) for details of the labor reform and conversion programs.

73. Private conversation with a Falun Gong follower in 2016. See also posts on two anticult websites, with the titles "An Exploration of the Methods to Educate and Deprogram Fanatical Falun Gong Followers" and "Use Traditional Culture to Walk Cult Victims Out of the Pit," https://www.zhanlu.org.cn/zlforum/962949.html and http://www.hnsfxjxh.net/v_zx.asp?id=353 (accessed August 1, 2023).

74. The term "most plagued areas" of Falun Gong refers to areas where the movement had a substantial following prior to the crackdown in 1999 and where members persisted in engaging in actions of protest, such as petitioning or distributing Falun Gong materials, even after the crackdown. This term has been used in China's official news reporting and official documents.

75. For the NRMs that have already gained broad recognition and become more or less established worldwide, the Chinese government usually would refrain from listing them as "evil cults." Because the Way of Unity has attained legal status in Taiwan and many countries, the Chinese government treats it in a way similar to how it treats Bahá'í and the Mormons (Palmer 2012; Vendassi 2014). These religions have also engaged in dialogues with Chinese authorities over the years, and some kind of understanding has been reached. The religions exercise a great degree of self-control in return for the government's tolerance.

76. Palmer (2007, pp. 278–80).

77. See https://www.cecc.gov/resources/legal-provisions/national-peoples-congress-standing-committee-decision-on-banning#body-chinese (accessed August 1, 2023).

78. See https://www.cecc.gov/resources/legal-provisions/supreme-peoples-court-supreme-peoples-procuratorate-interpretation-on-0 (accessed August 1, 2023).

Chapter 5

1. In addition to the dominant Chinese Buddhism (*hanchan fojiao*), there are other distinct Buddhist traditions in China, notably Theravada Buddhism, which is practiced primarily among several ethnic groups in Yunnan Province, and Tibetan Buddhism. These traditions fall outside the scope of this book.

2. On Buddhism's early transmission in China, see Y. Tang ([1938] 2017); Zürcher (1959); Ch'en (1964).

3. Attempts of rulers to employ Buddhism for political legitimation are mentioned in historical surveys of Buddhism in China such as that of Ch'en (1964). This theme receives particular attention in more recent works of Ku (2003) and Jülch (2016). There are also works examining several most notable rulers' attempts to style themselves as Buddhist monarchs. See Forte's (1976) and Chen's (2002) work on Wu Zhao (reigned 690–705), the only female emperor in Chinese history; Janousch's (1999) and De Rauw's (2008) work on Emperor Wu of the Liang Dynasty (reigned 502–49); and Hughes's (2021) work on Emperor Wen of the Sui dynasty (reigned 581–604) and on Wu Zhao.

4. Zhao (2015, pp. 331–42), in his synthesis of the advent of "a Confucian society" as a result of the neo-Confucian movement, highlights the strong element of competitive isomorphism in the neo-Confucianism movement in response to the Buddhist challenge.

5. Faure (2007, p. 279).

6. According to Goossaert (2000)'s study of a census of Buddhist and Daoist clergy conducted in 1736–1739, Daoist clerics made up approximately 13 percent of the total clerical population. This percentage closely aligns with census data from earlier periods, including the Song, Yuan, and early Ming dynasties. Across all provinces in China, Buddhist clergy constituted the majority.

7. For an overview of Chinese Buddhism in post-Mao China, see Birnbaum (2003); Sun (2011); Ji (2012).

8. For instance, Qin (2000); Ashiwa and Wank (2006).

9. Gildow (2014, 2020); Bianchi (2019); Nichols (2022); Campo (2023).

10. Fisher's (2011, 2014, 2017, 2019) studies have focused on this issue.

11. For instance, Nichols (2019, 2022); Vidal (2019).

12. Ji (2008); Ashiwa (2009); Wank (2009); Laliberté (2011, 2019).

13. McCarthy (2013); Laliberté (2022).

14. This study chooses to focus on Taiwan under Chiang Kai-shek's rule because this period overlapped with the time when Christianity enjoyed rapid growth in Taiwan, particularly between 1949 and 1965. Since the 1970s, the growth of Christianity has slowed.

15. Wood (1927).

16. Zürcher (1980); Skar (2000).

17. Kohn (2008, p. 69).

18. Bechert (1966); Bond (1988); Gombrich and Obeyesekere (1988).

19. This term was first coined in Obeyesekere (1970). In Gombrich and Obeyesekere's (1988) book, they reflect on the term and conclude, "The utility of the label 'Protestant Buddhism' lies in its double meaning. It originated as a protest against the British in general and against Protestant missionaries in particular. At the same time, however, it assumed salient characteristics of that Protestantism" (p. 7).

20. For the case of Meiji Japan, see Thelle (1987). For the case of Korea, see Nathan (2018).

21. Walters (1992); Learman (2005).

22. Warner (1994); Warner and Wittner (1998); Ebaugh and Chafetz (2000); Yang and Ebaugh (2001); Cadge and Sangdhanoo (2005); Cadge (2008).

23. Chesnut (2003).

24. DiMaggio and Powell (1983).

25. Powell and DiMaggio (1991); Mizruchi and Fein (1999); Drori, Meyer, and Hwang (2006); Krücken and Drori (2009); Scott (2014).

26. Chaves (1996, 1999); Wilde (2007); Wilde et al. (2010).

27. Goossaert (2008b); Ji (2008); Ashiwa (2009); Nedostup (2009); Palmer (2009); Goossaert and Palmer (2011).

28. Hannan and Freeman (1977).

29. Hannan and Freeman (1977); Gilbert (2005).

30. Bays (2012).

31. Gregg (1946); Standaert and Tiedemann (2009). The total population of China in 1910 is a highly debatable issue, with estimates ranging from 368 million to 420 million (Li 2020). I choose to use the rough estimate of 400 million.

32. For the sudden increase of Christian missionary activities in Taiwan, see Rubinstein (1991); Leung (2017, pp. 7–8).

33. The numbers are from Qu (1982a, 1982b) and Madsen (2012).

34. See Huang's (2008) review of relevant studies in China, and Jiang and Xu (1989).

35. Welch (1967, pp. 369–70); Chen and Deng (2000).

36. Welch (1967, pp. 359–60).

37. He (1992); Deng (1994); Chen and Deng (2000); Tang (2013); Ming (2005, 2014); Wu (2016); Xingyun (2016).

38. Li Bingnan (1891–1986), a renowned lay Buddhist leader, presided over the first Buddhist wedding in Taiwan in 1950 (S. Xu 2006).

39. Huang (2010); Yü (2013).

40. Chandler (2004, pp. 193–94).

41. Zürcher ([1999] 2012).

42. Zürcher ([1999] 2012).

43. See Zürcher (1959, [1999] 2012) and Ch'en (1964) for a general picture. On the role of itinerant monks in propagating Buddhism in the Northern dynasties, see S. Liu (2008, pp. 161–67); on the use of storytelling, see Mair (1989) and Z. Zhang (2014); on the use of wonder-making and telling wonderous stories, see Kieschnick (1997).

44. Chen and Deng (2000, p. 16).

45. Tang (2013, p. 121).

46. Chen and Deng (2000, pp. 103–4); Wu (2016, pp. 202–9).

47. Z. Liu (2015).

48. Ming (2016).

49. Chen and Deng (2000, pp. 105–6); Tang (2013); Scott (2016); H. Li (2017).

50. Jones (1999, p. 159); Kiely (2010, p. 202); Zhang (2016).

51. S. Li (2006).

52. Li and Wang (2005, p. 236).

53. Kan (2004, pp. 336–51).

54. There are a number of biographies of Xingyun, such as Fu (2000) and Deng and Mao (2013). Xingyun himself is a prolific author and has published several autobiographic accounts, among which the most notable is *Xingyun* (2013).

55. Deng (1994, pp. 117–18, 211, 219–20); Tang (2013, pp. 169–230).

56. Xu (2006, pp. 60–61).

57. He (2010, pp. 15–25).

58. On Zhengyan and Tzu Chi, see Huang (2009).

59. On Taixu's life and his reform, see Pittman (2001); Y. Chen (2003); Deng and Chen (2017); Ritzinger (2017).

60. Yinshun's autobiographical account has been translated into English; see Yinshun (2009). There are a number of studies on Yinshun's life and work, among which the most comprehensive is Bingenheimer (2004).

61. Taixu coined the term *rensheng fojiao* (Buddhism for the living) to counter the role to which Buddhism was reduced as provider of funerary rituals, and the preoccupation in traditional Chinese Buddhism with the dead/ghosts. Finding inspiration in an Agamas quote stating that "all Buddhas arise in the human realm; no one achieves Buddhahood in heavens," Yinshun used the term *renjian fojian* (Buddhism for the human realm) to criticize what he perceived as an overwhelming tendency in traditional Chinese Buddhism to deify the Buddhas and bodhisattvas and worship them as savior gods. Whatever their nuanced differences, both terms intend to chart a new course for Chinese Buddhism in the modern world, advocating a much more world-engaging role for Buddhism, urging its practitioners to create a pure land in this human realm through their own endeavors instead of seeking rebirth in a pure land through devotional acts. See Pittman (2001); Jones (2003); Bingenheimer (2004, 2007).

62. Mingyang (2004).

63. Deng (1994, pp. 164–69). On the life of Tanxu, see Carter (2014).

64. On the prevalence of the practice of Humanistic Buddhism in Taiwan, see Kan (2004). For analyses of general trends in Buddhism in Taiwan, see also Yang (1991) and Jiang (2009).

65. For an account of the situation of Buddhism under Mao, see Welch (1972).

66. The figures are from the official website of the Buddhist Association of China: https://www.chinabuddhism.com.cn/web/myjs.html (accessed June 12, 2023).

67. See Ji's (2012) assessment of the post-Mao revival of Chinese Buddhism.

68. This survey, carried out by the Chinese Buddhist Society in 1930, did not include data from Sichuan, Henan, Anhui, and Hunan provinces. Therefore, the actual numbers of clerics and temples must have been much larger. See Welch (1967, appendix 1).

69. Ashiwa and Wank (2005).

70. For discussions of the tension that developed between local officials and Buddhist temples due to tourism, see Sun (2009); Nichols (2019).

71. Temples with more than a hundred resident monastics are rare—a rough estimate places that number around forty. This estimate is made by assembling online information and interviews with several well-placed and widely connected monks.

72. Pushou Temple, with resident nuns up to one thousand, and Pingxing Temple, with more than four hundred resident monks, are the two largest monastic communities that have emerged in post-Mao China.

73. The Chan School is a Buddhist school of practice that originated in China during the Tang Dynasty (618–907). It rejects reliance on scriptures and doctrinal study in favor of a more immediate and experiential approach. For an explanation of Pure Land Buddhism, see chapter 3, note 36 and note 151 of this chapter. Chan and Pure Land Buddhism rose to be the dominant Buddhist schools in China in the mid–Tang dynasty and remain so to this day.

74. In interviews, I asked elite Buddhists on the mainland, including leaders and well-educated and aspiring young monastics, to list their top five model temples. Interestingly, their answers displayed great similarity. Even monastics from temples that are perceived by the Buddhist community as fairly commercialized place great value on ascetic monasticism.

75. See McCarthy's (2013) study of the Ren'ai Foundation.

76. Jinghui (1933–2013), abbot of Bailin Temple, was a good friend of Xingyun, founder of Fo Guang Shan. His idea of summer camp was inspired by the practices of Fo Guang Shan. See Yang and Wei (2005); G. Huang (2016). Xuecheng (born 1966), abbot of the Longquan Temple until he was forced to resign amid sex scandals, was hugely influenced by the Fuzhi (Bliss and Wisdom) Center, a Buddhist organization established in Taiwan in 1991. Both Jinghui and Xuecheng once

held important leadership positions in the Buddhist Association of China. See Zhang's (2024) study on Xuecheng's organization.

77. For instance, following the example of Bailin Temple, more and more Buddhist temples started to organize summer camps for college students. Some even offered camps for teenagers.

78. The rest were territorial cult temples registering as Buddhist sites to obtain legal status (see chapter 3). I classify a temple as Buddhist when it satisfies at least two criteria: (1) the principal deities are Buddhist; (2) the primary liturgical framework is Buddhist.

79. He passed away at the age of 91 in 2010.

80. At a well-functioning Buddhist monastery, daily life starts at 4:30 or 5 a.m. Monastics gather at the Main Buddha Hall to begin their morning chanting. This religious service usually lasts from forty minutes to an hour. Then the monastics would have breakfast.

81. The pricing structure for ritual services is often highly stratified. For instance, fees for Buddhist ceremonies could vary considerably based on the size, placement, and prominence of the spirit tablet (*paiwei*). Those who make larger contributions were formally acknowledged as "primary merit-makers" (*da gongdezhu*).

82. For example, for the popular rite to release the burning mouths (*fang yankou*, also known as the rite of feeding ghosts), temples charged 2,500–3,000 yuan (US$366–US$439) in 2009. The rite is a tantric ritual performed by Buddhist monks for the deceased. By the power of the ritual, the deceased who were reborn as hungry ghosts can be fed with sweet dew. The ritual usually lasts more than four hours. For detailed descriptions and analysis of the ritual, see Welch (1967, pp. 185–87).

83. At the occasion of this grand event, many monks outside River County would be invited to participate in hosting the ritual. Their participation would be compensated.

84. As its name indicates, *shuilu fahui* aims to provide universal deliverance to all sentient beings through the power of rites. It has ritual activities taking place simultaneously in the inner altar (*neitan*) and six outer altars (*waitan*). It is believed by Buddhists that *shuilu fahui*, by virtue of so many monks chanting sutras and performing powerful rituals, would generate a great amount of merit. The laity pay to install spirit tablets in the altars so that the merit can be transferred to their deceased relatives. In 2008, Cypress Shade Temple, one of the only two temples in the county that had the ability to organize this grand ritual event, charged a minimum of 50 yuan (US$7) for placing a spirit tablet in the outer altars and 1,000 yuan (US$146) for a spirit tablet in the inner altar, which was more elaborately decorated and had special rituals. For a more detailed description of the rite, see Welch (1967, pp. 190–97).

85. The Collection was compiled by Huang Xianian and his associates and published in 2006 and 2007.

86. The website is http://buddhistinformatics.dila.edu.tw/minguofojiaoqikan.

87. After some experimentation, I used the following keywords in my search because they capture most of the Christianity-related entries: *Tianzhu* (Heavenly Father), *Yesu* (Jesus), *Jidu* (Christ, Christians, Christianity), *Shangdi* (God), *Yejiao* (Christianity), *fuyin* (gospel), *shenfu* (Catholic priest), *mushi* (Protestant pastor), *Shengjing* (Bible), *Daofeng* (Tao Fong Shan Christian Centre), *yiduan* (heresy), *yang* (foreign).

88. The authors were a diverse group, encompassing well-known leaders and recent converts, monastics and lay Buddhists. A few authored hundreds of articles, and some only authored one. What distinguished them from many of their coreligionists is that they were educated, well-informed, and active, among the movers and shakers of the Chinese Buddhist community. In other words, they belonged to the Buddhist elite. Of the 112 articles whose publication dates are

recorded, 20 were published in the 1920s, 39 in the 1930s, and 53 in the 1940s. This shows that the awareness of the Christian challenge was present among the Buddhist elite throughout the entire Republican period and was possibly strengthening over time.

89. The attacks concentrate on Christianity's exclusivism (they questioned God's compassion and found the condemnation of unbelievers to hell totally unacceptable) and demand of "blind" faith from its followers (Christianity was thus denounced as a form of "superstition").

90. The Buddhists were especially infuriated by the practices of Tao Fong Shan Christian Centre, founded in Hong Kong in 1930 by Norwegian missionary Karl Ludvig Reichelt (1877–1952) with a mission of reaching out to Buddhist monastics and converting them. Prior to Tao Fong Shan, Reichelt had established Ching Fong Shan in Nanjing with a similar mission.

91. For instance, some authors urge Buddhists not to use the Christian calendar and object to translating Christmas as *shengdan jie*, arguing that the term—literally "holy birth festival"—implicitly affirms Christian religious claims.

92. The negative reports mainly made fun of Catholic priests unable to exorcise demons in the households of the Chinese converts.

93. Yinshun (1932).

94. Nie (1927).

95. Tanxu ([1954] 1993).

96. The quote is from his letter to Chiang, which is included in his autobiography (Xuyun 1953). On Xuyun's life, see Campo's (2016) study.

97. Cited in Li and Wang (2005, p. 239).

98. Shengyan founded Fagushan (Dharma Drum Mountain), one of the most influential Buddhist organizations in Taiwan, in 1989. He has an autobiography in English (Shengyan 2008). Shengyan's (1999a) autobiography in Chinese, *Guicheng*, provides a detailed account of his life and is a valuable source for understanding Buddhism in Republican China and post-1949 Taiwan.

99. Yinshun's polemical essays were compiled and published as a volume titled *Wo zhi zongjiao guan* (My views on religion; Yinshun 2000). Li Bingnan's critiques of Christianity are included in *Li Bingnan laojushi quanji* (Complete works of Li Bingnan; Li 1995). Shengyan's polemics were collected in *Jidujiao zhi yanjiu* (Study of Christianity; Shengyan 1999b). Zhuyun delivered a lengthy diatribe against Christianity in a public speech in 1955, and a transcript was widely circulated in Taiwan at the time (Zhuyun 1966).

100. Here, Huixiu invoked two Chinese idioms to express himself. Wangpo is a fictional figure known for aggressive self-promotion. Jiang was a military strategist in the twelfth to eleventh century BC who helped the kings of Zhou overthrow the Shang dynasty (c. 1600–1046 BCE). Legend has it that he fished in a river using a barbless hook, waiting for fish to come to the hook, just as he patiently waited for the king of Zhou to call upon him.

101. In my revisits to the field sites some ten years later, I found that Buddhism has been even more plagued by the aging and passing of its most devoted population.

102. See Nedostup (2009) for an in-depth study on the institutionalization of the binary religion-superstition paradigm in the Republic of China.

103. The quote is from Goossaert and Palmer (2011, p. 51). Cults of popular religion deities, feng shui, geomancy, spirit mediums, and other religious practices were labeled as superstitious. The states in Republican China and Taiwan under Chiang launched various campaigns to suppress "superstition" (Nedostup 2009).

104. Goossaert and Palmer (2011) coined the term "Christian-secular normative model" to emphasize the impact of the Christian model on religious policy in the Republic of China.

105. Bays and Widmer (2009).

106. Dunch (2014).

107. Goossaert and Palmer (2011, p. 70).

108. Bays (2012, p. 125).

109. Goossaert and Palmer (2011, p. 72).

110. Li (2007, p. 341).

111. The Ministry of the Interior was established in 1928 by the Nationalist government after it made Nanjing its capital. One of its responsibilities was to oversee religious affairs.

112. Xue (1928).

113. Dongchu (1974); Li (2006, pp. 289–91).

114. These were related in Madame Chiang's (1955) testimony of her spiritual journey, published in *Reader's Digest*.

115. Zhuyun (1966); Shengyan (2004); Xingyun (2013); Han (2018).

116. Nanting (1990).

117. Youguang (1936).

118. Taixu (1996).

119. Cai (1934).

120. Li (1995, pp. 139–46, 147–54); Shengyan (2004, pp. 73–75).

121. Zhuyun (1966); Li (1995, pp. 147–54).

122. Yinshun (2000).

123. Zhuyun (1966).

124. Ye (2009); He (2010).

125. Sun (2011).

126. Pittman (2001, p. 249). See also Taixu (1938).

127. Zhang (2016).

128. Anonymous (1946).

129. Chen (1920).

130. Shanyin (1948).

131. Liu (1947).

132. Chen (1947).

133. Zhuyun (1966).

134. Kan (2004, p. 467).

135. Wen (2009).

136. Han (2018).

137. A student of Taixu, Dongchu actively promoted Taixu's agenda for Buddhist reforms in Chiang's Taiwan.

138. Shengyan (2008).

139. The development of Buddhism in Taiwan is often regarded as an integral part of the broader global Engaged Buddhism movement. See Queen, Prebish, and Keown (2003); Hsiao and Schak (2005); Yao (2012).

140. Chandler (2004); Madsen (2007).

141. For discussion of the influence of Buddhism on the civil society and politics in Taiwan, see Jones (1999); Laliberté (2004); Madsen (2007).

142. For a fuller introduction to the biography and teachings of Jingkong, see Sun (2017b). On the evolution of the lay movement influenced by Jingkong's teachings in mainland China, see Xie (2013, 2017); Sun (2017b).

143. Y. He (1999).

144. Y. He (1999).

145. See chapter 4 for more discussion on the feverish conditions in the early post-Mao years.

146. They did so by taking control of Buddhist temples with weak or no clerical leadership, building large Jingkong centers at the sites of popular religious temples, or registering their sites as educational institutions, old-age homes, or libraries.

147. On the Lujiang Center and its relationship with popular Confucianism in post-Mao China, see Ji and Dutournier (2009).

148. The "harmonious society" served as the governing philosophy of the Hu–Wen administration in response to escalating social discontent stemming from rapid and uneven economic growth over the preceding decades. The Lujiang Center not only aligned itself with the prevailing political slogan for self-protection but also genuinely embraced the objective of a harmonious society, seeing its own contribution as instrumental in realizing this goal.

149. Changshengjiao is a sect that originated in Zhejiang Province in the mid-seventeenth century. Its doctrines were a blend of elements of Buddhism and Confucianism. Followers were urged to keep strict vegetarian diets and carry out meritorious deeds to attain longevity. The sect was severely suppressed by the Qing government in the eighteenth century, but it went underground and still existed in Zhejiang, Jiangsu, and Jiangxi provinces during the Republican era; see Seiwert (2003, pp. 316–17). It was persecuted in the campaign launched by the CCP in the 1950s.

150. The sutra is one of the primary sutras in the tradition of Pure Land Buddhism. The sutra describes the creation of the Pure Land of Amitābha Buddha and goes into great detail to describe this Land of Bliss and its inhabitants. The sutra also contains the Forty-Eight Vows made by the Amitābha Buddha to save all sentient beings. The eighteenth vow forms a basic tenet of Pure Land Buddhism; it states that if a sentient being makes even ten recitations of the Amitābha Buddha's name, his rebirth into the Pure Land is certain. Jingkong made every endeavor to promote this sutra, in effect elevating it above all other Buddhist texts.

151. The practice requires a group of devotees assembled together to chant the name of Amitābha incessantly by the bedside of the dying to help concentrate his/her mind on seeking rebirth in Amitābha's Pure Land.

152. Miller and Spoolman (2012).

153. For instance, see https://tianjian.org/tjw/jingkongxs/beizhipj2.htm (accessed June 12, 2023) for the article titled "Red Alert: The Hidden and Elusive Undercurrent of the 'Jingkong Cult.'"

154. Although it is at the discretion of the RAB to grant or refuse registration status to religious groups, the bureau would first consult the religious associations about the qualification of the applicants. Religious associations' endorsement is usually a perquisite for the RAB to approve the application.

155. Jingkong, in contrast to Li Hongzhi, never urged his followers in mainland China to resist or protest the government's proscription. He refrained from making complaints against the Chinese government and hinted that someone within the Buddhist establishment opposed his return to mainland China. In his lectures, he continued to curry favor with the government. He also placed hope in some of his well-connected lay disciples in mainland China to intercede on his behalf to persuade the government to lift the proscriptions.

156. Donglin Temple is one of the sacred sites of Pure Land Buddhism. Interestingly, Donglin Temple received patronage and support from Li Muyuan, head of the Singapore Buddhist Lodge, who was Jingkong's most important patron between 1997 and 2000. After a falling-out in 2000 with Jingkong, he turned to supporting Da'an and Donglin Temple.

157. I also note that none of Jingkong's emulators has been able to generate an enthusiastic lay movement on the scale Jingkong did.

158. Informant No. 99.

159. Informant No. 389.

Conclusion

1. Western media coverage, NGO documentation, government reports, and scholarly analyses abound on China's intensified religious persecution and repression. Examples include Fifield (2018); https://freedomhouse.org/report/special-report/2017/battle-chinas-spirit; https://www.govinfo.gov/content/pkg/CHRG-115hhrg32308/html/CHRG-115hhrg32308.htm; https://berkleycenter.georgetown.edu/posts/regulating-religion-in-china (accessed July 16, 2023); "Sinicization of Religion: China's Coercive Religious Policy" and a report by the US Commission on International Religious Freedom (https://www.uscirf.gov/publications/sinicization-religion-chinas-coercive-religious-policy, accessed October 24, 2024).

2. Johnson (2019).

3. Smith (2018); the report of the US Congressional-Executive Commission on China (2018), https://www.cecc.gov/publications/annual-reports/2018-annual-report (accessed July 16, 2023).

4. The campaign launched by the Zhejiang provincial government to remove crosses from the tops of church buildings was often cited as evidence of the Xi administration's repression of Christianity. However, we can reach a more contextualized understanding of this campaign by taking into account the following observations: First, although the crosses were removed, they were not demolished but allowed to be displayed on the facade of the church. Second, the cross-removal campaign did not affect worship and other aspects of church life. Third, the campaign mainly affected government-registered Three-Self churches and sparked widespread grievances, protests, and strong criticisms inside this sector. In effect, the campaign served to strengthen the solidarity between Three-Self churches and independent churches. Fourth, this campaign was mainly restricted to Zhejiang Province and remained largely confined there. Fifth, the Zhejiang provincial government claimed the cross-removal campaign was part of its urban renewal project—the so-called Three Rectifications and One Demolition Campaign, which targeted structures that violated the government's zoning regulations. While this claim is contestable, it is little disputed that only 0.26 percent of the demolished structures were religious, and among these, merely 2.3 percent were Christian (https://news.sina.cn/gn/2014-08-20/detail-iaxixtqn59 55251.d.html?from=wap, accessed August 1, 2023). Across the province, popular religion temples bore the brunt. If this religion has defenders as powerful as Protestantism, the campaign can very well be interpreted as persecution targeting popular religion. See Jiang's (2015) report on this campaign and Cao (2017) and Ying (2018) for differing interpretations.

5. The Doctrine of Four Confidences and the notion of the Chinese Dream are signature political philosophies of the Xi Jinping administration. The Doctrine of Four Confidences calls for CCP members, government officials, and the Chinese people to have confidence in the path, theory, system, and culture of socialism with Chinese characteristics. The Chinese Dream mainly refers to the "great rejuvenation of the Chinese nation."

6. An English translation of the revised *Regulations on Religious Affairs* can be found at https://www.loc.gov/item/global-legal-monitor/2017-11-09/china-revised-regulations-on-re ligious-affairs (accessed August 1, 2023).

7. In Zhejiang Province, this position is usually held by the deputy secretary of the CCP at the township level.

8. For instance, Zhejiang Province has developed and mandated the use of apps such as "Religion on the Palm" (Zhangshan Zongjiao), which requires different agencies to input their inspection reports of religious venues into the system and requires religious organizations to rectify any problems found in the inspections and to perform self-evaluations.

9. The RAB of River County, for instance, proudly listed installing surveillance cameras at registered religious sites as one of its achievements in 2017.

10. On the Sinicization campaign, see Chang (2018) and Madsen (2021).

11. For analyses of the core socialist values of China, see Gow (2017); Lin and Trevaskes (2019); Miao (2020).

12. On numerous occasions, Xi has spoken of the need to strengthen cultural confidence, promote traditional Chinese culture, and build a "spiritual home" for the Chinese people. For instance, https://news.cctv.com/2023/11/01/ARTIimc2FdFGgMUt40EIysFr231101.shtml; http://www.moe.gov.cn/jyb_xwfb/s6052/moe_838/202410/t20241008_1156272.html (accessed October 24, 2024).

13. On December 5, 2016, a national conference was convened to study key messages of Xi's speeches and the central government's work plan for popular religion. At the conference, Wang Zuoan, director of SARA and vice-minister of the UFWD from 2009 to 2022, praised the positive values of popular religion: "Doing the good work with popular religions has great significance for uniting the masses and fostering social harmony and stability, for safeguarding national and public interests and for resisting foreign infiltration, for promoting China's fine traditional culture and cultivating good social norms; for maintaining close contact with overseas Chinese and advancing the unification of the motherland." See the report "Jiji tansuo wenbu tuijin: Qieshi tigao minjian xinyang gongzuo nengli he shuiping" [Exploring actively and advancing steadily: Conscientiously improving capabilities and standards of the work on folk beliefs], *Zhongguo zongjiao* [China religion], 2016/12: 16–17.

14. Ashiwa and Wank (2023).

15. My analysis focuses on officials whose work is related to religious affairs, yet their behavior aligns with broader trends within China's bureaucracy. For example, Chinese officials today work much harder than they did a decade ago, though much of their energy is consumed by increasingly complex yet ultimately hollow bureaucratic procedures. They find themselves planning often unrealistic goals, struggling to cope with the demands of the very "plans" they created, and devising ad hoc solutions to the policy directives and bureaucratic requirements imposed by various levels and agencies of the government. These bureaucratic practices frequently yield outcomes that diverge from or even contradict the intentions of policymakers. See Zhao (2019) for an insightful analysis of the challenges facing China's bureaucracy.

16. Political positioning requires officials to align their actions, policies, or stance with the political goals and ideology of the CCP, emphasizing their ideological commitment and loyalty to, and support of, the Party's core objectives. Officials are also repeatedly urged to take initiative (*you suowei*), be bold in taking responsibility (*ganyu dandang*), and demonstrate diligence and dedication in their work (*qinzheng*).

17. An example from River County in 2019 illustrates this point. In that year, RAB officials, in collaboration with public security officers, raided a house church that had refused to register with the government. The authorities suspended the church service and confiscated furniture, resulting in a physical altercation. In response, the house-church leaders traveled to Beijing to

seek justice through the petitioning system. Upon their return, some were detained by local police on charges of "disrupting public order." Meanwhile, the RAB chief was reprimanded for mishandling the situation and subsequently reassigned to an insignificant post.

18. Red tourism in China involves visiting historical sites significant to the CCP's revolutionary past, such as Mao's former residences, battlefields of the Long March, revolutionary museums, and places like the Jinggang Mountains in Jiangxi Province, which was the birthplace of the Red Army, and Yan'an, which was the CCP's power base from 1937 to 1947. The practice has grown significantly since the 1990s, with a notable surge under the Xi administration, as it was promoted as an important means of political education. See Yan and Hyman (2023).

19. For instance, Yang (2021).

20. This is a nationwide phenomenon, as Chang (2018) notes. At times, the formalistic tendencies pushed the Sinicization campaign to the point of absurdity. Daoism, China's indigenous religion, has also been compelled to participate by devising ways to "Sinicize" itself. The Chinese Daoist Association even issued the *Outline of Five-Year Work Plan for Adhering to the Direction of Sinicization of Daoism (2019-2023)*. This absurdity highlights how bureaucrats often prioritize performative displays over the realization of policy objectives.

21. For Mao's war against the bureaucracy, see Lee (1978); Wu and Zhao (2007); Walder (2015).

22. See Zhao (2023) for an analysis of bureaucratic formalism under Xi.

23. As early as in 2004, religious regulatory agencies in Zhejiang, Fujian, Hunan, and Guangdong provinces experimented with ways to govern popular religion temples. However, it is under Xi Jinping that the legalization and registration of popular religion temples has been carried out forcefully across China. See Chen (2018).

24. Zhejiang, Fujian, Hunan, Guangdong, Jiangsu, and Shaanxi provinces took the lead in the registration process. Gansu, Sichuan, Guangxi, Anhui, Jiangxi, and other provinces have followed. Registering popular religion sites has become nationwide.

25. For instance, the governments of Hunan and Jiangsu provinces specified that temples with a main hall exceeding fifty square meters, or those hosting a single religious event with more than a thousand participants in the span of one year, were eligible for registration. The *Regulations on the Management of Folk Belief Activities Sites* in Jiangsu and Hunan provinces can be found, respectively, at https://mzw.jiangsu.gov.cn/art/2020/7/27/art_39793_9329448.html and https://www.faxin.cn/lib/dffl/dfflContent.aspx?gid=B1412339 (accessed August 1, 2023).

26. The government of Taizhou, a city in Zhejiang Province, began experimenting with temple registration as early as 2004. Their experimentation has given rise to the so-called Taizhou model and has greatly influenced how the Zhejiang provincial government formulated its policies toward popular religion. According to the Bureau of Religious Affairs of Taizhou, in their campaign to dismantle illegally constructed buildings in 2014, the Taizhou government demolished a total of 1,463 popular religion structures and converted 588 temples to other uses; http://www.zjsmzw.gov.cn/Public/NewsInfo.aspx?type=1&id=52ab70f5-d3e5-4cb5-a60e-956 b878779d0 (accessed August 1, 2023). See also Chen and Lin (2016).

27. See the measures adopted by the township officials of Xiangjiazhen of Pingjiang County in Hunan Province for an example: http://www.pingjiang.gov.cn/35048/35049/34957/36135/36 062/content_1793794.html (accessed August 1, 2023).

28. *Notice from the General Office of the People's Government of Hunan Province on Issuing the "Regulations on the Management of Folk Belief Activities Sites in Hunan Province"* (https:// www.faxin.cn/lib/dffl/dfflContent.aspx?gid=B1412339, accessed August 1, 2023).

29. Positive energy is another catchphrase in the Xi era, referring to "attitudes or emotions that are aligned with the ideological or value systems of the Chinese government, or any discourses that promote such an alignment" (P. Yang and Tang 2018).

30. Song (2018).

31. Take Dong's temple in River County (see chapter 3) as an example. In July 2023, I revisited this temple only to be informed that Dong passed away in 2017. Another elderly lady in her late eighties kept the keys of the temples. She was rather frail and, due to cataracts, had difficulty moving around. She became sentimental when recalling the good old days when Dong was in charge. With the older-generation female worshippers fading away, this temple has long ceased to hold ritual events. The fate of this temple is representative of many small popular religion temples in the region.

32. Xi Jinping's speech at UNESCO Headquarters on March 27, 2014, is available at http://www.xinhuanet.com//politics/2014-03/28/c_119982831_2.htm (accessed August 1, 2023).

33. The full Chinese text of the document *Several Suggestions on Further Addressing the Commercialization Problems in Buddhism and Daoism* can be found at https://www.gov.cn/zhengce/zhengceku/2017-11/23/content_5538962.htm (accessed August 1, 2023).

34. See https://www.youtube.com/watch?v=HmIW0SWx35A (accessed August 1, 2023).

35. The group cited Matthew 24, verse 27—"For as lightning that comes from the east is visible even in the west, so will be the coming of the Son of Man"—to support their central claim that Jesus has returned to earth to work and incarnated as a woman in China. See Dunn's (2015) in-depth study of this NRM.

36. Cardinal Joseph Zen, retired bishop of Hong Kong, has been one of the most outspoken critics of Pope Francis's attempt to make a deal with China. He penned a strongly worded opinion piece in the *New York Times* with the title "The Pope Doesn't Understand China." See Fraze (2017); Zen (2018).

37. Scammell (2016).

38. See https://www.vaticannews.va/en/vatican-city/news/2024-10/holy-see-china-provisional-agreement-appointment-bishops-extend.html (accessed November 30, 2024).

39. This placed the Vatican in a difficult position. In response, the Vatican's Secretariat of State issued an unsigned document offering "pastoral guidelines of the Holy See concerning the civil registration of clergy in China" in 2019. It acknowledged the plight of the underground Church and stated that "the Holy See understands and respects the choice of those who, in conscience, decide that they are unable to register under the current conditions." Yet the guidelines offered little practical aid to the pressed underground Church.

40. For instance, in April 2023, the China side unilaterally installed Joseph Shen Bin as bishop of Shanghai, and the Vatican learned of his appointment from the media. Shen is the head of the Council of Chinese Bishops, the state-sanctioned bishops' conference. Three months later, Pope Francis decided to recognize Shen's appointment, even though the Vatican protested to China about its violation of the bilateral agreement. The position of bishop in Shanghai had remained vacant since Bishop Ma Daqin was placed under house arrest, leaving the largest diocese in China in a state of paralysis (see chapter 2). This is perhaps why Pope Francis, despite his dissatisfaction with China's unilateral action, ultimately chose to compromise. The compromise damaged the credibility of the papacy, already under criticism for abandoning and sacrificing the underground flock who had paid a great price for their loyalty to the pope. For critical voices inside the Catholic community, see https://www.pillarcatholic.com/p/pope-francis-long-view-on-china-has (accessed August 1, 2023). The papacy has also been criticized by Western media

outlets and NGOs for remaining silent about China's worsening religious freedom and human rights violations.

41. Around US$4,500 based on the exchange rate at the time.

42. Similar sentiments and trends could be found among the Catholic communities.

43. I explored the variable success of Christianity in its global expansion since the Age of Exploration in another article (Sun 2014b).

Appendix I

1. See the conclusion for a discussion on the Eastern Lightning.

2. The sutra is an indigenous Chinese scripture composed in the sixth century, devoted to the worship of Avalokiteśvara. For an introduction on the origin of this scripture, see Chien (2022).

Bibliography

Aikman, David. 2003. *Jesus in Beijing: How Christianity Is Transforming China and Changing the Global Balance of Power*. Washington, DC: Regnery.

Anagnost, Ann. 1994. "The Politics of Ritual Displacement." In *Asian Voices of Authority: Religion and the Modern States of East and Southeast Asia*, edited by Charles Keyes, Laurel Kendall, and Helen Hardacre. Honolulu: University of Hawai'i Press.

Anderson, Eugene N. 1970. "The Boat People of South China." *Anthropos* 65 (1/2): 248–56.

Anonymous. 1946. "Jingren zhi Jidujiao xuanchuan jihua" [The alarming evangelism plan of Christians]. *Juequn zhoubao* [Awakening the multitude weekly news] 1 (14): 7. Reprinted in *Minguo Fojiao qikan wenxian jicheng* 101: 229.

Armstrong, Karen. 2006. *The Great Transformation: The Beginning of Our Religious Traditions*. New York: Knopf.

Asad, Talal. 2003. *Formations of the Secular: Christianity, Islam, Modernity*. Stanford, CA: Stanford University Press.

Ashiwa, Yoshiko. 2009. "Positioning Religion in Modernity: State and Buddhism in China." In *Making Religion, Making the State: The Politics of Religion in Modern China*, edited by David L. Wank and Yoshiko Ashiwa. Stanford, CA: Stanford University Press.

Ashiwa, Yoshiko, and David L. Wank. 2005. "The Globalization of Chinese Buddhism: Clergy and Devotee Networks in the Twentieth Century." *International Journal of Asian Studies* 2: 217–37.

Ashiwa, Yoshiko, and David L. Wank. 2006. "The Politics of a Reviving Buddhist Temple: State, Association, and Religion in Southeast China." *Journal of Asian Studies* 65 (2): 337–59.

Ashiwa, Yoshiko, and David L. Wank. 2023. "Chinese Buddhism and Soft Power: Geopolitical Strategy and Modality of Religion." In *The Geopolitics of Religious Soft Power: How States Use Religion in Foreign Policy*, edited by Peter Mandaville. New York: Oxford Academic Press.

Barnadas, Josep. 1984. "The Catholic Church in Colonial Spanish America." In *The Cambridge History of Latin America*, edited by Leslie Bethell. Cambridge: Cambridge University Press.

Baum, Richard. 1994. *Burying Mao: Chinese Politics in the Age of Deng Xiaoping*. Princeton, NJ: Princeton University Press.

Bays, Daniel H. 1996. "The Growth of Independent Christianity in China, 1900–1937." In *Christianity in China: From the Eighteenth Century to the Present*, edited by Daniel H. Bays. Stanford, CA: Stanford University Press.

Bays, Daniel H. 2003. "Chinese Protestant Christianity Today." *China Quarterly* 174 (3): 488–504.

Bays, Daniel H. 2012. *A New History of Christianity in China*. Malden, MA: Wiley-Blackwell.

Bays, Daniel, and Ellen Widmer. 2009. *China's Christian Colleges: Cross-Cultural Connections, 1900–1950*. Stanford, CA: Stanford University Press.

Beanman, W. F. 1901. "And Still It Saves." *Baptist Mission Magazine* 81 (8): 544–45.

Bechert, Heinz. 1966. *Buddhismus, Staat und Gesellschaft in den Ländern des Theravāda-Buddhismus*. Frankfurt am Main: Alfred Metzner Verlag.

Beckford, James A. 1978. "Accounting for Conversion." *British Journal of Sociology* 29 (2): 249–62.

Bell, Norman W. 1959. "Review of *Tokugawa Religion: The Values of Pre-Industrial Japan* by Robert N. Bellah." *Canadian Journal of Economics and Political Science / Revue Canadienne d'Economique et de Science Politique* 25 (2): 239–41.

Bellah, Robert N. 1957. *Tokugawa Religion: The Values of Pre-Industrial Japan*. Glencoe, IL: The Free Press.

Bellah, Robert N. 1970. *Beyond Belief: Essays on Religion in a Post-Traditional World*. New York: Harper & Row.

Bellah, Robert N., and Hans Joas, eds. 2012. *The Axial Age and Its Consequences*. Cambridge, MA: Harvard University Press.

Benedict XVI. 2007. "Letter of the Holy Father Pope Benedict XVI to the Bishops, Priests, Consecrated Persons and Lay Faithful of the Catholic Church in the People's Republic of China." https://w2.vatican.va/content/benedict-xvi/en/letters/2007/documents/hf_ben-xvi_let _20070527_china.html.

Berezkin, Rostislav. 2018. "Paying for Salvation: The Ritual of 'Repaying the Loan for Life' and Telling Scriptures in Changshu, China." *Asian Ethnology* 77 (1–2): 307–29.

Berger, Peter L. 1967. *The Sacred Canopy: Elements of a Sociological Theory of Religion*. New York: Doubleday.

Berkey, Jonathan Porter. 2003. *The Formation of Islam: Religion and Society in the Near East, 600–1800*. Cambridge: Cambridge University Press.

Bianchi, Ester. 2019. "Transmitting the Precepts in Conformity with the Dharma: Restoration, Adaptation, and Standardization of Ordination Procedures." In *Buddhism after Mao: Negotiations, Continuities, and Reinventions*, edited by Zhe Ji, Gareth Fisher, and André Laliberté. Honolulu: University of Hawai'i Press.

Billioud, Sébastien. 2020. *Reclaiming the Wilderness: Contemporary Dynamics of the Yiguandao*. New York: Oxford University Press.

Bingenheimer, Marcus. 2004. *Der Mönchsgelehrte Yinshun (1906*) und seine Bedeutung für den Chinesisch-Taiwanischen Buddhismus im 20. Jahrhundert*. Heidelberg: Edition Forum, Würzburger Sinologische Schriften.

Bingenheimer, Marcus. 2007. "Some Remarks on the Usage of Renjian Fojiao and the Contribution of Venerable Yinshun to Chinese Buddhist Modernism." In *Development and Practice of Humanitarian Buddhism: Interdisciplinary Perspectives*, edited by Mutsu Hsu, Jinhua Chen, and Lori Meeks. Hua-Lien: Tzuchi University Press.

Bireley, Robert. 1999. *The Refashioning of Catholicism, 1450–1700: A Reassessment of the Counter Reformation*. Washington, DC: Catholic University of America Press.

Birnbaum, Raoul. 2003. "Buddhist China at the Century's Turn." *China Quarterly* 174: 428–50.

Bol, Peter K. 1992. *"This Culture of Ours": Intellectual Transitions in T'ang and Sung China*. Stanford, CA: Stanford University Press.

Bol, Peter K. 2008. *Neo-Confucianism in History*. Cambridge, MA: Harvard University Asia Center.

Bond, George Doherty. 1988. *The Buddhist Revival in Sri Lanka: Religious Tradition, Reinterpretation, and Response*. Columbia: University of South Carolina Press.

Brandt, Loren, and Thomas G. Rawski, eds. 2008. *China's Great Economic Transformation*. Cambridge: Cambridge University Press.

Brim, John A. 1974. "Village Alliance Temples in Hong Kong." In *Religion and Ritual in Chinese Society*, edited by Arthur P. Wolf. Stanford, CA: Stanford University Press.

Brockey, Liam Matthew. 2009. *Journey to the East: The Jesuit Mission to China, 1579–1724*. Cambridge, MA: Belknap Press of Harvard University Press.

Brook, Timothy. 1996. "Toward Independence: Christianity in China under the Japanese Occupation, 1937–1945." In *Christianity in China: From the Eighteenth Century to the Present*, edited by Daniel H. Bays. Stanford, CA: Stanford University Press.

Brook, Timothy. 2005. *The Chinese State in Ming Society*. London: Routledge Curzon.

Bruce, Steve. 1999. *Choice and Religion: A Critique of Rational Choice Theory*. New York: Oxford University Press.

Bruce, Steve. 2002. *God Is Dead: Secularization in the West*. Oxford: Blackwell.

Brusco, Elizabeth E. 2011. *The Reformation of Machismo: Evangelical Conversion and Gender in Colombia*. Austin: University of Texas Press.

Bryant, Joseph M. 2000. "Cost-Benefit Accounting and the Piety Business: Is *Homo religiosus*, at Bottom, a *Homo economicus*?" *Method and Theory in the Study of Religion* 12: 520–48.

Burdick, John. 1993. *Looking for God in Brazil: The Progressive Catholic Church in Urban Brazil's Religious Arena*. Berkeley: University of California Press.

Bush, Richard Clarence. 1970. *Religion in Communist China*. Nashville, TN: Abingdon.

Cadge, Wendy. 2008. "De Facto Congregationalism and the Religious Organizations of Post-1965 Immigrants to the United States: A Revised Approach." *Journal of the American Academy of Religion* 76 (2): 344–74.

Cadge, Wendy, and Sidhorn Sangdhanoo. 2005. "Thai Buddhism in America: An Historical and Contemporary Overview." *Contemporary Buddhism* 6 (1): 7–35.

Cai, Huicheng. 1934. "Duiyu Yufojie Jidutu xuanjiang de ganyan" [My views on Christians' proselytization on Buddha's birthday]. *Zhengxin* 4 (8): 4. Reprinted in *Minguo Fojiao qikan wenxian jicheng* 61: 314.

Campbell, Colin. 1977. "Clarifying the Cult." *British Journal of Sociology* 28 (3): 375–88.

Campbell, John L., and Leon N. Lindberg. 1990. "Property Rights and the Organization of Economic Activity by the State." *American Sociological Review* 55 (5): 634–47.

Campo, Daniela. 2016. "Chan Master Xuyun: The Embodiment of an Ideal, the Transmission of a Model." In *Making Saints in Modern China*, edited by David Ownby, Vincent Goossaert, and Ji Zhe. New York: Oxford University Press.

Campo, Daniela. 2023. "Buddhist Monastic Regulations in Contemporary China: Adapting the Rules to a Changing Social and Political Context." In *"Take the Vinaya as Your Master": Monastic Discipline and Practices in Modern Chinese Buddhism*, edited by Ester Bianchi and Daniela Campo. Leiden: Brill.

Cao, Nanlai. 2007. "Christian Entrepreneurs and the Post-Mao State: An Ethnographic Account of Church-State Relations in China's Economic Transition." *Sociology of Religion* 68 (1): 45–66.

Cao, Nanlai. 2010. *Constructing China's Jerusalem: Christians, Power, and Place in Contemporary Wenzhou*. Stanford, CA: Stanford University Press.

Cao, Nanlai. 2017. "Spatial Modernity, Party Building, and Local Governance: Putting the Christian Cross-Removal Campaign in Context." *China Review* 17 (1): 29–52.

Carlin, J. W., and Mrs. Carlin. 1895. "Ungkung—1892." *Baptist Missionary Magazine* 75: 360.

Carter, James. 2014. *Heart of Buddha, Heart of China: The Life of Tanxu, a Twentieth Century Monk*. Oxford: Oxford University Press.

Casanova, José. 2011. *Public Religions in the Modern World*. Chicago: University of Chicago Press.

Castelli, Elizabeth A. 2004. *Martyrdom and Memory: Early Christian Culture Making*. New York: Columbia University Press.

Chan, Anita, Richard Madsen, and Jonathan Unger. 1984. *Chen Village Under Mao and Deng*. Berkeley: University of California Press.

Chan, Kam Wing, J. Vernon Henderson, and Kai Yuen Tsui. 2008. "Spatial Dimensions of Chinese Economic Development." In *China's Great Economic Transformation*, edited by Loren Brandt and Thomas G. Rawski. Cambridge: Cambridge University Press.

Chan, Shun-hing. 2012a. "Changing Church and State Relations in Contemporary China: The Case of Mindong Diocese, Fujian Province." *China Quarterly* 212: 982–99.

Chan, Shun-hing. 2012b. "Changing Church-State Relations in Contemporary China: The Case of the Fengxiang Diocese." *Chinese Sociological Review* 45 (2): 65–77.

Chandler, Stuart. 2004. *Establishing a Pure Land on Earth: The Foguang Buddhist Perspective on Modernization and Globalization*. Honolulu: University of Hawai'i Press.

Chang, Jianhua. 1988. "Lun 'Shengyu guangxun' yu Qingdai de xiaozhi" [On the *Amplified Instructions on the Sacred Edict* and governance through filial principles in the Qing Dynasty]. *Nankai shixue* [Nankai Historical Studies] 1: 147–72.

Chang, Jianhua. 2001. "Mingdai zongzu cimiao jizu lizhi jiqi yanbian" [The establishment and evolution of the sacrificial ritual at ancestral temples in Ming]. *Nankai xuebao* [Nankai Journal] 3: 60–67.

Chang, Jianhua. 2006. *Qingdai de guojia yu shehui yanjiu* [A study of state and society in Qing]. Beijing: Zhongguo renmin daxue chubanshe.

Chang, Kuei-min. 2018. "New Wine in Old Bottles: Sinicisation and State Regulation of Religion in China." *China Perspectives* 1–2: 37–44.

Chang, Patricia M. Y. 2003. "Escaping the Procrustean Bed: A Critical Analysis of the Study of Religious Organizations, 1930–2001." In *Handbook of the Sociology of Religion*, edited by Michele Dillon. Cambridge: Cambridge University Press.

Chao, Jonathan T'ien-en. 1986. "The Chinese Indigenous Church Movement, 1919–1927: A Protestant Response to the Anti-Christian Movements in Modern China." PhD diss., Department of Oriental Studies, University of Pennsylvania.

Charbonnier, Jean. 1992. *Histoire des chrétiens de Chine*. Paris: Desclée.

Charbonnier, Jean. 1993. "The 'Underground' Church." In *The Catholic Church in Modern China: Perspectives*, edited by Edmond Tang and Jean-Paul Wiest. Eugene, OR: Wipf & Stock.

Chartier, Roger. 2015. *The Cultural Origins of the French Revolution*. Durham, NC: Duke University Press.

Chau, Adam Yuet. 2005. "The Politics of Legitimation and the Revival of Popular Religion in Shaanbei, North-Central China." *Modern China* 31 (2): 236–78.

Chau, Adam Yuet. 2006. *Miraculous Response: Doing Popular Religion in Contemporary China*. Stanford, CA: Stanford University Press.

Chaves, Mark. 1996. "Ordaining Women: The Diffusion of an Organizational Innovation." *American Journal of Sociology* 101 (4): 840–73.

Chaves, Mark. 1999. *Ordaining Women: Culture and Conflict in Religious Organizations*. Cambridge, MA: Harvard University Press.

Chen, Baifeng. 2012. "Jidujiao chuanbo yu Zhongguo zongjiao zai renshi: Cong E'nan nongcun jinyan qieru" [The spread of Christianity and the rethinking of Chinese religions: A case study of rural Southern Hubei]. *Rural China: An International Journal of History and Social Science* 9 (1): 147–71.

Chen, Bing, and Zimei Deng. 2000. *Ershi shiji Zhongguo Fojiao* [Chinese Buddhism in the 20th century]. Beijing: Minzu chubanshe.

Chen, Cunfu, and Tianhai Huang. 2004. "The Emergence of a New Type of Christians in China Today." *Review of Religious Research* 46 (2): 183–200.

Chen, Faxiang. 1947. "Fojiaotu ji ying jiaru chuanjiao bisai: Fu shi" [Buddhists must urgently join the missionary competition: A comment]. *Jue Youqing* 179–80: 8. Reprinted in *Minguo Fojiao qikan wenxian jicheng* 89: 116.

Chen, Hsi-yuan. 1999. "Confucianism Encounters Religion: The Formation of Religious Discourse on the Confucian Movement in Modern China." PhD diss., Department of History, Harvard University.

Chen, Hui. 1920. "Ping Zhongguo Fojiao tu chuanjiao de taidu bing lun xuanchuan Fojiao de fazi" [A critique of Chinese Buddhists' attitudes toward proselytization and methods for propagating Buddhism]. *Xin Fojiao* 1 (6): 3. Reprinted in *Minguo Fojiao qikan wenxian jicheng* 7: 397.

Chen, Jinguo. 2009. "Bentu qinghuai yu quanqiu shiye: Gan, Xiang, Yun sansheng jidujiao xianzhuang diaocha baogao" [Local concern and global perspective: Field report on Christianity in Jiangxi, Hunan, and Yunnan provinces]. In *Zhongguo zongjiao baogao* [Annual report on China's religions], edited by Ze Jin and Yonghui Qiu. Beijing: Shehui kexue wenxian chubanshe.

Chen, Jinguo. 2018. "Zhongguo minjian xinyang ruhe zouxiang shanzhi" [How can good governance of Chinese popular religion be realized]. *Zhongyang Shehui Zhuyi Xueyuan Xuebao* [Journal of the Central Institute of Socialism] 3: 115–20.

Chen, Jinguo, and Minxia Lin. 2016. "Ruhe zouxiang 'shanzhi': Zhejiang sheng minjian xinyang shehui zhili zhuanxing de fasi" [Toward good governance: Reflections on the transformation in the management of popular religion in Zhejiang Province]. In *Zhongguo zongjiao baogao* [Annual report on China's religions], edited by Yonghui Qiu. Beijing: Shehui kexue wenxian chubanshe.

Chen, Jinhua. 2002. "Śarīra and Scepter: Empress Wu's Political Use of Buddhist Relics." *Journal of the International Association of Buddhist Studies* 25 (1–2): 33–150.

Chen, Yongge. 2003. Fojiao honghua de xiandai zhuanxing: Minguo Zhejiang fojiao yanjiu [Modernization of the proliferation of Buddhism: A study of Buddhism in Republican Zhejiang (1912–1949)]. Beijing: Zongjiao wenhua chubanshe.

Ch'en, Kenneth. 1964. *Buddhism in China: A Historical Survey*. Princeton, NJ: Princeton University Press.

Chen, Minghua. 2014. "Quanli bianqian yu xinxing zongjiao de yingdui: Yi Shijie Hongwanzihui Xuzhou fenhui huizhi jiufen weizhong de kaocha (1921–1936)" [Power shift and the responses of new religious movement: A case study of a site dispute involving the Xuzhou Branch of the Red Swastika Society (1921–1936)]. *Zhejiang daxue xuebao (shehui kexue ban)* [Journal of Zhejiang University (Humanities and Social Sciences)] 11 (5): 80–96.

Chen, Xingqiao. 1998. "Falun Gong: Yizhong juyou mingjian zongjiao tedian de fufo waidao" [Falun Gong: A pseudo-Buddhist heretical cult with attributes of popular sectarian religions]. *Fayin* [Voice of dharma] 3–4: 21–28.

Chen, Zhihua, and Qiuxiang Li. 2010. *Zhuge cun* [Zhuge village]. Beijing: Qinghua daxue chubanshe.

Cheng, Tiejun, and Mark Selden. 1994. "The Origins and Social Consequences of China's Hukou System." *China Quarterly* 139: 644–68.

Chesnut, R. Andrew. 1997. *Born Again in Brazil: The Pentecostal Boom and the Pathogens of Poverty*. New Brunswick, NJ: Rutgers University Press.

Chesnut, R. Andrew. 2003. *Competitive Spirits: Latin America's New Religious Economy*. New York: Oxford University Press.

Chien, Li-kuei. 2022. "Magnifying Statuettes: Reconsidering the Artistic Production of the Earliest Buddha Statues in Japan." In *Dynamics of Interregional Exchange in East Asian Buddhist Art, 5th–13th Century*, edited by Dorothy C. Wong. Wilmington, DE: Vernon Press.

Chow, Kai-Wing. 1994. *The Rise of Confucian Ritualism in Late Imperial China: Ethics, Classics and Lineage Discourse*. Stanford, CA: Stanford University Press.

Chow, Tse-tsung. 1967. *The May Fourth Movement: Intellectual Revolution in Modern China*. Stanford, CA: Stanford University Press.

Chu, Tung-tsu. 1962. *Local Government in China Under the Ch'ing*. Cambridge, MA: Harvard University Press.

Chuanjie. 1928. "Fojiao he yejiao de bijiao ji fojiaotu de zeren" [A comparison between Buddhism and Christianity and the responsibility of Buddhists]. *Xiandai sengqie* [Modern sangha] 1 (1): 9–14. Reprinted in *Minguo Fojiao qikan wenxian jicheng bubian* 139: 343–48.

Clark, Anthony E. 2010. "No Easy Answers: An Interview with Shanghai's Bishop Aloysius Jin Luxian, S. J." *Ignatius Insight*, July 23.

Clarke, Jeremy. 2013. *The Virgin Mary and Catholic Identities in Chinese History*. Hong Kong: Hong Kong University Press.

Clart, Philip. 2013. "'Religious Ecology' as a New Model for the Study of Religious Diversity in China." In *Religious Diversity in Chinese Thought*, edited by Perry Schmidt-Leukel and Joachim Gentz. New York: Palgrave Macmillan.

Cline, Erin M. 2010. "Female Spirit Mediums and Religious Authority in Contemporary Southeastern China." *Modern China* 36 (5): 520–55.

Coggins, Chris. 2003. *The Tiger and the Pangolin: Nature, Culture, and Conservation in China*. Honolulu: University of Hawai'i Press.

Cohen, Myron. 1990. "Lineage Organization in North China." *Journal of Asian Studies* 49 (3): 509–34.

Cohen, Paul A. 1963. *China and Christianity: The Missionary Movement and the Growth of Chinese Antiforeignism, 1860–1870*. Cambridge, MA: Harvard University Press.

Congressional-Executive Commission on China. 2018. "The Communist Party's Crackdown on Religion in China." https://www.congress.gov/event/115th-congress/house-event/LC64946/text?s=1&r=81.

Cooper, Gene. 2013. *The Market and Temple Fairs of Rural China*. London: Routledge.

Dai, Yingcong. 2019. *The White Lotus War: Rebellion and Suppression in Late Imperial China*. Seattle: University of Washington Press.

Daughton, J. P. 2008. *An Empire Divided: Religion, Republicanism, and the Making of French Colonialism, 1880–1914*. Oxford: Oxford University Press.

Davis, Deborah. 1995. *Urban Spaces in Contemporary China: The Potential for Autonomy and Community in Post-Mao China*. Washington, DC: Woodrow Wilson Center.

Dean, Kenneth. 1995. *Taoist Ritual and Popular Cults of Southeast China*. Princeton, NJ: Princeton University Press.

Dean, Kenneth. 1997. "Ritual and Space: Civil Society or Popular Religion?" In *Civil Society in China*, edited by Timothy Brook and B. Michael Frolic. Armonk, NY: M. E. Sharpe.

Dean, Kenneth. 2003. "Local Communal Religion in Contemporary South-East China." *China Quarterly* 174: 338–58.

Dean, Kenneth, and Zhenman Zheng. 2010. *Ritual Alliances of the Putian Plain*. Leiden: Brill.

de Bary, Wm. Theodore, and John W. Chaffee, eds. 1989. *Neo-Confucian Education: The Formative Stage*. Berkeley: University of California Press.

Deng, Zimei. 1994. *Chuantong Fojiao yu Zhongguo jindaihua* [Traditional Buddhism and the modernization of China]. Shanghai: Huadong shifan daxue chubanshe.

Deng, Zimei, and Qinyong Mao. 2013. *Xingyun dashi xin zhuan* [A new biography of Master Xingyun]. Beijing: Shehui kexue wenxian chubanshe.

Deng, Zimei, and Weihua Chen. 2017. *Taixu dashi xin zhuan* [A new biography of Master Taixu]. Beijing: Huawen chubanshe.

De Rauw, Tom. 2008. "Beyond Buddhist Apology: The Political Use of Buddhism by Emperor Wu of the Liang Dynasty (r. 502–549)." PhD diss., Department of Languages and Cultures, Ghent University.

Dikötter, Frank. 2008. *The Age of Openness: China Before Mao*. Berkeley: University of California Press.

DiMaggio, Paul J., and Walter W. Powell. 1983. "The Iron Cage Revisited: Institutional Isomorphism and Collective Rationality in Organizational Fields." *American Sociological Review* 48 (2): 147–60.

Dirlik, Arif. 1993. *Anarchism in the Chinese Revolution*. Berkeley: University of California Press.

Dobbelaere, Karel. 1981. *Secularization: A Multi-Dimensional Concept*. London: Sage.

Dongchu. 1974. *Zhongguo Fojiao jindaishi* [History of Buddhism in modern China]. Taipei: Chung-Hwa Institute of Buddhist Culture.

Drori, Gili S., John W. Meyer, and Hokyu Hwang. 2006. *Globalization and Organization: World Society and Organisational Change*. Oxford: Oxford University Press.

Du, Xiaotian. 2011. "Cong nongcun jidujiao shenxing kan nongmin shehui baozhang xuqiu: Jiyu Yu xinan H cun de diaocha" [Understanding the rise of Christianity in rural China through the lens of peasants' social security needs: Evidence from Village H in southwest Henan]. *Xibei renkou* [Northwest Population] 32 (4): 43–46.

Duan, Qi. 2010. "Zongjiao shengtai shiheng dui jidujiao fazhan de yingxiang: Yi Jiangxi Yugan xian de zongjiao diaocha weili" [The loss of equilibrium of religious ecology and its impact on the growth of Protestant Christianity: An investigation based on Yugan County in Jiangxi Province]. *Zhongguo minzu bao* [Chinese ethnic news], January 19.

Duara, Prasenjit. 1988. *Culture, Power, and the State: Rural North China, 1900–1942*. Stanford, CA: Stanford University Press.

Duara, Prasenjit. 1991. "Knowledge and Power in the Discourse of Modernity: The Campaigns Against Popular Religion in Early Twentieth-Century China." *Journal of Asian Studies* 50 (1): 67–83.

Duara, Prasenjit. 2001. "The Discourse of Civilization and Pan-Asianism." *Journal of World History* 12 (1): 99–130.

Dubois, Thomas David. 2005. *The Sacred Village: Social Change and Religious Life in Rural North China*. Honolulu: University of Hawai'i Press.

Dudbridge, Glen. 1992. "Women Pilgrims to Taishan: Some Pages from a Seventeenth-Century Novel." In *Pilgrims and Sacred Sites in China*, edited by Susan Naquin and Chün-fang Yü. Berkeley: University of California Press.

Dunch, Ryan. 2001. "Protestant Christianity in China Today: Fragile, Fragmented, Flourishing." In *China and Christianity: Burdened Past, Hopeful Future*, edited by Stephen Uhalley and Xiaoxin Wu. New York: Routledge.

Dunch, Ryan. 2014. *Fuzhou Protestants and the Making of a Modern China, 1857–1927*. New Haven, CT: Yale University Press.

Dunn, Emily. 2015. *Lightning from the East: Heterodoxy and Christianity in Contemporary China*. Leiden: Brill.

Durkheim, Émile. (1893) 1964. *The Division of Labor in Society*. Translated by W. D. Halls. New York: Free Press.

Durkheim, Émile. (1897) 1951. *Suicide: A Study in Sociology*. Translated by John A. Spaulding and George Simpson. New York: Free Press.

Durkheim, Émile. (1912) 1995. *The Elementary Forms of Religious Life*. Translated by Karen E. Fields. New York: Free Press.

Ebaugh, Helen Rose Fuchs, and Janet Saltzman Chafetz, eds. 2000. *Religion and the New Immigrants: Continuities and Adaptations in Immigrant Congregations*. Walnut Creek, CA: AltaMira.

Ebrey, Patricia Buckley. 1986. "The Early Stages in the Development of Descent Group Organization." In *Kinship Organization in Late Imperial China, 1000–1940*, edited by Patricia Buckley Ebrey and James L. Watson. Berkeley: University of California Press.

Ebrey, Patricia Buckley. 1991. *Confucianism and Family Rituals in Imperial China: A Social History of Writing About Rites*. Princeton, NJ: Princeton University Press.

Esherick, Joseph W. 1988. *The Origins of the Boxer Uprising*. Berkeley: University of California Press.

Fan, Lizhu. 2003. "The Cult of the Silkworm Mother as a Core of Local Community Religion in a North China Village: Field Study in Zhiwuying, Baoding, Hebei." *China Quarterly* 174: 359–72.

Fan, Lizhu, Na Chen, and Richard Madsen. 2015. "Chuantong de yishi yu fugui: Wenzhou nanbu xiangcun zongzu chuantong de tianye yanjiu" [The loss and renewal of cultural heritage: Ethnographic study on lineage traditions in southern Wenzhou]. In *Jiangnan diqu de zongjiao yu gonggong shenghuo* [Religion and public life in Greater Jiangnan], edited by Robert P. Weller and Lizhu Fan. Shanghai: Shanghai renmin chubanshe.

Fan, Zhengyi. 2005. "Jindai Fujian chuanmin xinyang tanxi" [A study of religious belief among boat people of Fujian in modern China]. *Putian xueyuan xuebao* 6: 37–40.

Fan, Zhengyi. 2015. *Zhongshen xuanhua zhong de shizijiao: Jidujiao yu Fujian minjian xinyang gongchu guanxi yanjiu* [The cross in the sound and fury of Chinese deities: A study on the relations of Christianity and folk beliefs in Fujian]. Beijing: Social Science Academic Press.

Faure, David. 2007. *Emperor and Ancestor: State and Lineage in South China*. Stanford, CA: Stanford University Press.

Feng, Erkang. 2011. *Zhongguo zongzu zhidu yu pudie bianzuan* [The institution of Chinese lineages and the compilation of genealogies]. Tianjin: Tianjin guji chubanshe.

Feng, Zigang. 1935. *Lanxi nongcun diaocha* [A survey of rural Lanxi]. Hangzhou: Zhejiang University.

Feuchtwang, Stephan. 1977. "School-Temple and City God." In *The City in Late Imperial China*, edited by G. William Skinner. Stanford, CA: Stanford University Press.

Feuchtwang, Stephan, and Mingming Wang. 2001. *Grassroots Charisma: Four Local Leaders in China*. London: Routledge.

Fifield, Anna. 2018. "With Wider Crackdowns on Religion, Xi's China Seeks to Put State Stamp on Faith." *Washington Post*, September 15.

Finke, Roger. 2006. "Religious Deregulation: Origins and Consequences." *Journal of Church and State* 48 (3): 477–503.

Finke, Roger, and Rodney Stark. 1992. *The Churching of America, 1776–1990: Winners and Losers in Our Religious Economy*. New Brunswick, NJ: Rutgers University Press.

Finke, Roger, and Patricia Wittberg. 2000. "Organizational Revival from Within: Explaining Revivalism and Reform in the Roman Catholic Church." *Journal for the Scientific Study of Religion* 39 (2): 154–70.

Fisher, Gareth. 2011. "Morality Books and the Regrowth of Lay Buddhism in China." In *Religion in Contemporary China: Revitalization and Innovation*, edited by Adam Yuet Chau. Abingdon, UK: Routledge.

Fisher, Gareth. 2014. *From Comrades to Bodhisattvas: Moral Dimensions of Lay Buddhist Practice in Contemporary China*. Honolulu: University of Hawai'i Press.

Fisher, Gareth. 2017. "Lay Buddhists and Moral Activism in Contemporary China." *Review of Religion and Chinese Society* 4 (2): 247–70.

Fisher, Gareth. 2019. "Places of Their Own: Exploring the Dynamics of Religious Diversity in Public Buddhist Temple Space." In *Buddhism after Mao: Negotiations, Continuities, and Reinventions*, edited by Zhe Ji, Gareth Fisher, and Andre Laliberte. Honolulu: University of Hawai'i Press.

Forney, Matthew. 2001. "Positioning Missionaries." *Time*, February 19. http://content.time.com /time/subscriber/article/0,33009,99019,00.html.

Forte, Antonino. 1976. *Political Propaganda and Ideology in China at the End of the Seventh Century*. Naples: Istituto Universitario Orientale.

Fraze, Barb. 2017. "China and the Vatican Have Reached an Agreement on Bishops, Says Cardinal." *Catholic Herald*, February 9. http://www.catholicherald.co.uk/news/2017/02/09/china -and-the-vatican-have-reached-agreement-on-bishops-says-cardinal.

Freedman, Maurice. 1979. *The Study of Chinese Society: Essays by Maurice Freedman*. Stanford, CA: Stanford University Press.

Fu, Zhiying. 2000. *Handing down the Light: The Biography of Venerable Master Hsing Yun*. Los Angeles: Hsi Lai University Press.

Gaetan, Victor. 2017. "The Vatican and China Reach a Promising Accord." *Foreign Affairs*, March 27. https://www.foreignaffairs.com/articles/2017-03-27/vatican-and-china-reach-promi sing-accord.

Gan, Mantang. 2007. *Cunmiao yu shequ gonggong shenghuo* [Communal temple and community public life]. Beijing: Shehui kexue wenxian chubanshe.

Ge, Zhaoguang. 2001. *Zhongguo sixiangshi* [A history of Chinese thought]. Shanghai: Fudan daxue chubanshe.

Ge, Qinghua. 2009. "Taipingtianguo zhanhou yimin yu Wannan jiaoan" [Post-Taiping Rebellion migration and the anti-Christian incident in southern Anhui]. *Lishi Dang'an* [Historical archives] 1: 75–78.

Gilbert, Clark G. 2005. "Unbundling the Structure of Inertia: Resource Versus Routine Rigidity." *Academy of Management Journal* 48 (5): 741–63.

Gildow, Douglas M. 2014. "The Chinese Buddhist Ritual Field." *Journal of Chinese Buddhist Studies* 27: 59–127.

Gildow, Douglas M. 2020. "Questioning the Revival: Buddhist Monasticism in China since Mao." *Review of Religion and Chinese Society* 7: 6–33.

Glock, Charles. 1964. "The Role of Deprivation in the Origin and Evolution of Religious Groups." In *Religion and Social Conflict*, edited by Robert Lee and Martin Marty. Oxford: Oxford University Press.

Glock, Charles, and Rodney Stark. 1965. *Religion and Society in Tension*. Chicago: Rand McNally.

Goldberg, Jeffery. 1997. "Washington Discovers Christian Persecution." *New York Times Magazine*, December 21. http://www.nytimes.com/1997/12/21/magazine/washington-discovers -christian-persecution.html.

Gombrich, Richard Francis, and Gananath Obeyesekere. 1988. *Buddhism Transformed: Religious Change in Sri Lanka*. Princeton, NJ: Princeton University Press.

Goossaert, Vincent. 2000. "Counting the Monks: The 1736–1739 Census of the Chinese Clergy." *Late Imperial China* 21 (2): 40–85.

Goossaert, Vincent. 2008a. "Irrepressible Female Piety: Late Imperial Bans on Women Visiting Temples." *Nan nü* 10 (2): 212–41.

Goossaert, Vincent. 2008b. "Republican Church Engineering: The National Religious Associations in 1912 China." In *Chinese Religiosities: Afflictions of Modernity and State Formation*, edited by Mayfair Mei-Hui Yang. Berkeley: University of California Press.

Goossaert, Vincent. 2015. "Territorial Cults and the Urbanization of the Chinese World: A Case Study of Suzhou." In *Handbook of Religion and the Asian City*, edited by Peter van der Veer. Berkeley: University of California Press.

Goossaert, Vincent, and David A. Palmer. 2011. *The Religious Question in Modern China*. Chicago: University of Chicago Press.

Gorski, Philip S. 2000. "Historicizing the Secularization Debate: Church, State, and Society in Late Medieval and Early Modern Europe, ca. 1300 to 1700." *American Sociological Review* 65 (1): 138–67.

Gorski, Philip S. 2003. "Historicizing the Secularization Debate: A Program for Research." In *Handbook for the Sociology of Religion*, edited by Michelle Dillon. Cambridge: Cambridge University Press.

Gow, Michael. 2017. "The Core Socialist Values of the Chinese Dream: Towards a Chinese Integral State." *Critical Asian Studies* 49 (1): 92–116.

Gregg, Alice H. 1946. *China and Educational Autonomy: The Changing Role of the Protestant Educational Missionary in China, 1807–1937*. Syracuse, NY: Syracuse University Press.

Greil, Arthur L., and David R. Rudy. 1984. "What Have We Learned from Process Models of Conversion? An Examination of Ten Case Studies." *Sociological Focus* 17 (4): 305–23.

Groesbeck, A. F. 1900. "South China Missionary Conference." *Baptist Mission Magazine* 80 (6): 206–8.

Guo, Lina. 2012. *Qingai zhongye Baili Waifang chuanjiaohui zai Chuan huodong yanjiu* [A study on the MEP's activities in Sichuan during the Mid-Qing]. Beijing: Xueyuan chubanshe.

Guo, Mutian. 1993. *Zhejiang sheng zongjiaozhi ziliao huibian* [A collection of records for the religious history of Zhejiang Province], vol. 1. Book for internal circulation in the Catholic Patriotic Association of Hangzhou, Zhejiang Province.

Guo, Mutian. 2011. *Zhejiang Tianzhujiao shilue* [Brief history of Catholicism in Zhejiang]. Hangzhou: Administrative Commission of the Catholic Church of Zhejiang Province.

Han, Guanqun. 2015. "Yi zu yi shen: Gudai Jiangzhe diqu de Xuyan wang xinyang" [As both ancestor and god: The cult of King Yan of Xu in pre-modern Jiangzhe regions]. *Shilin* [Historical review] 2: 86–96.

Han, Heng. 2012. "Chuanbo moshi yu nongchun jidujiao qunti tezheng de yanbian—jiyu Henan 14 ge diaochadian de fenxi" [Spread and development of rural Protestant groups: A study based on 14 sites in Henan]. *Shijie zongjiao wenhua* [Journal of the world religious culture] 5: 137–65.

Han, Huanzhong. 2018. "Cishan huodong yu Fojiao zhenxing: Qiantan Nanting zhanglao de zongjiao jingzhen yishi" [Charitable activities and the revival of Buddhism: A preliminary discussion of Venerable Nanting's awareness of religious competition]. *Mintai wenhua yanjiu* [Fujian-Taiwan Cultural Research] 3: 33–39.

Han, Songtao. 2015. "Zhongjiao ji Zhongjiaodaoyihui yanjiu" [A study of the Middle-Way Society or the Moral Society of the Middle Way]. *Shijie zongjiao yanjiu* [Studies in world religions] 3: 115–29.

Hannan, Michael T., and John Freeman. 1977. "The Population Ecology of Organizations." *American Journal of Sociology* 82 (5): 929–64.

Hansen, Valerie. 1990. *Changing Gods in Medieval China, 1127–1276*. Princeton, NJ: Princeton University Press.

Hansson, Anders. 1996. *Chinese Outcasts: Discrimination and Emancipation in Late Imperial China*. Leiden: Brill.

Hamrin, Carol Lee. 2004. "Advancing Religious Freedom in a Global China: Conclusions." In *God and Caesar in China: Policy Implications of Church-State Tensions*, edited by Jason Kindopp and Carol Lee Hamrin. Washington, DC: Brookings Institution Press.

Harrison, Henrietta. 2013. *The Missionary's Curse and Other Tales from a Chinese Catholic Village*. Berkeley: University of California Press.

Harvey, Peter. 2013. *An Introduction to Buddhism: Teachings, History and Practices*. 2nd ed. New York: Cambridge University Press.

Hastings, Adrian. 1979. *A History of African Christianity 1950–1975*. Cambridge: Cambridge University Press.

Hastings, Adrian. 1996. *The Church in Africa, 1450–1950*. Oxford: Oxford University Press.

Haveman, Heather A., and Yongxiang Wang. 2013. "Going (More) Public: Institutional Isomorphism and Ownership Reform Among Chinese Firms." *Management and Organization Review* 9 (1): 17–51.

He, Husheng. 2010. "Zhongguo tese sheshuizhuyi zongjiao lilun tixi yanjiu" [Research on the socialist theories of religion with Chinese characteristics]. *Hengyang shifan xueyuan xuebao* [Journal of Hengyang Normal University] 31 (4): 16–23.

He, Jianming. 1992. "Minchu Fojiao gexin yundong shulun" [A survey of the Chinese Buddhist reform movement in early Republican China]. *Jindaishi yanjiu* [Modern Chinese history studies] 4: 74–92.

He, Mianshan. 2010. *Taiwan Fojiao* [Buddhism in Taiwan]. Taiwan: Sonbooks.

He, Yun. 1999. "Jingkong fashi fangwen ji" [An interview with Venerable Jingkong]. *Fojiao wenhua* [Buddhist culture] 4: 4–7.

He, Zhangrong. 2013. "Shanjiao xia de Shizijiao: Guangdong Jiexixian Miaohuzhen Yushicun Tianzhujiao xinyang de kaocha" [Cross at the foot of the hill: A study of Catholicism in Yushi Village, Miaohu Township, Jieshi County of Guangdong Province]. *Zongjiao xue yanjiu* [Religious studies] 1: 200–209.

Hoornaert, Eduardo. 1984. "The Catholic Church in Colonial Brazil." In *The Cambridge History of Latin America*, edited by Leslie Bethell. Cambridge: Cambridge University Press.

Howe, Christopher, Y. Y. Kueh, and Robert F. Ash. 2003. *China's Economic Reform: A Study with Documents*. London: Routledge.

Hsu, Francis L. K. 1948. *Under the Ancestor's Shadow*. New York: Columbia University Press.

Hsu, Francis L. K. 1953. *Americans and Chinese: Two Ways of Life*. New York: Henry Schuman.

Hua, Hua. 2008. "Daxuesheng xinyang Jidujiao zhuangkuang diaocha: Yi Shanghai bufen gaoxiao daxuesheng wei li" [A survey of Christian belief among college students: A case study of several universities in Shanghai]. *Qingnian yanjiu* [Youth study] 1: 27–34.

Huang, C. Julia. 2009. *Charisma and Compassion: Cheng Yen and the Buddhist Tzu Chi Movement*. Cambridge, MA: Harvard University Press.

Huang, C. Julia, Elena Valussi, and David A. Palmer. 2011. "Gender and Sexuality." In *Chinese Religious Life*, edited by David A. Palmer, Glenn Landes Shive, and Philip L. Wickeri. Oxford: Oxford University Press.

Huang, Gongyuan. 2016. "Renjian Fojiao shenghuo chan zai dalu de kaizhan" [Development of life meditation of Humanistic Buddhism in Mainland China]. In *Fayu Zhongguo, purun Yazhou: Renjian fojiao zai Dongya yu Dongnanya de kaizhan* [The Dharma rain in China, spreading across Asia: The development of Humanistic Buddhism in East and Southeast Asia], edited by Centre for the Study of Humanistic Buddhism, Chinese University of Hong Kong. Hong Kong: Centre for the Study of Humanistic Buddhism, Chinese University of Hong Kong.

Huang, Jianbo. 2009. "Ershi nian lai Zhongguo dalu Jidujiao de jinyanxing yanjiu shuping" [A review on empirical studies of Christianity in mainland China in the last twenty years]. *Jidujiao sixiang pinglun* [Regent review of Christian thoughts] 9: 345–66.

Huang, Jianbo. 2012. *Xiangcun shequ de xinyang, zhengzhi yu shenghuo: Wuzhuang Jidujiao de renleixue yanjiu* [Faith, politics and social lives in a rural community: An ethnographic study of Protestants of Wuzhuang]. Hong Kong: Center for the Study of Religion and Chinese Society of Chung Chi College.

Huang, Jianbo. 2013. *Doushi li de xiangcun jiaohui: Zhonghua chengshihua yu mingong Jidujiao* [Rural churches in cities: Urbanization and Christianity of migrant workers in China]. Hong Kong: Daofeng shushe.

Huang, Jianbo. 2014. "Beijing Christians in Urbanizing China: The Epistemological Tensions of the Rural Churches in the City." *Current Anthropology* 55 (s10): s238–s247.

Huang, Jianbo, and Fenggang Yang. 2005. "The Cross Faces the Loudspeakers: A Village Church Perseveres Under the State Power." In *State, Market, and Religions in Chinese Societies*, edited by Fenggang Yang and Joseph B. Tamney. Leiden: Brill.

Huang, Philip C. C. 1985. *The Peasant Economy in Social Change in North China*. Stanford, CA: Stanford University Press.

Huang, Shiru. 2010. *Zhanhou Taiwan Fojiao de sensu guanxi: Yi dazhuan qinnian xuefo yundong wei beijin* [The monastic-lay relationship in post-1949 Taiwan: A case study of Buddhist studies movement among college students]. Taipei: Academia Historica.

Huang, Xianian, ed. 2006. *Mingguo Fojiao qikan wenxian jicheng* [Collection of Republican-Era Buddhist periodical literature]. Beijing: China National Microfilming Center for Library Resources.

Huang, Xianian, ed. 2007. *Minguo Fojiao qikan wenxian jicheng bubian* [Supplement to the complete collection of Republican-Era Buddhist periodical literature]. Beijing: China National Microfilming Center for Library Resources.

Huang, Yasheng. 2008. *Capitalism with Chinese Characteristics: Entrepreneurship and the State*. Cambridge: Cambridge University Press.

Hughes, April D. 2021. *Worldly Saviors and Imperial Authority in Medieval Chinese Buddhism.* Honolulu: University of Hawai'i Press.

Hunter, Alan, and Kim-Kwong Chan. 1993. *Protestantism in Contemporary China.* Cambridge: Cambridge University Press.

Hussey, J. M. 2010. *The Orthodox Church in the Byzantine Empire.* Oxford: Oxford University Press.

Hymes, Robert P. 2002. *Way and Byway: Taoism, Local Religion, and Models of Divinity in Sung and Modern China.* Berkeley: University of California Press.

Hymes, Robert P., and Conrad Schirokauer, eds. 1993. *Ordering the World: Approaches to State and Society in Sung Dynasty China.* Berkeley: University of California Press.

Iannaccone, Laurence R. 1991. "The Consequences of Religious Market Structure: Adam Smith and the Economics of Religion." *American Journal of Sociology* 96 (5): 1065–95.

Janousch, Andreas. 1999. "The Emperor as Bodhisattva: The Bodhisattva Ordination and Ritual Assemblies of Emperor Wu of the Liang Dynasty." In *State and Court Ritual in China*, edited by Joseph McDermott. Cambridge: Cambridge University Press.

Jaspers, Karl. (1949) 1953. *The Origin and Goal of History.* Translated by Michael Bullock. New Haven, CT: Yale University Press.

Jerolmack, Colin, and Douglas Porpora. 2004. "Religion, Rationality, and Experience: A Response to the New Rational Choice Theory of Religion." *Sociological Theory* 22 (1): 140–60.

Josephson, Jason Ānanda. 2012. *The Invention of Religion in Japan.* Chicago: University of Chicago Press.

Ji, Zhe. 2008. "Secularization as Religious Restructuring: Statist Institutionalization of Chinese Buddhism and Its Paradoxes." In *Chinese Religiosities: Afflictions of Modernity and State Formation*, edited by Mayfair Mei-Hui Yang. Berkeley: University of California Press.

Ji, Zhe. 2011. "Buddhism in the Reform Era: A Secularized Revival?" In *Religion in Contemporary China: Revitalization and Innovation*, edited by Adam Yuet Chau. New York: Routledge.

Ji, Zhe. 2012. "Chinese Buddhism as a Social Force: Reality and Potential of Thirty Years of Revival." *Chinese Sociological Review* 45 (2): 8–26.

Ji, Zhe, and Guillaume Dutournier. 2009. "Social Experimentation and 'Popular Confucianism.'" *China Perspectives* (December). https://doi.org/10.4000/chinaperspectives.4925.

Jiang, Canteng. 2009. *Taiwan Fojiao shi* [History of Taiwanese Buddhism]. Taipei: Wu-nan Book.

Jiang, Yannan. 2015. "1200 zuo shizijia beichai, Yazhou zuida jiaotang xian weiji" [1,200 crosses removed, Asia's largest church in crisis]. *Initium Medium*, August 20. https://theinitium.com/zh-hans/article/20150820-china-church-cross.

Jiang, Yufeng. 1991. "Taiping Tianguo shiqi Qingchao guanjun zai Lanxi de yichang da tusha" [A massacre committed by the Qing Army in Lanxi during the Taiping Rebellion]. *Zhejiang xuekan* [Zhejiang academic journal] 67: 25.

Jiang, Zhimin, and Zugen Xu. 1989. "Miandui shizijia de sikao: Zhongguo 'Jidujiaore' touxi" [Thoughts before the cross: An analysis of the 'Christianity fever' in China]. *Liaowang zhoukan* [Outlook weekly] 5: 6–9.

Jin, Luxian. 2012. *The Memoirs of Jin Luxian, Volume 1: Learning and Relearning, 1916–1982.* Hong Kong: Hong Kong University Press.

Jing, Jun. 1996. *The Temple of Memories: History, Power, and Morality in a Chinese Village.* Stanford, CA: Stanford University Press.

Johnson, Ian. 2019. "China's New Civil Religion." *New York Times*, December 22.

Jones, Charles Brewer. 1999. *Buddhism in Taiwan: Religion and the State, 1660–1990*. Honolulu: University of Hawai'i Press.

Jones, Charles Brewer. 2003. "Transitions in the Practice and Defense of Chinese Pure Land Buddhism." In *Buddhism in the Modern World: Adaptations of an Ancient Tradition*, edited by Steven Heine and Charles S. Prebish. New York: Oxford University Press.

Jones, Stephen. 2017. *Daoist Priests of the Li Family: Ritual Life in Village China*. St. Petersburg, FL: Three Pines.

Jülch, Thomas, ed. 2016. *The Middle Kingdom and the Dharma Wheel: Aspects of the Relationship between the Buddhist Saṃgha and the State in Chinese History*. Leiden: Brill.

Kan, Zhengzong. 2004. *Chongdu Taiwan Fojiao* [A reinterpretation of Buddhism in Taiwan]. Taipei: Darchen.

Kang, Xiaofei. 2009. "Rural Women, Old Age, and Temple Work: A Case from Northwestern Sichuan." *China Perspectives* 4: 42–52.

Kang, Xiaofei. 2016. "Women and the Religious Question in Modern China." In *Modern Chinese Religion II: 1850–2015*, edited by Jan Kiely, Vincent Goossaert, and John Lagerwey. Leiden: Brill.

Kang, Zhijie. 2006. *Shangzhu de putaoyuan: E xibei Mopanshan Tianzhujiao shequ yanjiu, 1634–2005* [The Lord's Vineyard: A study of the Mopanshan Catholic community in northwest Hubei, 1634–2005]. Xinzhuang: Furen daxue chubanshe.

Kasoff, Ira E. 1984. *The Thought of Chang Tsai (1020–1077)*. Cambridge: Cambridge University Press.

Keating, John Craig William. 2012. *A Protestant Church in Communist China: Moore Memorial Church Shanghai 1949–1989*. Plymouth: Lehigh University Press.

Kelley, Dean M. 1972. *Why Conservative Churches Are Growing: A Study in Sociology of Religion*. New York: Harper & Row.

Kelliher, Daniel. 1997. "The Chinese Debate over Village Self-Government." *China Journal* 37: 63–86.

Kiely, Jan. 2010. "Spreading the Dharma with the Mechanized Press: New Buddhist Print Cultures in the Modern Chinese Print Revolution, 1866–1949." In *From Woodblocks to the Internet: Chinese Publishing and Print Culture in Transition, Circa 1800 to 2008*, edited by Cynthia Brokaw and Christopher A. Reed. Leiden: Brill.

Kieschnick, John. 1997. *The Eminent Monk: Buddhist Ideals in Medieval Chinese Hagiography*. Honolulu: University of Hawai'i Press.

Kindopp, Jason. 2004a. "Fragmented yet Defiant: Protestant Resilience Under Chinese Communist Party Rule." In *God and Caesar in China: Policy Implications of Church-State Tensions*, edited by Jason Kindopp and Carol Lee Hamrin. Washington, DC: Brookings Institution.

Kindopp, Jason. 2004b. "Policy Dilemmas in China's Church-State Relations: An Introduction." In *God and Caesar in China: Policy Implications of Church-State Tensions*, edited by Jason Kindopp and Carol Lee Hamrin. Washington, DC: Brookings Institution.

Koesel, Karrie J. 2013. "The Rise of a Chinese House Church: The Organizational Weapon." *China Quarterly* 215: 572–89.

Kohn, Livia. 2008. *Introducing Daoism*. New York: Routledge.

Kraus, Richard Curt. 2012. *The Cultural Revolution: A Very Short Introduction*. Oxford: Oxford University Press.

Krücken, Georg, and Gili S. Drori, eds. 2009. *World Society: The Writings of John W. Meyer*. Oxford: Oxford University Press.

Kuhn, Philip. 1970. *Rebellion and Its Enemies in Late Imperial China: Militarization and Social Structure, 1796–1864.* Cambridge, MA: Harvard University Press.

Kuru, Ahmet T. 2009. *Secularism and State Policies Toward Religion: The United States, France, and Turkey.* Cambridge: Cambridge University Press.

Laliberté, André. 2004. *The Politics of Buddhist Organizations in Taiwan, 1989–2003: Safeguarding the Faith, Building a Pure Land, Helping the Poor.* London: RoutledgeCurzon.

Laliberté, André. 2011. "Buddhist Revival Under State Watch." *Journal of Current Chinese Affairs—China Aktuell* 40: 107–34.

Laliberté, André. 2019. "Buddhism Under Jiang, Hu and Xi." In *Buddhism after Mao: Negotiations, Continuities, and Reinventions,* edited by Zhe Ji, Gareth Fisher, and André Laliberté. Honolulu: University of Hawai'i Press.

Laliberté, André. 2022. *Religion and China's Welfare Regimes: Buddhist Philanthropy and the State.* Singapore: Palgrave Macmillan.

Lam, Anthony. 2011. "Recalling the 1981 Episcopal Ordinations and Their Consequences for the Chinese Catholic Church." *Tripod* 31 (163).

Lam, Anthony. 2016. "Catholic Population in China Since 2000 and Its Impact." *Tripod* 31 (180).

Lapidus, Ira M. 2002. *A History of Islamic Societies.* Cambridge: Cambridge University Press.

Latourette, Kenneth Scott. 1929. *A History of Christian Missions in China.* New York: Macmillan.

Learman, Linda. 2005. *Buddhist Missionaries in the Era of Globalization.* Honolulu: University of Hawai'i Press.

Lee, Hong Yung. 1978. *The Politics of the Chinese Cultural Revolution: A Case Study.* Berkeley: University of California Press.

Lee, Joseph Tse-Hei. 2014. *The Bible and the Gun: Christianity in South China, 1860–1900.* Abingdon: Routledge.

Leemans, Johan. 2005. *More Than a Memory: The Discourse of Martyrdom and the Construction of Christian Identity in the History of Christianity.* Dudley, MA: Peeters.

Legge, James, trans. 1885. *The Sacred Books of China: The Texts of Confucianism. Part IV. The Li Ki, XI–XLVI. The Sacred Books of the East,* vol. 28, edited by Max Müller. Oxford: Clarendon.

Leung, Beatrice. 2005. "China's Religious Freedom Policy: The Art of Managing Religious Activity." *China Quarterly* 184: 894–913.

Leung, Beatrice. 2017. "Introduction." In *The Catholic Church in Taiwan: Problems and Prospects,* edited by Francis K. H. So, Beatrice Leung, and Ellen Mary Mylod. New York: Springer.

Leung, Beatrice, and Marcus J. J. Wang. 2016. "Sino-Vatican Negotiations: Problems in Sovereign Right and National Security." *Journal of Contemporary China* 25 (99): 467–82.

Leung, Beatrice, and Patricia Wittberg. 2004. "Catholic Religious Orders of Women in China: Adaptation and Power." *Journal for the Scientific Study of Religion* 43 (1): 67–82.

Leung, Ka-lun. 1999. *Gaige kaifang yilai de zhongguo nongcun jiaohui* [Rural Protestant churches in reform-era China]. Hong Kong: Alliance Bible Seminary.

Lewis, James R. 2018. *Falun Gong: Spiritual Warfare and Martyrdom.* Cambridge: Cambridge University Press.

Li, Baochang. 2017. "Kangzhan shiqi Shanxi Yiguandao tanwei" [A study of the Way of Unity in Shanxi during the Sino-Japanese War]. *Kangri zhanzheng yanjiu* [Journal of studies of China's resistance war against Japan] 1: 72–86.

Li, Bingnan. 1995. *Li Bingnan laojushi quanji* [Complete works of Li Bingnan]. Taipei: Qinglian chubanshe.

Li, Hongzhi. 1994. *Zhuan Falun*. Beijing: Zhongguo dianshi guanbo chubanshe.

Li, Huawei. 2010. "Huabei zongzu de ruohua yu jidujiao zai xiangtu shehui de fazhan: Yi Yu xi Licun wei zhongxin de kaocha" [The decline of the lineage organizations and the growth of Christianity in rural North China: A case study of Li Village in western Henan Province]. *Zhongguo nongye daxue xuebao (shehui kexue ban)* [Journal of China Agricultural University (social sciences edition)] 27 (3): 18–32.

Li, Huawei. 2012. "Kunan yu gaijiao: Henan sandi xiangcun minzong gaixin jidujiao de shehui genyuan tanxi" [Suffering and conversion: An analysis on the social causes of peasants' conversion to Christianity in three sites of Henan Province]. *Zhongguo nongye daxue xuebao (shehui kexue ban)* [Journal of China Agricultural University (social sciences edition)] 29 (3): 81–91.

Li, Hui. 2017. "Foxue congbao yu Minguo Fojiao fuxin" [Journal of Buddhist miscellany and the revival of Buddhism in Republican China]. *Anhui daxue xuebao* [Journal of Anhui University] 5: 130–40.

Li, Kwok Sing. 1995. *A Glossary of Political Terms of the People's Republic of China*. Hong Kong: Chinese University Press of Hong Kong.

Li, Laura Tyson. 2007. *Madame Chiang Kai-Shek: China's Eternal First Lady*. New York: Grove Press.

Li, Shangquan. 2006. *Dangdai Zhongguo hanchuan Fojiao xinyang fangshi de bianqian* [Evolution of the forms of contemporary Chinese Buddhism]. Lanzhou: Gansu renmin chubanshe.

Li, Sher-shiueh. 2022. *Ovid in China*. Leiden: Brill.

Li, Shiwei, and Wang Jianchuan. 2005. "Dazhuan qingnina xuefo yundong de chuqi fazhan (1958–1971)" [The initial stage of Buddhist study movement among college students in Taiwan from 1958 to 1971]. In *Taiwan Fojiao de tansuo* [The exploration of Buddhism in Taiwan], edited by Chunwu Fan, Jianchuan Wang, and Shiwei Li. Taipei: Boyoung Culture.

Li, Xiaochen. 2012. *Jindai Hebei xiangcun Tianzhu jiaohui yanjiu* [A study of Catholic communities in rural Hebei in modern China]. Beijing: Renmin chubanshe.

Li, Yong, and Zihua Chi. 2006. "Jindai Sun'nan yumin de Tianzhujiao xinyang" [Catholicism among fisherman communities in south Jiangsu in modern China]. *Zhongguo nong shi* [Agricultural history of China] 25 (4): 98–104.

Li, Zhangpeng. 2020. "Qingmo Zhongguo de jindai renkou diaocha" [China's modern population survey in the late Qing dynasty]. *Qing shi yanjiu* [Qing history journal] 1: 25–44.

Lian, Xi. 2010. *Redeemed by Fire: The Rise of Popular Christianity in Modern China*. New Haven, CT: Yale University Press.

Lieberthal, Kenneth, and Michel Oksenberg. 1988. *Policy Making in China*. Princeton, NJ: Princeton University Press.

Lin, Delia, and Susan Trevaskes. 2019. "Creating a Virtuous Leviathan: The Party, Law, and Socialist Core Values." *Asian Journal of Law and Society* 6 (1): 41–66.

Lin, Fen. 2008. "Turning Gray: Transition of Political Communication in China, 1978–2008." PhD diss., University of Chicago.

Lin, Justin Yifu, Fang Cai, and Zhou Li. 2003. *The China Miracle: Development Strategy and Economic Reform*. Hong Kong: Hong Kong Centre for Economic Research and the International Centre for Economic Growth, Chinese University Press.

Lin, Mei-rong. 1987. "You jisi quan lai kan Tsaotun zhen de difang zhuzhi" [The religious sphere as a form of local organization: A case study from Tsaotun Township]. *Bulletin of the Institute of Ethnology, Academia Sinica* 62: 53–114.

Lin, Mei-rong. 1988. "You jisi quan dao xinyang quan: Taiwan minjian shehui de diyu goucheng yu fazhan" [From sacrificial sphere to devotional sphere: The territorial formation and development of local folk society in Taiwan]. In *Zhongguo haiyang fazhan shi lunwen ji* [Collection of papers on history of China's maritime development], vol. 3, edited by Yanxian Zhang. Taipei: Institute of Ethnology, Academia Sinica.

Lin, Mei-rong. 2008. *Jisi quan yu difang shehui* [Sacrificial ritual sphere and local society]. Luzhou: Boyang wenhua.

Lin, Xihao. 2003. "Guonei ge Jidujiao daxue zhi bijiao" [A comparison of Christian colleges in Taiwan]. *Xin shizhe zazhi* [New messenger] 76: 5–8.

Lin, Yueh-Hwa. 1947. *The Golden Wing: A Sociological Study of Chinese Family*. London: Routledge and Kegan Paul.

Lipton, Sara. 1999. *Images of Intolerance: The Representation of Jews and Judaism in the Bible moralisée*. Berkeley: University of California Press.

Litzinger, Charles A. 1996. "Rural Religion and Village Organization in North China: The Catholic Challenge in the Late Nineteenth Century." In *Christianity in China: From the Eighteenth Century to the Present*, edited by Daniel H. Bays. Stanford, CA: Stanford University Press.

Liu, Jianping. 2012. *Hongqi xia de shizijia: Xin Zhongguo chengli chuqi Zhonggong dui Jidujiao, Tianzhujiao de zhengce yanbian jiqi yingxiang (1949–1955)* [The cross under the red flag: The policy changes of the Chinese Communist Party toward Protestantism and Catholicism and their impacts in the early PRC (1949–1955)]. Hong Kong: Christian Study Centre on Chinese Religion and Culture, Chinese University of Hong Kong.

Liu, Kwang-Ching. 2004. "Religion and Politics in the White Lotus Rebellion of 1796 in Hubei." In *Heterodoxy in Late Imperial China*, edited by Kwang-Ching Liu and Richard Hon-Chun Shek. Honolulu: University of Hawai'i Press.

Liu, Peng. 2014. "Zhongguo you duoshao jidujiaotu? Qianxi 2010 nian zongjiao lanpishu guanyu Zhongguo jidujiao renshu de diaocha baogao" [How many Christians does China have? An examination of the survey report on the number of Chinese Christians in *Annual Report on Religions in China 2010*]. https://chinadigitaltimes.net/chinese/331867.html.

Liu, Shufen. 2008. *Zhonggu de fojiao yu shehui* [Medieval Chinese society and Buddhism]. Shanghai: Shanghai guji chubanshe.

Liu, Xianliang. 1947. "Fojiaotu jiying jiaru chuanjiao bisai" [Buddhists must urgently join the evangelism competition]. *Jue youqing* 179–80: 7–8. Reprinted in *Minguo Fojiao qikan wenxian jicheng* 89: 115–16.

Liu, Yonghua. 2013. *Confucian Rituals and Chinese Villagers: Ritual Change and Social Transformation in a Southeastern Chinese Community, 1368–1949*. Leiden: Brill.

Liu, Zhijun. 2007. *Xiangcun dushihua yu zongjiao xinyang bianqian: Zhangdian zhen ge'an yanjiu* [Rural urbanization and religious transformation: A case study of Zhangdian Town]. Beijing: Shehui kexue wenxian chubanshe.

Liu, Zhiquan. 2015. "Gudu de Taisuo yu qianjing: Minguo Fojiao xiaoshuo chuangzuo ji lilun chutan" [A lonely journey: A review of the composition and theory of Buddhist novels in Republican China]. *Nanjing shida xuebao* [Journal of Nanjing Normal University] 5: 135–43.

Lofland, John. 1966. *Doomsday Cult: A Study of Conversion, Proselytization, and Maintenance of Faith*. Englewood Cliffs, NJ: Prentice-Hall.

Lofland, John, and Rodney Stark. 1965. "Becoming a World-Saver: A Theory of Conversion to Religious Cults." *American Sociological Review* 30 (6): 862–75.

Lozada, Eriberto P. 2001. *God Aboveground: Catholic Church, Postsocialist State, and Transnational Processes in a Chinese Village.* Stanford, CA: Stanford University Press.

Lu, Yunfeng. 2008. *The Transformation of Yiguan Dao in Taiwan: Adapting to a Changing Religious Economy.* Lanham, MD: Lexington Books.

Luo, Jianjian. 2010. *Guilai zhishen: Yige xiangcun simiao chongjian de minzuzhi kaocha* [The returning gods: An ethnography on the rebuilding of a village temple]. Shanghai: Renmin chubanshe.

Lutz, Jessie Gregory. 1971. *China and the Christian Colleges, 1850–1950.* Ithaca, NY: Cornell University Press.

Lutz, Jessie Gregory. 1988. *Chinese Politics and Christian Missions: The Anti-Christian Movements of 1920–28.* Church and the World, vol. 3. Notre Dame, IN: Cross Cultural Publications, Cross Roads Books.

Ma, Guoqing. 2000. "Zongzu de fuxing yu renqun jiehe: Yi Minbei Zhanghu zhen de tianye diaocha wei zhongxin" [Lineage revival and group connections: A study based on fieldwork in Zhanghu Township in northern Fujian]. *Shehui xue yanjiu* [Sociological studies] 6: 76–84.

Ma, Xisha, and Bingfang Han. 1992. *Zhongguo minjian zongjiao shi* [History of popular sects in China]. Shanghai: Shanghai renmin chubanshe.

MacInnis, Donald E., ed. 1972. *Religious Policy and Practice in Communist China.* London: Hodder & Stoughton.

Madame Chiang, Chai-shek. 1955. "The Power of Prayer." *Readers Digest* 67: 52–58.

Madsen, Richard. 1998. *China's Catholics: Tragedy and Hope in an Emerging Civil Society.* Berkeley: University of California Press.

Madsen, Richard. 2001. "Saints and the State: Religious Evolution and Problems of Governance in China." *Asian Perspective* 25 (4): 187–211.

Madsen, Richard. 2003. "Catholic Revival During the Reform Era." *China Quarterly* 174: 468–87.

Madsen, Richard. 2007. *Democracy's Dharma: Religious Renaissance and Political Development in Taiwan.* Berkeley: University of California Press.

Madsen, Richard. 2012. "Taiwan Tianzhu jiaohui de chengzhang yu shuaitui: Yi Maliruohui de liangge chuanjiaoqu weili" [The growth and decline of the Catholic Church in Taiwan: An analysis of two Maryknoll mission areas]. *Taiwan xuezhi* [Monumenta Taiwanica] 6: 53–76.

Madsen, Richard, ed. 2021. *The Sinicization of Chinese Religions: From Above and Below.* Religion in Chinese Societies, vol. 18. Leiden: Brill.

Mair, Victor H. 1989. *Tang Transformation Texts: A Study of the Buddhist Contribution to the Rise of Vernacular Fiction and Drama in China.* Cambridge: Harvard University Asia Center.

Mann, Michael. 1984. "The Autonomous Power of the State: Its Origins, Mechanisms and Results." *European Journal of Sociology* 25 (2): 185–213.

Mann, Michael. 1986. *The Sources of Social Power: Volume 1, A History of Power from the Beginning to AD 1760.* Cambridge: Cambridge University Press.

Mao, Zedong. (1927) 1953. *Report of an Investigation into the Peasant Movement in Hunan.* Beijing: Foreign Language Press.

Mariani, Paul P. 2011. *Church Militant.* Cambridge, MA: Harvard University Press.

Mariani, Paul P. 2018. "The Extremely High Stakes of the China-Vatican Deal." *America: The Jesuit Review of Faith & Culture* 220, no. 1 (October 15): 18–25.

Martin, David. 1978. *A General Theory of Secularization.* New York: Harper & Row.

Martin, Emily. 1988. *Gender and Ideological Differences in Representations of Life and Death.* Berkeley: University of California Press.

McCarthy, Susan. 2013. "Serving Society, Repurposing the State: Religious Charity and Resistance in China." *China Journal* 70: 48–72.

McFarland, H. Neill. 1967. *The Rush Hour of the Gods: A Study of New Religious Movements in Japan*. New York: Macmillan.

McKinnon, Andrew M. 2013. "Ideology and the Market Metaphor in Rational Choice Theory of Religion: A Rhetorical Critique of 'Religious Economies.'" *Critical Sociology* 39 (4): 529–43.

Menegon, Eugenio. 2009. *Ancestors, Virgins, and Friars: Christianity as a Local Religion in Late Imperial China*. Cambridge, MA: Harvard University Asia Center.

Meng, Xin. 2000. *Labour Market Reform in China*. Cambridge: Cambridge University Press.

Mertha, Andrew. 2009. "'Fragmented Authoritarianism 2.0': Political Pluralization in the Chinese Policy Process." *China Quarterly* 200: 995–1012.

Merton, Robert K. 1938. "Social Structure and Anomie." *American Sociological Review* 3 (5): 672–82.

Merton, Robert K. 1957. *Social Theory and Social Structure*. Rev. ed. Glencoe, IL: Free Press.

Meulenbeld, Mark R. E. 2015. *Demonic Warfare: Daoism, Territorial Networks, and the History of a Ming Novel*. Honolulu: University of Hawai'i Press.

Miao, Ying. 2020. "Romanticising the Past: Core Socialist Values and the China Dream as Legitimisation Strategy." *Journal of Current Chinese Affairs* 49 (2): 162–84.

Miller, Donald E., and Tetsunao Yamamori. 2007. *Global Pentecostalism: The New Face of Christian Social Engagement*. Berkeley: University of California Press.

Miller, G. Tyler, and Scott Spoolman. 2012. *Essentials of Ecology*. 6th ed. Boston: Cengage Learning.

Ming, Chengman. 2005. "Mingguo Fojiao cishan xuexiao yanjiu" [Study of Buddhist charity schools in Republican China]. *Zhongguo kuangye daxue xuebao* [Journal of China University of Mining and Technology] 17 (2): 75–82.

Ming, Chengman. 2014. "Mingguo Fojiao de linzhong guanhuai tuanti yanjiu" [On Buddhist hospice care groups of the Republic of China]. *Shaoxing wenli xueyuan xuebao* [Journal of Shaoxing University] 34 (4): 91–95.

Ming, Chengman. 2016. "Minguo fojiao de jianyu jiaoyu yanjiu" [Buddhist prison evangelism in prisons in Republican China]. *Zongjiao xue yanjiu* [Religious studies] 2: 128–34.

Mingyang. 2004. *Chongding Yuanying dashi nianpu* [A revised chronicle of Master Yuanying]. Beijing: Zhonghua shuju.

Mizruchi, Mark S., and Lisa C. Fein. 1999. "The Social Construction of Organizational Knowledge: A Study of the Uses of Coercive, Mimetic, and Normative Isomorphism." *Administrative Science Quarterly* 44 (4): 653–83.

Mollier, Christine. 2008. *Buddhism and Taoism Face to Face: Scripture, Ritual, and Iconographic Exchange in Medieval China*. Honolulu: University of Hawai'i Press.

Morrison, Peter. 1984. "Religious Policy in China and Its Implementation in the Light of Document No. 19." *Religion in Communist Lands* 12 (3): 244–55.

Mungello, David E., ed. 1994. *The Chinese Rites Controversy: Its History and Meaning*. Nettetal: Steyler Verlag.

Nanting. 1990. *Nanting heshang quanji* [The complete collection of the writings of Venerable Nanting]. Taipei: Huanyan lianshe.

Naquin, Susan. 1976. *Millenarian Rebellion in China: The Eight Trigrams Uprising of 1813*. Yale Historical Publications 108. New Haven, CT: Yale University Press.

Naquin, Susan. 1981. *Shantung Rebellion: The Wang Lun Uprising of 1774*. New Haven, CT: Yale University Press.

Naquin, Susan. 2000. *Peking: Temples and City Life, 1400–1900*. Berkeley: University of California Press.

Nathan, Mark A. 2018. *From the Mountains to the Cities: A History of Buddhist Propagation in Modern Korea*. Honolulu: University of Hawai'i Press.

Nedostup, Rebecca. 2009. *Superstitious Regimes: Religion and the Politics of Chinese Modernity*. Cambridge, MA: Harvard University Asia Center.

Nguyen, Van Canh. 1983. *Vietnam Under Communism, 1975–1982*. Stanford, CA: Hoover Institution Press, Stanford University.

Nichols, Brian J. 2019. "Tourist Temples and Places of Practice: Charting Multiple Paths in the Revival of Monasteries." In *Buddhism after Mao: Negotiations, Continuities, and Reinventions*, edited by Zhe Ji, Gareth Fisher, and Andre Laliberte. Honolulu: University of Hawai'i Press.

Nichols, Brian J. 2022. *Lotus Blossoms and Purple Clouds: Monastic Buddhism in Post-Mao China*. Honolulu: University of Hawai'i Press.

Nie, Qijie. 1927. *Piye pian* [Book on refuting Christianity]. Beijing: Zhonghua shuju.

Norris, Pippa, and Ronald Inglehart. 2004. *Sacred and Secular: Religion and Politics Worldwide*. Cambridge: Cambridge University Press.

Oberschall, Anthony. 1993. *Social Movements: Ideologies, Interests, and Identities*. New Brunswick, NJ: Transaction.

Obeyesekere, Gananath. 1970. "Religious Symbolism and Political Change in Ceylon." *Modern Ceylon Studies* 1 (1): 43–63.

Oblau, Gotthard. 2005. "Pentecostals by Default? Contemporary Christianity in China." In *Asian and Pentecostal: The Charismatic Face of Christianity in Asia*, edited by Allan Anderson and Edmond Tang. Minneapolis: Augsburg Fortress.

Overmyer, Daniel L. 1976. *Folk Buddhist Religion: Dissenting Sects in Late Traditional China*. Harvard East Asian Series 83. Cambridge, MA: Harvard University Press.

Ownby, David. 2008. *Falun Gong and the Future of China*. New York: Oxford University Press.

Palmer, David A. 2007. *Qigong Fever: Body, Science, and Utopia in China*. New York: Columbia University Press.

Palmer, David A. 2008. "Heretical Doctrines, Reactionary Secret Societies, Evil Cults." In *Chinese Religiosities: Afflictions of Modernity and State Formation*, edited by Mayfair Mei-hui Yang. Berkeley: University of California Press.

Palmer, David A. 2009. "China's Religious Danwei: Institutionalising Religion in the People's Republic." *China Perspective* 4: 14–30.

Palmer, David A. 2011. "Chinese Redemptive Societies and Salvationist Religion: Historical Phenomenon or Sociological Category?" *Journal of Chinese Theatre, Ritual and Folklore* (Minsu quyi) 172: 21–72.

Palmer, David A. 2012. "From 'Congregations' to 'Small Group Community Building': Localizing the Bahá'í Faith in Hong Kong, Taiwan, and Mainland China." *Chinese Sociological Review* 45 (2): 78–98.

Pan, Hongli. 2006. "The Old Folks' Associations and Lineage Revival in Contemporary Villages of Southern Fujian Province." In *Southern Fujian: Reproduction of Traditions in Post-Mao China*, edited by Chee Beng Tan. Hong Kong: Chinese University Press.

Peng, Yusheng. 2004. "Kinship Networks and Entrepreneurs in China's Transitional Economy." *American Journal of Sociology* 109 (5): 1045–74.

Peng, Yusheng. 2010. "When Formal Laws and Informal Norms Collide: Lineage Networks Versus Birth Control Policy in China." *American Journal of Sociology* 116 (3): 770–805.

Penny, Benjamin. 2012. *The Religion of Falun Gong*. Chicago: University of Chicago Press.

Perry, Elizabeth J., and Tom Chang. 1980. "The Mystery of Yellow Cliff: A Controversial 'Rebellion' in the Late Qing." *Modern China* 6 (2): 123–60.

Pew Research Center. 2011. "Appendix C: Methodology for China." December 19. *Religion and Public Life Project, Pew Research Center*. http://www.pewforum.org/files/2011/12/Christian ityAppendixC.pdf.

Pittman, Don Alvin. 2001. *Toward a Modern Chinese Buddhism: Taixu's Reforms*. Honolulu: University of Hawai'i Press.

Poon, Shuk-Wah. 2004. "Refashioning Festivals in Republican Guangzhou." *Modern China* 30 (2): 199–227.

Poon, Shuk-Wah. 2008. "Religion, Modernity, and Urban Space: The City God Temple in Republican Guangzhou." *Modern China* 34 (2): 247–75.

Poon, Shuk-Wah. 2011. *Negotiating Religion in Modern China: State and Common People in Guangzhou, 1900–1937*. Hong Kong: Chinese University of Hong Kong.

Potter, Pitman B. 2003. "Belief in Control: Regulation of Religion in China." *China Quarterly* 174: 317–37.

Potter, Sulamith Heins, and Jack M. Potter. 1990. *China's Peasants: The Anthropology of a Revolution*. Cambridge: Cambridge University Press.

Powell, Walter W. 1991. "Expanding the Scope of Institutional Analysis." In *The New Institutionalism in Organizational Analysis*, edited by Walter W. Powell and Paul J. DiMaggio. Chicago: University of Chicago Press.

Powell, Walter W., and Paul J. DiMaggio, eds. 1991. *The New Institutionalism in Organizational Analysis*. Chicago: University of Chicago Press.

Putterman, Louis G. 1993. *Continuity and Change in China's Rural Development: Collective and Reform Eras in Perspective*. New York: Oxford University Press.

Qin, Wen-jie. 2000. "The Buddhist Revival in Post-Mao China: Women Reconstruct Buddhism on Mt. Emei." PhD diss., Harvard University.

Qu, Haiyuan. 1982a. "Taiwan diqu Jidujiao fazhan qushi zhi chubu tantao" [A preliminary exploration of the trends of development of Protestantism in Taiwan]. *Zhongguo shehui xuekan* [Chinese journal of sociology] 6: 15–28.

Qu, Haiyuan. 1982b. "Taiwan diqu Tianzhujiao fazhan qushi zhi yanjiu" [Research on the trends of development of Catholicism in Taiwan]. *Zhongyang yanjiuyuan minzuxue yanjiusuo jikan* [Bulletin of the Institute of Ethnology Academia Sinica] 51: 129–54.

Qu, Xiaoyu. 2015. "Shequ baohu shemiao de miaojie keyi yu xiangcun chongjian" [A boundary-crossing rite for a community-protecting temple and rural reconstruction: The case of baojie activities in the Mid-Taizhou villages]. In *Jiangnan diqu de zongjiao yu gonggong shenghuo* [Religion and public life in the Jiangnan region], edited by Robert Weller and Lizhu Fan. Shanghai: Shanghai Renmin.

Queen, Christopher S., Charles S. Prebish, and Damien Keown, eds. 2003. *Action Dharma: New Studies in Engaged Buddhism*. London; New York: RoutledgeCurzon.

Rankin, Mary Backus. 1986. *Elite Activism and Political Transformation in China: Zhejiang Province, 1865–1911*. Stanford, CA: Stanford University Press.

Regev, Eyal. 2016. "Early Christianity in Light of New Religious Movements." *Numen* 63 (5/6): 483–510.

Reny, Marie-Eve. 2018. *Authoritarian Containment: Public Security Bureaus and Protestant House Churches in Urban China*. New York: Oxford University Press.

Research Group of the Institute of World Religions, Chinese Academy of Social Sciences. 2010. "Zhongguo jidujiao ruhu wenjuan diaocha baogao" [Report on a household survey of Christianity in China]. In *Zhongguo zongjiao baogao* [Annual report on China's religions], edited by Ze Jin and Yonghui Qiu. Beijing: Shehui kexue wenxian chubanshe.

Riesebrodt, Martin. 2010. *The Promise of Salvation: A Theory of Religion*. Translated by Steven Rendall. Chicago: University of Chicago Press.

Rist, Rebecca. 2016. *Popes and Jews, 1095–1291*. Oxford: Oxford University Press.

Ritzinger, Justin. 2017. *Anarchy in the Pure Land: Reinventing the Cult of Maitreya in Modern Chinese Buddhism*. New York: Oxford University Press.

Roe, A. S. 1920. *Chance and Change in China*. New York: George H. Doran.

Rubinstein, Murray A. 1991. *The Protestant Community on Modern Taiwan: Mission, Seminary, and Church*. Armonk, NY: M. E. Sharpe.

Saich, Anthony. 2000. "Negotiating the State: The Development of Social Organizations in China." *China Quarterly* 161: 124–41.

Sangren, Paul Steven. 1983. "Female Gender in Chinese Religious Symbols: Kuan Yin, Ma Tsu, and the 'Eternal Mother.'" *Signs* 9 (1): 4–25.

Sangren, Paul Steven. 1987. *History and Magical Power in a Chinese Community*. Stanford, CA: Stanford University Press.

Scammell, Rosie. 2016. "Pope Francis Praises China in Latest Effort to Thaw Chilly Relations." *National Catholic Reporter*, February 3. https://www.ncronline.org/news/vatican/pope-francis-praises-china-latest-effort-thaw-chilly-relations.

Schak, David, and Hsin-Huang Michael Hsiao. 2005. "Taiwan's Socially Engaged Buddhist Groups." *China Perspectives* 59 (May–June): 43–55. https://doi.org/10.4000/chinaperspectives.2803.

Schiller, Anne. 1996. "An 'Old' Religion in 'New Order' Indonesia: Notes on Ethnicity and Religious Affiliation." *Sociology of Religion* 57 (4): 409–17.

Scott, Gregory Adam. 2016. "A Revolution of Ink: Chinese Buddhist Periodicals in the Early Republic." In *Recovering Buddhism in Modern China*, edited by Jan Kiely and J. Brooks Jessup. New York: Columbia University Press.

Scott, W. Richard. 2014. *Institutions and Organizations: Ideas, Interests, and Identities*. 4th ed. Los Angeles: SAGE.

Seaman, Gary. 1981. "The Sexual Politics of Karmic Retribution." In *The Anthropology of Taiwanese Society*, edited by Emily Martin and Hill Gates. Stanford, CA: Stanford University Press.

Seiwert, Hubert Michael. 2003. *Popular Religious Movements and Heterodox Sects in Chinese History*. Leiden: Brill.

Shanghai Municipal Public Security Bureau Editorial Committee. 1997. *Shanghai gongan zhi* [Gazetteer of Shanghai Public Security]. Shanghai: Shanghai shehui kexueyuan chubanshe.

Shao, Jiandong. 2011. *Zhezhong diqu chuantong zongci yanjiu* [A study of ancestral halls in the middle Zhejiang Region]. Hangzhou: Zhejiang daxue chubanshe.

Shanyin. 1948. "Fojiao ying ruhe wanjiu zhi jianyi" [Suggestions on how to save Buddhism]. *Haichaoyin* 29 (11). Reprinted in *Minguo Fojiao qikan wenxian jicheng* 204: 387.

Sharot, Stephen. 2002. "Beyond Christianity: A Critique of the Rational Choice Theory of Religion from a Weberian and Comparative Religions Perspective." *Sociology of Religion* 63 (4): 427–54.

Shaw, Victor N. 1996. *Social Control in China: A Study of Chinese Work Units*. Westport, CT: Praeger.

Shen, Hong. 2010. "Xinhai gemin qianhou de Zhejiang shehui sichao he biange—Yingguo nü zuojia Luo Anyi yanzhong de Hangzhou he Lanxi" [Social thought and transformation in Zhejiang around the time of the 1911 Revolution: Hangzhou and Lanxi through the eyes of British female writer A. S. Roe]. *Wenhua yishu yanjiu* [Research on culture and art] 3 (5): 16–31.

Shengyan. 1999a. *Guicheng* [The journey home]. 2nd ed. Taipei: Fagu wenhua shiye gufen youxian gongsi.

Shengyan. 1999b. *Jidujiao zhi yanjiu* [Study of Christianity]. Taipei: Dharma Drum.

Shengyan. 2004. *Shengyan fashi xuesi licheng* [The journey of learning and reflection of Venerable Shengyan]. Taipei: Dharma Drum.

Shengyan. 2008. *Footprints in the Snow: The Autobiography of a Chinese Buddhist Monk*. New York: Doubleday.

Sider, Ronald J., and Diane Knippers. 2005. *Toward an Evangelical Public Policy: Political Strategies for the Health of the Nation*. Grand Rapids, MI: Baker Books.

Siu, Helen F. 1990. "Recycling Tradition: Culture, History, and Political Economy in the Chrysanthemum Festivals of South China." *Comparative Studies in Society and History* 32 (4): 765–94.

Skar, Lowell. 2000. "Ritual Movement, Deity Cults, and the Transformation of Daoism in Song and Yuan Times." In *Daoism Handbook*, edited by Livia Kohn. Leiden: Brill.

Smith, Chris. 2018. "The World Must Stand Against China's War on Religion." *Washington Post*, December 27.

Smith, Thomas W. 2001. "Religious Freedom as Foreign Policy Priority." *International Studies Review* 3 (3): 152–56.

Snow, David A., and Richard Machalek. 1984. "The Sociology of Conversion." *Annual Review of Sociology* 10 (1): 167–90.

Song, Rui. 2018. "Zhejiang Taizhou: Jianghao 'Yimiao Yi Gushi' Chongsu Minjian Xinyang Jiazhi" [Taizhou City in Zhejiang Province: Launching the project of 'One Temple One Story' to reconstruct the value of popular religion]. *Zhongguo minzu bao*, September 19.

Spires, Anthony J. 2011. "Contingent Symbiosis and Civil Society in an Authoritarian State: Understanding the Survival of China's Grassroots NGOs." *American Journal of Sociology* 117 (1): 1–45.

Standaert, Nicolas, and R. G. Tiedemann. 2009. *Handbook of Christianity in China*, Vol. 2. Leiden: Brill.

Stanley, Brian. 1990. *The Bible and the Flag: Protestant Missions and British Imperialism in the Nineteenth and Twentieth Centuries*. Leicester: Apollos.

Stark, Rodney. 1996. *The Rise of Christianity: A Sociologist Reconsiders History*. Princeton, NJ: Princeton University Press.

Stark, Rodney. 2001. *One True God: Historical Consequences of Monotheism*. Princeton, NJ: Princeton University Press.

Stark, Rodney, and Roger Finke. 2000. *Acts of Faith: Explaining the Human Side of Religion*. Berkeley: University of California Press.

Stark, Rodney, and Laurence R. Iannaccone. 1994. "A Supply-Side Reinterpretation of the 'Secularization' of Europe." *Journal for the Scientific Study of Religion* 33 (3): 230–52.

Stark, Rodney, and Reid L. Neilson. 2012. *The Rise of Mormonism*. New York: Columbia University Press.

Stark, Rodney, and Xiuhua Wang. 2015. *A Star in the East: The Rise of Christianity in China*. West Conshohocken, PA: Templeton.

Stewart, Pamela J., and Andrew Strathern. 2009. "Growth of the Mazu Complex in Cross-Straits Contexts (Taiwan, and Fujian Province, China)." *Journal of Ritual Studies* 23 (1): 67–72.

Stockwell, Foster. 2002. *Westerners in China: A History of Exploration and Trade, Ancient Times Through the Present*. Jefferson, NC: McFarland.

Stoll, David. 1990. *Is Latin America Turning Protestant? The Politics of Evangelical Growth*. Berkeley: University of California Press.

Strand, Kenneth A. 1992. "Governance in the First-Century Christian Church in Rome: Was It Collegial?" *Andrews University Seminary Studies* 30 (1): 59–75.

Sun, Hao. 2009. "Shehui zhuanxing qi zongjiao shiwu guanli wenti yanjiu: Yi Xiaoshan jidujiao difang jiaohui weili" [A study of the management of religious affairs during the transitional period: A case of the Local Churches in Xiaoshan]. Master's thesis, Shanghai Jiaotong University.

Sun, Anna. 2013. *Confucianism as a World Religion: Contested Histories and Contemporary Realities*. Princeton, NJ: Princeton University Press.

Sun, Yanfei. 2011. "The Chinese Buddhist Ecology in Post-Mao China: Contours, Types and Dynamics." *Social Compass* 58 (4): 498–510.

Sun, Yanfei. 2014a. "Popular Religion in Zhejiang, Southeast China: Feminization, Bifurcation and Buddhification." *Modern China* 40 (5): 455–87.

Sun, Yanfei. 2014b. "Qiannian weiyou zhi bianju: Jindai Zhongguo zongjiao shengtai geju de bianqian" [The Christian expansion in modern China and beyond]. *Xuehai* [Academia bismestrie] 2: 11–25.

Sun, Yanfei. 2017a. "The Rise of Protestantism in Post-Mao China: State and Religion in Historical Perspective." *American Journal of Sociology* 122 (6): 1664–725.

Sun, Yanfei. 2017b. "Jingkong: From Universal Saint to Sectarian Saint." In *Making Saints in Modern China*, edited by David Ownby, Vincent Goossaert, and Ji Zhe. New York: Oxford University Press.

Sun, Yanfei. 2019a. "Reversal of Fortune: Growth Trajectories of Catholicism and Protestantism in Modern China." *Theory and Society* 48 (2): 267–98.

Sun, Yanfei. 2019b. "Linghe kuozhang siwei yu qian xiandai diguo de zongjiao kuanrong" [Zero-sum evangelism and religious toleration of pre-modern empires]. *Shehuixue yanjiu* [Sociological studies] 34 (2): 96–122.

Sun, Yanfei, and Dingxin Zhao. 2019. "Religious Toleration in Pre-Modern Empires." In *States and Nations, Power and Civility: Hallsian Perspectives*, edited by Francesco Duina. Toronto: University of Toronto Press.

Szonyi, Michael. 2000. "Local Cult, Lijia, and Lineage: Religious and Social Organization in the Fuzhou Religion in the Ming and Qing." *Journal of Chinese Religions* 28: 93–125.

Szonyi, Michael. 2001. "Translator's Preface." In *Family Lineage, Organization and Social Change in Ming and Qing Fujian*, by Zhenman Zheng, translated by Michael Szonyi. Honolulu: University of Hawai'i Press.

Szonyi, Michael. 2002. *Practicing Kinship: Lineage and Descent in Late Imperial China*. Stanford, CA: Stanford University Press.

Szonyi, Michael. 2015. "Lineages and the Making of Contemporary China." In *Modern Chinese Religion II: 1850–2015*, edited by Vincent Goossaert, Jan Kiely, and John Lagerwey. Leiden: Brill.

Taixu. 1938. "Zhongguo xu Yejiao yu Oumei xu Fojiao" [China needs Christianity while Europe and America need Buddhism]. *Haichaoyin* 19 (8): 4–7.

Taixu. 1996. *Taixu dashi zizhuan* [Memoir of Master Taixu]. Taipei: Fuzhi zhisheng chubanshe.

Tan, Chee Beng. 2006. *Southern Fujian: Reproduction of Traditions in Post-Mao China*. Hong Kong: Chinese University Press.

Tang, Edmond. 1993. "The Church into the 1990s." In *The Catholic Church in Modern China*, edited by Edmond Tang and Jean-Paul Wiest. Maryknoll, NY: Orbis Books.

Tang, Edmond, and Jean-Paul Weist. 2013. *The Catholic Church in Modern China: Perspectives*. Eugene, OR: Wipf & Stock.

Tang, Yongtong. (1938) 2017. *Han Wei liang Jin Nanbeichao Fojiao shi* [History of Buddhism in the Han, Wei, Jin, and Northern-Southern Dynasties]. Beijing: Zhonghua shuju.

Tang, Zhongmao. 2013. *Zhongguo Fojiao jindai zhuanxing de shehui zhiwei: Minguo Shanghai jushi Fojiao zuzhi yu cishan yanjiu* [The social dimension of the modern transition of Chinese Buddhism: Lay Buddhist organizations and charity in Republican Shanghai]. Guilin: Guangxi shifan daxue chubanshe.

Tanxu. (1954) 1993. *Yingchen huiyi lu* [Memories of shadows and dust]. Shanghai: Shanghai xinwen chubanshe.

Tao, Feiya. 2004. *Zhongguo de Jidujiao wutuobang: Yesu jiating, 1921–1952* [The Christian utopian commune in China: The Jesus family, 1921–1952]. Hong Kong: Hong Kong Chinese University Press.

Tao, Jin, and Vincent Goossaert. 2015. "Daojiao yu Suzhou difang shehui" [Daoism and local society in Suzhou]. In *Jiangnan diqu de zongjiao yu gonggong shenghuo* [Religion and public life in the Jiangnan region], edited by Robert Weller and Lizhu Fan. Shanghai: Shanghai Renmin.

Taveirne, Patrick. 2004. *Han-Mongol Encounters and Missionary Endeavors: A History of Scheut in Ordos (Hetao), 1874–1911*. Leuven Chinese Studies 15. Leuven: Leuven University Press.

Taylor, Romeyn. 1997. "Official Altars, Temples and Shrines Mandated for All Counties in Ming and Qing." *T'oung Pao* 83 (1/3): 93–125.

Teiser, Stephen F. 1996. *The Ghost Festival in Medieval China*. Princeton, NJ: Princeton University Press.

Teiwes, Frederick, and Warren Sun. 1999. *China's Road to Disaster: Mao, Central Politicians, and Provincial Leaders in the Unfolding of the Great Leap Forward, 1955–1959*. Armonk, NY: M. E. Sharpe.

ter Haar, Barend J. 2017. *Guan Yü: The Religious Afterlife of a Failed Hero*. 1st ed. Oxford: Oxford University Press.

Thelle, Notto R. 1987. *Buddhism and Christianity in Japan: From Conflict to Dialogue, 1854–1899*. Honolulu: University of Hawai'i Press.

Thompson, Laurence G. 1995. *Chinese Religion: An Introduction*. 5th ed. San Francisco: Wadsworth.

Thompson, Stuart E. 1988. "Death, Food, and Fertility." In *Death Ritual in Late Imperial and Modern China*, edited by James L. Watson and Evelyn S. Rawski. Berkeley: University of California Press.

Thornton, Patricia M. 2008. "Manufacturing Dissent in Transnational China: Boomerang, Backfire or Spectacle?" In *Popular Contention in China*, edited by Kevin J. O'Brien. Cambridge, MA: Harvard University Press.

Tiedemann, R. G. 2010a. "The Treaty System." In *Handbook of Christianity in China*, vol. 2, edited by R. G. Tiedemann. Leiden: Brill.

Tiedemann, R. G. 2010b. "Protestant Missionaries." In *Handbook of Christianity in China*, vol. 2, edited by R. G. Tiedemann. Leiden: Brill.

Tiedemann, R. G. 2011. *Huabei de baoli he konghuang: Yihetuan yundong qianxi Jidujiao chuanbo he shehui chongtu* [Violence and Fear in North China: Christian Missions and Social Conflict on the Eve of the Boxer Uprising]. Translated by Huiyi Cui. Nanjing: Jiangsu renmin chubanshe.

Tiedemann, R. G. 2016. *Reference Guide to Christian Missionary Societies in China: From the Sixteenth to the Twentieth Century*. Abingdon: Routledge.

Tilly, Charles. 1978. *From Mobilization to Revolution*. Reading, MA: Addison-Wesley.

Tilly, Charles. 1992. *Coercion, Capital, and European States, AD 990–1992*. Cambridge, MA: Blackwell.

Tong, James W. 2009. *Revenge of the Forbidden City: The Suppression of the Falungong in China, 1999–2005*. Oxford: Oxford University Press.

Tong, John. 2013. "The Church from 1949 to 1990." In *The Catholic Church in Modern China: Perspectives*, edited by Edmond Tang and Jean-Paul Weist. Eugene, OR: Wipf & Stock.

Tsai, Lily L. 2007. *Accountability Without Democracy: Solidary Groups and Public Goods Provision in Rural China*. Cambridge: Cambridge University Press.

Twitchett, Denis. 1959. "The Fan Clan's Charitable Estate, 1050–1760." In *Confucianism in Action*, edited by David S. Nivison and Arthur F. Wright. Stanford, CA: Stanford University Press.

Vala, Carsten T. 2018. *The Politics of Protestant Churches and the Party-State in China: God Above Party?* Routledge Research on the Politics and Sociology of China. Abingdon: Routledge.

Vala, Carsten T., and Kevin J. O'Brien. 2007. "Attraction Without Networks: Recruiting Strangers to Unregistered Protestantism in China." *Mobilization* 12 (1): 79–94.

van der Veer, Peter. 2012. "Market and Money: A Critique of Rational Choice Theory." *Social Compass* 59 (2): 183–92.

Vendassi, Pierre. 2014. "Mormonism and the Chinese State: Becoming an Official Church in the People's Republic of China?" *China Perspectives* 1: 43–50.

Vidal, Claire. 2019. "Administering Bodhisattva Guanyin's Island: The Monasteries, Political Entities, and Power Holders of Putuoshan." In *Buddhism after Mao: Negotiations, Continuities, and Reinventions*, edited by Zhe Ji, Gareth Fisher, and Andre Laliberte. Honolulu: University of Hawai'i Press.

Vogel, Ezra F. 2011. *Deng Xiaoping and the Transformation of China*. Cambridge, MA: Belknap Press of Harvard University Press.

von Glahn, Richard. 1993. "Community and Welfare: Chu Hsi's Community Granary in Theory and Practice." In *Ordering the World: Approaches to State and Society in Sung Dynasty China*, edited by Robert P. Hymes and Conrad Schirokauer. Berkeley: University of California Press.

Wagner, Rudolf G. 1982. *Reenacting the Heavenly Vision: The Role of Religion in the Taiping Rebellion*. China Research Monograph 25. Berkeley: Institute of East Asian Studies, University of California, Berkeley.

Wald, Kenneth D., and Allison Calhoun-Brown. 2011. *Religion and Politics in the United States*. Lanham, MD: Rowman & Littlefield.

Walder, Andrew. 1986. *Communist Neo-Traditionalism: Work and Authority in Chinese Industry*. Berkeley: University of California Press.

Walder, Andrew G. 2015. *China Under Mao: A Revolution Derailed*. Cambridge, MA: Harvard University Press.

Walls, Andrew F. 1996. *The Missionary Movement in Christian History: Studies in the Transmission of Faith*. Maryknoll, NY: Orbis.

Walters, Jonathan S. 1992. "Rethinking Buddhist Missions." *Journal of the American Academy of Religion* 60 (3): 429–53.

Wang, Chao. 2015. "Coordinated Compliance and Private Approach of International Engagement in China's Human Rights." In *International Engagement in China's Human Rights*, edited by Titus Chen and Dingding Chen. New York: Routledge.

Wang, Jing. 1996. *High Culture Fever: Politics, Aesthetics, and Ideology in Deng's China*. Berkeley: University of California Press.

Wang, Mingming, Ke Fan, Hongli Pan, Chee-Beng Tan, Khun Eng Kuah-Pearce, Siumi Maria Tam, Yuling Ding, and Chee-Beng Tan. 2006. *Southern Fujian: Reproduction of Traditions in Post-Mao China*. Hong Kong: Chinese University Press.

Wang, Yun "Ray." 2015. "The Changed and Unchanged in Chinese Religious Freedom Discourse and Its Responses to International Engagement of Protestant Advocacy." In *International Engagement in China's Human Rights*, edited by Titus Chen and Dingding Chen. New York: Routledge.

Wang, Xiaoyue. 2006. "How Has a Chinese Village Remained Catholic? Catholicism and Local Culture in a Northern Chinese Village." *Journal of Contemporary China* 15 (49): 687-704.

Wank, David L. 2009. "Institutionalizing Modern 'Religion' in China's Buddhism: Political Phases of a Local Revival." In *Making Religion, Making the State: The Politics of Religion in Modern China*, edited by Yoshiko Ashiwa and David L. Wank. Stanford, CA: Stanford University Press.

Warner, R. Stephen. 1993. "Work in Progress Toward a New Paradigm for the Sociological Study of Religion in the United States." *American Journal of Sociology* 98 (5): 1044-93.

Warner, R. Stephen. 1994. "The Place of Congregation in the Contemporary American Religious Configuration." In *American Congregations: New Perspectives in the Study of Congregations*, vol. 2, edited by James P. Wind and Lewis M. James. Chicago: University of Chicago Press.

Warner, R. Stephen, and Judith G. Wittner, eds. 1998. *Gatherings in Diaspora: Religious Communities and the New Immigration*. Philadelphia: Temple University Press.

Watson, James L. 1988. "The Structure of Chinese Funerary Rites: Elementary Forms, Ritual Sequence, and the Primacy of Performance." In *Death Ritual in Late Imperial and Modern China*, edited by James L. Watson and Evelyn S. Rawski. Berkeley: University of California Press.

Weber, Max. (1905) 2001. *The Protestant Ethic and the Spirit of Capitalism*. Translated by Stephen Kalberg. Chicago: Fitzroy Dearborn.

Weber, Max. (1915) 1946. "The Social Psychology of the World Religions." In *From Max Weber: Essays in Sociology*, edited and translated by H. H. Gerth and C. Wright Mills. New York: Oxford University Press.

Weber, Max. (1915) 1951. *The Religion of China: Confucianism and Taoism*. Translated by Hans H. Gerth. Glencoe, IL: Free Press.

Weber, Max. (1916) 1958. *The Religion of India: The Sociology of Hinduism and Buddhism*. Translated by Hans H. Gerth and Don Martindale. Glencoe, IL: Free Press.

Weber, Max. (1917–1919) 1952. *Ancient Judaism*. Translated by Hans H. Gerth and Don Martindale. Glencoe, IL: Free Press.

Weber, Max. (1922) 1963. *The Sociology of Religion*. Translated by Ephraim Fischoff. Boston: Beacon.

Weber, Max. 1978. *Economy and Society: An Outline of Interpretive Sociology*. Edited by Guenther Roth and Claus Wittich. Berkeley: University of California Press.

Wehrfritz, George, and Lynette Clemetson. 1998. "Missionaries Flock to China." *Newsweek*, June 29.

Welch, Holmes. 1967. *The Practice of Chinese Buddhism, 1900–1950*. Cambridge, MA: Harvard University Press.

Welch, Holmes. 1972. *Buddhism Under Mao*. Cambridge, MA: Harvard University Press.

Weller, Robert P. 1987. *Unities and Diversities in Chinese Religion*. Seattle: University of Washington Press.

Weller, Robert P. 1994. *Resistance, Chaos and Control in China: Taiping Rebels, Taiwanese Ghosts and Tiananmen*. Seattle: University of Washington Press.

Wen, Jinke. 2009. "Ji sanwei he Zhengyan fashi jiaotan de Zaixing zhongxue xiunü: Beidi, Huang Xuewen he Gaolingxia" [In memory of the three Catholic nuns from Haixing High School who talked with Venerable Zhengyan]. *Faguang* [Dharma light monthly] 239. http://enlight .lib.ntu.edu.tw/FULLTEXT/JR-BJ013/bj013212578.pdf.

Weng, Fei. 1985. "Wannan Jiaoan Shuping" [An account of the Wannan anti-Christian incident]. *Anhui Shifan Daxue Xuebao* 2: 94–101.

Wilcox, Clyde, and Carin Robinson. 2011. *Onward Christian Soldiers? The Religious Right in American Politics*. Boulder, CO: Westview.

Wilde, Melissa J. 2007. *Vatican II: A Sociological Analysis of Religious Change*. Princeton, NJ: Princeton University Press.

Wilde, Melissa J., Kristin Geraty, Shelley L. Nelson, and Emily A. Bowman. 2010. "Religious Economy or Organizational Field? Predicting Bishops' Votes at the Second Vatican Council." *American Sociological Review* 75 (4): 586–606.

Wilson, Bryan R. 1979. *Contemporary Transformations of Religion*. Oxford: Oxford University Press.

Wind, James P., and James Welborn Lewis. 1994. *American Congregations*. Chicago: University of Chicago Press.

Wittberg, Patricia. 1994. *The Rise and Fall of Catholic Religious Orders: A Social Movement Perspective*. Albany: State University of New York Press.

Wolf, Arthur P. 1974. "Gods, Ghosts, and Ancestors." In *Religion and Ritual in Chinese Society*, edited by Arthur P. Wolf. Stanford, CA: Stanford University Press.

Wolf, Arthur P. 1976. "Aspects of Ancestor Worship in Northern Taiwan." In *Ancestors*, edited by William H. Newell. The Hague: Mouton.

Wood, Irving P. 1927. "Borrowing Between Religions." *Journal of Biblical Literature* 46 (1/2): 98–105.

Wu, Hua. 2016. *Mingguo Chengdu Fojiao yanjiu: 1912–1949* [A study of Buddhism in Republican Chengdu: 1912–1949]. Beijing: Zongjiao wenhua chubanshe.

Wu, Keping. 2015. "Sunan Fojiao: Goujian hefaxing, zhengtongxing he daode shehui" [Buddhism in the making: The construction of legitimacy, orthodoxy and moral society in southern Jiangsu]. In *Jiangnan diqu de zongjiao yu gonggong shenghuo* [Religion and public life in the Jiangnan region], edited by Robert Weller and Lizhu Fan. Shanghai: Shanghai Renmin.

Wu, Lili, and Dingxin Zhao. 2007. "Kelisima quanwei de kunjing: Ningxia wenge de xingqi he fazhan" [The dilemma of charismatic authority: The rise and development of the Cultural Revolution in Ningxia]. *Ershiyi shiji* [Twenty-First century] 102: 58–70.

Wu, Tao. 2004. "Qingdai Suzhou diqu de cunmiao he zhenmiao: cong minjian xinyang toushi chengxiang guanxi" [Village temples and township temples in Suzhou in the Qing dynasty: On the urban-rural relationship from the perspective of popular religion]. *Zhongguo Nongshi* [Agricultural history of China] 2: 95–101.

Xiao, Tangbiao. 2001. *Cunzhi zhong de zongzu: Dui jiu ge cun de diaocha yu yanjiu* [Kinship organizations in rural governance: A study based on fieldwork in nine villages]. Shanghai: Shanghai shudian chubanshe.

Xiao, Tangbiao. 2010. *Zongzu zhengzhi: Cunzhi quanli wangluo de fenxi* [Kinship politics: An analysis of the power networks of rural governance]. Beijing: Shangwu yinshuguan.

Xie, Ming. 2010. "Dangdai daxuesheng jidujiao chuanbo xianzhuang diaocha: Yi Beijngshi mou gaoxiao daxuesheng tuanqi weili" [The spread of Christianity among college students in China: A research based on a student fellowship in a Beijing university]. *Minzu jiaoyu yanjiu* [Journal of research on education for ethnic minorities] 101 (6): 70–74.

Xie, Yanqing. 2013. "Sanshi xinian yu Jingkong pai jushi daochang: Yi Linjiang Jingkong pai mou jushi daochang weili" [Thrice yearning and chanting ceremonies and the Jingkong lay Buddhist groups: A case study of a lay Buddhist site in Linjiang]. In *Zongjiao renlei xue* [Anthropology of religion], edited by Ze Jin and Jinguo Chen. Beijing: Shehui kexue wenxian chubanshe.

Xie, Yanqing. 2017. "Zongjiao tuanti hefaxing chongjian: Yi Nanjing Majia jiedao weili" [Rebuilding legitimacy of a religious organization: A case study of a Buddhist community in Majia District in Nanjing City]. *Xibei minzu yanjiu* [Northwestern Journal of Ethnology] 92 (1): 142–47.

Xin, Ping. 1996. "Fandui Weikexue Yao Jingzhong Changming" [Alarm bells must ring continuously to fight against pseudoscience]. *Guangming ribao* [Guangming daily], June 17.

Xingyun. 2013. *Bainian foyuan* [A hundred years of affinity with Buddhism]. Kaohsiung: Buddha's Light.

Xingyun. 2016. "Dangdai renjian Fojiao de fazhan" [The contemporary development of humanistic Buddhism]. http://www.lnanews.com/news/%E7%95%B6%E4%BB%A3%E4%BA%BA%E9%96%93%E4%BD%9B%E6%95%99%E7%9A%84%E7%99%BC%E5%B1%95%EF%BC%88%E4%BA%94%E4%B9%8B%E4%BA%8C%EF%BC%89.html.

Xu, Xiaoqun. 2001. *Chinese Professionals and the Republican State: The Rise of Professional Associations in Shanghai, 1912–1937*. Cambridge: Cambridge University Press.

Xu, Shuhua. 2006. *Xuelu jushi Fojiao sixiang ji xingshu yanjiu* [A study on the thoughts and acts of the lay Buddhist Xuelu]. Taipei: Showwe Information.

Xu, Yihua. 2004. "'Patriotic' Protestants: The Making of an Official Church." In *God and Caesar in China: Policy Implications of Church-State Tensions*, edited by Jason Kindopp and Carel Lee Hamrin. Washington, DC: Brookings Institution.

Xue, Dubi. 1928. "Xue nei buzhang fu Fojiaohui han" [A reply from Interior Minister Xue]. *Fohua suikan* [Buddhistic occasional] 5: 5–6.

Xuyun. 1953. *Xuyun heshang zishu nianpu* [The annalistic autobiography of Master Xuyun]. Edited by Xuelü Cen. Hong Kong: Xuyun heshang fahui bianyin banshichu.

Yamada, Toshiaki. 2008. "Gengshen." In *The Encyclopedia of Taoism*, edited by Fabrizio Pregadio. London: Routledge.

Yamane, David. 1997. "Secularization on Trial: In Defense of a Neosecularization Paradigm." *Journal for the Scientific Study of Religion* 36 (1): 109–22.

Yan, Tony, and Michale R. Hyman. 2023. "Softly Enhancing Political Legitimacy via Red Tourism." *Journal of Heritage Tourism* 18 (4): 556–73.

Yan, Yunxiang. 2003. *Private Life Under Socialism: Love, Intimacy, and Family Change in a Chinese Village, 1949–1999*. Stanford, CA: Stanford University Press.

Yang, C. K. 1961. *Religion in Chinese Society: A Study of Contemporary Social Functions of Religion and Some of Their Historical Factors.* Berkeley: University of California Press.

Yang, Fenggang. 2005. "Lost in the Market, Saved at McDonald's: Conversion to Christianity in Urban China." *Journal for the Scientific Study of Religion* 44 (4): 423–41.

Yang, Fenggang. 2012. *Religion in China: Survival and Revival Under Communist Rule.* Oxford: Oxford University Press.

Yang, Fenggang. 2021. "Sinicization or Chinafication? Cultural Assimilation vs. Political Domestication of Christianity in China and Beyond." In *The Sinicization of Chinese Religions: From Above and Below,* edited by Richard Madsen. Leiden and Boston: Brill.

Yang, Fenggang, and Helen Rose Ebaugh. 2001. "Transformations in New Immigrant Religions and Their Global Implications." *American Sociological Review* 66 (2): 269–88.

Yang, Fenggang, and Dedong Wei. 2005. "The Bailin Buddhist Temple: Thriving Under Communism." In *State, Market, and Religions in Chinese Societies,* edited by Fenggang Yang and Joseph B. Tamney, 63–86. Religion and the Social Order, Vol. 11. Leiden: Brill.

Yang, Hongshan. 1994. "Wuandong nongcun 'Jidujiao re' diaocha yu sikao" [Research and reflection on 'Christianity fever' in rural East Anhui Province]. *Jianghuai luntan* [Jianghuai tribune] 4: 30–37.

Yang, Hua. 2014. "Nongcun dixia jidujiao de nanbei chayi" [Differences of rural underground churches in southern and northern China]. https://www.guancha.cn/YangHua/2014_07_05_243296.shtml?web.

Yang, Hua, and Xianhong Tian. 2010. "Nongcun jidujiao xinyang fasheng jizhi de sanceng jichu fenxi" [An analysis of the three premises of conversion to Protestant Christianity in rural China]. *Zhanglue yu guanli* [Strategy and management] 5/6: 1–21.

Yang, Huinan. 1991. *Dangdai Fojiao sixiang zhanwang* [Prospect of contemporary Buddhist thoughts]. Taipei: Dongtu tushu gongsi.

Yang, Mayfair. 2004a. "Spatial Struggles: Postcolonial Complex, State Disenchantment, and Popular Reappropriation of Space in Rural Southeast China." *Journal of Asian Studies* 63 (3): 719–55.

Yang, Mayfair. 2004b. "Goddess Across the Taiwan Strait: Matrifocal Ritual Space, Nation-State, and Satellite Television Footprints." *Public Culture* 16 (2): 209–38.

Yang, Peidong, and Lijun Tang. 2018. "'Positive Energy': Hegemonic Intervention and Online Media Discourse in China's Xi Jinping Era." *China: An International Journal* 16 (1): 1–22.

Yao, Yushuang. 2012. *Taiwan's Tzu Chi as Engaged Buddhism: Origins, Organization, Appeal and Social Impact.* Leiden; Boston: Global Oriental.

Ye, Xiaowen. 2009. "Zhengque renshi he chuli shehuizhuyi shehui de zongjiao guanxi" [To correctly understand and handle inter-religious relations in our socialist society]. *Qiushi* 16: 8–11.

Ying, Fuk-tsang. 1997. "Jidujiao yu Zhongguo zuxian chongbai: Lishi de kaocha" [Christianity and Chinese ancestor worship: A historical perspective]. In *Zhongguo jizu wenti* [Chinese ancestor worship], edited by Ying Fuk-tsang. Hong Kong: Alliance Bible Seminary.

Ying, Fuk-tsang. 2005. *Fandi, aiguo, shulingren: Ni Tuosheng yu Jidutu Juhuichu yanjiu* [Anti-imperialism, patriotism and the spiritual man: A study on Watchman Nee and the "Little Flock"]. Hong Kong: Christian Study Center on Chinese Religion and Culture, Chinese University of Hong Kong.

Ying, Fuk-tsang. 2018. "The Politics of Cross Demolition: A Religio-Political Analysis of the 'Three Rectifications and One Demolition' Campaign in Zhejiang Province." *Review of Religion and Chinese Society* 5 (1): 43–75.

Yinshun. 1932. *Fofa zhi weiji ji qi jiuji* [The crisis of Buddhism and its remedies]. *Haichaoyin* 13(9): 19–26.

Yinshun. 1985. *Yindu zhi Fojiao: Xu* [Buddhism of India: Preface]. Xinzhu: Zhengwen chubanshe.

Yinshun. 2000. *Wo zhi zongjiao guan* [My views on religion]. Taipei: Zhengwen chubanshe.

Yinshun. 2009. *A Sixty-Year Spiritual Voyage on the Ocean of Dharma*. Translated by Yu-Jung L. Avis, Maxwell E. Siegel, and Po-Hui Chang. Towaco, NJ: Noble Path Buddhist Education Fellowship.

Yip, Ka-che. 2003. "China and Christianity: Perspectives on Missions, Nationalism, and the State in the Republican Period, 1912–1949." In *Missions, Nationalism, and the End of Empire*, edited by Brian Stanley and Alaine M. Low. Grand Rapids, MI: W. B. Eerdmans.

Youguang. 1936. "Yejiaotu eyi xuanchuan" [Vicious disinformation of Christians]. *Zhengxin* 9 (11): 4. Reprinted in *Minguo Fojiao qikan wenxian jicheng* 63: 78.

Young, Ernest P. 1996. "The Politics of Evangelism at the End of the Qing: Nanchang, 1906." In *Christianity in China: From the Eighteenth Century to the Present*, edited by Daniel H. Bays. Stanford, CA: Stanford University Press.

Young, Ernest P. 2013. *Ecclesiastical Colony: China's Catholic Church and the French Religious Protectorate*. New York: Oxford University Press.

Yu, Ying-shih. 2004. *Zhu Xi de lishi shijie: Songdai shidafu zhengzhi wenhua de yanjiu* [Zhu Xi's historical world: a study on Song scholar officials' political culture]. Beijing: Sanlian Shudian.

Yü, Chün-fang. 2001. *Kuan-Yin: The Chinese Transformation of Avalokiteśvara*. New York: Columbia University Press.

Yü, Chün-fang. 2013. *Passing the Light: The Incense Light Community and Buddhist Nuns in Contemporary Taiwan*. Honolulu: University of Hawai'i Press.

Zen, Joseph Ze-Kiun. 2018. "The Pope Doesn't Understand China." *New York Times*, October 24.

Zhang, Hua. 2016. "Ershi shiji shangbanye Fojiao xuexi Jidujiao zhi xin fuxing: Yi Shanghai weili" [The refashioning of Buddhism in Shanghai in the first half of the 20th century: Learning from Christianity]. In *Ershi shiji Zhongguo Fojiao de liangci fuxing* [Two revivals of Chinese Buddhism in the 20th century], edited by Ji Zhe, Daniela Compo, and Qiyuan Wang. Shanghai: Fudan daxue chubanshe.

Zhang, Kevin Honglin, and Shunfeng Song. 2003. "Rural-Urban Migration and Urbanization in China: Evidence from Time-Series and Cross-Section Analyses." *China Economic Review* 14: 386–400.

Zhang, Liping, and Yong Guo. 2005. "Diguo wangyang zhong de 'gudao': Cong Qingdai Sichuan kan Tianzhujiao zai Handi de nonggeng shequ" [Lonely islets in the ocean of the Chinese empire: The agrarian Catholic communities in Sichuan in the Qing dynasty]. *Zongjiao xue yanjiu* [Religious studies] 3: 168–74.

Zhang, Yu. 2006. "Wanqing shi Shengmu shengxin hui zai Neimenggu diqu chuanjiao huodong yanjiu (1865–1911)" [The CICM Mission in Inner Mongolia: 1865–1911]. PhD diss., Jinan University.

Zhang, Yuehe. 2024. "Xin meiti xia de dangdai Zhongguo fojiao: Yi neidi fojiao Longquan jiaotuan (2004–2018) weili" [Contemporary Chinese Buddhism in the age of new media: A case study of Longquan Monastic Community in mainland China (2004–2018)]. PhD diss., Chinese University of Hong Kong.

Zhang, Yunhou, Xuli Yin, Qingxiang Hong, and Yunkai Wang. 1979. *Wusi shiqi de shetuan* [Mass organizations during the May Fourth era]. Beijing: Sanlian.

Zhang, Zhenjun. 2014. *Buddhism and Tales of the Supernatural in Early Medieval China: A Study of Liu Yiqing's (403–444) Youming Lu.* Leiden: Brill.

Zhang, Zhongcheng. 2010. "Hangzhou Jidujiao diaocha yanjiu fengxi baogao: Hangzhou Jidujiao de xianzhuang, fazhan qushi he duice" [An analysis of the current situations and trends of Protestant churches in Hangzhou]. *Jinling shenxue zhi* [Nanjing theological review] 2: 111–34.

Zhao, Dianying. 2002. "Mingmo Qingchu zaihua Tianzhujiao ge xiuhui de chuanjiao celue shulun" [A review of the policies of different Catholic orders working in China in late Ming and early Qing dynasties]. *Hanshan shifan xueyuan xuebao* [Journal of Hanshan Teachers College] 1: 48–59.

Zhao, Dingxin. 2001. *The Power of Tiananmen.* Chicago: University of Chicago Press.

Zhao, Dingxin. 2006. *Shehui yu zhengzhi yundong jiangyi* [Social and political movements]. Beijing: Shehui kexue wenxian chubanshe.

Zhao, Dingxin. 2015. *The Confucian-Legalist State: A New Theory of Chinese History.* Oxford: Oxford University Press.

Zhao, Dingxin. 2019. "Jiazhi queshi yu guodu youwei: Cong gujin yitong kan dangqian guanliao zhi de kunjin" [Value deficiency and overperformance: The predicament of the bureaucracy in contemporary China in a historical comparative perspective]. *Wenhua Zongheng* 10: 30–36.

Zhao, Hanyu. 2023. "Overstretched Leviathan: Bureaucratic Overload and Grassroots Governance in China." PhD diss., Department of Government, Harvard University.

Zhao, Shiyu. 2002. *Kuanghuan yu richang: Ming Qing yilai de miaohui yu minjian shehui* [Carnivals and everyday life: Temple festivals and local society during and after the Ming and Qing]. Beijing: Sanlian.

Zheng, Zhenman. 2001. *Family Lineage, Organization and Social Change in Ming and Qing Fujian.* Honolulu: University of Hawai'i Press.

Zhou, Feizhou. 2009. "Creating Wealth: Land Seizure, Local Government, and Farmers." In *Creating Wealth and Poverty in Postsocialist China*, edited by Feng Wang and Deborah Davis. Stanford, CA: Stanford University Press.

Zhou, Li'an. 2007. "Zhongguo difang guanyuan de jinsheng jinbiaosai moshi yanjiu" [The tournament model of promotions of Chinese local officials]. *Jingji yanjiu* [Economic research journal] 7: 36–50.

Zhou, Zhuwei. 2005. "Zhongguo chuantong xiangcun de shehui texing jiqi jiazhi quxiang: Yi jindai Zhejiang sheng Lanxi xian Sanquan cun wei ge'an" [The social characteristics and value orientations of traditional Chinese villages: A case study of Sanquan Village in Lanxi County, Zhejiang Province]. *Zhejiang xuekan* [Zhejiang academic journal] 3: 64–73.

Zhou, Zhuwei, Shundao Lin, and Dongsheng Chen. 2001. *Zhejiang zongzu cunluo shehui yanjiu* [Lineage-based villages in Zhejiang]. Beijing: Fangzhi chubanshe.

Zhu, Haibing. 2009. "Minjian xinyang de diyu xing: Yi Zhejiang Huze shen weili" [The territoriality of popular religion: A case of God Huze in Zhejiang]. *Shehui kexue yanjiu [Social science research]* 4: 141–46.

Zhu, Haibing. 2011. *Jinshi Zhejiang wenhua dili yanjiu* [Culture and geography of Zhejiang in later imperial China]. Shanghai: Fudan University Press.

Zhuyun. 1966. *Fojiao yu Jidujiao de bijiao* [A comparison of Buddhism and Christianity]. Kaohsiung: Huacheng shuju.

Zito, Angelo. 1997. *Of Body and Brush: Grand Sacrifice as Text/Performance in 18th Century China*. Chicago: University of Chicago Press.

Zürcher, Erik. 1959. *The Buddhist Conquest of China: The Spread and Adaptation of Buddhism in Early Medieval China*. Leiden: Brill.

Zürcher, Erik. 1980. "Buddhist Influence on Early Taoism: A Survey of Scriptural Evidence." *T'oung Pao* 66 (1/3): 84–147.

Zürcher, Erik. 2012. "Buddhism Across Boundaries: The Foreign Input." In *Buddhism Across Boundaries: The Interplay of Indian, Chinese, and Central Asian Source Materials*, edited by Jan Nattier and John McRae. Philadelphia: Department of East Asian Languages and Civilizations, University of Pennsylvania.

Index

Page numbers followed by "f" and "t" refer to figures and tables, respectively.

www.ingramcontent.com/pod-product-compliance
Lightning Source LLC
Chambersburg PA
CBHW032116020426
42334CB00016B/974